ALMANAC
OF
WORLD
CRIME

Jay Robert Nash

ALMANAC
OF
WORLD
CRIME

BONANZA BOOKS
New York

This 1986 edition is published by Bonanza Books, distributed by Crown Publishers, Inc., 225 Park Avenue South, New York, New York 10003, by arrangement with Doubleday and Company, Inc.

Printed and Bound in the United States of America

Library of Congress Cataloging-in-Publication Data

Nash, Jay Robert.
  Almanac of world crime.

  Reprint. Originally published: Garden City, N.Y. : Anchor Press/Doubleday, 1981.
  Bibliography: p.
  Includes index.
  1. Crime and criminals—Case studies. I. Title.
HV6025.N33 1986   364.1′09   86-26806

ISBN: 0-517-62530-X

h g f e d c b a

This book is for my friends—
Curt Johnson, Marc Davis, Jim
McCormick, Dan McConnell,
Chicago authors all.

CONTENTS

ALMANAC
OF
WORLD
CRIME

Tony Accardo, Chicago syndicate chieftain, better known as "Big Tuna."

ALIASES
AND
MONIKERS

HOW THE MONIKER TAKES HOLD

Those sinister-sounding monikers umbilically attached to criminals do not, as popularly thought, evolve through weird cabalistic rites. The origin of a criminal's nickname is usually attributable to an odd event, or a misunderstood word.

Jacob "Gurrah" Shapiro, murderous sidekick of New York's one-time crime czar Louis "Lepke" Buchalter (the only board member of the syndicate to be executed) came to his nickname via a marble mouth. Shapiro, in his awful youth, terrorized Bowery pushcart peddlers, scooping up their wares in gargantuan arms and shouting, "Get out of here," only it roared from his throat as "Gurrah here!"

The recently deceased Chicago hoodlum Sam "Teets" Battaglia also received his nickname in youth when he was a member of the 42 Gang. Sam's way of threatening store owners to pay extortion money came out, ". . . or I'll bust ya in da teets." *Voilà:* "Teets" Battaglia was born. Syndicate sachem Tony Accardo was labeled "Joe Batters" by his own ilk after they had witnessed his skill with a baseball bat while in the employ of Al Capone. For a period, Tony took to deep-sea fishing, once posing with a giant marlin he had hooked off Miami. Veteran newsman Ray Brennan of the Chicago *Sun-Times* spotted the photo and dubbed Accardo "Big Tuna," a name that has clung to the mob chieftain like an unwanted talisman ever since.

Late of New York and now of Tucson, Arizona, crime chieftain Joseph

"Joe Bananas" Bonanno received his *nom de guerre* through an obvious distortion of his last name. California's Benjamin "Bugsy" Siegel (as well as Chicago's George "Bugs" Moran) received his nickname because of the insane methods and emotional displays he made when dispatching gang rivals.

The press aside, many criminals pick their own names before some wisenheimer does it for them. California stage robber Charles E. Bolton signed the bits of doggerel he left in empty strong boxes, "Black Bart." Jesse James, while cleaning a pistol when he rode with Bloody Bill Anderson's guerillas during the Civil War, accidentally shot off the tip of a finger and exclaimed: "Well, ain't that the dingus-dangest thing!" The name "Dingus" stuck and was used by close associates thereafter.

Bank robber and berserk killer Lester Gillis of the 1930s insisted everyone call him "Big George," perhaps because he only stood five feet four. His request was ignored and "Baby Face Nelson" came out instead. Robert Leroy Parker called himself Butch Cassidy after an old-time outlaw he long admired. His pal, Harry Longbaugh, was called the Sundance Kid after having spent a brief time in the Sundance, Wyoming, jail. Another member of the Wild Bunch, Harvey Logan, insisted upon being called Kid Curry, a name adopted from another, older outlaw, George "Flat Nose" Curry.

In the gangster era, monikers abounded. There was Vincent "Mad Dog" Coll, termed thusly by fellow hoodlums because he shot down several children at play on a New York street while gunning for another gangster. And Nathan "Kid Dropper" Kaplan, who told his boys (and his wife, Veronica) to "call me Jack the Dropper or Kid Dropper, that's all." Kid Dropper had been a turn-of-the-century heavyweight boxer Kaplan had long admired. Jack Diamond was called "Legs" because of his ability to escape pursuing police.

Then there was Eddie Sterch, who served time in Joliet Prison for armed robbery and went on to become close pals with Joey DiVarco and "Big Joe" Arnold, both of whom were named as members of the Chicago crime syndicate by the U. S. Senate's Permanent Subcommittee on Investigations. Sterch also wound up in a posh job as Title Officer in the Cook County Recorder's Office.

At one booking, police told Sterch to face the camera, take off his hat and throw away his cigar.

"Naw, I ain't gonna do that," Sterch responded.

"Tough guy, huh?"

"That's right, copper."

He was "Tough" Eddie Sterch forevermore.

Contrary to popular belief, the most notorious and successful confidence man in the twentieth century, Joseph "Yellow Kid" Weil, re-

"Black Bart" is how Charles E. Bolton signed his taunting notes to pursuing posses. (University of Oklahoma, Western History Collection)

ceived his moniker not for any addiction to yellow apparel but from a quipping political hack in Chicago. Weil died at the age of 101 and claimed to have bilked more than $12 million from suckers. The author's estimate, after talking with him and many of those who worked for him in his illustrious scams, tallies about $8 million.

In his conning youth, Weil hung about the Silver Dollar Saloon on Clark Street, which was owned and operated by a colorful political boss named "Bathhouse John" Coughlin. The "Bath" noticed one day in 1903 that his most dapper regular—Weil was partial to winged collars, colorful cravats spliced by a diamond stickpin, cutaway coat, striped trousers, spats and patent leather shoes—could always be found at his bar sipping a beer and reading, over and over again, a popular cartoon strip called "Hogan's Alley," in which the Yellow Kid was a major character.

Coughlin stepped behind the bar and pointed to the capricious character in the strip and boomed: "Joe, that guy in the cartoon is just like you, always foolin' people, taking their money, making suckers out of 'em.

Joseph "Yellow Kid" Weil, the greatest con man of them all, was named after a cartoon strip character.

That's you, Joe . . . from now on you're the 'Yellow Kid!' " And so he was.

Another, much more sinister criminal in Chicago was known as the "Torture Doctor," an evil moniker that fit its owner like the tight bowler hat he always wore. This was Herman Webster Mudgett, also known as the "arch fiend" of the nineteenth century. Using the name "H. H. Holmes," Mudgett set himself up as a pharmacist on Chicago's South Side (he had studied medicine at the medical school at Ann Arbor, Michigan, before being expelled for stealing bodies in an insurance swindle). Next Holmes-Mudgett had an elaborate house built—later termed "Murder Castle." The building was as sinister in design as its proprietor: doors that opened on blank walls, rooms without doors, an elevator without a shaft, a shaft without an elevator, a chute that spiraled from his bedroom through many rooms and ended in the basement.

All of this crazy-quilt building was meant for one thing: Murder. The "Torture Doctor" went to work with a vengeance in 1893, the year of the Columbian Exposition in Chicago. The city was overrun with young girls from out of town seeking jobs and opportunities that the Fair was sure to offer, a fact Mudgett knew well. He inveigled scores of these young women to his murder castle on the promise of either jobs or marriage and, after obtaining their savings, insurance and valuables, he systematically murdered them, more than two hundred of them, becoming America's ultimate mass murderer. Mudgett was finally captured in Philadelphia and hanged in 1896, but that wasn't the end of the "Torture Doctor."

The memory of the "arch fiend" was kept alive at least by one person, whose dark humor was unrelenting. For years, a book reviewer for the New York *Times* used Mudgett's alias, "H. H. Holmes" when signing his reviews. Perhaps it was this reviewer's logic that such a moniker was appropriate for the kind of reviews he wrote—"Hatchet Jobs."

Other notable monikers:

Adonis, Joe "Joey A" (née Doto), New York syndicate gangster, 1906–72; after the beautiful lover of Aphrodite, self-chosen.
Aiuppa, Joseph John "Mourning Doves," Chicago syndicate gangster, 1907–   ; after illegally transporting mourning doves from Kansas to Chicago, by police.
Alderisio, Felix Anthony "Milwaukee Phil," Chicago syndicate gangster, 1922–71; after his interests and sometime residency in Milwaukee, Wisconsin, named by press.
Alterie, Louis "Two-Gun," Chicago gangster, 1920s, 1892–35; after his habit of always carrying two revolvers, by press.

Felix "Milwaukee Phil" Alderisio got his name from his favorite town.

Anastasia, Albert "Lord High Executioner," New York syndicate-Mafia gangster, 1902–57; after his position of primary enforcer for the New York syndicate, by press.

Anderson, William "Bloody Bill," pro-Southern Civil War guerilla, ?–1864; after his murderous treatment of Union prisoners, by his own men.

Bailey, Harvey "Old Harve," bank robber, 1920s–30s, 1889–1979, after his durability as a bank robber, by cohorts.

Barker, Arizona Donnie Clark "Kate," "Ma," gang leader, 1872–1935; after her ostensible leadership of the Barker gang of the 1930s, by her sons.

Barker, Arthur "Dock," or "Doc," 1930s bank robber, kidnapper, 1899–1939; reasons unknown, by his brothers Fred, Herman and Lloyd.

Barter, Richard "Rattlesnake Dick," California bandit, 1834–59; after his venomous temperament, by members of his gang.

Benders, The "Bloody," a murderous four-member family headed by John Bender, the father, and Kate Bender, the daughter, who murdered perhaps more than fourteen travelers for their money when they stopped at the Bender wayside inn in Cherryvale, Kansas, in 1872–73; after their slaughtering ways, by the press.

Bonney, William H. "Billy the Kid," southwestern robber and murderer, 1859–81; after his youth, by friends and the press.

Brocius, William "Curly Bill," gunfighter, 1857–82; after his curly locks, by friends.

Buchalter, Louis "Lepke," one of the organizers of the national crime syndicate and head of Murder, Inc., 1897–1944; after a NYC street nickname picked up as a youth, by his friend and fellow killer, Jacob "Gurrah" Shapiro.

Burke, Elmer "Trigger," free-lance killer, hired to murder a member of the Brink's robbery gang in 1954, 1917–58; after his impulsive trigger finger, by the press.

Capone, Alphonse "Scarface," crime czar of Chicago during the 1920s, 1899–1947; after receiving three slashes on the left side of the face with a stiletto wielded by one Frank Galluccio in a Brooklyn bar in 1917 (Capone had insulted Galluccio's sister), by the press.

Chessman, Caryl "The Red Light Bandit," robber and sex offender, 1921–60; after using a red light flashed on his victims, by the press.

Colosimo, James "Big Jim," early-day Chicago gang chieftain, 1877–1920; after his position of importance in the underworld, by the press.

John Bender, of the "Bloody Benders" of Kansas.

Crime czar of the 1920s in Chicago, Al Capone—no one ever called him "Scarface" to his face.

Coppola, Michael "Trigger Mike," New York gangster, 1904–66; after his willingness to use automatic weapons in disputes with opponents, by the press.

Costello, Frank "The Prime Minister," high-ranking NYC Mafia-syndicate chieftain, 1893–1973; after his alleged role of mediator of gang disputes, by the U. S. Senate Committee to Investigate Organized Crime in Interstate Commerce, headed by Estes Kefauver.

Crowley, Francis "Two-Gun," youthful NYC robber and killer, 1911–31; after a prolonged gun battle waged with police while he employed two guns, by the press.

Drucci, Vincent "The Schemer," one of Dion O'Bannion's chief gangster gunners in Chicago during the 1920s, 1895–1927; after his penchant to plan robberies, chiefly the hijacking of liquor, by O'Bannion.

Esposito, Joseph "Diamond Joe," Chicago bootlegger of the 1920s, 1872–1928; after his habit of wearing diamonds—stickpins, cuff links, diamond belt buckle, etc., by the press.

Fish, Albert "The Cannibal," a monstrous old man who preyed upon children for decades, killing and cannibalizing them, 1870–1936; by the press.

Floyd, Charles Arthur "Pretty Boy," 1930s bank robber, 1904–34; after his good looks, by a Kansas City, Missouri, madam, Ann Chambers, who refused to let any of the girls in her brothel service him, remarking: "I want you for myself, pretty boy."

Genovese, Vito "Don Vitone," NYC Mafia chief, 1897–1969; after his exalted position in the Mafia hierarchy, by his followers.

Goldsby, Crawford "Cherokee Bill," western bandit, 1876–96; this killer of thirteen men before the age of twenty was nicknamed after his Indian heritage, by the press and law enforcement officers.

Jones, William "Canada Bill," old-time confidence man, ?–1877; after his one-time Canadian residence, by George H. Devol, his long-time confederate.

Albert Fish, "The Cannibal."

Karpis, Alvin "Old Creepy," 1930s bank robber and kidnapper, 1908–79; after his appearance following a botched plastic surgery operation on his face, by his lover, Fred Barker.

Kelly, George "Machine Gun," robber and kidnapper of the 1930s, 1897–1954; after his so-called ability to wield a submachine gun, a reputation wholly invented, as was the sobriquet, by his wife, Kathryn Kelly.

Ketchum, Thomas "Black Jack," western bandit, 1866–1901; after a then popularly commonplace name for robbers (his brother Sam was also called "Black Jack"), by the press.

Lingley, William "Big Bill," head of NYC's Car Barn gang in the 1910s, ?–1915; after his big ideas, by opponents.

Lowe, Joseph "Rowdy Joe," gambler, gunfighter, ?–1880; after his brawling nature, by rivals.

Lucchese, Thomas "Three-Finger Brown," much-feared NYC syndicate chieftain, 1903–67; after losing three fingers as a youth in an accident and being given the name of a popular baseball pitcher who was also missing three fingers, by his enemies. (A one-time Lucchese sidekick, Joe Valachi, testified: "I never heard *anyone* call him 'Three-Finger Brown' to his face!")

Charles "Lucky" Luciano; the scars on his throat earned him his moniker.

William "Old Bill" Miner, who robbed trains until the 1910s.

Luciano, Charles "Lucky," Mafia leader and one of the organizers of the crime syndicate, 1897–1962; after having his throat cut by rival gangsters in October 1929 and being fortunate enough to survive, by his associates.

McGurn "Machine Gun Jack," Chicago killer in Al Capone's elite bodyguard during the 1920s–30s, 1904–36; after his repeated and deadly use of the submachine gun (he was thought to be one of those machine gunners who slaughtered the seven members of Moran's North Side gang on St. Valentine's Day, 1929), by the press.

Mandelbaum, Fredericka "Marm," early-day fence in NYC, 1818–89; after the motherly image she showed to the press, by her colleagues.

Martin, Michael "Captain Lightfoot," early-day highwayman, 1775–1822; after his ability to escape following a robbery, by his fellow bandits.

Metesky, George Peter "The Mad Bomber," malcontent who planted bombs all over New York in 1940–41, then in 1951, 1903–   ; by the press.

Miner, William "Old Bill," western bandit, 1847–1913; after his premature look of old age, by his friends.

Moran, Thomas B. "Butterfingers," legendary pickpocket, 1892–1913; an unjust slur, according to Moran, on his ability to pick pockets, by jealous rivals.

Roger "The Terrible" Touhy, 1920s bootlegger.

O'Connor, Thomas "Terrible Tommy," Chicago gunman of the 1920s, 1886–?; after his conscienceless murders, by the press; O'Connor escaped jail only days before his scheduled hanging, and was never found.

Poole, William "Bill the Butcher," old-time NYC gangster, ?–1855; after killing several opponents with a carving knife, by the press.

Ricca, Paul "The Waiter," Chicago Mafia-syndicate chief, 1897–1972; after the fact that he had once worked in a restaurant as a waiter, by the press.

Rothstein, Arnold "Mr. Big," "The Big Bankroll," top NYC gambler, claimed to have fixed the 1919 World Series, 1882–1928; after the amount of cash he carried and his high financing of rackets, by friends and the press.

Schmid, Charles Howard, Jr., "The Pied Piper of Tucson," youthful murderer, 1942–   ; after his ability to entice other youths to lonely areas, where he murdered them, by press.

Schultz, Dutch (née Arthur Flegenheimer), NYC bootlegger, rackets king, 1902–35; after a prizefighter named Dutch Schultz, self-chosen.

Smith, Jefferson Randolph "Soapy," early-day confidence man, 1860–89; after his ability to convince "suckers" of his money-grabbing schemes, by his colleagues.

Sutton, Willie "The Actor," bank robber, 1901–80; after his use of actor's make-up, garb and disguises in robbing banks, learned from Broadway actors and actresses during the early 1920s, by associates.

Touhy, Roger "The Terrible," Chicago bootlegger, 1898–1959; after his alleged brutality with kidnap victims (Touhy was exonerated of any kidnappings after spending twenty-five years in prison on a false conviction), by the press.

Watson, Ella "Cattle Kate," early-day cattle rustler, who was lynched, 1866–88; by the press.

Weiss, Earl "Hymie," Chicago gang chief of the North Side during the 1920s, 1898–1926; after an affectionate name, by his friends O'Bannion and Bugs Moran.

Wortman, Frank "Buster," St. Louis bootlegger and gangster, 1903–70; after his sometimes childlike antics, by the press.

Zelig, Jack "Big Jack," early-day NYC gangster, 1882–1912; after his size and his ideas of becoming the city's crime overlord, by the press.

Zwerbach, Max "Kid Twist," NYC gangster of the 1900s, 1882–1908; after his ability to slip out of the law's grasp, by associates.

Zwillman, Abner "Longy," syndicate chief of New Jersey, 1899–1959; after his long-on-talk reputation, by associates.

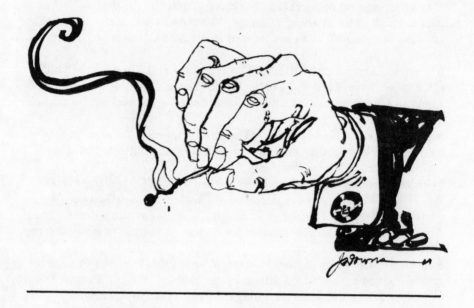

ARSON

FATAL FIREBUGS, PAST AND PRESENT

Perhaps the most insidious and elusive criminal is the ubiquitous arsonist. Although the FBI does not classify arson as a major crime (the Bureau groups it with drunken driving, forgery and vagrancy), this lethal offense consistently increases each year in loss of property and life and widespread injuries. In one recent year more than twelve thousand lives were lost to arson, along with more than $11 billion in loss of property. Almost a half million persons were seriously injured in 1978 due to the work of arsonists.

The problem with combatting arsonists is their erratic patterns, if they be psychological torchers, or for the lack of hard evidence, should the arsonist be a professional doing the job for the failing businessman eager to recoup through insurance claims. Further, in every major city in the United States, only a small per cent of fire and police personnel are even superficially trained to investigate arson (2 per cent of the state police and 10 per cent of the firemen in Illinois, for example). An historical look at the problem of arson only reaffirms the ongoing dilemma facing hopelessly undermanned arson squads of today. In the earliest accounts of recorded arson, the motives for the great fires appear to be largely rooted in political and social unrest, or the fires were perpetrated as acts of military frustration.

Arson by colonial times had become largely a matter of military reprisal and continued so in the nineteenth century with increasing sporadic outbursts of incendiaries seeking to settle personal grudges via the torch.

Toward the end of the nineteenth century, arson became a predominantly personal crime, no longer laid at the feet of ambiguous marching armies. Profits, thrills and the inexplicable were the motives. Many of those arsonists in the gaslight era went on to spectacular, horrendous criminal careers with arson as only a criminal harbinger of offenses to come.

As arson spread as a major crime deeper into this century, it became clear that, in addition to criminal motivation, arsonists were employing fire as a revolutionary tactic. Also on the obvious increase were acts of arson stemming from the vengeful to the deranged until the setting of fires has become commonplace, a popular method of "expressing oneself," as one current-day psychiatrist haphazardly put it. (Such "expressions" he would undoubtedly not welcome from his patients.) The death penalty, or even lynching by an outraged populace in the past, studies show, confined widespread arson to the lunatic element who incoherently burn their way through any age. Punishments for arson, particularly where deaths occur, modern records testify, are comparatively lenient and sadly encouraging to the would-be arsonist.

Here, from the ancient past to the present, are the most notable acts of incendiarism:

Babylon, Mesopotamia, 538 B.C.: Invading Persians captured the city and, in vengeance of the stiff resistance, set fire to the resplendent metropolis, destroying most of the buildings, including the hanging gardens, one of the ancient seven wonders of the world. Thousands perished in the flames.

Alexandria, Egypt, 48–47 B.C.: Julius Caesar, besieged in the royal palace with four thousand men, ordered the Egyptian fleet burned. Flaming ships at dockside ignited piers and houses, the blaze spreading to the magnificent 250-year-old Alexandrine library, which, along with its priceless manuscripts and ancient scrolls, was utterly destroyed. Caesar could have easily had the fire extinguished but allowed the great library to be consumed, earning himself the label of "arsonist."

Rome, Italy, A.D. 64: Mad Emperor Nero thought to destroy Rome in order to rebuild it on a grand scale, reserving a vast area at the south end of the Forum for his personally designed private palaces and gardens. He ordered the fires set in the Circus Maximus, and, from that point, the flames spread rapidly, shooting across narrow streets and consuming, within eight days, more than 75 per cent of the city, most of which was built of rotting timber. Hundreds died in the flames, but Nero escaped the wrath of his blood-lusting people by blaming the fire on the Christians, thus bringing about their long persecutions. That the demented Nero "fiddled while Rome burned," is undoubtedly apocryphal, but he may have plucked his favorite lute as he watched, glassy-eyed, his city burn.

Boston, Massachusetts, 1653, 1676, 1679: For almost twenty-five years, beginning in 1653, when several homes were torched, the infant city of Boston was plagued by great fires set by arsonists. In 1676, fifty homes, warehouses and shops were burned down, including the church of Increase Mather, the rabid religious zealot. No one was apprehended. Three years later a man was seen to set a tavern sign afire. As he undoubtedly knew it would, the fire spread quickly to many buildings until eighty houses and several warehouses were reduced to cinders. The arsonist was not identified but enraged authorities proclaimed the death penalty for any arsonist caught in the future. Moreover, at least a dozen suspected arsonists were routed from their beds and driven at the muzzles of guns from the city, banished. So on guard against arsonists were Bostonians that city fathers compelled one and all to give an oath of allegiance every three months.

Roxbury, Massachusetts, 1681: A slave named Marja set fire to two houses on July 12; a child burned to death in one building but Marja, quickly apprehended, was not convicted of murder but of arson and *witchcraft,* it being the time of the Salem mania. She was executed in Boston on September 22, burned at the stake before a huge gathering. Among the crowd was the witch-hunter Cotton Mather, who marked the deranged woman's fate as having been brought about because she did not have "the fear of God before her eyes" and was "instigated by the Devil."

New York City, 1741: Blacks by the score were labeled arsonists in March 1741, when several fires broke out. Of a population of 10,000, one fifth were slaves. The whites were suspicious and distrustful of all blacks. One slave named Mary, to save her own life, began naming dozens of blacks as part of a mass murder conspiracy through arson to wipe out the white population. She was readily believed by plot-fearing British authorities. Wholesale executions of so-called arsonists saw thirteen blacks burned at the stake, eighteen more hanged, and seventy-one others deported.

Lisbon, Portugal, 1755: Following a devastating earthquake and seismic sea wave on November 1, 1755, in which Lisbon was all but destroyed, and 50,000 persons were either crushed, drowned or burned to death, authorities began to round up looters, hanging them after summary hearings in the rubble. Many of these were prisoners who escaped from the city jail when its walls collapsed, and, by the score, before their executions, admitted to committing arson to spread confusion and thus aid them in their looting. One was identified by a reporter as a Moor who "confessed at the gallows that he has set fire to the king's palace with his own hand; at the same time glorying in the action, and declaring with his last breath, that he had hoped to have burnt all the royal family."

New York City, 1776: When the British fleet anchored in New York Harbor on August 22, 1776, preparatory to landing an army, Washington petitioned the Continental Congress for permission to burn the strategic town to prevent the city from being comfortably occupied by the enemy; he was refused. British soldiers occupied New York on September 16 with many pro-British inhabitants greeting them with open arms. Five days later fires broke out all over New York, obvious acts of sabotage. Though Washington feigned ignorance, he undoubtedly gave secret orders for New York to be razed. So devastating were the fires raging through the old city of wooden structures that one fourth of the town—more than five hundred buildings—was obliterated.

Further, when British troops raced to church steeples to sound the alarm, they found all the bells had been removed by the Revolutionaries (to be melted down for use as cannons), and thousands of buckets grabbed up by the British troopers were without bottoms. Washington had planned well. Several suspected arsonists were actually driven into the flames at bayonet point by infuriated British troops.

Moscow, 1812: Following his triumph over the Russian army at Borodino, Napoleon, at the head of 500,000 troops, entered Moscow on September 14. The following day, at the orders of the retreating Russian commanders, the great ancient capital was put to the torch, leaving Bonaparte to occupy a city of ashes and cinders. Almost all the city, more than 31,000 buildings with $150 million in damages, was destroyed. This "scorched earth" tactic, later used against the Nazis in World War II to murderous effect, contributed greatly to Napoleon's crushing defeat in Russia.

Washington, D.C., 1814: British troops, under the command of General Robert Ross, took a leaf from Washington's book on military arson during the War of 1812, setting Washington, D.C., on fire on August 24, 1814, after fleeing militiamen dared to fire on the British. All of the great buildings—the President's House, the Treasury, the Capitol—were reduced to ashes.

New York City, 1842: The Tombs prison in New York suddenly caught fire in November 1842, only a few days before murderer John C. Colt was scheduled to hang. The flames were extinguished but much of the prison was destroyed. Many, including city officials, suspected arson on the part of the killer's brother, Samuel Colt, the famous inventor of the revolver, who had been working on a new explosive, but proof was lacking, the eternal problem with all cases of suspected arson. It mattered little since John Colt committed suicide in his cell on November 18 only hours after marrying his childhood sweetheart, who smuggled a knife into his cell.

St. Louis, Missouri, 1849: A disgruntled, unidentified sailor who was refused work was blamed for the great waterfront fire in St. Louis on the night of May 17, 1849, when fire broke out on board the *White Cloud*. The blaze quickly spread to the host of wooden vessels moored closely together. Within hours, twenty-five steamships, all the wharves and fifteen square blocks of St. Louis were wrecked, with a loss of $4 million. Further, the arsonist's revenge was indirectly more devastating than he could

George Washington committed arson for patriotic reasons in 1776.

have conceived in that the loss of housing forced congested living conditions which allowed cholera to reach epidemic proportions and scores died.

New York City, 1859: Another arsonist heaped his hatred upon New York by firing the elegant Crystal Place on October 5, 1859. The blaze destroyed the greatest museum in the country, wrecking more than $2 million in precious antiquities and works of art as two thousand persons fled the massive iron and glass structure in panic.

New York City, 1863: The Draft Riots, occurring in July 1863, brought devastation and death to hundreds in New York. At the time, thousands of New York men rebelled against conscription into the Union Army and, in acts of mob violence, set many buildings on fire, including the Orphan Asylum for Colored Children. Chief John Decker arrived too late to save the building (the children had been evacuated only moments before the mob burst through the front door). Rioters seized him, put a rope around his neck and prepared to hang Decker on the spot. The nerveless fireman stared at his would-be executioners and coolly commented: "Gentlemen,

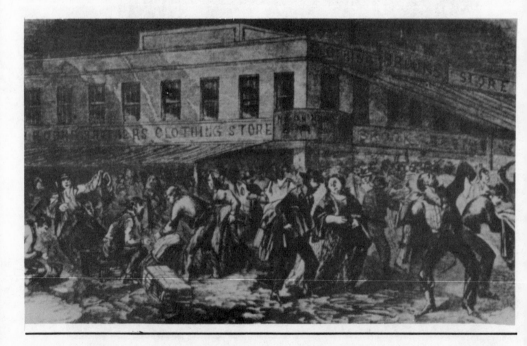

Draft rioters in New York looting Brooks Brothers in 1863 before torching the building.

Union troops under the command of General William T. Sherman, encamped just after burning Atlanta. (Library of Congress)

do you think you can stop the government's draft by stopping mine?" The clever remark saved his life as the rioters let him go.

Atlanta, Georgia, 1864: Union General William T. Sherman, after promising the occupants of Atlanta that their city would not be harmed, entered Atlanta on September 2, 1864, as Confederate troops retreated. Sherman ordered the torch put to the city on November 15. More than five thousand homes, churches and businesses, along with the industrial plants Sherman had specifically designated for destruction, went up in smoke; the city was gutted and Sherman would be forever known in the Deep South as "The Arsonist."

New York City, 1864: In retaliation against Sherman's fiery March to the Sea, Confederates attempted to burn down the whole of New York City on November 25, 1864, setting fire to eleven hotels, two theaters, and Barnum's Museum, but the damage brought about by these arsonists was minimized by quick-responding volunteer firemen who put out all the blazes with little loss.

Richmond, Virginia, 1865: Confederate defenders of Richmond decided to burn their city rather than let it fall intact into Union hands. Munition stores, warehouses, bridges and businesses were selected for the torch but the fires got out of hand and spread throughout the residential district. When firemen attempted to put out the fires, citizens, half berserk with rage over the defeat of their armies, cut their hoses. Ironically, Union troops entering the city put out the fires, but, by then, Richmond was in ashes.

London, Ontario, Canada, 1878: Dr. Thomas Neill Cream, who was later to murder at least a half dozen women, dosing them with strychnine, set several fires in the London, Ontario, area, collecting insurance money on his own torched property. Cream would later die on the gallows as a mass murderer. Just before he fell through the trap, his last words were: "I am Jack—[the Ripper?]."

Silver Plume, Colorado, 1884: The prosperous mining boomtown of Silver Plume had been subjected to several attempts at arson (over mining claims), the last, in September 1884, effective enough to cause the entire business section to be burned. Reported the local press: "The citizens are very much excited, and if the guilty one is found, he will certainly participate as principal actor in a special necktie sociable."

New York City, 1886: On February 4, 1886, a tenement house on East Sixty-fourth Street was set afire by Edward and Henry Kohout, who were apprehended while running away from the blaze which killed a Mrs. Fialla and her two children. The torch scheme was to collect insurance; instead, the Kohout brothers were sent to Sing Sing for life.

Greensburg, Pennsylvania, 1888: Frank Baer, eager to expand his mills, torched two mills in the area, causing the owners to declare bankruptcy and giving him a monopoly in the area. An accomplice, William Richardson, informed police of Baer's arson, and the miller was arrested, tried and sent to prison for six years. Richardson was given eight years.

New York City, 1892: Patrick Mullins, a thirty-five-year-old laborer, was caught in the act of setting fire to a stable at 161st Street and Eleventh Avenue on the night of May 1, 1892. Mullins quickly confessed that he and four others had been burning stables for two years. They first purchased a stable, stocked it with first-rate horses, and had each place highly insured. They then replaced the good horses with broken-down, sickly animals and torched the stable, collecting large sums from insurance companies. All five men were sent to jail.

Chicago, Illinois, 1892–93: Herman Webster Mudgett, alias H. H. Holmes purchased several cheap houses on Chicago's South Side, insured them heavily, then torched the buildings to collect heavy insurance monies. He went on to build a three-story monstrosity later called "Murder Castle," in which he systematically murdered more than two hundred women for their money and property within a year, becoming America's all-time mass murderer. He torched the building housing his victims' bones but able firemen put out the blaze. Holmes fled to Pennsylvania and was subsequently hanged in Philadelphia for other murders.

Cologne, Germany, 1904: Sex pervert and future mass murderer Peter Kurten set fire to dozens of barns and hayricks in the Cologne area. As he later stated, he was delighted by "the agitation of those who saw their property being destroyed." Kurten was to murder almost at will for thrills, dragging his pyromania into the realms of killing, for another twenty-five years, responsible for the deaths of more than two dozen persons all over Germany. He was beheaded in Cologne on July 2, 1931.

Red Wing, Minnesota, 1905: Carl Panzram, an eleven-year-old incorrigible inmate of the Minnesota Training School, set fire to a school warehouse on July 7, 1905, causing $100,000 damage. "The whole place burned down," he later laughed. "Nice, eh?" Panzram went on to establish a staggering criminal career of burglary, robbery and murder. He confessed to killing twenty-one persons in his lifetime of thirty-nine years before he was hanged in Leavenworth in 1930.

Bolshevik troops like these were responsible for widespread arson during the Russian Revolution of 1917.

Russia, 1917: Bolsheviks attempting to overthrow the brief democratic premiership of Alexander Kerensky set many fires to spread terror and confusion among his supporters. On September 9, in the town of Laishev in Kazan, Bolsheviks broke out of a small prison and torched the city; twenty of the Bolsheviks were lynched. Days later, in the village of Nicholivak, two hundred Bolsheviks attempted to burn the town, but dallied in a large wine cellar, where they staged a drunken orgy. All two hundred burned to death in the fire of their own making.

Walnut Creek, California, 1925: Charles Henry Schwartz, a chemist whose business was failing, interviewed a bum seeking work, Gilbert Warren Barbe. Noticing the almost identical appearance of Barbe to himself, Schwartz murdered him, then set fire to his plant, on July 30, 1925, thinking the authorities would find the body and conclude it to be his. Heavy insurance payments would then be made to his wife. Authorities, however, determined Barbe's identity through a dental check; Schwartz was run to ground in an Oakland rooming house where he had been hiding. As police broke down the door, Schwartz sent a bullet into his brain.

Columbus, Ohio, 1930: On April 21, 1930, a raging fire broke out in the Ohio Penitentiary. The ancient buildings went up in flames quickly despite valiant attempts to put out the blaze. Killed were 322 inmates. Prisoners Clinton Grate, Hugh Gibson and James Raymond were found guilty of setting the fire. All confessed that they set the fire to escape. Grate and Raymond committed suicide in their cells after all three were convicted of second-degree murder.

Buenaventura, Colombia, 1931: Revolutionaries on January 26, 1931, set scores of fires throughout Buenaventura, Colombia, a solid wall of flames covering a square mile of the business district, which wiped out hundreds of buildings. Looters then raced through the flames, stealing at will. Two Chinese shopkeepers were murdered by looters and the city's fire chief, attempting to stop the thieves, was knifed. The damage went beyond $3 million. Government troops arrived at the scene, firing at the arsonists, all of whom escaped.

Salt Lake City, Utah, 1937: Clifford Bramble, forty-five, had an unhappy homelife; to achieve "relief from the pressures," he set, his later confession stated, thirty-one fires in Sacramento, California, and five fires in Salt Lake City, causing more than $2 million in damage. Bramble was sent to an asylum.

Chatsworth, Georgia, 1942: Mark Pulliam, wanting to rid himself of family responsibilities, set fire to his farm home in November 1942, in which his wife and five of his eight children burned to death. Pulliam was sent to prison for life.

Oakland-San Francisco, California, 1944: Twenty-two persons died when pyromaniac George Holman set eleven fires in Oakland and San Francisco, mostly in the sleazy tenement and hotel districts, from March

25 through March 28, 1944. He was identified by a janitor as running from the scene of one fire with a can of kerosene in his arms. Holman was convicted and sent to San Quentin, given twenty-two consecutive life sentences for arson-murder.

London, England, 1949: Clifford Alexander Weallans, a London policeman, was apprehended after setting eight fires all at Jewish-owned shops in the East End. His only explanation before being sent to prison for five years was that he "hated the Jews," having fought in Palestine in the days of the Jewish wars for independence.

Chungking, China, 1949: Enormous fires raged through Chungking on September 3–4, 1949, after Communist underground workers put the city to the torch. One of the Communist arsonists was caught and shot on the spot. The fire killed 1,700 persons and left 100,000 homeless.

San Francisco, California, 1951: A seventeen-year-old substitute newsboy, Kenneth Skinner, set fire to an apartment complex on July 22, 1951, a fire in which eight persons died. When questioned by fire inspectors and police, Skinner denied being at the scene during the fire, but a newspaper photo showed him standing within the staring crowd. Skinner, confronted with the photo, confessed; he was sent to San Quentin for ten years.

Chicago, Illinois, 1953: On December 4, 1953, Vincent Ciucci, seeking to rid himself of his family for another woman, chloroformed his wife, Anne, and his three children, shot all four in the head, then set fire to his three-room apartment, but firemen found the bodies and the murder wounds. "How could a man kill his own children?" protested Ciucci when arrested. He was electrocuted in 1962.

Murderer and arsonist Vincent Ciucci (center) tried to conceal the mass killing of his family by torching his Chicago home in 1953; Ciucci later went to the electric chair, executed on March 23, 1962.

Chicago, Illinois, 1955: George Fisher, desperate to cash in on his huge twelve-room house, fixed up an elaborate gadget to his phone, traveled 1,500 miles to Florida, where he stayed a week to establish an alibi, then called his own house, the gadget in the phone box setting off a searing fire which gutted the house. Fisher put in his claim for $75,000 but insurance investigators, leery of Fisher's past shady dealings, investigated and found the phone box with special wiring. The claim was not paid.

Watts, California, 1965: The black community of Watts erupted in wholesale outbreaks of arson to aid looting on August 8, 1965. Arriving firemen were greeted with Molotov cocktails. The fires raged out of control for four days, at the end of which thirty-four persons had died, 1,033 were injured, more than 4,000 were arrested and damages soared beyond $34 million.

New York City, 1971: Albert Epstein hired Benjamin Warren, a former tenant of his five-story brick apartment building, to burn the building down so he could collect insurance money. Warren, in turn, hired three youths to help him. After the fires were started, Warren locked the boys in a closet, where they burned to death. Epstein was sent to prison for ten years; Warren got twenty years.

Chicago, Illinois, 1978: A "Mr. Goodbar" murder in reverse occurred on June 3, 1978, when a thirty-year-old Loop secretary, Bobbie Ryan, went home with Peter Hoban, a Democratic precinct captain. After Hoban fell into a drunken stupor, Ms. Ryan waited an hour and a half. She then stripped the man, looted the apartment and set fire to the flat. Hoban was roasted to death. Bobbie Ryan was convicted of arson-murder and given a twenty-two-year prison sentence. "The judge might as well have handed her a book of matches as she left the court," lamented one police officer.

ASSASSINATION

RAY AND BOOTH, THE DANGEROUS PARALLELS

Nobody has truly answered the question of conspiracy in the killing of Martin Luther King, Jr., as he stood on a motel balcony in Memphis on April 4, 1968. James Earl Ray remains enigmatic in a silence that screams conspiracy. One eight-month Justice Department report which cost $2,000,000 and led lawyer-investigators through fifteen cities and 200,000 documents (mostly FBI reports) but strangely involved interviewing only forty persons, concludes that Ray acted alone. The self-confessed assassin was not initially questioned, refusing any interviews with federal authorities (which is his right since he is serving a ninety-nine-year sentence in Brushy Mountain State Prison in Petros, Tennessee, a state-controlled institution).

What is unanswered by the Justice Department report and remains unanswered by the Congressional probe into the killing, is how Ray managed, from the time of the shooting to the time he was arrested at London Airport on June 8, 1968—sixty-five days after the King assassination—to move so freely and expensively around the world.

Precision of movement, detailed planning, cleverly arranged escape routes were not in the make-up of the uneducated Ray, whose IQ is less than average and whose only recommendation for killing King was his hatred for Negroes and King in particular. "If I ever get to the streets, I'm going to kill him," Ray was heard several times to say while in prison. But it took more than a racist's wrath to engineer King's death, many argue. It took a great deal of intelligent scheming and a young fortune to set in motion and finance Ray's role.

Looking back to another conspiracy, the same kind of protective funding and political shielding was inherent in the great plot to assassinate

President Abraham Lincoln. John Wilkes Booth, John Surratt and four other men had planned to murder Lincoln and most of his Cabinet on April 14, 1865. Of the plotters, only Booth was successful in killing his victim, Lincoln, as the President sat in a box at Ford's Theater watching a comedy, *Our American Cousins*.

A set of startling events began to occur minutes before Booth made his way down a dark passageway to the President's box. Lincoln's bodyguard, John F. Parker, was not on duty, so that Booth could enter the box wholly unmolested. Parker later told authorities that the play bored him, so he went to a nearby saloon for a drink! He was never reprimanded, dismissed or prosecuted for such gross misconduct.

Booth's escape, even with an injured leg resulting from his dramatic leap from Lincoln's box to the stage of the theater, was unbelievably smooth. He raced a horse through the streets and was allowed to pass over the heavily guarded Anacostia Bridge as he made for Maryland. The commercial telegraph wires leading from Washington were mysteriously crossed and put out of commission for two hours from almost the moment Booth pulled the trigger.

When Booth was finally trapped in the Garrett barn by a troop of federal officers he was informed that he could surrender. Yet he was killed by a Union soldier, Boston Corbett, even though some claimed the assassin died by his own hand. Corbett was a strange case, a religious monomaniac who castrated himself in 1858 after a prostitute solicited his attentions, a man, one report had it, who was in the exclusive service of Secretary of War Edwin McMasters Stanton.

It was to Stanton that Corbett brought the diary found on Booth's person. The Secretary of War kept this diary until compelled to turn it over to investigators. By then eighteen pages of the diary were missing. Perhaps overlooked was one still intact line: "I have a greater desire and almost a mind to return to Washington, and in a measure clear my name, which I feel I can do."

Stanton is the pivot to answers about the Lincoln conspiracy. A trucu-

John Wilkes Booth leaping from the presidential box in Ford's Theater, April 14, 1865, after shooting President Lincoln.

lent, seething man who violently opposed Lincoln's pacifist plans for the South's reconstruction, Stanton's conduct following the assassination was nothing less than hysterical. He ramrodded the trials of the conspirators and made sure Mrs. Surratt, apparently innocent of the plot, was hanged with the guilty parties. Stanton also confiscated the only photo ever taken of Lincoln in his coffin, ordering the master plate destroyed. All prints but one were burned and the remaining photo did not surface until eighty-seven years later.

More important, Stanton acted strangely in his handling of the case against John H. Surratt, Booth's co-conspirator. Several times government agents located the fugitive and informed Stanton of his whereabouts. The Secretary either refused to order his arrest or delayed decision. Tracking down Surratt developed into a world chase. He was ultimately found in Egypt and was returned to the United States (against Stanton's orders).

Surratt's trial was a farce and he was acquitted through the clever loophole picking of his lawyers, men who "incidentally" happened to be Stanton's friends. Surratt lived to a ripe old age in Baltimore.

A few years following Lincoln's murder, his son, Robert Lincoln, was found in his Manchester, Vermont, home burning many of his father's papers in the fireplace. When asked why he was destroying such historic

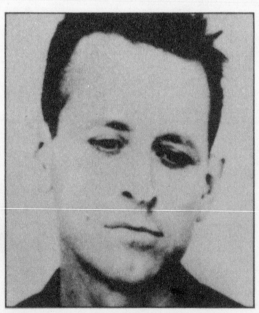

James Earl Ray, Martin Luther King's assassin: his exploits suggest conspiracy.

documents, Robert Lincoln replied: "These papers contain the documentary evidence of the treason of a member of my father's cabinet . . . it is best for all that such evidence be destroyed."

One might also ask how much paper has been burned in the case of James Earl Ray.

END OF A MAD MONK

Where he came from and what he really was no one will ever know. His name, Rasputin, was not given to him at birth. Rasputin means "debauchee," a name that this strange, unpredictable creature certainly earned. Born in a peasant home near Pokrovskoye, western Siberia, about 1872, Rasputin was to become Russia's most powerful leader, a sex-mad lunatic, and suffer not one, but four assassinations, all on the night of December 29, 1916.

Rasputin's given name was Grigory Yefimovich Novykh and early in his youth he joined and finally became a leader of a sex cult called Khlysty. The members of this demented group first beat themselves into bloody, pulpy messes (like the superstition-stricken flagellants of the Black Plague era) and then danced frantically around the earthen floors of peasant huts.

Overcome by exhaustion the members collapsed and in a prone position ripped away their clothes like mad dogs attempting to catch their tails. Males and females then carelessly copulated. Husbands ignored their wives and grabbed the nearest female. Wives thrust themselves upon the closest male stranger. This weird rite ended when the dozens of pretzelized couples would at last climax down to the last dynamic duo.

Rasputin was usually in the center of the goings-on and he took one woman after another. He was capable of having nonstop sex with as many as thirty women each night, it was said.

The Orthodox Church of Russia finally condemned the excesses of the Khlysty sect. Through fear, most of its members ceased their orgies— everyone except Rasputin. His sexual appetite had increased so enormously that no man's wife was safe from his assaults. In addition, his sexual prowess caused him to believe that he was inspired by God and that he could actually work miracles if he chose.

The Church branded Rasputin a heretic and he was tried by the Church. But since little evidence and no witnesses (people were afraid even then of Rasputin's odd hypnotic powers) against him could be found, he was released. Rasputin suddenly took on the role of a roving holy man common in those days—referred to as *staretz*—and began a pilgrimage to St.

Petersburg. It was really a way of escaping punishment for his gross offenses in western Siberia.

He walked more than a thousand miles until he came to the majestic home of the czars. He arrived in 1903 and immediately ingratiated himself with high-ranking churchmen, who introduced him to the flighty, fanciful aristocracy who lived in St. Petersburg's dream world. Here, Rasputin went back to old ways of debauchery. But this time he was more subtle. Seducing some count's wife under the guise of religious cultism could be dangerous.

The monk first gained a reputation as a hypnotist who could perform miraculous cures (mysticism then being in fashion). Discreetly, he led the high society women who patronized him into believing that anyone coming into physical contact with his body would be healed and purified. Naturally, complete purification would only come through intercourse and, according to reliable reports, almost all the ranking women of Russia's aristocracy in St. Petersburg had more than one round with him in bed.

There was one problem for these women other than secrecy: Rasputin smelled like an open latrine. The Mad Monk did not believe in bathing and sometimes went for months without washing his hands and face. He felt (or so he told his gullible patrons) that washing diminished his supernatural powers. His stench was so powerful that women literally bathed in perfume before going to see him, so that their own smells overpowered his.

Rasputin's fame or infamy spread until the empress heard of the strange holy man with the gleaming power in his eyes. She was told that Rasputin could work miracles and that no physical problem was too difficult for him to overcome. This intrigued Empress Alexandra, who was a desperate woman. Her son, Alexis, heir to the most powerful throne in all Europe, was afflicted with hemophilia.

Alexandra and her husband, Czar Nicholas II, had consulted the finest doctors in Europe and found no cure for the small boy. They had tried every conceivable religious prayer and his condition never changed. Perhaps, the empress thought, even though he be a mystic, this Rasputin could cure or at least protect her son. She sent for him.

Rasputin arrived at the Royal Palace in 1905, ironically just in time to hear that the czarevitch had fallen and had begun to bleed. He was led into the boy's room and, holding only one candle in the darkness to his eyes, hypnotized the child into a trance.

The empress gasped in wonder as the boy stopped bleeding immediately. She had found her cure and Rasputin soon had the freedom of the palace, coming and going as he chose, always on hand should the boy have an attack. This placed Rasputin in a power position he was never to relinquish except once, when he was banished for a brief time in 1912.

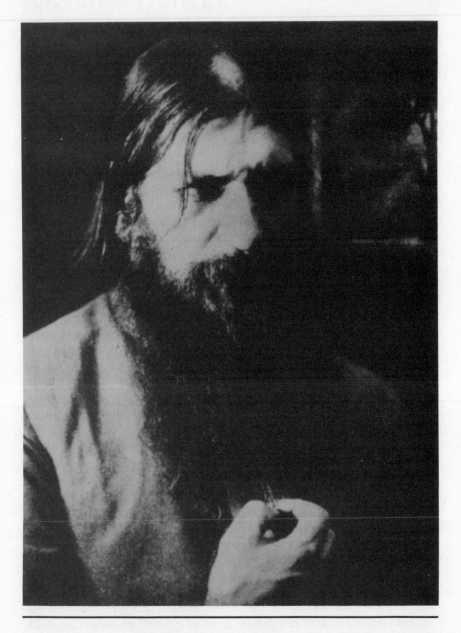

Russia's notorious "Mad Monk," Grigory Rasputin, whose resistance to assassination was almost miraculous.

For the most part, Rasputin actually named, through the empress, anyone he chose to an important governmental position.

When World War I broke out and Emperor Nicholas (who had tried to reduce Rasputin's power) went to the front, the Mad Monk became the untitled ruler of Russia. Through the empress he fired and named ministers.

Newspapers that attacked him for the immoral and insane person he was were destroyed. Members of the aristocracy who urged the empress to get rid of this lunatic were banished.

A rabid nationalist, Rasputin caused severe rationing of food, and massive drafts of men for the fighting fronts, while all the while wasting fortunes on his lavish private parties. The monk ignored criticism. He felt he was the most powerful man in Russia and he could do as he pleased. He controlled the empress and therefore the government.

One man, Prince Felix Yusupov, thought differently. He, along with several other noblemen, concluded that the only way Russia's monarchy would be saved was with the assassination of Rasputin. Even the czar's cousin, Grand Duke Dimitry Pavlovich, helped to plan the killing.

On the night of December 29, 1916, Yusupov lured Rasputin to his castle, saying that he was giving a party. The Mad Monk wanted to know if Yusupov's wife would be present. He had always coveted Yusupov's attractive wife, the Princess Irene. Yusupov said she would. Thus, using his wife as a lure, the prince convinced Rasputin to attend.

When the Mad Monk arrived, he was already drunk. He gave off a foul odor. "Where is the woman?" he grunted to Yusupov. The prince showed him into an empty banquet hall, its long table littered with dirty plates.

"You're late. You missed the feast. But my wife will be right down. Here, sit down here and have some of these delicious cakes."

The prince pushed forth a plate of specially made brown cakes. Each one of them had enough cyanide to kill ten men, the poison personally prepared by a Dr. Lazovert. Rasputin popped one and then two into his mouth.

Yusupov could not believe his eyes as the Mad Monk ate all of the cakes rapidly and then belched. "Good. Is there more?"

"Yes, I'll get them." Trembling, Yusupov went to an adjoining room. "He's eaten all the cakes," he hurriedly told fellow plotters.

"The wine, have him drink the wine," urged Lazovert. The wine jug contained several ounces of cyanide; a sip of it would mean instant death for most men. But Rasputin was not most men.

After encouraging him, Yusupov watched Rasputin down six goblets of madeira wine without showing any signs of discomfort.

"Where is your wife, Yusupov? You told me she would be here."

"She's preparing herself."

Rasputin got up and walked back and forth before the huge fireplace in the banquet hall. "I don't like to be kept waiting. You promised."

The prince was frantic. The poison had failed. (Of course, the assassins had no way of knowing that Rasputin had dyspepsia, a condition where his stomach did not secrete hydrochloric acid, which is necessary to activate cyanide.) Yusupov drew a large dagger and rushed the Mad Monk from behind, stabbing him a half dozen times until Rasputin fell. Then he tied him hand and foot and went back to get his fellow conspirators.

When the assassins re-entered the room and bent to lift the still form, Rasputin suddenly came to life, his pawlike hands firmly around Yusupov's neck, his fierce eyes blazing. One of the conspirators drew his pistol and emptied it into the Mad Monk, who collapsed.

Rasputin's body was tied with chains and rope and his body was taken to the frozen river Neva. There, six men hacked away at the ice until there was a hole large enough through which the body could be dumped. Yusupov kicked him through the hole with relief.

But that was not the end of Rasputin. To their horror, the assassins learned the next day that the Mad Monk had almost survived. His body was found on the opposite shore of the Neva. From what they could discover, he had gotten free of his bonds and smashed through the ice with his head.

But the effort had been too much. It wasn't the poison, stab wounds, or six bullets that had killed him. Rasputin had swallowed too much water and drowned. Ignoble as was his end, Rasputin's memory was fairly venerated by the empress. While ordering a chapel built to house his much damaged body at the czar's estate, Tsarkoye Selo, she turned her wrath upon the conspirators, but Yusupov and his wife quickly left Russia to save the crown embarrassment, as well as their own lives, it appears, since the prince felt sure that revolution would soon topple the Romanov dynasty. He was right. Yusupov traveled widely for some time, the assassin dabbling in the dubious arts of faith healing. He died in New York City in 1967 at age eighty-one.

Rasputin's body, like his reputation, was horribly violated when the czar fell. Revolutionaries broke into his chapel, dragged out his casket, pried it open with sticks and, after soaking the remains with kerosene, burned it on a huge log pyre as a large, silent throng gathered to watch the blaze throughout the night, perhaps making sure, as it were, that the Mad Monk was truly finished.

ASSASSINATION IN MEXICO

Nowhere in the world were assassinations of the military as spectacular and bizarre as in Mexico, particularly in the early years of the twentieth century, when that country was plagued by ceaseless anarchistic civil war. The Latin temperament for execution and/or annihilation showed itself in Mexico as both erratic and calculating, an unpredictable brand of extermination that usually cloaked itself in the shining but bloodied name of patriotism.

The death of Emiliano Zapata, the folk-hero farmer who successfully rose against the dictator Porfirio Díaz in 1910 in the backward state of Morelos, was indicative of the passionate treachery practiced so ardently during the revolution and subsequent civil wars. By 1919 Zapata's ranks were depleted, his supply of arms dwindling. The wary Zapata was made a tempting offer by a colonel in the army of Pablo González and under the command of Zapata's then archenemy, Venustiano Carranza. The colonel, a half-breed Yaqui named Jesús Guajardo, offered in April 1919 to bring his eight hundred troops into Zapata's camp, deserting Carranza with enormous supplies of new rifles and ammunition.

Suspicious, Zapata asked Guajardo to prove his loyalty. The colonel wasted no time. He ordered his troops to attack their fellow Carrancistas and then executed the prisoners taken at Jonacatepec. Zapata was then convinced of Guajardo's stated intentions and journeyed on April 10, 1919, with ten followers to meet him at the hacienda of San Juan Chinameca near Cuautla. Bugles and drums bleated and thrumped as Zapata and his men rode through the gate at 2 P.M., an honor guard of two hundred of Guajardo's soldiers drawn up before him. The colonel stood to one side of his ranks, smiling. Zapata stood directly in front of the troops to take their salute.

Drawing his sword, Guajardo shouted: "Present arms!" The troops raised their rifles and then, as Zapata and his friends stared in shock, leveled them at the revolutionary hero and let loose a terrific volley that shot Zapata and the others to pieces. Guajardo was promoted to brigadier general and given $50,000 for his betrayal.

The man who had worked out this black farce with Carranza, General Alvaro Obregón, survived all of the bombastic revolutionaries and later became President of Mexico. But he did not escape the same kind of bloody end that he had so enthusiastically arranged for his one-time

Emiliano Zapata, Mexico's noblest hero, assassinated in 1919.

comrade-in-arms. Early in 1928, fanatical religious sects, suppressed under Obregón's regime, began to devise ways of assassinating him. One elaborate plan, concocted by a mystic called Madre Conchita, involved poisoning Obregón. In April, Obregón attended a huge dance in Mexico City and one attractive girl was so persistent in demanding that he dance with her that she had to be taken away by armed guards. It was later discovered that the girl had hidden in the bouquet she wore on the front of her dress a hypodermic needle loaded with fluid cyanide. Conchita's plan called for the girl to press close to Obregón while dancing and inject him with the lethal poison.

The setback did not discourage Madre Conchita, who coached another religious zealot, José de León Toral, in various methods designed to rid Mexico of the ruthless Obregón. (Ignoring his own constitution, Obregón decided to be re-elected to the presidency, executing Arnulfo R. Gómez and Francisco R. Serrano; as the only candidate of note running for the office, Obregón naturally won in a landslide on July 1, 1928.)

On July 16, the twenty-six-year-old Toral, an amateur artist, followed Obregón's triumphant cortege through the streets of Mexico City in a taxi, tossing flowers and crying: *"Viva Obregón!"* That's as close as Toral got to the President-elect that day. The next day, however, proved more opportune. Obregón attended a political fete thrown for him in La Bom-

Francisco "Pancho" Villa, the most feared man during the Mexican Revolution.

bita (The Little Bomb), a cafe in San Angel, a few miles outside of Mexico City. Toral appeared at the entrance and explained that he was an artist and wanted to sketch the President.

Allowed inside, Toral worked his way to the table where Obregón sat. He quickly explained his artistic mission, showing the President his sketches. Would the great Obregón be kind enough to pose for a few minutes? The President agreed and Toral began to doodle on a pad, standing up and just behind his victim. With a rubbery smile, Obregón turned in his seat to face Toral, saying, "I hope you make me look good, kid." Toral jammed a pistol into Obregón's nose and fired five times, blowing away the President's face. Obregón died in his seat at the table of honor.

The fleeting glimpse Obregón did have of the pistol being leveled at him may have given him a moment's thought of the end he arranged for Zapata's equal in northern Mexico, Francisco "Pancho" Villa (Doroteo Arango), the Centaur, as he was known to the rabid revolutionaries who marched in the menacing dust of his victorious Division of the North. Villa and his lieutenants were a fierce lot who had snuggled up to death with taunting grins for almost a decade. Next to Villa, the worst of the northern revolutionaries was General Rodolfo Fierro, who earned with relish the title of "Pancho Villa's butcher." It was the fiery Fierro's staunch contention that "there is no end but death for a traitor." When Villa's oldest companion, General Tomás Urbina, looted Villa's war chest and fled to his hacienda in Durango, the Centaur, accompanied by his faithful butcher, Fierro, tracked him down.

Hoofbeats of Villa's horsemen aroused Urbina, who stepped from the house rubbing sleep from his eyes. Fierro shot Urbina down as he rode up, but Villa stopped his butcher short of killing. Urbina pleaded with his boyhood friend to spare him. Villa took out his pistol but could not bring himself to execute Urbina. Fierro rushed up and insisted that Urbina be shot as a traitor. Pancho moved away, weeping. In a whisper he said to his butcher: ". . . all right . . . but find a way, so he won't know it. Tell him . . . tell him you're taking him to see a doctor. Don't let him suffer any more."

Fierro bundled the wounded Urbina into a carriage and drove off with a squad of *dorados* at his side, telling the disgraced general that he was being taken to a hospital in Chihuahua City. Villa stood in the courtyard of the hacienda as his men brought him millions in gold and jewels which Urbina had taken from him. As the carriage bumped down the road, Urbina shouted gratefully to the Centaur: "I knew it, Pancho! I knew you'd help me! We're compadres, aren't we? You're the best friend I ever had!" Villa did not reply. He was crying.

Some distance up the road, Fierro ordered the carriage stopped and the escort to dismount. He then told Urbina to get up and walk to a nearby tree. "Why should I do that?" Urbina asked, but he apparently knew the answer, for he said his last words in a rush: "I enlisted you, Rodolfo. Remember? I made you a captain. We were friends . . ."

According to one of Villa's better biographers, William Douglas Lansford, the compassionless Rodolfo Fierro snorted: "I'm not interested in old time's sake. To me you're just a goddamn traitor, and you cost us Celaya [the battle from which Urbina deserted]. Because of you and *piojos* like you, Villa's lost almost everything. Get over here, you sniveling sonofabitch! That walk will buy you ten more seconds of life!"

Urbina staggered forward without a word and Fierro signaled the execution squad to fire. Riddled, Urbina was still alive, writhing on the ground. Rodolfo Fierro, who once saved bullets by lining up prisoners three in a row and killing each closely pressed threesome with a single slug from his pistol, squandered two shots on Tomás Urbina, sending them through the back of his head.

Fierro enjoyed killing Pancho's enemies. Once he captured three hundred Huerta men and offered them a grim opportunity to save their lives. If they could reach a wall in the courtyard where they were held and climb it before he could pick them off with a single shot, they were free.

"Don't worry," he lied to the three hundred, "I'm a terrible shot."

Fierro spread a blanket on the earth, had wine and food brought to him and sat down with three hundred cartridges—one per man. Then the captives, one by one, started their run for the wall. All day and into the night, Fierro picked them off until his hands were swollen from holding the pistol and shooting.

The last man almost made it over the wall but Fierro picked him off, too, and he fell back into the courtyard among the huge litter of dead. It was an inky night. An aide came up.

"What if the last one is not dead, General?"

Fierro snorted, stretched out on the blanket. "When I shoot a man, he's dead," the butcher said. Then, with no signs of conscience or remorse, he went to sleep in the middle of his own carnage.

But by 1920, even the terrible Fierro was dead. He insisted on fording a small lake while wearing several weighty bands of ammunition, four guns and a money belt loaded down with pounds of raw gold.

When Fierro's men hesitated, he spurred his mount into the water, screaming at his terrified men: "Here! I'll show you! You are cowards! Watch me!" He dashed into the Laguna de Guzmán but his men refused to follow the madman. The waters instantly trapped him and his horse. "You stupid sons of the mother-whore!" Fierro, a non-swimmer, yelled. "Don't just stand there looking at me. Can't you see I'm drowning? Throw me a rope!"

But his troops mutely looked on from the shore, watching the waters slosh upward. None moved. Fierro's own men were in holy terror of him; they preferred to let him drown.

After the waters engulfed the bloodiest murderer of the revolution, Fierro's men rode back to report to Villa.

"He was superb, he never cracked," one soldier with a strange sense of the ironic told Pancho.

Villa's own sense of death was cavalier. He hanged most of the prisoners he took in his various battles and wars. He thought nothing of ordering anyone's execution for the slightest reason. When he learned that one of his generals, Dionisio Triana, had an uncle who commanded a brigade in Obregón's army, he had Triana brought before him. Looking the innocent officer over as he stood at attention, Pancho Villa barked to his guards to take the general out and shoot him. His only comment was: "I saw in his glance that he was a traitor."

Death had breathed heavily in the face of the Centaur through all the bloody years of the Mexican Revolution but never as close as on June 4, 1912. General Villa was shaken from his sleep that morning, arrested on orders of President Madero's strongman General Victoriano Huerta. Charged with insubordination and refusing to return stolen horses, Villa was dragged from his bed, and, following a fake trial, led to a wall where he faced a firing squad. Martín Luis Guzmán, in the *Memoirs of Pancho Villa,* gives us the Centaur's own reactions as one of the few men ever to survive a firing squad: "As I stood in the square the first sergeant of the platoon went up to the wall and made a cross on it with a mattock . . . The sergeant ordered me to stand at the foot of the mark . . . I asked . . . 'Why are they going to shoot me? If I am to die, I must know why. I have served the government faithfully.' . . .

"I could not continue for the tears that choked me. At the time I hardly knew whether I was weeping from fear or mortification, but I see now it was because of the wrong they were doing me . . . Again the sergeant ordered me to stand at the foot of the cross, and again, with tears in my eyes . . . I demanded to be told why they were shooting me. As the sergeant tried to force me to the wall I threw myself to the ground, pretending to beg but only fighting for time."

During the stall, Villa began pulling things out of his pockets. He offered Captain Hernández, who was in charge of the firing squad, the coins in his pocket, then his gold watch. He asked for a priest. Patiently, Hernández listened to all the pleas and then gently moved Villa back into position. Hernandez walked to his squad of men. He drew his sword and flashed it upward into the sun, singing out: *"Attención! . . . Listos . . . Apunten . . ."*

Several horses rode into the square and a man jumped from his moving mount and raced forward. "Wait!" he yelled. "Don't fire! I have authorization here to halt the execution!" It was Raúl Madero, the President's brother, in company with Colonel Rubio Navarrete. President Madero had ordered a stay of execution, and a re-examination of the charges brought by Huerta (whom Villa and Zapata would later defeat in the field and chase into exile).

The experience almost overcame the lion-hearted Centaur. He sagged against the wall and mumbled to Madero: "My God, Raúl. I was that close to it, that close, *amigo*. And it really shook the hell out of me."

Villa's luck, however, ran out on July 20, 1923. By then, the revolutionary general had gone into retirement, settling at Canutillo, a vast estate of thousands of rich farming acres.

A young and violent rancher of means, Melitón Losoya, nursed a grudge against Villa. Canutillo had once been part of his family estates, he claimed. Villa was a usurper, Losoya grumbled; he had become like the very gentry he had fought, killed and conquered for years. Losoya resolved to assassinate Villa.

The man who egged on Losoya was the cunning plotter and arch foe of Villa, Obregón. His greatest fear was that Villa would once more become

An incredible photo showing Pancho Villa attempting to talk his way out of being executed as he stands before a firing squad.

restless, take issue with the incoming puppet President Calles, and raise another army bent on revolution.

Revolution was the farthest thing from Pancho Villa's mind as he roared along the road toward the small town of Parral, which bordered his ranch. He was driving a big 1919 Dodge touring car which had been presented to him by the government. There were three bodyguards sitting in the back seat. Two more hung on the running boards.

At his side in the front seat sat Villa's secretary and close friend, Colonel Miguel Trillo. All of the men were armed with large pistols and rifles.

"General," Trillo said, "did you ever dream that some day you'd be traveling up to forty-five miles an hour in a machine?"

"Never," Villa laughed. "Impossible!" He drove into the little white town like a child enjoying a new toy. In many ways, the Centaur was a child, who stuffed himself on canned sardines, peanut brittle and candy.

It was 8 A.M. and the streets of Parral were almost deserted except for a young man who crossed the street where the car slowed down to a crawl. The young man, a pumpkinseed vendor, respectfully removed his sombrero in a salute to the moving car. He shouted: "Viva Villa!" (The plan called for the vendor to shout once if Villa was driving, twice if he was in the back seat.)

A large adobe building directly in front of the Dodge was jutting rifle barrels. Losoya and seven of his relatives, fanatically whipped up with hatred for Villa, were behind the guns.

A shot rang out, splintering the windshield of the Dodge and hitting Villa square in the chest. He slumped onto his bodyguard Trillo, who, with the others, frantically reached for their pistols.

The eight men inside the adobe building ran outside with their Winchesters whistling bullets. Trillo stood halfway up but a bullet ripped into him and he fell backward over the car door, dead.

Medrano, a bodyguard, spilled into the street, his brains blown from his head. Another bodyguard, Hurtado, slid from the side of the Dodge as it bounced upward on the sidewalk and slammed into a tree. Hurtado's chest was split down the middle with a hail of bullets from the assassins led by Losoya, now berserk with screams of vengeance.

Big Ramón Contreras, last of the bodyguards, jumped from the running board of the Dodge. A shot had smashed his left arm. Still, he managed to pump shot after shot from his Winchester at the assassins as he staggered away down a side street, the only survivor.

Except one more. Pancho Villa, his head resting against the dead Trillo, had sixteen bullets in him—twelve in his body, four more in his head. One of his arms was hanging by only shreds of flesh, his intestines were spilling onto the floorboards of the Dodge. His entire massive chest was torn apart as if by a can opener.

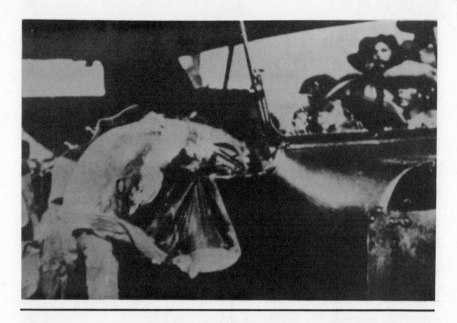

Villa's car shot to pieces by assassins on July 20, 1923; Villa died behind the wheel, his trusted bodyguard Trillo is sprawled dead halfway out of the big Dodge touring car.

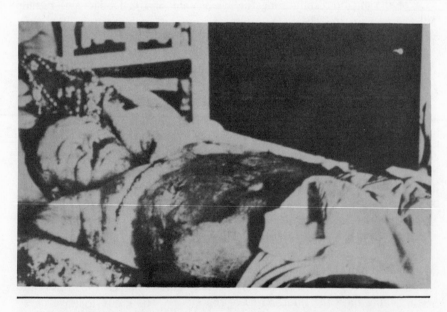

Villa dead in a Parral hotel room; his assassins claimed to be patriots.

The eight assassins closed in, amazed at their good luck. They had killed all but one and Pancho Villa was smashed to pieces behind the wheel. Ramón Guerra began to laugh. "The dirty pig, we taught him. We taught the bastard!" He came closer.

It was as if he were waking from a dream. Villa's eyes fluttered open, his mouth snarled wide and with one gigantic, superhuman gesture, the Centaur forced himself upward. His arm crossed his torn belly and yanked the big Colt from its holster.

Ramón Guerra's eyes bulged in disbelief as he watched the dying man raise the big weapon. It roared only once, like a cannon, and blew Guerra's face away, killing him instantly.

More shots were pumped into Villa. Then a long, deep sigh escaped from Pancho Villa's mouth as his shattered body slumped against the seat of the car.

Villa was not to be left in peace, even in death. His body was not taken to the magnificent mausoleum in Chihuahua City that he had prepared for himself and his comrades, but was buried in a plain grave outside Parral. For some arcane reason, ghouls broke into the Centaur's grave in 1926 and cut off his head. The head was never recovered.

Jesús Salas Barraza, an Obregón henchman who admitted goading Losoya into the murder of Villa and organizing the execution party and plan, was arrested shortly after the shooting and given a twenty-year prison term. He was released in six months. Obregón made him a colonel in the army, a post he held until his death in 1951. Barraza's own last words formed a shout of self-vindication: "I'm not a murderer! I rid humanity of a monster!"

KILLING THE KINGFISH

Perhaps no other American politician fully embodied the image of demagogue more than Huey Pierce Long, the dictator of the sovereign state of Louisiana. His power in his backward home state was absolute and he exercised that power with the kind of ruthlessness that had kept his sharecropper followers in bondage for a century. It was that ruthlessness that brought him to assassination at the hands of one of the most unlikely killers in political murder in America.

Long's political dynasty in Louisiana began with his election as governor in 1928, when the state became his private domain. He was, perhaps, the most flamboyant politician America has ever seen, a wild man who was charged, while in his offices of governor and U. S. Senator, with participation in incessant drunken revels, womanizing with the insatiable lust of a satyr, bribing state legislators to push through his pet bills which ostensibly benefited his "little people," and even ordering one of his body-guards to murder an opposing senator. The Kingfish was the virtual dictator of Louisiana, his motorcades and his person protected by a private army of armed thugs against the many who accused him and others who wanted him dead. (He was the prototype for figures in many Hollywood films, chiefly, Frank Capra's superb *Mr. Smith Goes to Washington,* where Edward Arnold, surrounded by a private army of cops, controls the state government, and in scores of books, the best of which is Robert Penn Warren's *All the King's Men.*)

Long developed the idea of a "share-the-wealth" program whereby all wealthy people would be mercilessly taxed. Ostensibly the Kingfish wanted to declare everyone in America debt-free and begin all over again by giving everyone $5,000.

Long said nothing about his own vast holdings in the southlands, which ran into the millions. He did not outline how his impractical plan could work. The Kingfish just said what he was thinking and let it go.

His real concern was holding on to power in Louisiana, to which he commuted regularly from Washington. Back home, he had a stooge governor who followed his instructions to the letter.

By 1935, the huge taxations Long had pushed through to build his beautiful superhighways, capitol buildings and lush leisure spas had the state almost bankrupt. The people rioted when he advocated new and heavier taxes to bail out himself and his party.

The Square Deal Association, organized by anti-Long people, swelled in membership and swarmed into the streets, armed with everything from pitchforks to shotguns. Huey hurried home. He called out the state troopers, the militia, hundreds of his goon squads, and put down this mini-rebellion with dozens of broken heads and blood-splashed streets.

Days later, presiding at a board of inquiry, Long shouted down his opposition. "You have all joined together to kill me!" he screamed as the lunatic aspects of his character surfaced. He was a strange-looking sight. Huey Long, U. S. Senator, argued against his accusers from inside a ring of men holding rifles with fixed bayonets and machine guns on his audience. Naturally, the Kingfish made his point. He sauntered from the hearing flushed with confidence. He still had his authority in Louisiana even though it was at the end of a gun.

At the end of another gun on September 8, 1935, down one of the hallways of the capitol building, stood quiet, meek-looking Dr. Carl Austin Weiss. He waited, unobserved, next to a granite pillar.

Why Dr. Weiss was there with a gun in his pocket and murder in his mind has always been a matter of mystery. Some said that Long had sexually assaulted someone in his family and Weiss wanted vengeance. It was also thought that Weiss was motivated by family loyalty in that he was married to Yvonne Pavy, daughter of Judge Benjamin Pavy, who was a

A newspaper recreation of Dr. Weiss's attack on Huey Long in 1935.

bitter foe of Huey Long and who, it was rumored, was about to be ruined by Long through a smear campaign which would employ the baseless rumor that the Pavy family was "tainted by Negro blood." Others maintained that Weiss hated the Kingfish for his anti-FDR campaigns.

There were others who insisted that Weiss felt Long to be a powerful and cruel demagogue, a madman destroyer of constitutional government. Today, with all eyes darting about for peeks at conspirators in the wake of Watergate, some misinformed revisionists are rumoring that Weiss was part of a vast political plot, or that he never pulled a trigger, which, of course, is nonsense.

No one ever really knew what motivated the mild-mannered Weiss to murder. He didn't live long enough to tell anybody. When Huey Long jovially marched down the hallway with his aides, he stopped to turn into the governor's office. As he did so, Dr. Weiss came at him with a drawn automatic.

Without a word, Weiss squeezed off two shots. His aim was thrown off by the movement of a bodyguard, but one bullet hit Huey in the abdomen.

Four of Long's bodyguards shot furiously into Weiss, emptying their pistols into his slight body. He fell, sixty-one bullet wounds spouting blood, and he was dead before he crashed to the marble floor.

Long, popeyed, his mouth sagging in disbelief, staggered down the hallway, out the massive capitol doors and down the stairs. He held on to his torn stomach, the blood jetting between his fingers. "Why did he do it?" he mumbled to an aide. "Why would anyone want to shoot me?"

The Kingfish never got an answer to that one. He died thirty hours later in a hospital on September 9, 1935. He was buried in a fabulous tomb on the capitol grounds.

Dr. Weiss was buried in an unknown graveyard. Not too many people remember the doctor who killed the demagogue. But everybody remembers Huey Long, the Kingfish, which is just the way he wanted it.

Other notable assassinations, chiefly those murders of heads of state through history, include:

Xerxes II, 424 B.C.: After ruling only one month, Xerxes II was murdered by his half brother Sogdianus, who claimed the throne, only to be assassinated by his brother Ochus six and a half months later. Ochus changed his name to Darius II.

Philip of Macedonia, 336 B.C.: The warrior king of Macedonia, having alienated his son Alexander and his wife, Olympias, by threatening to wed one of his concubines who would present him with a "legitimate heir," attended a wedding feast, jeopardizing his life by sauntering in front of his bodyguards to show his confidence in the people. The assassin Pausanias raced up to him and drove a dagger into Philip's side. The murderer was promptly killed before he could make any confessions, though it was widely assumed that the assassin was in the pay of Olympias, whose twenty-year-old son, later to be known as Alexander the Great, was assured of inheriting the Macedonian throne.

Darius III, 330 B.C.: After fleeing the battle of Arbela-Gaugamela and leaving his armies to the slaughtering whims of the Grecian army under Alexander the Great, Darius escaped to Bactria (now modern Afghanistan), where he was assassinated by Bessus, a satrap throwing his support to Alexander.

Julius Caesar, 44 B.C.: Thinking to proclaim himself king of the Roman Empire before the Senate, Caesar, on March 15, entered a hall in the theater of Pompey, and was beset by a score or more of militant senators, led by Brutus, Cassius Longinus, Trebonius, Tillius Cimber and others; all took turns plunging a dagger into Caesar—there were twenty-three bloody wounds on his body—until he crumpled to a gory heap beneath the statue of Pompey, his former adversary. In his dying moment, Caesar allegedly identified Brutus, his one-time friend, attacking him, uttering the immortal words: *"Et tu, Brute?"* The ringleaders of the assassination were at first offered amnesty by the Senate (a total of fifty senators, all Republican aristocrats, were involved in the plot), but the indicting words of Marc Antony in his funeral oration over Caesar's body inflamed the Roman mobs to revenge. All the chief conspirators were tracked down and killed.

Caligula (Gaius Caesar Germanicus), A.D. 41: The demented and obscene emperor Caligula was undoubtedly the most obstreperous of all the Caesars. His cruelty was only matched by his insanity. During his almost four-year reign, Caligula, who suffered from epilepsy, slept only three hours a night, and, in a half-somnambulistic state, roamed the corridors of the palace screaming commands for the sun to rise. He proclaimed himself a god, ordering any who displeased him murdered, often administering poison to the victim himself (he ordered his father-in-law, Marcus Silanus, to cut his own throat with a razor, stating that Silanus was plotting to seize power). A sadist, Caligula often ordered the canopies removed during the gladiatorial combats when the sun was at its hottest, commanding the suffering spectators to burn at his pleasure; he more than once whimsically closed the granaries of Rome to starve his subjects for the joy it would bring him. He once led an enormous army to the sea, ordering his befuddled soldiers to "dig for shells," so he could collect mussels.

On January 24, A.D. 41, two colonels in Caligula's guard, Chaerea and Sabinus, who had been constantly ridiculed by the emperor, repeatedly stabbed him to death, many of the Praetorian Guards gleefully rushing forward to redden their swords with the blood of the monster. "I am still alive!" Caligula shouted as he squirmed on the marble floor of the palace. The soldiers then stabbed him into silence. He was twenty-nine.

Claudius, A.D. 54: Caligula's uncle Claudius was a weak-willed emperor controlled by ambitious courtiers and, chiefly, by his wives, Messalina, whose gross sexual exploits caused the vacillating Claudius to have her executed, and the ruthless Agrippina, who tired of him in A.D. 54 and prepared a dish of mushrooms for him, his favorite dish, liberally spiced with poison. Claudius vomited the meal but Agrippina, an enterprising sort, told him soothingly that she could cure his upset stomach. She gave him the juice of a colocynth (a wild gourd from Palestine), which she administered to her husband both orally and as an enema, a "remedy" that killed him.

Nizam-al-Mulk, Grand Vizier of Turkey, October 1092: Following an audience in his tent, Nizam-al-Mulk, surrounded by a bevy of heavily armed guards, was carried outside on a litter to his caravan. A half-naked holy man approached, gesturing for permission to kiss the Grand Vizier's ring as a sign of respect. The guards parted, allowing the holy man to approach. He suddenly withdrew a dagger and plunged it into Nizam-al-Mulk's heart, killing him. The guards slashed him to pieces. This assassin, it was later learned, had been sent by an evil religious fanatic, Ala-u-d-Din Muhammed, commonly known as the Old Man of the Mountain, whose impregnable fortress was located in the mountains of Persia. The Old Man's character was not unlike that of the Ayatollah Khomeini of today's Iran. He was a vicious, self-aggrandizing despot who trafficked in political murder to gain power. According to the writings of Marco Polo, the Old Man gave wine laced with hashish to those members of his religious sect (the Ismailis) he had selected to perform his assassinations. They followed his instructions to the letter, knowing full well they would forfeit their lives in enemy camps. To amuse himself, the Old Man would receive foreign guests, then order one of his drugged followers to jump from a high window of his fortress to his death. According to Polo this made the Old Man feel he possessed the absolute power, that of life and death.

King William Rufus of England, August 1100: The forty-three-year-old English king, a tyrant by all standards, was assassinated by Walter Tirel, a knight, who sent an arrow through his breast while the king was riding alone in his private forest preserve near Winchester. No one seemed concerned with this assassination; Tirel explained that he was shooting at a deer and the king accidentally got in the way, an explanation that was accepted with gratitude by highborn and peasant alike, for, as one account put it, Rufus was "the kind of man who would collect enemies like other men collect the trophies of war . . . he was vicious, blasphemous, rapacious, violent and lustful."

Thomas à Becket, December 29, 1170: Thinking to control the English clergy and sanction his own excesses with the blessings of the Catholic Church, the corrupt Henry II of England made his free-living friend Thomas à Becket the Archbishop of Canterbury. Becket, however, repented his wastrel ways, taking his vows seriously. He imposed excommunications upon dissolute nobles, enraging Henry. After a seven-year exile in France, Becket returned to England, though warned that Henry meant to have him killed. Four knights—Reginald Fitzurse, William Tracy, Hugh de Morville and Richard Briton—visited Canterbury, seeking an audience with Becket. Undoubtedly Henry's emissaries, they were all heavily armed and supported with a large retinue of warriors. When Becket refused to withdraw the excommunications following their pleas, Fitzurse slashed Becket as he stood in the Cathedral in front of the altar of St. Benedict, the other knights eagerly putting the truculent churchman to death by the sword.

William of Orange, July 10, 1584: This prince of the Netherlands, who vowed to protect Dutch citizens accused of heresy by the Spanish Inquisition and marked for extermination, was himself ordered assassinated, Philip II of Spain offering a reward equivalent to $1 million to any assassin who could take the prince's life. This prompted several wild attempts upon William but the prince miraculously survived. Then, on July 10, 1584, one Balthazar Gérard entered William's court, requesting a passport. The request was granted and Gérard, instead of leaving the palace, hid in a small anteroom. When William entered this room Gérard shot him once. William shouted to his running guards: "My God, have pity on my soul! My God, have pity on these poor people!" He died before anyone could reach him.

Gérard tried to escape the palace but was quickly apprehended and taken to prison, where his joints were dislocated on the rack and his body was "seamed and scarred with flames." Gérard showed no emotion at his torturous execution. He mounted the scaffold with seeming indifference. One report had it that, on the scaffold, before a huge throng, Gérard's "right hand was burned off by a red-hot iron [the hand that committed the deed of regicide was invariably destroyed first], yet, although suffering the most excruciating agony, not a groan escaped his lips. Red-hot pincers then tore his flesh from his body in six different places. His abdomen was next cut open, and the bowels torn out. His legs and arms were then chopped off close to the trunk of his body. He yet lived. He ceased to breathe only when his heart had been cut out and thrown in his face. Finally the head was severed from the body, and the sentence had been executed."

Henry III of France, August 1, 1589: The son of the ruthless Catherine de Medici, who had indirectly caused the assassination of Admiral

Coligny and almost 70,000 of his fellow Huguenots in France in 1572, was himself an oppressor of Catholics in his own land, taking the side of the Huguenots in 1589, when he advanced on Paris with an army. A fanatical young Dominican brother, Jacques Clément, begged an audience with Henry before the siege of Paris began, stating that he had a message of great importance to deliver personally to the king. The message was a long knife which he plunged to the hilt in Henry's body, killing him instantly.

Henry of Navarre, May 14, 1610: Successor to Henry III, Henry of Navarre continued to oppress France's Catholics, the dominant religious group of the country. After attending mass at a church in the Rue St. Honoré in Paris on May 14, 1610, Henry departed by carriage for the palace. A religious fanatic, François Ravaillac, leaped upon the back of the king's carriage when it slowed down in a narrow street then known as the Rue de la Ferronnèrie. Ravaillac jumped upon the royal carriage's rear wheel, deftly leaned over the shoulder of the duke of Épernon, who was accompanying the king, and plunged a long-bladed knife into

An old print depicts the assassin Ravaillac attacking Henry IV as his coach halted for traffic on a Paris street.

François Ravaillac, who assassinated French King Henry IV in 1610. (from an old print)

France's monarch. "I am wounded!" cried Henry as Ravaillac jumped to the ground. Had he run, the assassin would, no doubt, have made his escape, but the killer was petrified by his act, holding the bloody knife in his hand and staring at it, standing as motionless as a statue in the street next to the carriage. A guardsman drew his sword to run the assassin through but the duke of Épernon shouted to him: "Save him, on your life!" Henry was taken to the Louvre, where he died within hours.

Ravaillac's punishment was even more gruesome than that meted out to Gérard, assassin of William of Orange. The killer was tied to a cross. His right hand was burned off in a slow fire. "The fleshy parts of his body were torn with red-hot pincers and into the gaping wounds were poured melted lead, hot oil, pitch and rosin." Before the wretch was beheaded he was dead.

Peter III of Russia, July 1762: Peter, grandson of Peter the Great, harbored hatred for his Russian subjects throughout his brief life, his sympathies lying with Germany, to which he was tied through strong bloodlines. When the empress Elizabeth died, Peter's six-month reign began with buffoonery and balderdash. The childish emperor spent most of his time playing with toy soldiers. He found a rat gnawing on one of his favorite puppets on one occasion and held a full-scale court-martial, executing the rat on a small gibbet he had ordered constructed. Peter had many mistresses and flaunted his affairs in front of his wife, Catherine, a much-abused princess from the small German principality of Anhalt-Zerbst.

Peter traveled to his palatial lodgings in Oranienbaum in June 1762, taking with him his favorite whore, Lizanka. Catherine received word that when Peter returned to St. Petersburg he would send off his wife to a Siberian exile. Catherine, with the help of the palace guard led by the brothers Aleksei and Grigori Orlov—Grigori was her some-time lover—left Peterhof and was proclaimed empress in St. Petersburg in a swift coup. Peter was seized and sent to confinement in Ropsha. He wrote groveling letters to Catherine, begging for his violin, pet monkey and his mistress, Lizanka. The violin and monkey were sent to him; Lizanka was shipped to a Siberian prison.

Some time in early July 1762, Aleksei Orlov, at Catherine's certain instigation, visited the deposed "Peter the Mad" in his quarters, getting the puerile sovereign drunk, and then strangling him. Aleksei and his brother were given huge cash endowments by Catherine, rewards for the assassination. The empress went on to become the greatest scandal of European royalty, her sexual appetite unappeased until she tottered into old age with the dubious sobriquet "Catherine the Great."

Jean Paul Marat, July 13, 1793: During the French Revolution, the Reign of Terror was conducted by chiefly three men, Danton, Robespierre and Marat, the latter being the most merciless in sending hundreds, many of them innocent, to their deaths on the guillotine as traitors to the revolution. A high-principled and beautiful young woman from St. Saturnin, Charlotte Corday (Marie Anne Charlotte Corday D'Armont), incensed with the revolutionary slaughter, walked the two hundred miles to Paris, resolved to assassinate Marat, who was busy hounding her Girondist friends.

Corday was shown into Marat's bath chamber. The "Father of the People," as Marat was called by his followers, sat in a bathtub, his chest bare, a bandanna soaked in vinegar to relieve his headaches, wrapped about his head, a board stretched across the tub with paper, ink and quill on it; Marat's labors, especially his elaborate orders of executions, did not escape him even in his ablutions. Marat motioned the attractive twenty-five-year-old Corday to be seated on a stool next to the tub, asking what she wanted. Corday coolly told him she had come from Caen and that she possessed important information about the uprising there. Marat gleefully seized his pen and began to write down a new list of traitors. As Corday spoke, Marat wrote; the woman, unseen by her victim, edged the stool closer to his tub.

Having finished the death list provided by Corday—all the names she supplied were fictional—Marat put down the pen triumphantly, turned to the woman and grinned, saying: "Excellent. In a few days' time I shall have them all guillotined in Paris!"

Corday's response to this was to withdraw a large knife from a sheath hidden in her blouse. With one movement, the woman rose, and plunged the knife downward into Marat's chest, where it cleanly penetrated a lung and cut into the aorta. She jerked the knife free and dropped the bloody blade upon Marat's writing board. The murderous Marat cried out with his dying breath: *"À moi, ma chère amie; à moi!"* (Help, dear friend; help!) He was dead by the time his servants rushed into the room.

Corday had left the bathroom but was stopped in an antechamber before she could reach the front door, a servant, Laurent Bás, crashing a chair on top of her head, then grabbing her brutally by the breasts and holding her until revolutionaries rushed in and dragged the assassin off to prison and a speedy trial. Charlotte Corday was humiliated at her trial, her dress torn away from her to expose her breasts before a drooling court of revolutionary cretins who quickly condemned her to death. She was beheaded on July 17, 1793. Her executioner, Sanson, stated in his memoirs that the alluring assassin met her death with womanly virtue. Another account supports this claim: "After her head fell into the basket, one of the attendants—a most brutal and inhuman wretch—lifted it up by the hair and struck the beautiful face—the face flushed with indignation."

Paul of Russia, March 24, 1801: The much neglected, dissolute son of Catherine the Great, Paul I, was a petty tyrant when he came to the throne at the age of forty-two in 1796. His hatred for his mother caused him to eradicate her memory by destroying statues, paintings and coins created in her memory. He inexplicably turned on England, sided with Napoleon, and brought down the wrath of Russian aristocracy. Fearful of assassinations, Paul left the Winter Palace and moved into the gloomy St. Michael's Castle outside of St. Petersburg, a seemingly impregnable fortress of massive gray stones, surrounded by a moat, large contingents of guards from Paul's favorite Gatchina regiments patrolling the castle's five drawbridges.

But the plotters against the emperor's life were the most powerful in Russia, including Count Nikita Panin, the vice-chancellor, and Count Peter Pahlen, the military governor-general of St. Petersburg. No castle could withstand their assassination attempt.

Paul's guards were simply bribed to allow nine conspirators to enter the castle on the night of March 24, 1801. Only one loyal guard, an elderly hussar who slept in front of Paul's bedroom, challenged the intruders; he was cut down by their swords. As the assassins burst into the royal chambers, Paul, who had taken to sleeping in his uniform and boots, jumped up, grabbed a chair and fought for his life, smashing the chair into the sword-thrusting killers. Pinned against a window, the monarch realized his desperate situation. He promised his attackers that he would abdicate, make them all princes of the empire, and reward them with estates. Several in the group seemed to reconsider until one in their number shouted: "We have passed the Rubicon. If we spare his life, before the setting of tomorrow's sun we shall be his victims." A sash was produced and Paul was then strangled with it. The assassins quietly left the castle, returned to their homes and went unpunished.

Juan Prim, Prime Minister of Spain, December 1870: A liberal politician, Prim was shot down while leaving the government chambers in Madrid by an unknown assassin who escaped.

Alexander II of Russia, March 13, 1881: Many attempts were made upon the life of Alexander II, even though he was known as the country's "Emancipator," having freed the serfs. His private train was blown up on December 4, 1879, but he escaped. The dining room in the Winter Palace was dynamited two years later only minutes before the czar was to take his meal. Nine soldiers were killed instead. Travel for the emperor became so hazardous that his ministers refused to allow him to leave his quarters unless he traveled on water.

The czar finally revolted against the restrictions of his police guards, booming: "I am a man. I will go and come as I please. I will eat and drink what I like, and do as I choose. If I am to be murdered in the end, that is the destiny which God himself has reserved for me. I have already lived longer than any of my race; as to death, I do not personally fear it."

What Alexander had no fear of occurred on March 13, 1881, as he and members of his family rode in carriages along the Nevsky Prospect after having viewed a military parade in St. Petersburg. Members of a violent nihilist sect called "The Will of the People," which had been conducting "an emperor hunt," hid in crowds waving to the emperor as his carriages crossed a bridge near the Michael Palace.

A young man dressed as a peasant leaped forward and threw a bomb, which exploded behind the czar's carriage. It completely shattered the carriage, killed two cossack guards riding escort nearby, an errand boy in the crowd, and several horses, and wounded several soldiers. Miraculously, Alexander emerged from the wrecked carriage unharmed. He tended to the wounded and then turned to get into another carriage. A second terrorist ran forward throwing another bomb two minutes later, shouting as he came toward the czar: "It is too early to thank God!"

The bomb landed squarely between Alexander's legs. It went off with a terrific explosion, described in one horrific account as producing "a havoc which the thrower could have scarcely expected. Columns of glittering snow arose high in the air, interspersed with which were flying fragments of wood and glass; the windows of the imperial stables broke with a crashing reverberation upon the still air, blown into myriads of pieces; the white mantle of the earth, gleaming with refractions such as diamonds themselves can scarcely produce, was dyed red with the blood which flowed from the death wounds of twenty killed and wounded men." The bomb-thrower himself had been killed. The czar was mortally wounded, his legs in shreds, one eyeball blown from its socket, his clothes in tatters.

To Grand Duke Michael, who rushed to his side, Alexander murmured: "Cold—cold—To the palace, quick—die there." The czar was removed to the Winter Palace, dying in the midst of his family, including his thirteen-year-old grandson Nicholas, who would himself be the victim of assassins' bullets.

President James A. Garfield, July 2, 1881: A political malcontent who had unsuccessfully sought an appointment as ambassador to France, Charles Julius Guiteau, vowed to murder President Garfield, who, Guiteau imagined, had denied him his foreign post. Guiteau stalked the President through the capital. The unbalanced assassin learned through the newspapers that Garfield would be taking the train to Williams College, his alma mater, to deliver an address. Guiteau hid in the Baltimore and Potomac train station and when Garfield, accompanied by Secretary of State Blaine, entered the waiting room, the assassin ran forward and fired a shot into the President, who lingered for over two months before dying.

President Garfield dying of an assassin's bullet in 1881. (*Frank Leslie's Illustrated Weekly*)

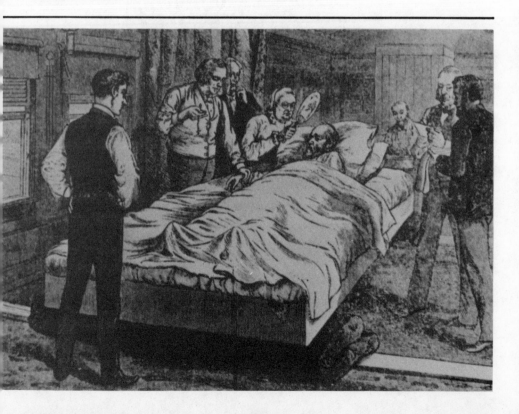

A railroad brochure seeking to sell tickets from President Garfield's assassination.

Guiteau went on trial, acting as his own defense attorney, cursing both judge and jury and lambasting the prosecutor. He was found guilty and hanged on June 30, 1882, reciting on the scaffold a poem he had written.

President Marie François Sadi Carnot, June 24, 1894: France was plagued by anarchists attempting political assassinations in the early 1890s, first by an anarchist named Ravachol, who tried to blow up the homes of a judge and public prosecutor involved with the trial of some Parisian anarchists. Anarchist Auguste Vaillant then tried to blow up the French Chamber of Deputies but his infernal machine exploded prematurely, injuring no one. He was nevertheless condemned. Because President Carnot would not grant Vaillant a reprieve, another anarchist, an Italian named Santo Geronimo Caserio, planned to assassinate him. Carnot attended the sprawling French Colonial Exhibition in Lyons on June 24, 1894, as Caserio knew he would. The assassin waited along the route of the French President's carriage as Carnot was being driven to the theater from a banquet. Fondling an expensive dagger with a six-inch blade, the assassin waited until the President's carriage came abreast of where he stood. He then easily pushed past the police cordon, jumped up on the President's landau and drove the knife up to the hilt in Carnot's body. The President died within a few hours. Caserio was almost lynched by the

Anarchist Santo Caserio assassinating French President Sadi Carnot in Lyons, France, in 1894.

irate mobs but he lived to face trial. He was condemned and brought to the guillotine on August 16, 1894. So terror-struck with his fate was the assassin that guards had to carry the quaking killer to the blade.

King Humbert I of Italy, July 29, 1900: While distributing prizes at Monza, near Milan, King Humbert was approached by Gaetano Bresci, a weaver who had saved his wages to travel from Patterson, New Jersey, to Italy. Bresci calmly walked up to the king and shot him dead.

President William McKinley, September 6, 1901: President McKinley, a much-respected and well-liked man, attended the Pan-American Exposition in Buffalo, New York, where, in the Temple of Music, he decided to greet visitors with traditional handshakes. In the line of anxious citizens waiting to press their palms to that of the President was twenty-eight-year-old anarchist Leon Czolgosz, who carried in his hand a short-barreled .32 caliber Iver Johnson revolver. He had the revolver covered with a handkerchief, wrapped in such a way as to indicate that his hand had been injured. Handkerchiefs were very much in evidence inside the hall; it was hot and everyone seemed to be mopping his brow. As Czolgosz approached the affable McKinley, who was surrounded by at least fifty guards, from policemen to secret service agents and soldiers, the assassin reached forward as if to shake the President's hand. McKinley, suspecting nothing, extended his hand. The assassin suddenly slapped it away and fired twice, the bullets striking the President, one ricocheting off a button, the other plowing through McKinley's abdomen. The shots caused the handkerchief in the killer's hand to be set on fire. "I done my duty," said Czolgosz as a dozen guards jumped on him, one punching him in the face. The mortally wounded McKinley looked up from the floor and, as was his compassionate nature, said: "Be easy with him, boys." He was dead eight days later. "It's God's way," the President told his wife on his deathbed. "His will be done."

Czolgosz told his prison guards that he first got the notion to kill McKinley when reading about a New Jersey working man who traveled to Italy to assassinate King Humbert of Italy on July 29, 1900. The hardships endured by his Polish immigrant family had caused him to hate America, he said. But why McKinley? Czolgosz shrugged. "I thought it would be a good thing for this country to kill the President." He had nothing more to say. He was executed on October 29, 1901, in New York's Auburn Prison, the first assassin to be electrocuted. Sulfuric acid was poured into his coffin to destroy his remains.

Leon Czolgosz assassinating President McKinley in Buffalo, New York, in 1901.

J. DAT. WALKER
BUFFALO

King Alexander of Serbia, June 10, 1903: After suspending the new constitution of Serbia when the country's radicals refused to support him, King Alexander and Queen Draga were marked for assassination by the country's elite army corps. Several officers led by a Colonel Apis broke into the royal couple's bedroom chamber in their Belgrade palace on June 10, 1903, and, following lengthy indictments about betraying the populace, shot both Alexander and Draga dead. Queen Draga had long had visions of their assassinations, warning her husband repeatedly to leave the country. "They are only dreams," he had told her.

King Carlos I of Portugal, February 1, 1908: A mob of revolutionaries swarmed around the carriage of the disliked King Carlos I of Portugal on February 1, 1908, in Lisbon. Scores of shots were fired, killing the king and his young son, Crown Prince Luis, while the queen helplessly beat the assassins with a bouquet of flowers.

Archduke Francis Ferdinand, June 28, 1914: During a state visit to the city of Sarajevo in Bosnia-Herzegovinia (now Yugoslavia), an Austrian protectorate, Archduke Francis Ferdinand, heir to the once all-powerful Austro-Hungarian Empire of the Hapsburgs, was marked for assassination by a small but determined Serbian nationalist group headed by nineteen-year-old Gavrilo Princip. He, Nedjelko Čabrinović and Trifko Grabez and others obtained arms and grenades from the same Colonel Apis (Dragutin Dimitrijević) who had engineered the assassinations of Alexander and Draga eleven years earlier.

The conspirators stationed themselves along the much publicized route the archduke and his morganatic wife, Countess Sophie, would take through Sarajevo, traveling in a slow-moving open touring car, on the morning of June 28, 1914. Čabrinović, a dull-witted fellow, calmly asked a policeman which car was the archduke's. When the auto was pointed out to him, Čabrinović casually pulled the pin from a grenade and hurled it at the car. It bounced off a fender, rolled beneath the car behind it and exploded, injuring several officials. The archduke and his party continued on to the town hall, oblivious to the attack.

Moments after he had tossed the grenade, Čabrinović, police in pursuit, raced to the nearby river Miljacka, leaping into the water. At the same moment he tried to swallow a cyanide capsule but it only burned his mouth. He was dragged screaming from the river.

Gavrilo Princip was more fortunate in carrying out the murderous plot. The archduke refused to be intimidated by Čabrinović's attack and insisted on continuing his tour of the town. Ferdinand and Sophie undoubtedly felt immune; both wore amulet charms to ward off danger. The royal couple left the town hall in the same touring car, which suddenly took a wrong turn, halting, as if by plan, directly in front of where Princip was standing in the crowd. Princip lost no time, approaching the car and firing his Browning revolver twice. Countess Sophie was struck by the first bullet, which drove through the car door and into her side, a mortal wound. The second shot struck Ferdinand in the neck.

"For God's sake, what has happened to you?" cried Sophie to her sagging husband, almost unaware of the fact that she had been hit.

Ferdinand saw the blood seeping from his wife's side and, as he crumpled into her lap, moaned, "Soferl, don't die. Live for my children."

By the time the speeding car roared into the courtyard of the Governor's Residence, Ferdinand and Sophie were dead. Princip had been seized immediately by officers after firing the fatal shots. Beaten by guards, his face running blood, the young assassin was rushed to the local jail and thrown into a cell next to Čabrinović. He shortly informed on his fellow conspirators, twenty-five persons in all, who were rounded up and, because of their youth, were given long prison sentences. Only Danila Ilic, a teacher, was hanged. Princip languished in jail, dying of tuberculosis in 1918. The motions of monolithic dynasties toward World War I were speeded up by this assassination, two shots that ended the old European world forever. Only weeks after Princip killed Ferdinand and his wife the world was at war.

Nicholas II of Russia, July 16, 1918: Following his abdication in 1917, the last of the Romanovs and his immediate family members were held prisoner, first by Kerensky's polite keepers, then by Bolsheviks, who removed Nicholas, his wife, children and personal servants to the gloomy town of Ekaterinburg in the eastern Urals. Nicholas and the others were led to believe that they would receive a public trial and then be banished. Lenin, Trotsky and especially the "butcher" of the Bolshevik Revolution, Jacob Sverdlov, had no such intentions.

On the night of July 16, 1918, Jacob Yurovsky, in charge of the royal captives at the Ipatiev House (the finest house in the primitive town, built by a one-time successful merchant N. N. Ipatiev)—the Soviets had ominously renamed the two-story building "The House of Special Purpose"—woke the czar, telling him and his family to dress. Nicholas was told that the Czech Legion and the White Army, who were attempting to liberate the royal family, were drawing dangerously near to Ekaterinburg and that the Romanovs would have to be moved. The czar and his family dressed and were taken to a semi-basement room of the house. Yurovsky, a watchmaker by profession, courteously asked the czar to wait in the basement room until the cars were brought around for them. The czar asked for chairs for his wife and his young son Alexis, who was ill (the boy was a hemophiliac). The empress sat on one chair, Nicholas, holding the boy, sat on another. His daughters, Tatiana, Olga, Marie and Anastasia, stood behind them with Dr. Eugene Botkin, the family physician, the empress' maid, Demidova, the czar's valet, Tropp, and the family cook, Kharitonov. The eleven captives had only moments to wait before Yurovsky returned with ten men, all of them professional executioners like himself, members of the new Soviet Secret Police, the Cheka.

"Your relations have tried to save you," Yurovsky blurted indifferently. "They have failed. We must now shoot you."

Incredulous, the czar began to rise from his chair, his son still in his arms, only one word escaping his mouth: "What?"

With that the assassins opened fire, mercilessly shooting the entire family and servants. The maid escaped the first volley but she was pursued screaming about the small basement room, finally bayoneted to death by the methodical assassins. When Alexis was found to be alive, Yurovsky leaned forward and fired two bullets into his ear. Thinking the carnage over, the guards prepared to leave, when they noticed the czar's youngest daughter, Anastasia, move; she had only fainted at the first shots. One account relates that "with bayonets and rifle butts, the entire band turned on her. In a moment, she too lay still."

The bodies were removed in the dead of night and taken to a mine shaft where 150 gallons of gasoline were poured upon them; they were burned for hours. The remains were hacked and sawed to pieces, then shoved down the shaft, with clothes and jewelry, four hundred pounds of sulfuric acid dumped over it all to dissolve the evidence of assassination.

Not until 1919, when the White Army took Ekaterinburg, did the world learn of the atrocity. Sifting through the skeletal remains in the mine shaft, investigators positively determined the deaths of the Romanovs, albeit only one slender, manicured finger—that of the empress—was found intact.

Since that time many theories have been advanced that not only did the Grand Duchess Anastasia survive the massacre but that the entire family somehow managed to escape the mass assassination, but conclusive proof has never been forthcoming.

The Soviets long denied the assassination but when the royal family's remains were discovered and identified, the Bolshevik leaders ordered the arrest and trial of twenty-eight people for the murders, even though Lenin and Sverdlov had secretly ordered the mass execution. The killers, the Soviets cried, were "Social Revolutionaries" bent on discrediting the Revolution by assassinating the czar. Five persons were executed.

Sverdlov was dead six months after the basement room slaughter, of pneumonia, his fellow Soviets insisted, but he was most likely murdered.

Those seeking to find the dismal town of Ekaterinburg on any present-day map will hunt in vain. The city has been renamed after Jacob Sverdlov, the chief architect of the czar's assassination, now known as Sverdlovsk.

Sir Henry Wilson, June 22, 1922: Wilson had been military adviser to the pro-British Belfast factions in Ireland during the Irish Civil War. He had incurred the wrath of the Irish Republican Army for his racist remarks and cruelty against the Irish Catholics fighting for their freedom from British rule. Wilson retired from the Army in 1922 but he continued to voice his hatred for the Irish. On Thursday, June 22, 1922, Wilson was returning to his home in Eaton Place by taxi. He got out, paid the cabbie, then walked to his front door to unlock it.

Two men, Reginald Dunne and Joseph O'Sullivan, who had been waiting for their target for more than an hour, shot Wilson dead on the doorstep. Dunne and O'Sullivan fled in a carriage but were soon overtaken and carried off to prison. Although neither assassin implicated the IRA at their trial, it was known, at least by authorities in Ireland, that the pair had done the bidding of Michael Collins, one of the leaders of the Irish Provisional Government. Both men had fought in the British Army during World War I. O'Sullivan had lost a leg at Ypres; he knew he had no chance of escape following the assassination. Both men were executed at Wandsworth Prison on August 10, 1922. Before he died, Dunne wrote out a statement to the British courts which read, in part, "You may, by your verdict, find us guilty, but we go to the scaffold justified by the verdict of our own conscience."

Sir Lee Stack, November 19, 1924: Stack, the British sirdar, or commander-in-chief, of the Egyptian Army, was attacked by several assassins on November 19, 1924, as his car slowed while moving through the congested streets of Cairo. The assassins fired dozens of bullets into the car, killing Stack and wounding other officers, before leaping into a taxi to escape. The Egyptian police learned through informants that a group of Egyptian nationalists led by Shafik Mansur had committed the murder, the actual shooting done by two brothers named Enayat and Mahmoud Rashid. The assassins were apprehended as they attempted to flee the country by train. Four pistols were found in a basket of fruit they were carrying. These weapons were matched to the bullets that killed Stack by ballistics expert Sidney Smith. His testimony helped to send the killers to their executions.

Mayor Anton J. Cermak, February 15, 1933: A political malcontent, Joseph Zangara, attempted to shoot President-elect Franklin Roosevelt on February 15, 1933, in Miami as the President's open car moved slowly through the streets. Zangara rushed to the car and, at a distance of eight feet, shouted: "There are too many people starving to death!" He fired his rounds wildly, missing Roosevelt and accidentally hitting Mayor Anton J. Cermak of Chicago with two bullets. Zangara was beaten to the ground by spectators and dragged away by police. Cermak was dead within hours. It was later suggested that Zangara had been hired by members of the Chicago syndicate to kill the mayor, but these theories were ground-

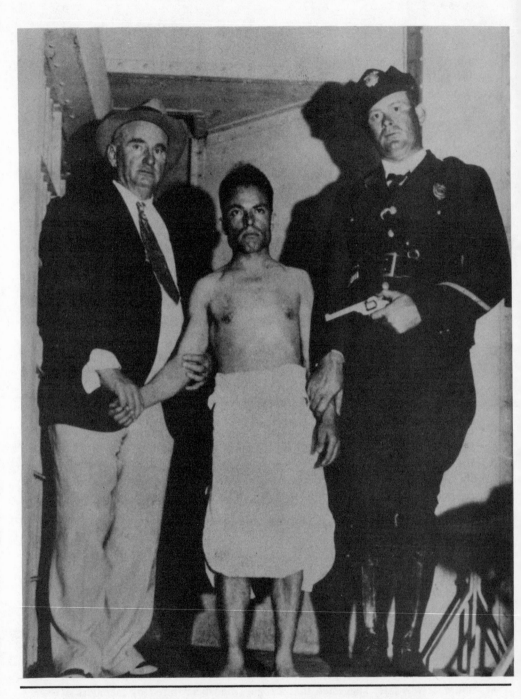

Joseph Zangara (center) under guard just after assassinating Mayor Anton
Cermak of Chicago in 1933; he was later executed.

less. The assassin was electrocuted on March 21, 1933. He went to his execution without remorse, stating that "If I got out I would kill him [Roosevelt] at once."

Chancellor Engelbert Dollfuss of Austria, July 25, 1934: The diminutive fascist leader of Austria had long resisted the rise of Nazi power in his country. In an attempted coup, Austrian Nazis (about 150 men of the SS Standarte 89), with Hitler's secret backing, tried to take over the Austrian Government on July 25, 1934, seizing Vienna's main radio station and important government buildings, including the Chancellery. Austrian leaders had been warned minutes beforehand and all but Chancellor Dollfuss had left the Chancellery. As he was preparing to flee, a gang of SS men led by Franz Holzweber and Otto Planetta burst into the Yellow Salon, Dollfuss' private offices. The chancellor at first tried to reason with them but Planetta brushed through the SS men and raised a pistol. Dollfuss shielded his face with his hands. Planetta fired two shots through his hands, one penetrating his throat, the other going through his spinal column, leaving Dollfuss alive but paralyzed from the hips down. He lived for several hours, begging his captors, who were by then under siege by government troops, for a doctor. His pleas were ignored. He died with the words: "Children, be good to one another. I always wanted to do only the best." The coup was quickly put down. Most of the assassins were executed. When Planetta and Holzweber mounted the scaffold, they stood to attention, faced Germany and shouted: "Heil Hitler!" But Hitler refused to recognize their attempt to unify Austria with Germany through revolt and assassination, denouncing the very men he had sent to kill Dollfuss. Four years later, Hitler took over Austria in a bloodless *Anschluss*.

King Alexander I of Yugoslavia, October 9, 1934: Alexander I was a monarch of a patchwork nation, pieced together following World War I, mostly from the defeated Austro-Hungarian Empire and made up of Serbia, Croatia-Slovenia, Montenegro, Bosnia and Herzegovina, all of it renamed Yugoslavia. The king was a Serbian to the core, a hard-line militarist who dissolved parliament in 1928 when Croatian representatives were shot to death in their parliamentary chambers. In turn, Croatian nationalists, under the leadership of Ante Pavelić, resolved to assassinate Alexander at the first opportunity.

That opportunity came in Marseilles on October 9, 1934, when Alexander, attempting to obtain a strong treaty with France, was motoring through a large throng with Louis Barthou, the French Foreign Minister, and French General Alfonse Georges at his side. Racing from the crowd lining the street, Vlada Chernozamsky, a professional assassin in the employ of Pavelić, leaped to the running board of the limousine carrying Alexander and emptied his pistol into the occupants of the car, striking Alexander twice, Barthou once, and Georges with four superficial wounds. The king died within two minutes in the back seat of the car as newsreel cameramen recorded his grim fate. Barthou, for lack of proper medical attention, bled to death hours later.

The assassin did not long survive. The furious crowd crushed him to the ground; he was shot in the head, most likely by a policeman. Chernozamsky died later that day. Others in the conspiracy were arrested and given life imprisonment. Pavelić scurried back to Italy, where he had planned the assassination with Mussolini's blessing. The architect of the murder remained free.

Leon Trotsky, August 20, 1940: The one-time co-leader of the Russian Revolution (with Lenin), exiled to Mexico for his political differences with the Soviets, chiefly Stalin, was assassinated on August 20, 1940, in his villa outside of Mexico City. His killer was a shadowy figure, one Jacques Mornard, a man of many aliases who claimed to be Belgian. Mornard took three years to ingratiate himself to Trotsky's friends before he became a minor confidant of the ousted revolutionary.

The assassin entered Trotsky's library at 5 P.M. on August 20, 1940. He asked Mrs. Trotsky for a glass of water. When she went to get it, Mornard slipped behind the unsuspecting Trotsky, removed a pickaxe from his long overcoat and brought it down full force into Trotsky's head. Instead of dying instantly, as Mornard had expected, the victim leaped up with a wild yell, throwing books and paperweights at the startled assassin. Guards caught the killer as he tried to escape. "They made me do it," he screamed, telling the guards that "they" had his mother in prison. He was undoubtedly a Stalinist assassin but he never clearly admitted it. Trotsky lingered for hours, dying on August 21, 1940. Mornard was sent to prison for twenty years. He was released in 1960, leaving Mexico for Czechoslovakia.

Reinhard Heydrich, May 27, 1942: Heydrich, chief of the Nazi Security Police, deputy chief of the Gestapo, Himmler's right-hand terrorist and one of the architects of Hitler's "final solution" to the so-called Jewish problem, was assassinated by two Czech freedom fighters, Jan Kubis and Josef Gabcik. Both men had parachuted from an RAF bomber with specific orders to kill Heydrich, who, it was felt by the Czechoslovak Government in exile, was becoming too popular in Czechoslovakia as that country's "Protector."

Kubis and Gabcik, along with two other partisans, waited in the Prague suburb of Holesovice along the Dresden–Prague road near to Troja bridge, a route Heydrich daily drove from his villa to his headquarters in Hradschin castle. When the Nazi's green Mercedes convertible slowed at a hairpin curve, the Czechs opened up with their guns; Kubis hurled a grenade, which struck the back of the car, wrecking it. Heydrich stumbled from the smashed auto swearing and firing his pistol at his assassins. He then grabbed his hip, staggered and fell. Steel springs from the car's seat had been driven into the Nazi's ribs and stomach. He died of his wounds on June 4, 1942.

Kubis and Gabcik escaped momentarily but they were killed, unknown to the Nazis, when the Germans retaliated for the assassination by liquidating 1,331 Czechs, which included the utter obliteration of the village of Lidice and its entire male population.

King Ananda of Siam, June 9, 1946: On the morning of June 9, 1946, a shot was heard from the bedchambers of the twenty-year-old Ananda, king of Siam. Officials hurrying into the Bangkok palace found the king with a single bullet through his head. Although the assassin was never apprehended, British authorities on the scene attributed the killing to a communist plot.

Mahatma Gandhi, January 30, 1948: Following a long fast, the seventy-eight-year-old spiritual leader of India, Mohandas Karamchand Gandhi, called affectionately Mahatma (meaning in Sanskrit "Great Soul"), was shot three times in the chest and abdomen by Nathuram Vinayak Godse, a thirty-seven-year-old newspaper editor and member of the violently anti-Moslem organization Mahasabha.

Godse had long feared that Gandhi's attempt to unite all of India's millions, Hindu and Moslem alike, would lead to a Moslem takeover of the country. He and six others conspired to kill the great Mahatma in early 1948.

At 5:15 P.M. on January 30, 1948, Godse pushed his way through the several hundred spectators awaiting the Hindu leader in the garden of his sanctuary, the Birla House, outside of New Delhi, India. Without a word, he rushed to Gandhi's side and shot him to death. Gandhi's only remarks to the two nieces at his side were: *"Hai Rama! Hai Rama!"* ("Oh, God! Oh, God!")

Godse was set upon by the crowd, beaten, then taken to jail. His trial and that of his fellow conspirators dragged on for months. He and Narayan Apte were condemned, five others given life sentences. Godse told the court that he considered Gandhi, who had, more than any other Indian leader, ended British rule of the country through nonviolent rebellion, a "curse to India, a force for evil . . . the master brain guiding the civil disobedience movement." Godse died slowly by the rope. Instead of having his neck snapped, Godse strangled to death for fifteen minutes on November 15, 1949.

Today, Gandhi is honored in India as Christians revere a saint. Though he once stated that he wanted to live to the age of 125, Gandhi remarked shortly before he was murdered: "I do not want to die . . . of creeping paralysis of my faculties . . . a defeated man. An assassin's bullet may put an end to my life. I would welcome it."

King Faisal II of Iraq, July 17, 1958: In a military coup, Iraqi General Qassim and small detachments stormed the royal palace in Baghdad at dawn on July 17, 1958, but the palace guard put up a stiff resistance. Faisal and his family were trapped; the king was guaranteed safe conduct by Qassim if his guard would cease fire. Faisal, to save the lives of his men, agreed. When the palace guards put down their arms, Qassim's men rushed into the palace and machine-gunned the entire royal family, brutally slaying several baby princesses. Qassim's dictatorship lasted a little less than five years, his regime being overthrown on February 8, 1963, the general being executed the following day.

Patrice Lumumba, January 17, 1961: The controversial Prime Minister of the newly established Republic of the Congo, Lumumba, was made a prisoner by President Joseph Kasavubu and sent by plane to the province of Katanga, an area teeming with Lumumba's enemies. Although Lumumba's assassination on January 17, 1961, was never made clear, one believable version is that he was beaten to death on the plane before it landed.

Rafael Trujillo, May 30, 1961: Strongman and dictator, Rafael Leonidas Trujillo Molina had ruled the Dominican Republic with an iron hand for thirty years, a reign of cruel repression, replete with torture and murder. Several abortive attempts to overthrow Trujillo had been made over the years, the CIA, as it had with Lumumba's downfall, actively seeking to have him assassinated and providing dissidents with arms.

Trujillo put on his elegant army uniform on May 30, 1961, which meant he was traveling from Ciudad Trujillo to his home town of San Cristobal to visit his sprawling ranch and one of his two mistresses. His car was ambushed along the road just outside Ciudad Trujillo as a car full of dissidents pulled alongside the generalissimo's blue and gray sedan, the assassins pumping dozens of bullets into Trujillo's auto.

"I am wounded!" Trujillo shouted to his driver. "Let's stop and fight!" He pulled his revolver and emptied it at the other car as both autos came to a halt. The driver fired a machine gun at the assassins. By then Trujillo was dead, slumped in the back seat. His driver was then overpowered. The killers mutilated the strongman's face, then dumped his body into the trunk of their car, which they drove back to Ciudad Trujillo, where it was deserted. The assassins, led by Pedro Cedeno, and Lieutenant Amado Garcia, were eventually caught and executed but the Trujillo regime was all but finished.

Ngo Dinh Diem, November 2, 1963: Diem, elected President of South Vietnam in 1955, quickly established a virtual dictatorship, and was overthrown in 1963 by military leaders aided by the CIA. A Vietnamese major, whose identity was never made public, executed Diem and his political adviser and brother Ngo Dinh Nhu as they rode in the back of an armored personnel carrier with their hands tied behind their backs.

President John F. Kennedy, November 22, 1963: Political subversive Lee Harvey Oswald, a sometime believer in Communism, shot and killed President Kennedy on November 22, 1963. His fire was directed from the sixth floor of the Texas School Book Depository Building in Dallas, Texas, where Oswald worked as a stock boy at $1.25 an hour. Using a 6.5 mm bolt-action, clip-fed 1938 Mannlicher-Carcano rifle, Oswald mortally wounded Kennedy, and injured Texas Governor John Connally as the President's motorcade passed beneath the depository building on Elm Street. Oswald did not live long enough to explain his motivations for the assassination.

Rafael Trujillo, dictator of the Dominican Republic, shortly before his assassination in 1961.

Following the shooting, Oswald calmly went to the building's lunch-
room on the second floor, where he sipped a soda. He then left the
building quietly as police raced to the sixth-floor perch where he had
gunned down the President. The assassin went home, changed his jacket
and put a pistol in his pocket. Officer J. D. Tippit stopped Oswald for unknown reasons near his home. The assassin shot him dead with four bullets. He then went to a movie at the Texas Theater, where he was arrested
(he had aimed his pistol at the officers in the lobby but it misfired).

On November 24, before millions of television viewers, Oswald was
himself shot to death by Dallas nightclub owner Jack Ruby as more than
seventy policemen were moving him to the county jail. Ruby, who
claimed to have acted out of patriotism, died of cancer in jail while awaiting execution after being found guilty of murder.

The President's Commission on the Assassination of President Kennedy, popularly known as the Warren Commission, determined that Oswald had acted alone and no conspiracy to kill Kennedy existed, but the
issue is hotly debated to this day.

Martin Luther King, Jr., April 4, 1968: The great civil rights leader,
Dr. King, was shot and killed as he stood on the balcony of a Memphis,
Tennessee, motel on April 4, 1968, his assassin firing from a nearby
building, using a .30-06 Remington pump rifle, sighting through a pair of
binoculars. Weeks later the assassin, who had fled to Canada, then to Lisbon and subsequently London, was identified as an habitual criminal,
James Earl Ray. He was extradited from England, tried and given a
ninety-nine-year prison term.

Ray's unsophisticated background coupled with his ability to flee the
country in what appeared to be an elaborately planned escape suggests a
conspiracy in the King assassination, but definite proof is lacking at this
date.

Robert Kennedy, June 5, 1968: Brother of the slain President John
Kennedy, Senator Robert F. Kennedy showed all the signs of winning the
Democratic nomination for the 1968 presidential campaign when, on
June 5, 1968, after winning the California primary, he was shot to death
by Palestinian Sirhan Bishara Sirhan, whose motives remain unclear to
this day. Kennedy had just finished a victory speech in the Ambassador
Hotel and was leaving the podium of the Embassy Ballroom when Sirhan
approached him with a rolled-up Kennedy campaign poster in his hand
which concealed a .22 caliber revolver, using the same method to disguise
his murder weapon as had Leon Czolgosz sixty-seven years earlier in the
assassination of President McKinley. Sirhan fired several times, one bullet
striking Kennedy in the head; he died twenty-five hours later.

Kennedy's guards leaped upon the assassin but too late. He was taken
battered to jail. Sirhan was condemned to death after a fifteen-week trial
at which time he openly confessed the assassination. Sirhan escaped the

gas chamber when the U. S. Supreme Court abolished capital punishment; he is currently in prison and actively seeking a parole.

King Faisal of Saudi Arabia, March 25, 1975: The king of the Saudis was executed by his nephew, twenty-seven-year-old Prince Faisal Bin Musaed Bin Abdulaziz, a drug-taking playboy who claimed to be motivated by the killing of his brother Prince Khalid nine years earlier while storming a Riyadh TV station (as a protest against the Koranic ban of human images). The assassin merely slipped into a delegation paying homage to Faisal in a reception room at the Ri'Assa Palace, firing three shots at the king, the first two finding the mark, one killing Faisal with a bullet wound in the head. The prince then screamed: "My brother is avenged!"

Prince Faisal was first declared deranged but was later thought fit enough to stand trial. He was condemned and later beheaded, his head placed on a stake for throngs to see.

President Park Chung Hee, October 26, 1979: The South Korean President Park Chung Hee was invited to dinner by the country's Central Intelligence Agency chief, Kim Jae Kyu, on the night of October 26, 1979. The President and five aides sat down to a food-laden table in the KCIA's two-story annex near the presidential Blue House compound. Kyu immediately fired on all six men, killing President Park and four others. Four more Park bodyguards were shot by Kyu's aides in a waiting room when Kyu's shots were heard.

At first, authorities in Seoul stated that the President and his aides had been killed "accidentally," but one of Kyu's aides quickly confessed the assassination. Kyu, now under arrest and awaiting trial at this writing, planned to complete a military coup, establish martial law, then take over the South Korean Government. Said one Korean authority, Kyu had taken his drastic measures because "he was afraid of losing his job."

BOMBINGS

BOMBERS IN OUR MIDST

The use of bombs, as a political weapon, a crime of passion, murder for profit, or the act of a lunatic seeking revenge for real or imagined wrongs, is a relatively current criminal exercise. Almost all such lethal activity has been confined to this century, the illogical outgrowth of Alfred Nobel's dubious invention of dynamite.

In the latter part of the nineteenth century the planting and throwing of bombs was wholly employed by political malcontents and directed at European royalty and American business kingpins. Such devastating and desperate techniques on the part of political radicals did not re-emerge until political activism, particularly in America, became almost a profession in the late 1960s, chiefly among anti-intellectual, anti-social students whose megalomania for self-identification was solely manifested in the mass death and destruction their bombs could produce.

For a two-year period, roughly from January 1969 to the end of 1970, more than 40,000 bomb threats, attempted bombings and actual bombings were recorded by local and federal law enforcement agencies throughout the United States. After eliminating the lunatics in this number, *at least* 8,000 involved direct political terrorism. In one five-day nightmare in 1970 bombs were exploded in a New York courthouse, at the base of a statue in Chicago honoring those police officers killed in the Haymarket anarchist bombings of May 4, 1886 (the first time dynamite was used as a weapon in America), in California at Santa Barbara in an armory, and in a San Rafael courtroom, and in Seattle, Washington, inside an ROTC building on the campus of the University of Washington.

Although the number of bombings has dwindled appreciably since that period, the ease with which explosive elements are obtained and constructed as bombs has allowed such so-called "political statements" to continue. In the first half of 1976 law enforcement personnel recorded

The Haymarket Riot in Chicago, May 4, 1886; Samuel Fielden, a teamster, harangues the anarchistic as the notorious bomb explodes in the middle of a police phalanx.

549 bombs exploding in the United States, almost all attributable to political maniacs, explosive devices that murdered twenty-three persons, injured another 108 people and caused more than $6 million in damage.

The bomb problem is still agonizingly with us, a worldwide dilemma that appears uncheckable. On May 31, 1979, forty-two bombs, set to go off one after another with intervals of only seconds between, exploded all around Paris, France, fortunately resulting in only minor injuries and damage. This was the work of a fanatical separatist organization demanding total independence for the French-held island of Corsica. In the United States, in early June 1979, five bombs were sent nationwide to the headquarters of neo-Nazi organizations, two to that of Chicago's Nazi leader Frank Collin, by a Jewish militant organization.

In the past the motives for bombings have been diversified, shocking and, for those responsible for answers, downright puzzling.

The hanging of the Haymarket "conspirators" in Chicago, November 11, 1887; (left to right) August Spies, Adolph Fischer, George Engel, Albert Richard Parsons.

Some of the more spectacular and notable bombings in this century include:

1903–05: Harry Orchard, born Albert E. Horsley, and using a half dozen more aliases, became the chief dynamiter for the anarchist wing of the violent IWW (Industrial Workers of the World; the "Wobblies," or "I Won't Works"), headed by ex-cowboy and miner Big Bill Haywood, whose rough-and-tumble union credo was "Good Pay or Bum Work."

Orchard's first assignment was to go to Cripple Creek, Colorado, to punish the owners of the Vindicator Mine who had locked out the Wobblies. He blew up the mine shaft opening in early 1903, killing a superintendent and a shift boss. With Haywood providing him with money and encouragement, Orchard next visited Independence, Colorado, where strikebreaking miners had shut out the Wobblies. Haywood had told Orchard that "something ought to be blown up."

Checking the work schedule of the strikebreakers, Orchard discovered that five minutes after the 2:30 A.M. shift was over, scores of men gathered on a nearby railroad platform, waiting to be shuttled to their quarters. The dynamiter stole two fifty-pound boxes of dynamite from a Cripple Creek storehouse and lugged them to nearby Independence. In a later confession, Orchard was to detail his setting of the infernal machine with devilish pride: "Late that night I prepared a bomb under the station platform. The mechanism was a simple job and consisted of the powder, some caps, a bottle of acid, and a little windlass which, when turned, would pull the cork from the bottle and permit the acid to run out. This would explode the charge.

"But setting the bomb in place took some work. I had to crawl a long way on my belly under the platform. It was dark, and cold. Hooking up the windlass to the cork was a ticklish job, but I managed it. Then I attached one end of a long wire to the windlass, and backed out from under the platform with the other end. I ran this wire into the bushes and up to an abandoned ore house on a siding. Then I sat down to wait.

"Through the dark I could hear the strikebreaking miners—quite a crowd of them—coming out of the mine and going to the depot. The train was on time. I heard her whistle for the station at 2:35, and a moment later she drove in. Just then I pulled on the wire. A second later the charge went off with a tremendous roar."

Harry Orchard had murdered another twenty-six men; more than fifty other miners were crippled for life in the flesh-ripping blast. Haywood, according to Orchard, heartily complimented him on the Independence bombing, next ordering him to murder one Fred Bradley, a member of the Mine Owners Association living in San Francisco. Orchard first put strychnine in a bottle of milk delivered to the Bradley family but the cook sipped the milk, found it bitter and threw it out. He next affixed a bomb between the double doors of the Bradley home and when the mine official left for work the following morning, he was blown across the street, the entire facade of this three-story home destroyed. Bradley miraculously survived.

Judge Luther M. Goddard, a Colorado Supreme Court justice who had ruled unfavorably for the Wobblies in the past, was selected as the next bombing victim of the Wobblies in 1904. In Denver, Orchard planted a bomb inside a purse along a snow-swept path the judge habitually crossed on his way to work. Goddard, however, was hailed by a friend before he moved across the lot, and walked a different way. However, Merritt W. Walley, a Denver citizen, minutes later, did walk along the path, spot the purse and pick it up. His body was blown in pieces over a radius of a half block.

Frank Steunenberg, ex-governor of Idaho, had incurred the enmity of Haywood and others in the past by calling federal troops in to quell riotous IWW miners; he was slated for death via bombing. Orchard placed a large charge of dynamite near the front gate of Steunenberg's home in Caldwell, Idaho, on December 30, 1905. When Steunenberg emerged he was exploded into tiny fragments. Orchard, whose previous escapes from bombing sites were always by a hair, was leaving Caldwell only minutes later when a sheriff from Baker, Oregon, Harvey K. Brown, recognized him as a union terrorist and had him arrested by local police. (Brown was later blown up by Wobbly dynamiters for identifying Orchard.)

Harry Orchard was tried for the Steunenberg bombing, found guilty of murder and condemned to the gallows. Through powerful union influence, however, his sentence was commuted to life in prison. Big Bill Haywood was also tried with Orchard, along with other Wobbly officials named by Orchard in his non-stop confession. Masterfully defended by Clarence Darrow, Haywood was freed for lack of corroborative evidence beyond Orchard's confession.

1908: Police corruption in New York City, especially the wholesale extortion of prostitutes in the Tenderloin District, had reached such horrendous proportions that massive public meetings were held to find remedies. Disgusted with the ineffectiveness of such gatherings, twenty-year-old M. Silverstein, a Russian immigrant, tossed a homemade bomb into a squad of police officers milling about in Union Square. Spotting the infernal machine, the cops dashed to safety, but a bystander was blown to pieces. Silverstein was captured on the spot and sent to prison. Authorities branded him an anarchist, but, as was later learned, Silverstein had been incensed over the brutal treatment of prostitutes by extorting police, particularly that of his own sister!

1916: Ignoring President Woodrow Wilson's "Too-Proud-to-Fight" credo, San Francisco, on July 22, 1916, caught up in the patriotic war fever sweeping the nation, held a giant Preparedness Day parade, replete with impressive Army and militia units marching down the main streets to the strump of drums. Hundreds of thousands turned out to hoot their approval. The streets were suddenly rocked with the sound of an explosion heard throughout the city. A fireball of immense proportions, followed by sickening black smoke, shot upward at the corner of Market and Steuart streets, leaving in its wake fifty stricken spectators, nine of whom were lying dead, bodies in ribbons.

Although he had a perfect alibi, labor leader Tom Mooney and his assistant, Warren K. Billings, were quickly indicted for the crime. (Only part of Mooney's defense was a photo showing him and his wife, Rena, watching the parade at a site 6,008 feet from the location of the bomb with a large clock behind them showing the exact time of the explosion.) Mooney had been selected by powerful business leaders in San Francisco as the likeliest suspect. Labor, in this boss era, was considered unpatriotic. The bombing was reminiscent of the Los Angeles *Times* explosion engineered by the McNamara brothers, labor agitators, on October 1, 1910. Billings, Mooney's protégé, had once been convicted in a bomb plot.

The thirty-two-year-old Mooney was railroaded, as was Billings, to a sentence of life imprisonment, largely on the testimony (later proved perjured) of Frank C. Oxman, who lied openly in court when he stated that he witnessed Mooney and Billings placing a black satchel against a Steuart Street saloon wall, quoting Mooney as saying: "We must run away; the cops will be after us." (Oxman, it was later proved, was ninety miles from San Francisco at the time of the explosion.) President Wilson, reviewing the case, declared that "the utilities sought to get Mooney . . . with Oxman discredited, the verdict was discredited."

Through archaic laws—California courts were prevented from considering perjury evidence after the rendering of a verdict—Mooney was kept in prison until January 7, 1939, when he was pardoned, a period of twenty-two years, one of the great injustices of modern jurisprudence. Billings was released some months later.

1920: An unidentified man drove a wagon to the corner of Broad and Wall streets, the core of America's financial power, shortly before noon on September 16, 1920. He stepped from the wagon and began to push his way through the dense crowds of businessmen. At exactly 11:59 A.M. a terrific explosion tore apart the street as the wagon, loaded to the hilt with dynamite and scrap iron, exploded with a deafening roar. Found in the smoking carnage were thirty-eight dead; hundreds more had been injured, scores maimed for life. The offices of J. P. Morgan Company, thought to be the target, were heavily damaged. The bomb planter, his motives unknown to this day, was never apprehended.

1922: John Magnuson, a farmer living outside of Marshfield, Wisconsin, after feuding with his neighbor, James A. Chapman, over the rights to a creek drain, sent a parcel to Chapman on December 27, 1922, which blew up when the farmer opened it; the blast permanently injured Chapman and killed his wife, who was leaning over his shoulder as he untied the package.

A piece of the package's wrapping paper was found with Chapman's address penciled on it. John F. Tyrrell, one of the foremost document detectives in the United States, identified Magnuson through his handwriting. Magnuson was sentenced to life.

1927: James Belcastro, known in the Chicago underworld of the 1920s as "King of the Bombers," served as one of Al Capone's most trusted terrorists. In addition to Black Handing, Belcastro's specialty with explosives was blowing up saloons whose owners refused to peddle Scarface's beer. Belcastro was particularly active in the 1927 Chicago primary, called the "Pineapple Primary," largely due to his bombings, in which he planted bombs in polling places and on the porches of political adversaries opposing William Hale "Big Bill" Thompson, Capone's hand-picked mayoral candidate. Five deaths were attributed to Belcastro's exploding devices; hundreds were injured. Thompson was elected. Belcastro, decades later, died in bed.

1930: A prominent lawyer in Amarillo, Texas, A. D. Payne, so that he could spend the rest of his days with one of his secretaries, blew up his wife and young son by planting a powerful explosive device in the family car on June 27, 1930. Sentenced to die, Payne beat the electric chair only a few days before his scheduled execution by igniting an explosive charge he had secretly strapped to his chest.

In this same year someone planted a bomb on the back porch of Baltimore's Mayor Broening which blew up half the building but injured no one. Though police insisted it was the work of an anarchist, anti-Prohibitionists in Baltimore, where speakeasies were rampant, joked that the mayor's private still had blown up.

1939: Two lovers, Lacene McDowell and Earl Austin, got into a car and went for a morning drive on March 20, 1939, motoring along the back roads of Hardin County, Illinois. An hour later an explosion roared through the floorboards of the car, sending the vehicle off the road and onto its side, hurling its occupants a dozen feet into the air. Austin died almost immediately, his attractive girl friend, Lacene McDowell, lingered for some hours in a hospital, despite the loss of one leg. State's Attorney Clarence E. Soward quickly determined solid suspects in Alice Austin and Ted Simmons. Austin was suing his wife for divorce on grounds of desertion at the time of the bombing; Alice Austin was counter-suing in an action that named Miss McDowell as "the other woman." The legal action was known to be violent. Further, Ted Simmons, Mrs. Austin's sweetheart, had been heard to threaten Austin.

Through a tip, police were informed that a farmer named Ira Scott had

All that remains of the cell occupied by A. D. Payne, an Amarillo lawyer who murdered his wife by blowing up her car in 1930, then blew himself to pieces with a small charge strapped to his chest while in jail.

something to do with the bombing. Confronted, the farmer broke down, blubbering: "I didn't mean to. I didn't know there was going to be anybody in the car. Alice and Ted Simmons gave me fifty dollars to bomb it for the insurance. They didn't tell me there would be anyone in it." Scott had planted three sticks of dynamite under the car. His stated ignorance about someone being in the car was belied by his admission that he had run the fuse from the dynamite back into the exhaust manifold, where it was impossible to ignite unless someone was driving the car.

Simmons and Alice Austin stubbornly refused to admit to their guilt in the bombing. They were each given fourteen years in prison; Scott was sentenced to the same amount of time behind bars.

1949: Albert Guay of Quebec, Canada, had decided to get rid of his wife, Rita Morel Guay, a plump twenty-eight-year-old woman with whom he had been constantly quarreling. Guay had several times in the past schemed to obliterate his wife, having fallen in love with a waitress, Marie-Ange Robitaille, a curvacious nineteen-year-old. On one occasion, Guay had offered a friend $500 if he would dose his wife's cherry wine with poison; the friend laughed uproariously, thinking it all a joke. The frustrated husband next went to his best friend, an oddball spinster named Marguerite Pitre, who lived on Monseigneur Gauvreau Street in Quebec's Lower Town. Miss Pitre, a petty crook and sometime abortionist, listened to Guay's tale of woe and then, in the spirit of friendship, readily agreed to help him murder his wife.

Marguerite's first plan was to have the woman blown up. It was quite simple, she said, merely take her for a taxicab ride in the country. To that end, Miss Pitre contacted a cabdriver she knew. She outlined the murder plan: He and Guay would drive Mrs. Guay to the country with a load of dynamite. At a lonely spot, Guay and the driver would get out of the cab under some pretext, leaving the wife in the auto. At a safe distance they would detonate the dynamite in the cab with a remote-control device. The cabdriver wanted no part of it, but his refusal had nothing to do with murder. "I don't want my cab damaged," he grunted.

Next, Miss Pitre enlisted the aid of her brother, a weird-acting watchmaker, Genéreaux Ruest. Though he happily agreed to make the bomb, Ruest was unsure of its construction. He stupidly remarked to one and all when a miner entered his jewelry shop: "Now, here's a man who can tell us about dynamite!" The bomb finally completed, Guay put the next part of the plan into action, buying his wife a round-trip ticket for Baie Comeau, asking her to pick up two suitcases of jewelry—his salesman's samples—which he had stored there while on a business trip. Mrs. Guay was more than happy to do so, thinking their reconciliation would be made stronger through such co-operation.

The night before Mrs. Guay was to depart, her husband gave her a night on the town. He had also taken out a $10,000 flight insurance policy on her life. Mrs. Guay flew from Quebec the next morning, Friday, September 9, 1949, on Flight 108 of Canadian Pacific Airlines. The DC-3 was airborne at 10:45 A.M. When the plane was only forty miles out of Quebec, several persons on the ground saw a small burst of smoke come from the ship. Seconds after this, an explosion was heard and the plane began to go to pieces, crashing into a steep hill. Killed instantly with Mrs. Guay were fifteen other adult passengers, four crew members and three children.

At first, the crash was listed as an accident but when investigators probing the crash site found pieces of a dry battery cell and evidence of dynamite they realized the aircraft had been bombed. Checking the cargo manifest, police found that one package had been sent to a nonexistent address. The person shipping this parcel was identified by a cabdriver who had driven a woman dressed all in black carrying a package—Miss Marguerite Pitre. She, her brother and Guay were subsequently arrested and charged with murder. All were found guilty and hanged. While sentencing Guay to death, the chief justice thundered: "Your crime is a crime of infamy. For what you did there is no name!"

1955: For what Jack Gilbert Graham did on November 1, 1955, when Flight 629 of United Airlines blew up over a Colorado beet farm, there was a name, murderer of forty-four humans—thirty-eight adults, a crew of five and an infant. Graham had long made money on insurance frauds, blowing up his service station for the insurance, then parking his car on a railroad track, where it was smashed to bits, also for the insurance. He had but one thing left on earth in late 1955 to exchange for more insurance money, his mother, Mrs. Daisie King. In addition to the $37,500 Graham had taken out on his mother's life just before a Denver takeoff (the desperate policy that made him a prime suspect), Graham, authorities quickly learned following the crash, stood to inherit his mother's $150,000 estate. A quick search of Graham's home revealed copper wiring he had used in the making of his bomb.

Interrogated by the FBI, Graham cracked within a few hours, admitting he had planted his homemade bomb in his mother's suitcase, twenty-six sticks of dynamite, connected with copper wire to two electric primer caps, a timer and a six-volt battery.

Convicted of this incredible bombing, Graham was sent to the gas chamber in the Colorado Penitentiary on January 11, 1957. He went to his death wordlessly, not a whisper of sorrow, not a murmur of regret.

The same year Graham committed his mass bombing murder, the national crime syndicate eradicated one of its most troublesome informers, Willie Bioff, who had extorted with the Chicago mob millions of dollars from the film industry through union infiltration. Exposed, Bioff turned state's evidence which resulted in the conviction of crime kingpins Paul "The Waiter" Ricca, Louis "Little New York" Campagna, Charles "Cherry" Gioe, Francis Maritote, John Roselli and Frank Nitti. (Nitti— Al Capone's "Enforcer"—chose to shoot himself while walking along the Illinois Railroad tracks in Chicago on March 19, 1943, rather than go to jail.)

Jack Gilbert Graham, who placed a bomb aboard an airplane in 1955 to murder his mother for insurance money; he succeeded in killing forty-four passengers and crew members. (Wide World)

Bioff went free and into hiding with more than $3 million taken from the film industry extortion, living in a comfortable ranch outside of Phoenix, Arizona, under the name of Al Nelson. He thought himself safe from Mafia retribution. On November 4, 1955, while Graham was building the bomb that killed his mother, Bioff-Nelson got into his pickup truck, stepped on the accelerator and was blown to death by a dynamite bomb planted beneath the hood of the truck.

1960: In the fall of 1960, on Sundays and holidays, several bombs were planted about New York City. The Staten Island Ferry was almost wrecked in one of these explosions. Most lethal of the "Sunday Bomber's" targets was the bombing of a subway at the 125th Street Station. Eighteen were killed and injured. Not only was this lunatic bomber never apprehended but his motives were also never stated.

1966: A black-boxed bomb was found on November 13, 1966, on board *The Grand Integrity,* a freighter five days out of Portland, Oregon. When the captain and crew members, all Chinese, took the box onto the main deck to inspect it, the bomb blew up in their faces, killing Captain Ho Lien-Siu and a motorman, and blinding the chief and second mate. U. S. Coast Guard inspectors could turn up no suspects or even reasons for the bomb.

On January 29, 1966, Yugoslavian dissidents, enraged at the regime of Communist dictator Tito, bombed five Yugoslavian consulates in the United States and the embassy in Washington, D.C. (This was the first massive display of political bombing in America.)

1967: Richard James Paris, twice deserting from the U. S. Army, married an unsuspecting young woman and honeymooned in the multimillion-dollar Orbit Inn in the heart of Las Vegas' casino district on January 7, 1967. Once in room 214, as a present to his bride, Christine Paris, the deranged GI produced a neatly wrapped bundle containing fourteen sticks of dynamite. He aimed a .38 caliber automatic at the bundle and fired, blowing up himself, his wife and five other persons (also on their honeymoons), as well as destroying two floors of the hotel.

1968: From March through the fall of 1968, an anti-Castro organization of Cubans, called Poder Cubano, set off scores of bombs throughout the United States, aiming them at businesses of non-communist countries trading with Castro.

1968: A customer, angry at being ejected from a Fort Worth, Texas, nightclub called The Grave, on May 6, 1968, returned a half hour later, tossing a gasoline fire bomb into the establishment. Seven were killed, a half dozen more patrons horribly burned. The bomb thrower was never identified.

1968: A rash of KKK-inspired bombings in Alabama and Mississippi left Jewish temples and black churches and homes in ruins. Sheriff Roy Gunn of Meridian, Mississippi, after receiving a tip, surrounded the home of a

Jewish businessman on June 30, 1968, and caught Thomas Albert Tarrant, of Mobile, Alabama, and Kathy Ainsworth, a one-time fifth-grade teacher, in the act of planting twenty-two sticks of dynamite. In an escape attempt, Ainsworth, firing a submachine gun, was killed. Tarrant was wounded. He was later sent to prison. The terrorist bombings ceased.

1968: Gambling czar Richard Chartrand, of Lake Tahoe, Nevada, stepped from his home on August 27. Once inside his new Cadillac, Chartrand turned the key in the ignition, his last living gesture. His car blew up with such force that it took hours for medical examiners to separate Chartrand's body from the wreckage.

1970: One of the most devastating of the many political bombings in the 1960–70 period was that of Karleton Armstrong, who, in August 1970, blew up the mathematics building at the University of Wisconsin in Madison as an anti-military gesture, killing in the process Robert Fassnacht, a thirty-three-year-old physicist and father of three. After some two years as a fugitive, Armstrong surrendered and pled guilty to second-degree murder. Daniel Ellsberg attempted to persuade the court to free Armstrong, but he received a twenty-three-year sentence in the penitentiary. He was released in 1979.

1970: David Rice, Duane Peak and Edwin Poindexter, fanatics of an offshoot group of the Black Panther Party, called on the citizens of Omaha, Nebraska, to kill on sight, policemen, their avowed enemies. When no one responded, the trio planted a bomb in a vacant house and then made an emergency call to police. Three officers responded. The bomb was set off when they entered the empty building. Two were critically injured, officer Larry Minard was blown to pieces. Rice received life, the others lesser sentences.

1976: Investigative reporter Don Bolles, probing connections between businessmen and organized crime in Phoenix, Arizona, was blown up in his car on June 2, 1976. A national team of reporters from several newspapers helped to indict John Harvey Adamson and others for the killing.

1977: A Puerto Rican independence group planted bombs in New York City in the summer of 1977. Two skyscrapers were selected. The bombs produced one dead, seven injured and dubious achievements for the unknown bombers.

BURGLARY

THE SUBTLE BURGLARY OF THE U.S. MINT

Robberies of the U.S. mints have been rare. The most puzzling was the burglary of $130,000 in gold bars from the Philadelphia Mint in the summer of 1893. No intruders were caught, no seals were broken and yet authorities, in their semiannual inventory, discovered the missing amounts and were utterly perplexed. Try as they might to figure out how thieves managed to smuggle out the gold, the method and the robbers remained a total mystery. Philadelphia authorities sent for A. L. Drummond, head of the Secret Service in Washington, D.C.

Upon his arrival, Drummond inspected the one compartment from which the gold bars had been taken. The storage area contained $9 million in gold bars piled six feet high. Each bar weighed about fourteen pounds and was worth approximately $5,000. The compartment was enclosed inside wire wickerwork. The door was fastened with a combination lock and sealed with a piece of tape. The lock remained untouched and the tape unbroken.

The only persons knowing the combination of the lock were Henry S. Cochrane, chief weighing clerk, and his assistant, a Mr. Robbins. Cochrane was regarded as incorruptible, as was his aide. A benevolent-looking man of sixty-seven, Cochrane had been the chief weighing clerk for thirty-seven years. After working for the mint for five years, Cochrane found the chief clerk stealing and turned him in, for which he was rewarded with his position. Robbins was thought to be as unimpeachable as his boss.

Drummond did learn, however, that Cochrane had recently complained about the uselessness of weighing the gold bars under his supervision even though the task was a mandatory ritual. The Secret Service chief called Cochrane in and asked him to open the combination lock. The old man bent to his job but seemed confused. Twirling the combination, Cochrane tried several times to open the lock but gave up in five minutes, and his assistant, Robbins, finally had to open the lock.

Asked to explain how he thought the gold might have been taken, Cochrane rambled through an almost incoherent theory which more or less suggested that the laborers who helped count the bars every six months were probably responsible for the theft. "No," he finally said shrugging. "It couldn't have been done that way."

Drummond, a steely-eyed detective of the old school, the kind who took unprecedented chances, played out a bold gamble with the chief weighing clerk. Without a shred of evidence to prove his point, he told Cochrane: "Do you know the superintendent suspects a certain person of having committed this crime?"

"He doesn't suspect me, does he?"

"Yes, he does, and so do I."

The old man stared in silence at Drummond, refusing to speak. "You are an old man," Drummond intoned. "You have long been in the services of the government. Your duty has been to take care of the public funds that are entrusted to your keeping. A large amount of this money is missing. I know you have taken it. You know I know you have taken it. Do the best you can to make up for the wrong you have done by telling me where the money is. It is your duty—do it!"

Tears were streaming down Cochrane's face by the time Drummond finished. Still he was speechless.

Drummond looked his prey square in the eye. "Tell me where the gold is."

"Part of it," blubbered the chief weighing clerk, "is hidden in the mint, and part of it is at home."

Cochrane then unraveled his simple but ingenious method of filching gold bars over several decades from the U.S. mint. He had stolen from between $50,000 and $60,000 in gold bars by first reaching a bent wire through the wickerwork and yanking the bars off the pile. He then reached beneath the wickerwork door, through a space of about eight inches, and merely pulled the bars out. Cochrane took no more than two bars home each night, affixing them to suspenders he had sewn onto his pants with reinforced thread.

Melting the bars down in a crucible in his attic at home, Cochrane would pour the molten metal into receptacles that would give them a different shape. He would then go to a small town and, using an assumed name and phony address, send the gold by express to the Philadelphia Mint, asking that the equivalent of gold coin be sent to him. When the gold arrived at the mint, Cochrane himself received it and sent the double eagles to himself.

When Cochrane learned that the gold bars in the compartment he had been raiding were going to be weighed, he took twenty-one bars and threw them through the skylight of the vault into a small, dark chamber between the ceiling of the vault and the floor above.

"I did this," the old man replied, "so that when the shortage was discovered the officials would think the amount too great for any one man in the mint to have gotten away with it."

The bars in the small chamber were recovered and much of the gold Cochrane had stolen was found hidden in the walls of his 150-year-old home at Darby, seven miles from Philadelphia. The master thief received seven years in the state prison. Upon his release, he was seen wandering about the mint on many occasions, eyeing the place "with a covetous look." He died at age eighty in 1906.

Most amazing in this mint robbery was the reason why Cochrane took the money in the first place. He used it to buy shopgirls presents.

After Cochrane was exposed, a salesgirl in a Philadelphia department store was heard to shout to her neighboring clerk: "Oh, Lizzie. What do you think? That old fool of a Cochrane who used to send me candy has robbed the mint."

THE BANK BURGLAR WHO WAS TRAPPED FROM OUTER SPACE

He was a burly man, handsome in a virile way, some women said. The press looked upon him as a lothario and an adventurer. The police of Canada and the United States thought of him as a criminal mastermind. Perhaps Georges Lemay was a bit of all these things but his historical distinction in crime is that his case was a scientific first in tracking down modern miscreants.

Lemay's beginnings were inauspicious. The suave Canadian was first jammed into the public eye in 1952. A skilled sailor and fisherman, Lemay loved to visit Florida, and it was during one vacation that his nineteen-year-old wife, Huguette Daoust, a one-time Montreal beauty queen, vanished forever while fishing from a bridge on the Overseas Highway in the Florida Keys.

Deputy Sheriff James A. Barker, investigating the mysterious disappearance of the first Mrs. Lemay, was convinced that she was "the victim of a violent end," but neither he nor a county grand jury could induce Georges Lemay to return from Canada to testify in the case. The Canadian, oddly enough, published a book in Canada entitled *Je Suis Coupable*, or *I Am Guilty*. Lemay claimed the title meant he was guilty merely of losing his wife's love. He related that Huguette complained of being cold while the two were fishing from the Florida bridge and went to the car and never returned, that he could prove that she was still alive but it would be futile since he planned to divorce her.

For the next five years, the world heard little of Georges Lemay but in July 1957 he was rounded up with others in connection with yet another disappearance, that of one Larry Petrov, a Montreal resident who had been charged with narcotics violations. Police arrested Lemay for carrying two unregistered pistols.

The elusive underworld figure again dropped out of sight until headlines across North America bannered the story of an astounding Montreal burglary of a branch of the Bank of Nova Scotia on July 1, 1961. The first estimates of the incredible burglary stated that anywhere from $500,000 to $4 million in cash, negotiable securities and jewels were taken from hundreds of safe deposit boxes, making the theft the largest in Canadian history. (Amounts, as always in such burglaries, were hard to establish because of the reluctance of depositors to talk, which is what all bank burglars rely upon. The final take was fixed at $633,605.)

Suspects were quickly rounded up and one of the gang members, Jacques Lajoie, was later to state that none other than Georges Lemay had "been the big wheel behind the bank job." The gang members had practiced endlessly for weeks with equipment and special walls, related

Lajoie and Yvon Belanger, another gang member, with Lemay supervising every move. When the burglars began to drill and jackhammer their way through the concrete ceiling and walls of the bank, Lemay was secreted across the street, directing them each step of the way with a walkie-talkie. Said Lajoie, "Lemay called all the shots and never showed his face inside the bank until it was time to take the money from the vault."

And the money, almost all of it, evaporated with Georges Lemay, who became Canada's most wanted man, the thirty-five-year-old bank burglar hunted on four continents. Four years passed and had it not been for a scientific experiment, Georges Lemay might never have been apprehended. In May 1965, the Royal Canadian Mounted Police flashed pictures of the fugitive on an Early Bird satellite experimental television program. A Fort Lauderdale, Florida, boat repairman recognized the man as one Rene Roy whose forty-three-foot yacht was anchored at the posh Bahia Mar basin. Roy-Lemay had been living on the boat for six months, paying his bills with a choking wad of hundred-dollar bills.

Tipped by the repairman, police surrounded the yacht and captured Lemay without a struggle, although he had vowed, friends stated, that he would shoot it out with police to the end. The master burglar had just enough time to slip on a pair of pants over his swim trunks and don a dapper straw hat. He was led bare-chested off the yacht and taken to Miami, where he was locked in the modern Dade County Jail. On the way, Lemay turned to Police Captain Bob Smith and inquired: "How did you people catch me? . . . I seldom make mistakes."

"You are the first man to be captured through the new worldwide communications facilities of the Early Bird."

Lemay was stunned. "Is that your word of honor?"

"It's the truth."

"Well, isn't that something," Lemay said, shaking his head. "It took a satellite to catch me."

Of course, authorities grilled the tight-lipped burglar as to the whereabouts of the enormous loot taken from the Montreal bank. They got nowhere. Lemay did demonstrate his respect for the fortune he had stolen. When asked how he managed to get a passport in the name of Rene Roy he cracked: "When you have money, you can get anything."

It was money again, insisted Dade County Sheriff T. A. Buchanan, which enabled the slippery Lemay to escape from the towering Dade County Jail in Miami on September 21, 1965. Shortly after Lemay's capture, a sultry twenty-eight-year-old brunette from Canada, Lise Lemieux, who had been convicted in 1962 of receiving part of the Montreal bank money, suddenly appeared in Miami. She and Georges would marry, even though he was a prisoner, Lise stated. The two attempted to shout their marriage vows through a jail window but guards stopped them.

Master bank burglar Georges Lemay of Canada being taken off his yacht under arrest in Fort Lauderdale, Florida, after being identified via a space satellite.

Officials were flabbergasted, however, on June 1, 1965, when Lemay was brought into an immigration office just before a hearing. Waiting was Lise and the couple hurriedly recited their marriage vows in French in front of an official paid to be there for that purpose. Before Miami authorities knew it, bank burglar Georges Lemay had been married in one of history's fastest recorded weddings. He had also made sure that Lise, as his wife, could not testify against him. As his wife, Lise was allowed to visit the prisoner regularly. According to Sheriff Buchanan, Lemay paid $35,000 in bribes to arrange his next disappearance.

On September 21, Lemay somehow managed to get out of his maximum security first-floor holding cell, take an elevator to the seventh floor of the jail and then slip out a window and onto an electric cable. Dozens of popeyed Miami witnesses watched the barrel-chested Lemay shinny down ninety feet to the ground and then casually hop into a waiting 1965 white sedan, which sped away northward with three other men. Again an international alarm went out. Not until August 19, 1966, was the fugitive recaptured, picked up by FBI agents at the Golden Nugget casino in Las Vegas, Nevada. Lemay was using the alias Robert G. Palmer and he and his wife were carrying almost $10,000 in American and Canadian currency, most of it in big bills.

Lemay was returned to Montreal, Canada, where he was tried for the spectacular 1961 bank burglary. He was finally convicted in December 1968, sentenced to eight years in the penitentiary. The slippery thief served his time and was released in 1975. He is in Montreal at this writing. Though the money from the bank burglary has never been recovered, Lemay is not under police surveillance.

For a man who "seldom makes mistakes," Georges Lemay, mastermind criminal, made the worst error of his life when he embarked upon bank burglary; he is now stone broke.

The electrocution of William Kemmler, the first in American history, at Auburn Prison, August 6, 1890.

CAPITAL
PUNISHMENT

ELECTROCUTION IN THE UNITED STATES:
TRAUMATIC FIRSTS

The first electrocution in America occurred in New York's Auburn Prison on August 6, 1890. The condemned murderer was one William Kemmler, who had taken a hatchet to his mistress, Tillie Zeigler, in Buffalo on March 29, 1889. The performance of the newly developed electric chair was much in debate and Kemmler's execution drew a host of doctors. On execution day the physicians sat in a circle around the chair.

Warden Charles F. Durston ushered Kemmler into the death room with solicitous decorum. The short, black-haired murderer was wearing a new suit, "dressed better than he had ever been before," in the words of one eyewitness. He enjoyed being the center of attention and Warden Durston acted out a role similar to that of a master of ceremonies. "Gentlemen," Durston announced dramatically, "this is William Kemmler."

The murderer walked quietly to the chair, gave a little bow and sat down. He crossed his legs and calmly stated: "The newspapers have been saying a lot of things about me which were not so. I wish you all good luck in the world. I believe I am going to a good place."

"Now we'll get ready, William," Durston said, and the killer stood up for a moment at the warden's motion. "Let me take off your coat." With the warden's help, Kemmler took off his coat and casually placed it on the back of the chair in which he was to die. He began to undo his vest but the warden reminded him that it was unnecessary to shed this since it was split up the back. The killer's shirt was then torn to expose the flesh where the lower electrode would be placed. Deputy Sheriff Joseph Veiling then began to strap Kemmler down, his hands shaking terribly. Kemmler looked at Veiling and said soothingly: "Don't get excited, Joe. I want you to make a good job of this."

Durston then fixed the electrodes. Kemmler moved his head from side to side to indicate that the head electrode was too loose. "I guess you'd better make that a little tighter, Mr. Durston," he advised the warden. The head gear tightened, Durston affixed the lower electrodes to the base of the back (this electrode is now fixed to the leg). A mask was then placed over Kemmler's head.

"Good-by, William," Durston said.

"Good-by," Kemmler said in the same calm voice.

Durston then moved to the door of a small adjoining room, where the unseen executioner waited. The warden banged on the door twice and the switch was immediately thrown, sending 1,000 volts tearing through the killer. The juice stayed on for seventeen seconds (it now takes two to three seconds to electrocute a human).

A reporter for the New York *World* watched as doctors gathered about Kemmler's body. He stared bug-eyed as "suddenly the breast heaved. There was a straining at the straps which bound him . . . The man was alive. Warden, physicians, everybody, lost their wits. There was a startled cry for the current to be turned on again. Signals, only half understood, were given to those in the next room at the switchboard. When they knew what had happened, they were prompt to act, and the switch-handle could be heard as it was pulled back and forth, breaking the deadly current into jets."

Though Kemmler was finally pronounced dead, the bungled execution was the cause of diatribes from the press, condemning this new form of execution as inhuman and torturous. The New York *Times* was a holdout, commenting: "It would be absurd to talk of abandoning the law and going back to the barbarism of hanging." But even the *Times* was appalled when almost three years later, on August 27, 1893, the execution of William G. Taylor turned into a horror show.

Taylor was condemned for slaying a fellow inmate in cold blood in Auburn Prison. He was strapped into a hopelessly inadequate chair and when the first electric shock ripped into him, his legs stiffened so that he tore away the front part of the chair where his ankles had been strapped. A screaming warden turned off the current and a box was brought by a guard and placed beneath the chair for support. Again the switch was thrown but there was no current. Taylor was still breathing. The generator in the powerhouse had burned out, a running guard informed the warden. Taylor was taken out of the chair, placed in a cot and given drugs to ease whatever pain he may have had, albeit he was unconscious.

By the time the power was restored, electricians, reporters and doctors frantically restringing electric lines over the prison walls from the city's power plant, Taylor had died. The law, however, had not been carried out according to officials, so the dead man was strapped into the chair once more and the current was sent into him for thirty seconds. "Gentlemen," a satisfied warden finally announced. "Justice has been done."

THE MORE THAN WILLING OF CAPITAL PUNISHMENT

Gary Gilmore's and Jesse W. Bishop's downright fanatical attempts to have themselves executed for murder recall a legion of American criminals who, either out of bravado or an idea of self-retribution (or plain stupidity), insisted upon the final solution of the law. Many went out without demanding their execution, but their attitudes, their final words and actions, convinced journalists, historians and executioners all that their bizarre ends were to them nothing more than casual, almost mundane occurrences.

The earliest of these "routine" happenings in our history was the execution of the New England highwayman Michael Martin, better known in saga and song as "Captain Lightfoot." Condemned to death in 1822 for stealing a horse, Martin stood upon a horse-drawn cart with a noose about his neck, the other end tied firmly to the limb of a sturdy oak outside of Cambridge, Massachusetts, scores of curious spectators gathered to witness his finish. Captain Lightfoot cavalierly withdrew a long piece of silk from his pocket and politely asked the hangman: "When shall I drop the handkerchief?"

"Whenever you're ready," replied the sheriff.

Martin studied the crowd for a moment with a smile playing about his lips and, while the enormous throng gasped, raised the handkerchief on high and let it flutter to the ground. The second the silk touched the earth, the cart driver whipped the horse forward and Captain Lightfoot dangled into eternity.

The outlaw Black Jack Ketchum met a similar fate on the gallows in Clayton, New Mexico, on April 25, 1901, executed for train robbery. His outlook was identical to Michael Martin's, but his demeanor and verbal farewells proved much more colorful. The witnesses to Black Jack's end were hardened Westerners and yet they were shocked when Ketchum took the stairs two at a time, eagerly racing upward to the scaffold. As the sheriff placed the noose around his neck, Black Jack shouted to all present: "I'll be in hell before you start breakfast, boys!" He then glanced sideways at the sheriff and ordered: "Let her rip!"

Black Jack's vernacular expression was, because of misplaced weights, realized in gruesome order. His body shot down and his head was torn from the trunk. Others possessed Ketchum's air of braggadocio, murderer

The hanging of Thomas "Black Jack" Ketchum, Clayton, New Mexico, April 25, 1901. (Western History Collections, University of Oklahoma Library)

and jewel thief Gerald Chapman in particular. Executed on a Connecticut scaffold in 1926 for killing a guard, Chapman's final words were obviously intended to instill respect in his executioners for his bold perspective. Commented Chapman through the black hood before he went through the drop: "Death itself isn't dreadful, but hanging seems an awkward way of entering the adventure."

Sing Sing was the site of many a celebrated execution during the 1920s and 1930s. The most spectacular was that of the twenty-year-old mass killer Francis "Two-Gun" Crowley, who was electrocuted in 1931.

Crowley's partner-in-crime, the hulking Rudolph "Fats" Duringer, had informed on "Two-Gun" but went to the chair anyway. When Crowley sauntered into the death chamber, he squinted at the chair which had claimed his associate, and then turned to Warden Lewis Lawes and said: "I got a favor to ask you."

Lawes nodded: "Name it."

"I want a rag."

"A rag? What for?"

"I want to wipe off the chair after that rat sat in it."

Lawes ignored the youthful killer's request as Crowley plopped indifferently into the chair. He was given a cigar and puffed heartily. He suddenly hissed out his hatred at the reporters seated in front of him and flipped the burning cigar into their ranks. The burning stogie hit one reporter in the forehead but he was too startled to protest. A second later, Crowley smiled at the warden and said: "Give my love to Mother." Another second and he was dead.

Rapist and murderer Harvey Murray Glatman, like Gilmore, demanded that his lawyers stop trying to save his life as he awaited the gas chamber in San Quentin. "It's better this way," Glatman intoned as he stepped inside the gas chamber in August 1959. "I knew this is the way it would be."

No convicted murderer, however, including Gary Gilmore, ever matched the self-destructive determination of Carl Panzram, burglar, robber and self-proclaimed murderer of at least twenty-one human beings. Condemned for killing a civilian foreman in Leavenworth, Panzram suddenly found himself in 1930 a *cause célèbre* of the Society for the Abolishment of Capital Punishment, its members zealously fighting to save his life with petitions and pleas. The murderer wrote to the society: "I do not believe that being hanged by the neck until dead is a barbaric or inhuman punishment. I look forward to that as real pleasure and a big relief to me . . . when my last hour comes I will dance out of my dungeon and on to the scaffold with a smile on my face and happiness in my heart . . . the only thanks you or your kind will ever get from me for your efforts on my behalf is that I wish you all had one neck and that I had my hands on it . . . I believe the only way to reform people is to kill 'em!"

Panzram lived up to these words. On the day of his execution, September 5, 1930, the killer pushed spectators out of the way and actually ran up the gallows stairs, dragging the hangman after him and yelling: "Let's get going! What are we stalling around for?"

"Anything you want to say?" inquired the executioner.

"Yes!" Panzram spat out, grabbing the rope and putting it about his own neck. "Hurry it up! I could hang a dozen men while you're fooling around!" The hangman finally kicked the trap open and the arch killer dropped to his death, tardy by his own schedule.

THOSE ENDEARING LAST WORDS

The execution of criminals for capital crime has produced a strange code where final words and actions form a sort of traditional literature. Gary Gilmore's recent execution by a firing squad in Utah embodied such melodrama with his statement, "Let's do it!"

The "tough guy" approach presents the eloquence of false courage, since the condemned are cut off from lengthy monologues, and their bluster remains to haunt. Would they, given time, have cracked and blurted their guilt or asked for forgiveness?

One would never know from the conduct of Raymond Flores, who hurled a young girl from a New York tenement house. Flores plopped into Sing Sing's electric chair with impatience. "Just hurry it up," he ordered the executioner. "I want to get my troubles over with."

William Deni, who murdered a Philadelphia, Pennsylvania, police officer, said, "I guess the Big Bad Wolf is going to get me!" as he was strapped into the chair.

In 1930, killer Michael Sclafoni entered the execution chamber and ran a finger over the arm of the electric chair. The gum-chewing gunman sneeringly remarked: "Dust. They at least could give a man about to die a clean chair."

When murderer Jesse Thomas walked into the death chamber, he waved at the witnesses in pews before him. "Well, well, well!" he shouted. "I can walk through and die like a man." From the chair he called out, "I'll see you all in hell some day. Let 'er go!" William Force, one of Thomas' partners, smiled at the executioner and purred, "What are you so nervous about, boy? Take it easy. I'm in no hurry."

Claude Udwine, the third member of this killing trio, sought to rival the brag of his friends, stating: "The good thing about this thing is that they carry you out—you don't have to walk." As the executioner began to adjust the head electrode, Udwine quipped: "So this is a football game. Oh, well, it's just a joke. Let's go!"

The witnesses at executions sometimes take verbal and/or physical abuse from the condemned. For example, Buffalo gangster Stephen Ziolkowski puffed on a cigar in the chair and then hurled it at reporters, igniting the trousers of one.

Sometimes, seemingly trivial matters concern the condemned. Before his electrocution in New Jersey, killer Charles Fithian blurted: "I want to make a complaint. The soup I had for supper tonight was too hot." A condemned killer named Smith in Pennsylvania shouted at the executioner adjusting the head electrode: "It hurts . . . you're pinching my ear." When the electrode was readjusted, the condemned man smiled and said, "That's better. There's no pain now."

Females facing execution have generally conducted themselves with more concern for their fate. Mrs. Martha Place, the first woman to be electrocuted, on March 20, 1899, could only utter the words "God, save me" before the current was sent into her. The notorious Ruth Snyder merely repeated over and over, "Jesus, have mercy." Mrs. Mary Creighton, who had poisoned her brother, two in-laws and her lover's wife, also sank into prayer at the end. Eva Coo, who murdered the janitor of her apartment house, waved calmly from the chair to the matrons who had kept the death watch with her, saying blithely, "Good-by, darlings."

Perhaps the most selfless condemned woman, though, was Irene Schroeder, the first woman to die in Pennsylvania's electric chair. Called

"Iron Irene" and the "Tiger Girl," Schroeder was to die days before her lover, Glenn Dagus, for the killing of a policeman.

As she was strapped into the chair February 23, 1931, Schroeder was asked if anything could be done for her. "Yes, there is something," she replied. "Tell them in the kitchen to fry Glenn's eggs on both sides. He likes them that way."

Undoubtedly the most absurd last words by a condemned person emanated from Carl Otto Wanderer, a convicted Chicago murderer who had befriended newsmen and future playwrights Ben Hecht and Charles MacArthur.

Before his death by hanging on March 19, 1921, Wanderer agreed to read from the gallows attacks on their editors which Hecht and MacArthur had written. The newsmen, though, had forgotten that people executed on the gallows were tied hand and foot. Hence, Wanderer could only look down helplessly to the typewritten speeches strapped to his side.

Wanderer shrugged at the dismayed reporters and thought to do the next best thing. As the rope was placed about his neck, Wanderer broke into song, belting out an ancient ditty entitled "Dear Old Pal o' Mine."

Following the execution, MacArthur turned to Hecht and quipped, "You know, Ben, that son-of-a-bitch should have been a song-plugger!"

Chicago gunman George Appel undoubtedly cracked the worst and most macabre pun of all time of those being executed. As he was being strapped into the chair, the cop-killer gave the spectators in the death room a sickening smile and gritted: "Well, folks, you'll soon see a baked Appel!"

TO KILL OR NOT TO KILL, THE PROS KNOW

As the argument about capital punishment continues to rage, it is more than academic to take a hard look at a segment of the underworld that risks death for profit: the professional criminal. It has long been the contention of the author that such persons are fully aware of their responsibility in taking a life while enacting a crime for which they may forfeit their own.

Ruth Snyder, who killed her husband with Judd Gray, her lover; she was electrocuted at Sing Sing, calling on God at the last second before being pronounced dead at 11:04 P.M., January 12, 1928; Gray died in the same chair ten minutes later.

The professional criminal plans his or her acts far in advance and within the organization of such premeditated activities, he or she decides whether the taking of lives is in the interest of success. It is this type of criminal for whom capital punishment should justly loom.

Testimony and personal confessions of professional criminals have confirmed that capital punishment is a deterrent. True, justice has erred in the past and some innocent lives have been taken, but such instances are so rare that to withhold capital punishment from the hardened professional criminal who takes a life becomes a travesty of justice, an irresponsible decision that further burdens a crime-oppressed society.

The blanket indictment of capital punishment by many has led to the ridiculous. One such case is the attempt to discredit the conviction of Bruno Richard Hauptmann, murderer of the Lindbergh baby. Hauptmann was no innocent carpenter living out a peaceful life as his defenders now claim. He was a professional burglar and thief who had learned the art of killing as a German soldier during World War I.

As a man who approached crime as a business, Hauptmann carefully selected his victims, men of prestige and wealth. That is why he burglarized the home of the mayor of Kamenz, Germany, in 1919, thirteen years before he kidnapped the Lindbergh child. His modus operandi in the enactment of both crimes is almost identical. Since he was armed in the earlier crime, it was evident that Hauptmann was prepared to take a life to complete the burglary. The slaying of the Lindbergh child only proved his professional resolve.

Hauptmann's subsequent conviction and execution was based on a concrete case wherein he was found with most of the marked ransom money and the ladder cut from the floorboards of his attic used in the crime (experts analyzed and identified the wood). Also, he was identified as the kidnapper by eyewitnesses.

Although Hauptmann never admitted his guilt, his fear of execution was as real as that of the professional criminal who would not kill because of that same fear. One such crook was confidence man Joseph "Yellow Kid" Weil.

Weil, the dean of confidence men in the twentieth century, often told the author that to "kill someone" while committing a crime was a ridiculous risk.

"Anyone who goes armed might kill someone, and for that you pay," the confidence man said. "We all know the price . . . the chair."

His words were echoed by Willie "The Actor" Sutton, who once admitted to the author that he carried automatic weapons while robbing banks. The Actor added, however, that he vowed never to use them.

"It was the chair," Sutton said. "I never used those guns because of the chair. It was a deterrent all right, it had that effect."

But during Sutton's heyday, the laws were tougher and capital punishment was not in debate. In fact, in 1934, the nation's top confidence men met at the Sherman House in Chicago, to sweep their grift of professional criminals who had taken to guns.

Said the weapons-loathing Yellow Kid, ". . . there's that Earl Christman [who had joined the Barker gang], a good confidence man as long as he stuck to his racket. But no, he has to get tough. Wanted to rob banks. Well, what happened to him? He got killed.

"And Dick Galatas [who figured prominently in the well-known Kansas City, Missouri, Massacre]—he's been getting heavy for a year or so . . . he's even carrying a gun. . . . I'm telling you, we've got to clean house! Got to throw out these people who are ruining our profession!"

Such sentiments among the ranks of professional criminals have altered drastically, however, as laws have been softened. Today, it is believed that many criminals, realizing they probably won't face the death penalty, won't hesitate to kill.

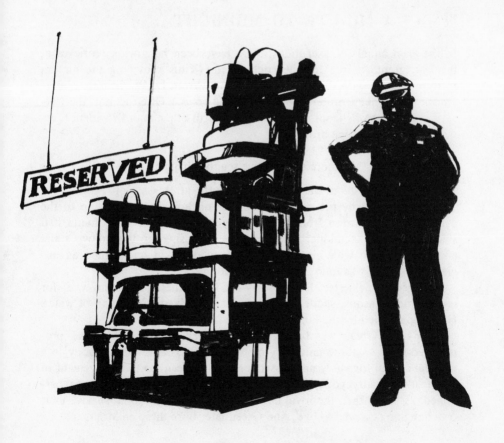

'TWAS A MINUTE TO MIDNIGHT

In the grim annals of executions, there have been harrowing reprieves at the last minute of life for the condemned. (Thus providing the motion picture industry with the grist of great drama from D. W. Griffith's *Intolerance* to Warner Brothers' countless crime epics.) Often as not, the last-second reprieve was from no authority on earth other than Providence, especially when the rope broke.

Here are some of the more provocative scaffold-hangers, if you will:

• Inetta de Balsham was hanged promptly at 9 A.M. on August 16, 1264, as decreed by the courts. A courier on horseback raced up to the gallows with a pardon from King Henry some seconds after Inetta had swung off. The executioner read the reprieve, dashed up the gallows stairs and cut the rope with his sword. Inetta, whose skin had turned an unglamorous blue, was found to be still breathing.

• Hanged at Leicester, England, in 1363, Matthew of Endeby was, for unexplained reasons, suddenly cut down and revived with a pail of water. He was pardoned by the king a short time later.

• One Ann Green was hanged on December 14, 1650. She was pronounced dead by three university physicians, who removed her body to a medical school for study and dissection. Miss Green, to the amazement of her academic surveyors, suddenly began to breathe. She, too, was pardoned, as it was then the royal notion that anyone who could survive their own hanging deserved to live. Ann Green later bore three children.

• In 1696 one rogue, Richard Johnson, devised a method to cheat the hangman. A half hour after Johnson was sent through the trapdoor, the executioner noticed his chest heaving slightly. Upon inspection, it was learned that Johnson had wrapped ropes around his body, connecting these with hooks at his neck, the hooks fashioned by himself to the hangman's rope, the clever apparatus hidden beneath Johnson's "perriwig and double shirt." He was cut down and "properly" hanged an hour later.

• One Margaret Dixon was hanged in 1700, but as she was being carted off for burial she came to life and was released. Like Ann Green, Margaret Dixon later gave birth to several children.

• The noted pirate Captain William Kidd mounted the London gallows for his innumerable crimes on May 23, 1701, along with one of his swashbuckling mates, Darby Mullins. When both were sent through the trapdoor, Mullins instantly met his fate, but Captain Kidd fell straight through to the ground. The rope had broken. He was again hauled up the gallows stairs and the ritual again commenced. Incredibly, the rope broke once more. Several in the large throng witnessing this spectacle cried out for a reprieve, that the badly knotted ropes giving way had been a sign from on high to spare the cutthroat. British authorities pooh-poohed such superstition and ordered Kidd up to the gallows for a third time. At last the rope held and the pirate ended life by the neck.

Half-hanged Maggie Dixon (or Dickson) recovering from her own execution in Edinburgh, terrifying her would-be burial party.

• A burglar, John Smith, was sentenced to death for housebreaking, a decision of the court which found little favor among the common people of London. At the hanging on the morning of December 24, 1705, a large throng watched the malefactor dangle for fifteen minutes, before many began to chant in a menacing tone at the executioner: "A reprieve! A reprieve!" Just as the crowd began to surge forward, Smith was cut down. In keeping with the zany medical concepts of the day, doctors applied leeches to Smith, "bleeding him of impurities." Despite the rope and the leeches, Smith regained consciousness. He was later pardoned, and became a low-life celebrity, known far and wide as "Half-hanged Smith."

• Thomas Reynolds, a highwayman, was hanged in London on July 26, 1736. After being cut down, Reynolds was placed in a coffin. As workmen were nailing the box shut, Reynolds came to life, threw back the lid and grabbed one of the workmen by the arm (causing him, naturally, to faint). The executioner thought to hang Reynolds again but the crowd prevented it. The condemned man was carried to a nearby house, where, according to a contemporary report, "he vomited three pints of blood, but on giving him a glass of wine he died."

• On November 24, 1740, William Duell, convicted of the murder of Sarah Griffin, was hanged in London with four others. Duell's body was taken to the Surgeons Hall to be anatomized, where it was stripped and laid upon a board. Just before he was to be cut, an attendant washing the corpse noticed slight breathing. In two hours Duell was sitting up, groaning, saying he had had a bad dream. He became a local curiosity and was later deported.

• In another London hanging in 1752, an unnamed nineteen-year-old traitor, only minutes after his execution, sat upon the dissecting table, but a quick-thinking surgeon struck the youth with a mallet, killing him. The mallet was later put on exhibit.

• A young girl hanged in Paris in 1766 was turned over to a doctor who had purchased her body for study. She came to life a few hours later, telling a priest who had been called that she thought she was in heaven.

• Patrick Redmond, who had been sentenced to death for a street robbery, was executed on February 24, 1767, in Cork, Ireland, hanging for twenty-eight minutes. A doctor, six hours later, performed a tracheotomy and Redmond began to breathe. That night Redmond, attired in his best finery, attended the theater.

• John Whitefield was gibbeted in Cumberland, England, in 1771, but, after swinging in chains for an hour, came back to life. He was pardoned.

• In Columbia, Mississippi, on February 7, 1894, Will Purvis, suspected of being a member of the White Caps, a branch of the KKK, was hanged for the murder of a Negro, one Will Buckley. Purvis, who had shouted to a mob of hundreds gathered at the scaffold that he was innocent, was sent through the trap, but utterly confounded his executioners when the hangman's knot around his neck untwisted, sending him to the ground. The boy blinked and staggered to his feet.

Purvis, who was bound hand and foot, was ordered to hop once again up the gallows stairs, which he awkwardly did. A Dr. Ford examined the instrument of death beneath the gallows. Ford, who had serious doubts about Purvis' guilt, stared up at the executioner, who yelled to him: "Toss that rope up here, will you, Doc?"

Ford threw the rope down. "I won't do any such damn thing. That boy's been hung once too many times now!"

The Reverend J. Sibley, a friend of the Purvis family, seized the dramatic moment, and jumped up to the scaffold. "All who want to see this boy hanged a second time," intoned Sibley in the awe-struck silence, "hold up their hands!"

Not a hand in the crowd went up. Purvis was taken back to his cell, and his sentence was later commuted to life imprisonment. He received a full pardon on December 19, 1898. In 1917, a Mississippi farmer, one Joe Beard, became a fervent member of the Holy Rollers religious sect and, in a zealous moment of confession, admitted that he and a man named Louis Thornhill were the killers of Will Buckley. Purvis was voted $5,000 by the Mississippi Legislature as compensation for his jail time and the rope burn around his neck which he wore until the day he died.

Clarence Darrow, the indomitable criminal lawyer, at the time of the McNamara trial.

COURTS AND
TRIALS

CLARENCE DARROW AND THE MAD BOMBERS

It was long past midnight, October 1, 1910. In the bowels of the sprawling Los Angeles *Times* building labored dozens of men, working overtime at the presses. Their jobs were not made any easier by the thought that their publisher, Harrison Gray Otis, had, along with the building housing his newspaper, been openly threatened by union bombers.

A war was in progress and the *Times* squatted uncomfortably between the battle lines. On one side was Otis and his self-organized merchant and manufacturers association, which loudly bellowed: "We employ no union men." On the other were the struggling unions, whose frustrated leaders felt compelled to retaliate with dynamite . . . and bombs.

One of these infernal machines exploded in the *Times* building on October 1, blowing away an entire wall and creating an inferno in which twenty-one frantic workmen met screaming, flaming deaths. Otis, incensed, was no stranger to such terror tactics. He had previously mounted a small cannon to the running board of his car, ready to do battle in the street with any union anarchists. The bombing was no accident, Otis thundered publicly. It was the work of organized labor, now responsible for the murder of his men.

Two union men, brothers Jim and John McNamara, were quickly charged with the crime. Throughout the nation, public sentiment ran in favor of the brothers. They were being victimized, most felt, made scapegoats by autocratic businessmen. Defense funds for the brothers poured into union offices and the unions turned as one toward grimy Chicago and Clarence Darrow, the great white hope in the cause of labor.

Darrow, then fifty-three, had been making headlines for ten years as the nation's leading labor lawyer. His defense of striking anthracite coal miners in 1902 had been masterly. His appearance on behalf of Big Bill Haywood and his bomb-loving Wobblies in a 1907 bombing trial in Idaho was sensational. At first, Darrow declined to represent the McNamaras; he was through with labor murders, he said.

Pressure and money (a promised $50,000 fee) caused him to change his mind, and he went reluctantly into the case. In Los Angeles, Darrow began to gather piecemeal evidence and shortly concluded that the McNamara brothers were guilty of the bombing murder. Coupled to this unhappy deliberation was a maze of subversive activity. Rampant bribery was practiced by the district attorney's minions and the Burns Detective Agency (working for the Otis forces). Darrow's people bribed back.

Above it all, Darrow wrestled with his gigantic conscience. To quit the case meant fraud and deceit. Clarence Darrow was a moral man. A friend, writer Lincoln Steffens, who had journeyed to L.A. to cover the trial, suggested the lawyer plead his clients guilty if life imprisonment would be guaranteed. Otis reluctantly agreed and the brothers stood up in court at the trial's inception and announced their guilt.

William J. Burns, one of America's foremost detectives, threw the weight of his agency against Darrow and the McNamaras. (UPI)

Labor accused Darrow of selling out its members. The law accused Darrow of bribery. On the second count, the lawyer was arrested and held for trial; one of his own workers, he learned, had overzealously attempted to bribe two possible jurors in the McNamara trial on a city street.

Darrow's subsequent trial was a shabby finale to the McNamara defense, in which the lawyer was heralded as the man who "turned cases into causes." Otis and his advocates urged Darrow's conviction and imprisonment. As the long, dreary trial prattled onward, Darrow defended himself, assisted by the flashy, eloquent Earl Rogers, who summed up the defense with: "Will you tell me how any sane, sensible man who knows anything about the law business—and this defendant has been at it for thirty-five years—could make himself go to a detective and say to him: 'Just buy all the jurors you want. I put my whole life, my reputation, I put everything I have into your hands. I trust you absolutely. I never knew you until two or three months ago and I don't know much about you now. But there you are. Go to it!' "

Darrow, following this and a second trial, was acquitted, glumly returning to Chicago and vowing never again to practice labor law. The murdering brothers McNamara had wrecked him in this field. He would practice criminal law, he gritted. He certainly would.

TWELVE MILLION WORDS FOR A LOVER'S LANE MURDER CASE

One of America's most sensational murder trials, the Hall-Mills fiasco of 1926, created an insatiable national appetite for news of the killing of lovers.

The impassioned ones lacked the svelte images of Valentino and Garbo, but by the time the scandal-hugging press of the day finished with the Reverend Edward Wheeler Hall and his lead choir singer, Eleanor Mills, these two very dead sweethearts had become the Romeo and Juliet of American murder.

It was, at best, a dowdy affair from the start. The Reverend Mr. Hall, forty-one, bald and beefy, was the popular pastor of St. John the Evangelist Protestant Episcopal Church in New Brunswick, New Jersey.

Not for a moment did any of his parishioners suspect that he had for several years been carrying on with Eleanor Mills, thirty-four, a plain woman but the sweetest singer in the church choir.

Also unsuspecting, it seemed, were Mrs. Frances Stevens Hall, the pastor's homely, dumpy wife, seven years his senior, and Eleanor's husband, James Mills, the thirty-five-dollar-a-week sexton at St. John's.

The events on the night of September 16, 1922, however, certainly proved that someone was angrily aware of the trysting lovebirds. Their bodies were found stretched beneath a crab apple tree on De Russey's Lane outside of New Brunswick by a young couple.

The Reverend Mr. Hall was clad in a neat dark suit with a clerical collar, his face covered with an expensive panama hat. There was a single .32 caliber bullet in his brain.

Nestled in the crook of the pastor's arm was choir singer Eleanor Mills, adorned in a blue dress with red polka dots. A scarf covered her face. She had been shot three times in the forehead and her throat was slashed so deeply that the head was nearly decapitated. In a last grisly act, the killer, as if in contempt of her one great talent of singing, had removed Eleanor's voice box, tongue, larynx and upper windpipe.

Love letters the victims had sent each other were ripped and scattered about their bodies. Almost as an impish final gesture, the murderer had propped Rector Hall's calling card at his feet.

Despite the sensational slaying, police bungled the entire case, allowing thousands of curious spectators to trample the grounds of the murder site, strip the crab apple tree bare and destroy any clues that might have existed. Further, no autopsies of the bodies were made, and no coroner's inquest held.

The murders went unsolved and the case faded only to burst wide again at midnight on July 17, 1926, when squads of police suddenly surrounded the home of Mrs. Frances Stevens Hall and dragged the fifty-two-year-old widow out of bed, charging her with the murder of her husband.

Also indicted for murder were Mrs. Hall's two brothers, Henry Stevens, a retiring stockbroker, and Willie Stevens, who was thought to be a half-wit.

Philip Payne, managing editor of the reckless tabloid the New York *Mirror,* had prompted the arrests and trial after obtaining the calling card left at the feet of the slain Reverend Hall. Payne produced a fingerprint expert who swore that Willie Stevens' prints were on the card.

Willie proved to be no mental defective when testifying, but rather an expert in botany, metallurgy and entomology.

Mrs. Hall was equally convincing before the jury. Her tranquil composure under the most ruthless cross-examinations caused one newsman to dub her "the iron widow."

More than a hundred reporters from every prestigious newspaper in the country were present, a regular Who's Who in journalism and crime writing—H. L. Mencken, Dudley Nichols, Mary Roberts Rinehart, Billy Sunday, Peggy Hopkins Joyce and the sage of Broadway, Damon Runyon.

Even James Mills, Eleanor's husband, was pressed into service as a newsman, his flapper daughter typing out his copy. Sixty leased wires in the courtroom basement hummed for twenty-four days, all funneled through a giant switchboard which had been built for the Dempsey–Tun-

De Russey's Lane, where the bodies of the Reverend Mr. Hall and Eleanor Mills were found in 1926.

ney championship fight in Philadelphia. Along these wires the frantic scribes filed more than twelve million words on the sordid trial.

The courtroom highlight was the appearance of Jane Gibson, who ran a pig farm on De Russey's Lane. Ailing with cancer, "the pig woman," as the inventive press named her, was rolled into the packed courtroom on a stretcherlike bed. She croaked out the claim that she had been chasing runaway pigs on the murder night. She insisted that she had seen Mrs. Hall and her brothers kill the pastor and the choir singer.

The defense counsel, however, proved that she could not even remember who and when and where she had married or whether or not she had been divorced.

The spectacle was complete but the case unsolved. Mrs. Hall and her brothers were acquitted. They promptly sued the *Mirror* for $3 million, obtaining an out-of-court settlement. "The pig woman" went to her grave four years later, insisting to the last that Mrs. Hall and the Stevens brothers had gotten away with murder.

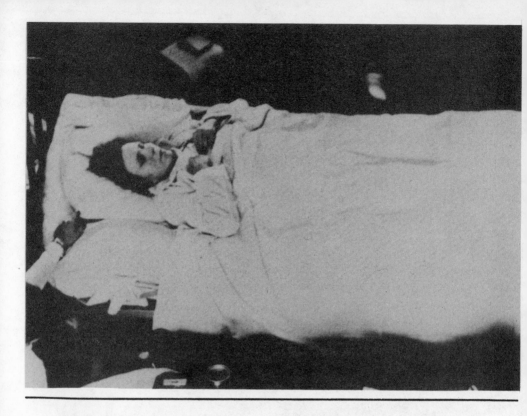

Testifying from a portable bed at the sensational Hall-Mills trial of 1926, Jane Gibson, known as "the pig woman," unfailingly groaned that Mrs. Hall and her brothers were murderers.

GETTING AWAY WITH MURDER

In the annals of murder trials there has been many an infamous acquittal that has stirred the public, enraged the press and raised the question of insanity in the American judicial system. Other acquittals, such as that of Lizzie Borden in 1893, only served to confuse prosecutors and posterity (albeit the author, after years of study of this case is unconvinced of Lizzie's guilt, despite the fact that she was tried and convicted by the press; there remain too many options, including the possible guilt of the Borden maid, Bridget Sullivan).

From such early court lore came America's first sensational acquittal, that of Levi Weeks in 1800. Miss Julianna Elmore Sands, a beautiful young woman, had been found murdered, at the bottom of a New York well. Weeks, who lived in the same Manhattan rooming house as Miss Sands, was accused of the slaying. He was defended by no less blinding political lights than Alexander Hamilton and Aaron Burr. The evidence against Weeks was minimal but prejudice against him high. It was Burr's moving address to the jury which freed Weeks. (Judge John Lansing, who presided at this case, completely vanished thirty days after the trial.)

A few years later, public feeling in Boston earmarked Thomas O. Selfridge for the hangman. Selfridge bumped into Charles Austin on State Street on August 4, 1806. Austin's father, Benjamin Austin, had been waging political battle with attorney Selfridge, the dispute loudly carried on by his son when meeting the lawyer on Boston's "public exchange." Both men drew pistols and fired; Austin died. Selfridge's case became the first *cause célèbre* on the law of self-defense. He was acquitted by a jury that had insisted he be indicted for manslaughter instead of murder, the most esteemed member of the jury being Paul Revere.

Some of the more startling acquittals in nineteenth-century America include:

• George Coombs, who, while drunk, beat his mistress Maria Henry to death in Boston, on June 15, 1816. Coombs's defense attorney cited his client's sterling navy record (he had served on board the *Enterprise* and the *Constitution* during the War of 1812) and referred to the dead Maria as "an abandoned woman." Despite that fact that four persons testified against Coombs, identifying him as the killer, he was acquitted. The jury ignored the witnesses since they were "known prostitutes."

• Also in 1816, George Bowen, an inmate at the Hampshire, Massachusetts, prison, was tried for the murder of Jonathan Jewett, a fellow prisoner. Jewett had been condemned to death for the murder of his father and Bowen had suggested he cheat the hangman by killing himself; Jewett took his advice, and committed suicide on November 9, 1815. Bowen was acquitted of the murder charge but remained in prison to serve out his term for another offense.

• Kentucky justice triumphed in September 1818, when Samuel Daviess was acquitted of stabbing to death one Henry Pendleton Smith on the street in Harrodsburg. The accused never denied the murder, but felt that he had just provocation. Daviess, at the time, was running for the state legislature, and Smith, encountering him on the street, upbraided him for his political beliefs, adding insufferable shame to Daviess by slapping him in the face. Murder was the only answer to such an offense. The jury agreed.

• Medad M'Kay was tried twice in 1820 and 1821 in Allegany, New York, after he had been accused of murdering his wife. M'Kay's own words presented the strongest case against him. When Mrs. M'Kay's body was being exhumed for examination, Medad commented to officials at the graveside: "I will not say that they won't find arsenic in her; but if they do, I did not put it there, for I have enemies enough to put it there." His self-condemning statements notwithstanding, M'Kay was acquitted.

• In 1830 Daniel H. Corey was tried for the murder of Mrs. Matilda Nash, who had attempted to break up an argument between Corey and his wife in their Sullivan, New Hampshire, home. Corey's response to such neighborly aid was to beat out Mrs. Nash's brains. Corey's own brains had been somewhat scrambled for years, as everyone knew. The farmer had been forever claiming that hosts of killers were after him because of the fabulous gold mine he had discovered on his barren farm, an El Dorado that existed only in his deranged mind. Further, Corey had been seen to make a silver bullet, with which he killed his pet cat; the animal, he moaned, was "bewitched." Corey's well-known history of such irrational conduct helped his lawyers to acquit him on the grounds of insanity, one of the first such acquittals in American jurisprudence.

• The strange death of Sarah M. Cornell in Tiverton, Rhode Island, in December 1832, almost brought the Reverend Ephraim K. Avery to the hangman's rope. Sarah was found hanging from a haystack frame; her alleged suicide note read: "If I should be missing, enquire of the Rev. Mr. Avery, of Bristol—he will know where I am."

Although acquitted of murder, the Reverend Ephraim K. Avery is shown killing his lover Sarah Cornell in a newspaper cartoon of the day, a universal belief by the residents of Tiverton, Rhode Island, in 1832.

Though Avery had been seen wandering about the bleak countryside on the day of Sarah's death, and her note seemed to incriminate him, magistrates hearing his first trial released him. When it was discovered that Sarah was five months pregnant at the time of her death, public resentment was so hotly pitched that Avery was brought back from Rindge, New Hampshire, where he had been in hiding, and tried once more. His trial in Rhode Island set a record in that era, twenty-seven days, with 196 witnesses testifying. In the end, with most residents angrily convinced that Avery had impregnated Sarah and murdered her to cover his deed, the parson was acquitted, suspicion and accusation haunting him until the end of his days.

• Mary Harris, whose Washington, D.C., trial in 1865 created a sensation, was the living proof that "hell hath no fury like a woman scorned." Adonirum J. Burroughs had promised to marry Miss Harris. He inveigled his fiancée into accompanying him to a brothel, where he "compromised" her, and then called off the engagement on the grounds that she "was an immoral female." Mary, when learning that Burroughs had married someone else, tracked him to Washington, where, in front of startled passersby, she shot and killed the scheming Burroughs in a hall of the Treasury Building. Jury members to a man felt Mary justified in ridding the world of such a scurrilous cad, and acquitted her. She responded by politely curtsying to the jury while holding a large bouquet of posies in her arms; the flowers had been sent to her by none other than Mrs. Abraham Lincoln.

• Frank Kelly murdered Octavius V. Cato, a Negro, in a Philadelphia race riot on October 10, 1871. Kelly, who had been clean-shaven at the time of the killing, appeared in court wearing a rich, full beard. None of the witnesses could identify him and he was released.

• Fanny Hyde, a forelady in a New York hairnet factory, shot and killed the owner, George W. Watson, in 1872. Her brother, who worked in the same factory, found Fanny standing over Watson with a steaming pistol, and remarked: "Fanny, I told you not to do this." In court Miss Hyde sobbed a tearful tale of being seduced by the callous Mr. Watson and was quickly freed. A woman's chastity had been violated, the jury concluded, and that was reason enough to kill.

• On November 6, 1872, two barrels were found floating in the Charles River off Cambridge, Massachusetts, inside of which was the dismembered body of Abijah Ellis. Packed around the gory contents were wood shavings which were later traced to a billiard table maker, who reported giving the shavings to one Leavitt Alley, who said he would use the shavings as bedding for the horses in his livery stable.

Since it was known that Alley owed Ellis a good deal of money, the state prosecuted the stable owner on a first-degree murder charge. The defense, almost conceding guilt, argued that dismembering a body after death did not indicate premeditated first-degree murder. No one was more surprised when Alley was acquitted than his own lawyer.

• Peter P. Wintermute, a banker involved with railroad expansion in the Dakota Territory, took issue with Edwin S. McCook over railway right-of-ways in 1873. The argument, held inside the district courtroom in Yankton, ended when Wintermute produced a pistol and shot McCook to death. McCook's supporters were legion; he was one of the "Fighting McCooks" of the Civil War and lynching Wintermute almost became a reality on several occasions.

Wintermute was first convicted of manslaughter, but the decision was reversed. In a second trial, Wintermute was acquitted. There was much talk of jury bribing. The defendant did not wait for public acceptance, fleeing the territory on a mule while his neighbors searched about for a rope. For years, the McCook–Wintermute case was the most hotly debated murder trial in the Dakotas.

• Sixteen years before the Borden case put Fall River, Massachusetts, on the murder map in 1892, another woman, Rosalie A. Thyng, caused a sensation in that town when her husband, George H. Thyng, died of massive poisoning on July 9, 1876. Although she was the only person who could have administered the poison, Mrs. Thyng's lawyers won an acquittal in that no one could trace the poison to the accused murderess, and, like Lizzie Borden after her, Rosalie went free.

• In 1879, Mary Stannard, a servant girl in the home of Rev. Herbert

H. Hayden in Madison, Connecticut, was found in a field belonging to
Hayden with her throat cut. Mary had told half the town she was pregnant by Hayden and was planning an abortion. She had also stated that
she was to meet the parson in the field to pick berries and discuss the future; the reverend was the likely suspect. He was released after a prelimi-
nary hearing, but rearrested and put on trial for murder after arsenic was
found in Mary Stannard's stomach.

At Hayden's trial a clairvoyant gave testimony which indicated the defendant's innocence, perhaps the first such soothsaying before an American court. A hung jury permitted the parson's acquittal.

• Oran A. Carpenter of Lincoln, Illinois, found himself in straits identical to those of Reverend Hayden when, on October 14, 1883, the attractive twenty-two-year-old Zura Burns was found stabbed to death on a
lonely road outside of town. Zura's pregnancy at death was attributed to
Carpenter but he was acquitted in a speedy trial for lack of evidence. The
townsfolk, however, insisted at shotgunpoint that Carpenter leave town.
The accused hurriedly left for the Dakota Territory.

• A Temperance fanatic, George C. Haddock, led a violent crusade
against saloons in Sioux City, Iowa, in 1886. John Arensdorf, a local sa-
loonkeeper and brewer, took exception to Haddock tearing up his place
on August 3 and shot him to death. Arensdorf was quickly acquitted by a
jury comprised mostly of his customers. Following the acquittal, the
drinks were "on the house."

• Ira G. Struck of New Albany, Indiana, picked up his hometown news-paper one day in 1886 and learned that Charles V. Hoover, the lead choir singer in his church, was pitching woo to Mrs. Struck, the church organ-ist. Struck, encountering Hoover in a store some days later, shot at the youth, who ducked. The irate husband went off to Florida on business but was called back to Indiana to face an assault charge. On the steps of the New Albany courthouse, July 27, 1886, Struck spotted Hoover and his father. Cursing, Struck withdrew a pistol and shot both men, killing the son. The accused was acquitted as being insane at the time of the shoot-ing.

• For years fireman Samuel Rhodehouse resented being "bossed about" by his superior, engineer Mat Van Devander, as they toiled in a steam en-gine for the Cincinnati, Jackson & Mackinaw Railroad. Outside of Van Wert, Ohio, in 1894, Rhodehouse convinced engineer Van Devander that something was wrong with the cowcatcher. The engineer got out to check, and, standing in front of the train, was promptly run down and crushed to death.

Rhodehouse was acquitted of first-degree murder, but the jury did find him guilty of assault, for which he served a few weeks in jail. (A hobo saw the fireman "lean on the throttle.") It was the first and only time in American murder annals that a train was used as a murder weapon!

CRIMINALS

THE CRIMINAL AS A WRITER

"I wish I could write a book and not have to make a living." With these words, convicted Watergate criminal John W. Dean III echoed the monetary sentiments of almost every malefactor in American history. Either white collar or blue, American criminals have left no margin for financial loss in capitalizing on their crimes by writing about how they were committed.

Henry Tufts began it all by writing the first American criminal autobiography in 1807. The book was widely read, especially by horse thieves, for whom Tufts had actually written a manual. Five years later, counterfeiter William Stuart duplicated Tufts's success by detailing his own life of roguery. Michael Martin, known better as "Captain Lightfoot," didn't have the time to describe his life of crime, being hanged as a highwayman on December 22, 1822, near Cambridge, Massachusetts. Captain Lightfoot did have enough hours, however, to dictate his strange tales to Boston reporter Frederick W. Waldo, who went on to publish his own best seller.

By the mid-1830s, such cunning miscreants as hotel thief Sile Doty and gambler George H. Devol popularized the criminal autobiography. Gunfighter John Wesley Hardin, with forty notches on his pistols, authored his own story after spending sixteen years in the Huntsville, Texas, prison for murder. The book was published in 1894, just a year before Hardin was shot to death in the back while rolling dice in an El Paso saloon, and the one-time outlaw realized little profit. Hardin was the exception among writing criminals. His chief aim was to vindicate himself with such claims as "I swear before God that I never shot a man except in self-defense." Few believed him.

Another outlaw of the Old West, Emmett Dalton, wrote the terrible tale of the Dalton Brothers, vividly recounting in 1931 how his brothers Bob and Grat were killed (and Emmett wounded) in their last bank raid at Coffeyville, Kansas, in 1892. Emmett had been sent to prison for life but was pardoned after serving fourteen years. His lurid book reaped great rewards from avid readers and was made into a movie, *When the Daltons Rode.*

Many outlaws strangely sought not to write their own stories but to receive good press. Jesse and Frank James were forever sending letters to newspaper editors explaining how and why they were not present when certain banks and trains were robbed; Jesse made a point of giving an interview to a St. Louis *Dispatch* reporter in Galveston, Texas, in 1874.

Thirties outlaws Bonnie Parker and Clyde Barrow were fond of writing letters to the editor (both shown here enjoying their gun-happy brief lives as Bonnie "arrests" Clyde in 1933); Bonnie penned their bloody saga in a long poem, "Suicide Sal."

The most wanted man in the country let it be known that he had married Miss Zerelda "Zee" Mimms.

"Notwithstanding the lies that have been told upon me and the crimes laid at my door," Jesse announced, "her [Zee's] devotion to me has never wavered a moment." The *Dispatch* ran the interview under the banner head "All the World Loves a Lover."

Jesse's habit of writing to newspapers was duplicated, like everything else they mimicked of the Old West, by most of the Depression-era robbers. John Dillinger wrote letters denouncing the police. Bonnie Parker, of Bonnie and Clyde infamy, not only wrote to newspapers but submitted maudlin poetry for publication. One of her poems, "The Story of Suicide Sal," was printed by the press almost coast to coast.

Charles Arthur "Pretty Boy" Floyd, the Oklahoma bank robber, outstripped of all his contemporaries, busying himself with writing dozens of letters to the press, especially denying the FBI claim that he was the deadly machine gunner who slew five men in the "Kansas City Massacre." One of Floyd's postcards read: "Dear sirs: I—Charles Floyd—want it made known that I did not participate in the massacre of officers at Kansas City. Charles Floyd."

Floyd was tracked down by the FBI and killed for that crime on October 22, 1934, yet Kansas City hoodlum James Henry "Blackie" Audett claimed in 1954 that Floyd, although the culprit of innumerable crimes, was never at the site of the massacre.

The list of criminal autobiographies fattened with each decade. Alvin Karpis, known as "Old Creepy" when he robbed banks with the Barker brothers and kidnapped millionaires for a living, emerged from a federal prison to write in 1971 his own story. In the book he claimed he never hurt anyone, a statement his myriad victims might dispute, if they were alive. Karpis' book, however, was a great success, as was the autobiography of super bank burglar Willie "The Actor" Sutton. Both men died celebrities.

The success of the books written by the Watergate conspirators is not a new phenomenon but merely typical of criminal autobiography. John Dean, along with Richard Nixon, John Mitchell, Ehrlichman and others, have capitalized on their crimes handsomely, more than $3 million being dispersed by publishers for their sales. No, Mr. Dean did not have to make a living for a long time after receiving a $300,000 advance from his publisher (not to mention $5,000 he was given for a *Playboy* interview and his wife, "Mo," receiving $100,000 for her story).

What could be more inspiring, one might ask any budding young writer, than witnessing such staggering incomes from criminal autobiographies? All of it might lead to a startling new course in college literature entitled: "Commit the Crimes, Then Write the Book."

THE CRIMINAL AND SHOW BUSINESS

As if to polish their tarnished images, criminals, particularly the American variety, have deeply involved themselves with legitimate show business, befriending super stars and often sponsoring the budding careers of talented hopefuls, as was the case with singer Frank Sinatra. It is widely known that his first sponsor was the New Jersey rackets king Willie Moretti, alias Moore.

More than providing a comfortable place where mobsters can mingle with union bosses, politicians and businessmen to whisper, unhampered, one shady deal after another, nightclubs, and show business in general, have provided American criminals with status. They will gingerly step into the limelight to scrape legitimate luster onto corroded character, as well as reap financial benefits and sexual pleasures.

The criminal as a show business buff is not a recent role but trails back to our earliest beginnings. The first play ever performed in newly developed Louisiana was based upon a murder.

In 1752 a Colapissa Indian killed a Choctaw and fled to the stockaded settlement of New Orleans. Angry Choctaws followed and demanded that the French governor turn over the killer to be executed. Before the governor could order the youthful Indian handed over, the Colapissa's father stepped from the fort and offered himself as a substitute victim for his murdering son. The Choctaws accepted, and before the horrified citizens of New Orleans the father was beheaded by the Choctaw chief.

An officer of the garrison, Le Blanc de Villeneuve, wrote a verse play called *The Indian Father,* which was performed in the governor's mansion in New Orleans in 1753. The son of the executed victim sat in the first row at the premiere performance, the first recorded murderer to attend the theater in America. (One account has it that the Indian youth, so moved by the play, died by his own hands some weeks later.)

Theater, or rather vaudeville shows, attracted almost every gunslinger of the Old West. Killers-for-hire such as Clay Allison and John Wesley Hardin were partial to melodramas. Gunman Ben Thompson, however, was no lover of comics and once burst into comedian Eddie Foy's dressing room in Dodge City's Comique Theater, bent on shooting off his head until peace officer Bat Masterson persuaded him to allow "the miserable actor" to live.

High art was not ignored. Scores of Black Handers flocked to see Enrico Caruso perform at New York's Metropolitan Opera House at the turn of the century. First the killers listened and applauded. Next came the Black Hand notes demanding enormous secret payments under the threat of death. Caruso paid $1,000 of each $10,000 he earned per performance.

Lawman William Barclay "Bat" Masterson once rescued actor Eddie Foy from the wrath of gunman Ben Thompson.

By the 1920s the gangster made the nightclubs and the theater his home, as well as a large part of his income. Milk racketeer Larry Fay opened up several clubs in New York, starring Texas Guian, whose "Hello, Sucker" to customers meant exactly that. Fay did not fare too well in show business. He was shot to death by his doorman after refusing to give the fellow a one-dollar-a-day raise.

Al Capone had great interests in various nightclubs and plays. Though he was an avowed friend of singer-comedian Joe E. Lewis, Capone did not object to his right-hand goon, "Machine Gun Jack" McGurn, almost killing Lewis by slashing his throat when the comic refused to move from one night spot to a Capone club. He once had his goons kidnap the talented Ritz brothers, to perform exclusively for him until dawn at the Hawthorne Hotel, Capone's sanctuary in Cicero, Illinois.

Two decades later the syndicate chieftains were everywhere in show business, from Florida palaces like the Colonial Inn with owners Meyer Lansky and Joe Adonis at ringside to the Las Vegas pleasure spas inspired by Benjamin "Bugsy" Siegel.

By then the most dangerous criminals in America moved openly with celebrities. The Fischetti clan from Chicago accompanied Frank Sinatra

The great operatic star Enrico Caruso (shown here in the role of Pagliacci) was constantly plagued by Black Handers.

Al Capone's love of nightclubs often led him to kidnap entertainers.

Benjamin "Bugsy" Siegel, who brought show business and the syndicate to Las Vegas.

on a trip to Cuba, where homage was paid to deported crime czar Charles "Lucky" Luciano.

Gangsters at the next table came to surprise few. But one startled and embarrassed fellow was the vulnerable J. Edgar Hoover, who made the Stork Club his favorite watering hole when in New York. One New Year's Eve, Hoover was asked to pose for a photo with one of the club's guests. The photographer thought it would be humorous if the guest held a toy submachine gun on Mr. Hoover. The FBI chief thought so too, and encouraged the guest to point the gun at him.

Not only did the guest angrily refuse, but he raced madly from the Stork Club. The reluctant first-nighter, Hoover later learned with a red face, was Terry Reilly, one of the most vicious killers on the syndicate's payroll and then on parole after serving time for extortion—and impersonating an FBI agent.

THE CRIMINAL'S SENSE OF HUMOR

Down through the history of American crime, U.S. miscreants have displayed a fascinating, albeit warped, sense of humor, one uncommon to the criminal world at large. From our inception as a country, criminals have been having the loud guffaw, but seldom the last laugh.

In the Old West, Charles E. Bolton, better known to lawmen as "Black Bart," thought himself quite the joker by leaving bits of doggerel scratched upon yellow note paper inside the Wells Fargo boxes he looted from California stagecoaches in the 1870s. One such note read:

> I've labored long and hard for bread,
> For honor and for riches
> But on my corns too long you've tred,
> You fine-haired sons-of-bitches.

The ever popular Jesse James, a cold-hearted killer if ever one existed, committed pranks he thought hilarious, especially when robbing trains. On January 31, 1874, Jesse and his band robbed the Little Rock Express outside of Gads Hill, Missouri, of $22,000 in cash and gold. He left what he thought to be an uproariously funny message. Jesse had written his own press release of the robbery, leaving the appropriate blank spaces to be filled in by the editors. It read:

THE MOST DARING TRAIN ROBBERY ON RECORD

The southbound train of the Iron Mountain Railroad was stopped here this evening by five [there was ten] heavily armed

America's most infamous bandit of the Old West, Jesse Woodson James, who
went so far as to send out his own press releases on robberies. (State Historical
Society of Missouri)

men and robbed of (   ) dollars.

The robbers arrived at the station a few minutes before the arrival of the train and arrested the agent and put him under guard
and then threw the train on the switch. The robbers were all
large men, all being slightly under six feet. After robbing the
train they started in a southerly direction. They were all
mounted on handsome horses. PS: They are a hell of an excitement in this part of the country.

The old street gangs of New York were equal to such snarling snickers.
The Car Barn Gang, which controlled an area encompassing Ninetieth to
100th streets, and Third Avenue to the East River, posted humorous no-

tices to police (which the latter took quite seriously) on the old car barns on Second Avenue and Ninety-seventh Street. They read:

NOTICE—COPS KEEP OUT!

No policemen will hereafter
be allowed on this block.

BY ORDER OF THE
CAR BARN GANG

Bank robber John Dillinger was another of those merry pranksters of the underworld who could not resist what he thought to be a good joke. Dillinger was forever phoning his nemesis, Captain Matt Leach of the Indiana State Police, to tell him what a poor job he was doing in tracking down Public Enemy Number One.

Dillinger reportedly sent Leach a subscription to a magazine which irked the captain no end. It was entitled: *How to Be a Good Detective.*

Gambler Nicky Arnstein, the great love of Ziegfeld Follies star Fannie Brice, pulled off perhaps the most spectacular joke in the modern history of criminal dragnets. Wanted for masterminding huge securities thefts from Wall Street, Arnstein chose a most unusual way to surrender to authorities.

He waited until the day of New York's Fifth Avenue Police Parade and as the last platoon of policemen marched by, his chauffeur-driven, top-down car swung in behind. As the car passed the main reviewing stand, high-ranking dignitaries discovered to their red-faced chagrin that they were doffing silk top hats to the most wanted man in New York.

As the mayor roared in apoplexy, the dapper Nicky waved cheerily back at him and then casually rode to police headquarters and turned himself in.

SUPERSTITION AND CRIMINALS, THE NUMBER 22

In that tear-streaked big house movie *20,000 Years in Sing Sing,* tough Tommy Connors (Spencer Tracy) complains of his jinx day: "I was born on a Saturday, I got caught on a Saturday, I was sent up to this crummy joint on a Saturday." He refuses to go along on a jailbreak on a Saturday but, as the jinx will have it, he goes to the chair on a Saturday. And he had it easy.

Research into the hard data of American crime uncovers a similar, but realistic phenomenon, not with a day of the week, however, but with a particular number, one that seems to work itself significantly into the lives of many important American criminals: 22.

In her book on numerology, Sybil Leek states that the number 22 represents "elements of treachery, causing impulsive action without thought and so leading to imperfect judgement." Criminals more than fit such a description.

Syndicate boss Joe "Joey A" Adonis (née Doto) was born on 11/22/1906. Felix Anthony "Milwaukee Phil" Alderisio, one of the worst of the Mafia's hit men, was born in 1922. The Barker gang held up a federal reserve mail truck, 8/22/1933, killing patrolman Miles A. Cunningham. A Barker brother, Lloyd, was captured after sticking up a rural Oklahoma post office, and sent to prison for life in 1922. Clyde Barrow was paroled from Eastham Prison in Texas, teaming up with Bonnie Parker to begin their killing/robbing spree on 2/2/1932. (They robbed, among others, the Alma, Texas, State Bank, 6/22/1933, eluded a posse near Grand Prairie, Texas, 11/22/1933; their betrayal to police was set up on 5/22/1934.)

Then there's Charles Arthur "Pretty Boy" Floyd, who was gunned down by FBI agents near East Liverpool, Ohio, 10/22/1934. Another bank robber, Harvey Bailey, who died in 1979 as a retired cabinetmaker, pulled off his first big crime in 1922, heisting $500,000 from the Denver Mint with Jim Ripley and others.

That number of "treachery" did not sit too well with Al Capone either. Scarface's first arrest in Chicago for carrying a concealed weapon occurred in 1922; he was arrested again on the same charge, 12/22/1927. Capone, as the world learned, operated the notorious Four Deuces speakeasy/brothel/murder den in Chicago at 2222 S. Wabash.

Throughout America's history of crime, the number is there, lurking. The notorious murderer and pirate Charles Gibbs was hanged for his crimes at Ellis Island, 4/22/1831. The infamous highwayman Michael Martin (known throughout New England as "Captain Lightfoot") was hanged at Cambridge, Massachusetts, 12/22/1822. Murderer Marion Ira Stout was executed at Rochester, New York, 10/22/1858. Jesse James, his brother Frank, the Younger brothers, in their first significant robbery —the Richmond, Missouri, bank of $4,000 in gold—shot down three men, killing them on 5/22/1867. Ella Watson, best known in Wyoming as "Cattle Kate," was hanged by vigilantes for rustling. She was 22-years-old.

The number rampantly appears in the lives of this century's criminals, which may or may not be due to more accurate record keeping.

Trunk murderess Winnie Ruth Judd was released from the Arizona State Prison, 12/22/1971. Alvin "Old Creepy" Karpis, the last man to commit a major train theft, robbed, in 1935, train number 622 at Gar-

Trunk murderess Winnie Ruth Judd, who slaughtered her best friends in 1932, then shipped them piecemeal from Phoenix to Los Angeles, was released from prison on that ominous date.

rettsville, Ohio, his last robbery before being apprehended. George "Machine Gun" Kelly kidnapped millionaire oilman Charles F. Urschel on 7/22/1933, the crime for which he went to prison for life. George "Baby Face" Nelson shot and killed an FBI agent near Rhinelander, Wisconsin, on 4/22/1934, a murder which brought down the wrath of the Bureau and led to Nelson's death.

California's first syndicate boss, Benjamin "Bugsy" Siegel murdered his first man on the West Coast, one Harry "Big Greenie" Greenberg on 11/22/1939. In another insane rub-out, seven men were killed in Chicago, the macabre St. Valentine's Day Massacre, at the S-M-C Cartage Co. (a front for George "Bugs" Moran), the address of which was 2122 N. Clark St. One who might have been wielding a machine gun there was Paul "The Waiter" Ricca, Mafia don who died 12/22/1972.

Ricca's one-time boss, father of the national syndicate, Johnny Torrio, received his first important arrest for income tax evasion at White Plains, New York, 4/22/1936. The man Torrio and Capone so much vexed,

John Dillinger—the number 22 amazingly reappears throughout his career.

bootlegger Roger "The Terrible" Touhy, married his wife Clara on 4/22/1922. Touhy's first trial for kidnapping Jake "The Barber" Factor (later proved a hoax) ended 2/2/1934. Another kidnapper, for real, Thomas Harold Thurmond, was lynched in San Jose, California, in 1933 by irate residents. His murder victim was Brooke Hart, age 22.

The underworld's most durable canary, Joe Valachi, wasn't ignored by this most sinister of numbers (black at roulette). He murdered John Joseph Saupp in the federal prison at Atlanta on 6/22/1962, an event which directly led to his revelation of the existence of the Cosa Nostra.

In crimes of passion, the number 22 abounds. Mad millionaire Harry K. Thaw, in 1906, murdered the great and girthsome architect Stanford White over the affection of one-time Floradora Girl Evelyn Nesbit, who at the time was age 22. Peoria's (Illinois) mass rapist and murderer Gerald Thompson was apprehended on 6/22/1935. Two of the eight nurses brutally slain by Richard Speck in Chicago in 1966 were 22-year-olds.

Even political assassinations are not exempt. President Kennedy, of course, was killed by Lee Harvey Oswald on 11/22/1963. His brother Robert was murdered by Sirhan Bishara Sirhan in 1968; the assassin wielded a .22 caliber revolver.

Winner and champion possessor of this spiritually rankling number is the Hoosier bandit John Dillinger. He was born 6/22/1903. He left home the day after committing his first robbery, a stolen car, 7/22/1923. He was paroled 5/22/1933 from the Michigan City, Indiana, State Prison. Dillinger was arrested for bank robbery in Dayton, Ohio, 9/22/1933. FBI agents in a one-sided battle attempted to capture him at Little Bohemia Lodge in Wisconsin, 4/22/1934. The shooting outside Chicago's Biograph Theater in which the FBI claimed to have killed him occurred 7/22/1934. Oh yes, John Dillinger's prison number at Michigan City was 13225.

DUAL PERSONALITIES IN CRIMINALS

William Stanley Milligan, suspected Ohio rapist, was recently found to be insane and was sentenced to life in a mental institution. Milligan's insanity, however, was piecemeal, psychiatrists insisting that he had as many as ten personalities, from a twenty-three-year-old man (his own age), with decided artistic talents, to a three-year-old girl who can only express herself in crude line drawings. He is a heady and frightening specter of Robert Louis Stevenson's Jekyll and Hyde, but certainly not an exclusive real-life representative.

There have been more than one such spectacular criminal whose sinister side (or sides) manifested an evil destiny, while another side kept up the appearances of respectability and clean living. One of the earliest dual personalities in American crime was that of Thomas W. Piper, sexton of the Warren Avenue Baptist Church in Boston, Massachusetts.

Outwardly, Piper was a dutiful church servant, performing his duties promptly and extending a pleasant personality to the congregation. He made it a point to greet churchgoers each Sunday by standing in the open belfry of the church, waving and smiling to all who entered.

Yet, like the potion-gulping Jekyll of his era, Piper was often seen to drink from a bottle during services as he sat in the last pew of the church. (The concoction, a brew of his own making, contained whiskey and laudanum.) At such time, Piper's personality altered abruptly; he became a sneering, dark-faced creature, twisting his long black mustache at women in church, and leering at little girls.

Parishioners shrugged off such behavior as the quirks of a lonely man. Then, on the night of December 5, 1873, a local servant girl, Bridget Landregan, was found murdered at the outskirts of town, her assailant surprised by a curious resident. The killer went whooping into the darkness, black cape flying over his shoulders. Then another girl, named Sullivan, was attacked, her head smashed, the victim of a yelping maniac dressed all in black who escaped pursuers. The girl died hours later in a hospital. Mary Tynam, a streetwalker, was next.

These attacks continued in and about Boston for almost two years, residents badly frightened by the same lurking killer. By May 23, 1875, there was little pretense of decency left in the laudanum-swilling Piper. In broad daylight he led five-year-old Mable H. Young to his belfry after services and attacked her. Witnesses intervened but too late. The girl died from the assault.

Piper confessed all he could remember shortly before his execution in May 1878, how his drugged whiskey had made him into a night creature that murdered at least three women and one girl. "I am a very bad man," he concluded darkly.

Almost thirty years later, America was treated to the schizoid antics of another killer, one of Society's elite, coke multimillionaire Harry K. Thaw. This playboy was to all a charming bon vivant who pleasantly squandered away his fortune of $40 million on good food, gilded mansions, and tall, leggy showgirls.

The dark, utterly secret side of his personality, however, belied the manners of the cultured gentleman. Thaw, late at night, would slip out of his Manhattan mansion and stroll to apartments he kept in a luxurious brothel. There he gave vent to the insane rage that simmered beneath his placid exterior.

What strange sexual practices he exercised were soon revealed when the madam, Susan Merrill, could no longer bear the piercing cries coming from his apartments.

She later swore: "I could hear the screams coming from his apartment and once I could stand it no longer. I rushed into his room. He had tied the girl to the bed, naked, and was whipping her. She was covered with welts. Thaw's eyes protruded and he looked mad."

Such fine madness leaped beyond beatings on the night of June 25, 1906. By then Thaw had married showgirl Evelyn Nesbit, who had once been mistress to Stanford White, the great architect. Thaw had whipped out of Evelyn the most lurid tales her tortured mind could invent concerning White's liaison with her.

Finding White attending a gay musical on the roof of Madison Square Garden, Thaw coolly walked up to the architect and shot him dead. At his trial, Thaw's dual personality was glibly explained away by his lawyer, the feisty Delphin Delmas, who pled his client as temporarily insane at the time of the murder. Thaw, Delmas insisted to a bewildered jury, suffered from a peculiar malady, an involuntary seizure that could result in murder; he called it "dementia Americana," indigenous to American males who held every man's wife as sacred.

The jury accepted such gobbledygook and returned a verdict of not guilty on grounds of insanity. Thaw was sent to an asylum for life, but his fortune was used to free him. This one-eyed wealthy Jack spent the rest of his life roaming the world in comfort, young attractive women constantly clinging to his withering body. Occasionally a strange gleam would come into his eye and he would reach for the whip.

One of the nicest visitors to Wheaton, Illinois, in the summer of 1914 was Henry Spencer, an ingratiating young man who spent a great deal of time talking about God and sin, while he applied for various positions as a salesman. In the course of his town travels, Spencer encountered a spinster named Allison Rexroat, a woman ten years his senior with a blossoming bank account. In no time, Spencer began to court the lady.

The bespectacled Spencer quietly took his bride-to-be on a picnic lunch which he preapred himself; he was never able to explain why he packed a hammer next to the egg salad and pickles. While the amorous Ms. Rexroat sprawled next to a quiet stream awaiting her lover, Spencer inexplicably took the hammer from the picnic basket and crushed her skull with it.

He hastily buried the body in a shallow grave and then prepared to leave Wheaton on the 1 P.M. train. Residents, suspicious of Spencer's strange actions, called the sheriff, who arrested the young man at the depot. After a week in jail, Spencer admitted the murder, almost as an afterthought. He was convicted and sentenced to hang.

While awaiting the gallows, Henry Spencer regained his religious zeal, telling one and all that he had embraced God. A Chicago reporter, Wallace Smith, interviewed him in his cell. Spencer told him that he had "joined God's holy crusade."

"Cut out the act," said Wallace.

"It's not an act," replied the offended killer. "I've rejoined the ranks of God's children."

"Have you admitted the killing?"

"That's not important anymore. I was a sinner, a black sinner. I did evil. Evil was in me. Now it's gone."

Spencer maintained his religious composure until mounting the gallows. Before the noose was put about his neck he gave a long, impassioned speech about good and evil before a great throng (this was still the era of public executions). Then, before the eyes of thousands, Henry Spencer seemed to change, his character slipping into an entirely different posture. He suddenly screamed: "I'm innocent of the murder of Allison Rexroat. It's a lie! I never killed her! You're all dirty bastards! You got no right! I never touched her! So help me God, I never harmed a hair on her head, so help me God!"

With the murderous side of his nature fully exposed, a sight more shocking than the hanging itself, Henry Spencer went through the trap to his dark eternity.

The same was true of Carl Otto Wanderer, a much-decorated hero of

World War I. Wanderer returned to Chicago to medals, parades and his adoring sweetheart, whom he married in 1919. The following year his wife was ruthlessly gunned down by a robber, whom Wanderer killed with his service automatic.

But reporters and police were suspicious of the war hero. Only days after his beloved was buried he was seen to be in ebullient spirits, whistling down the street; in fact he appeared blatantly happy. Through gritty investigations, authorities learned that Wanderer had actually hired the robber to stage a holdup.

The war hero had killed the hired assailant (a nameless bum paid five dollars for the deed), and then turned his weapon on his wife, shooting her to death. The causes, when sifted, seemed arcane, but before Wanderer was hanged in 1920, it was learned that he was a closet homosexual and the thought of his wife, then pregnant, giving birth, drove him to murder, the dark side of him finding it impossible to accept the birth of his own child, an affirmation of a heterosexual existence he found intolerable.

The most pronounced dual personality among American killers in recent times is undoubtedly that of William Heirens, who, as a youth, from 1945 to 1946, murdered two women while burglarizing their Chicago apartments. At such moments, he became another person entirely, standing outside of himself, as it were, once the bloody acts were performed. It was Heirens who, after stabbing Mrs. Frances Brown to death in her apartment, wrote on the bathroom mirror: "For heaven's sake, catch me before I kill more. I cannot control myself."

Following the abduction of six-year-old Suzanne Degnan, whom Heirens tried to ransom, then strangled and dissected, the killer was caught. He insisted that he was not the murderer, that his friend "George Murman" was the fiend. Murman, of course, did exist, but only in Heirens' mind (George Mur-*der*-man).

To this day, Heirens woefully begs release from the Joliet State Penitentiary in Illinois, parole board members thankfully shaking their heads. "George is a bad boy," whines Heirens. "George did it all."

A WHO'S WHO OF AMERICAN CRIMINALS IN FACT AND FICTION

There is an old saying that behind every great fortune there is a great crime. The same certainly applies in one way to many of the finest novels, plays and films. Crime has repeatedly provided authors and screenwriters with fascinating grist for their mills. Edgar Allan Poe, that crime-haunted scribe, who died drunk while stuffing ballot boxes in Baltimore, they say, launched his career with a story called "The Mystery of Marie Rogêt." Poe's tale was based upon the celebrated murder of Mary Cecilia Rogers, who was mysteriously strangled to death on July 28, 1841, one of the greatest unsolved murders in New York history.

Mary Rogers, a stunning beauty, had sold cigars at a popular snuff and cigar stand at 319 Broadway. Some of her customers included James Fenimore Cooper, Washington Irving and the brooding Poe, who actually dated her. When Poe heard of Mary's murder, he began to write the "Marie Rogêt" story, astounding authorities by suggesting that the girl had been pregnant and had been killed by a butchering abortionist. Poe's pregnancy theory was eventually proved to be true and even Poe became a suspect in the minds of some literary sleuths, this author included, but the case remained unsolved. Poe had instituted a crime cycle in American letters which to this day draws with incredible dependence upon the actual criminals in our midst, characters crawling not out of the searing imagination of inventive writers but from the living streets and byways of America, all chillingly real.

The hard-living Stephen Crane based his *Maggie, A Girl of the Streets* on a prostitute he encountered in Manhattan's Tenderloin in the 1890s. The police officer he profiled as beating up Maggie in order to obtain his kickbacks from her earnings was none other than the crooked police lieutenant Charles Becker, who was electrocuted in 1915 for the murder of a gambler.

Author Theodore Dreiser heard of a twenty-two-year-old youth named

F. Scott Fitzgerald, whose major work *The Great Gatsby* was based upon the author's one-time neighbor Larry Fay, a notorious New York bootlegger.

Gambler Arnold Rothstein became the character Wolfsheim in *The Great Gatsby*. (UPI)

Chester Gillette being tried for the murder of his sweetheart, Grace Brown, a girl Gillette had drowned in Big Moose Lake, New York, in 1906. Dreiser sat through the long trial taking notes. The case gave birth to his finest novel, *An American Tragedy*. When F. Scott Fitzgerald lived in Great Neck, New York, in the early 1920s he had as a suburban neighbor, a high-stepping bootlegger named Larry Fay. It was Fay who became the ill-starred protagonist of *The Great Gatsby;* the character Wolfsheim in the same book was undeniably the gambler Arnold Rothstein, the man who fixed the 1919 World Series and who financed some of Fay's rackets.

A plethora of books based upon real criminals from all eras in our history has developed since then. Meyer Levin's *Compulsion* drew wholly from the Leopold and Loeb killing of Bobbie Franks in Chicago in 1924. *The Harder They Fall* by Budd Schulberg, which aptly portrayed the crime-ridden sport of boxing, was based upon the gangster-controlled "champion" Primo Carnera. Even the Western became a writing genre where the real criminal was roped, hog-tied and offered up as a creative character. In the cowboy opus *Whispering Smith,* the lawman portrayed was based upon Joe Lefors, the man who doggedly tracked Butch Cassidy and his gang across the West; Harvey Dushayne in the same book was none other than the Wild Bunch's deadliest killer, Harvey Logan, better known as Kid Curry.

The movies, almost since their inception with such silent classics as *The Great Train Robbery*—based upon America's first train robbers, the Reno brothers—have ceaselessly presented "fictional" characters who were made from the whole cloth of actual criminals. The first great gangster epic was the silent film *Underworld,* written by Ben Hecht. The machine gun-wielding thug, enacted by George Bancroft, was based upon "Terrible Tommy" O'Connor, a Chicago killer who escaped the gallows only moments before he was scheduled to hang. (O'Connor was never found and a court order is still on the books which compels Chicago authorities to retain the gallows until the gangster's fate is determined; the timbers are stored to this day in the boiler room of the Criminal Courts Building at Twenty-sixth and California streets.)

Another Chicago underworld figure, the corrupt Chicago *Tribune* reporter Jake Lingle, who was gunned down in 1930, was portrayed by none other than screen idol Clark Gable in the now obscure crime melodrama *The Finger Points,* produced by First National in 1931. W. R. Burnett's classic *Little Caesar* was based upon Chicago's old Glorianna gang and its most ardent killer.

During the heyday of the gangster films, real-life criminals were the major sources of material for desperate film writers. James Cagney portrayed New York's Francis "Two-Gun" Crowley, especially in the wild shoot-out scene between "Rocky Sullivan" and the police in *Angels with Dirty Faces*. Again Cagney portrayed a lunatic criminal in 1949 in *White*

Heat; his Arthur Cody Jarrett was a loose version of the headache-hounded Arthur "Dock" Barker of the infamous Barker brothers and his exploits were gleaned from the actual Jarrett gang of California.

Humphrey Bogart played many a gangster but his most convincing roles involved his oblique performances as John Dillinger. As Duke Mantee in *The Petrified Forest* Bogart, a dead ringer for.Dillinger, studied short newsreels of Dillinger taken while he was a prisoner at Crown Point, Indiana (inside the "escape-proof" Crown Point Jail, from which Dillinger promptly escaped). Bogart dressed like Dillinger in the newsreels, wearing an open collar and an unbuttoned vest, holding his hands high and jutting his elbows, a trait of Dillinger's. He again played Dillinger, albeit an aging Dillinger, in Raoul Walsh's *High Sierra,* the film

The gangster film *Underworld* starred George Bancroft in a role modeled after "Terrible Tommy" O'Connor of Chicago.

James Cagney waiting to walk the last mile to the chair with Pat O'Brien at his side in *Angels with Dirty Faces;* Cagney's "Rocky Sullivan" was in real life Francis "Two-Gun" Crowley.

that brought Bogart to stardom in 1941. (The entire exploits of the Dillinger gang, as well as the events surrounding the real Kansas City Massacre of 1933 were incorporated in the James Cagney law-and-order film *G Men* in 1935.)

The list is almost endless, but such drawing upon real criminals is not without risks to authors and screenwriters. Ben Hecht, who wrote the screenplay *Scarface* in 1932, which was obviously based upon Al Capone, received a visit in his Hollywood home by two gun-toting goons from Chicago shortly after the picture was released. They wanted to know whom Hecht had in mind when he wrote *Scarface.*

"It wasn't Al, was it?" one of the gangsters asked with a scowl.

Hecht thought fast. "No, no," he said. "That was some other guy I knew back in Chicago."

"Who?" the thug demanded.

"Ahhh, Deanie O'Bannion," Hecht said.

"Oh, that's all right, then," the goon said. "We already killed him."

When the hooligans departed, Hecht poured himself a stiff drink, and vowed to obtain his material elsewhere than from lives of living criminals.

Humphrey Bogart modeled many of his gangster roles after John Dillinger.

Other notable Who's Who entries include:

In Classical Fiction and Drama

The roots of crime run deep, twining about classical literature, so deep in fact, that many classics are not only based upon real-life criminals but are often taken verbatim from reality and transplanted into some of the world's greatest novels and plays.

The moody Russian author Feodor Dostoyevski knew well the worth of crime in literature. His *Crime and Punishment* is an examination of self, and, given the fact that Dostoyevski's own father, a rural doctor of questionable moral habits, died under mysterious circumstances—there were

Al Capone was the role model for Ben Hecht's film script *Scarface*. (Capone is shown at Chicago's Wrigley Field in a rare photo displaying the scars on his left cheek; he would normally refuse to be photographed from this position. Signing a ball for Capone's son while bodyguards glare is Gabby Hartnett of the Chicago Cubs.) (UPI)

rumors of murder—it is not hard to believe that the author was all four of his tortured *Brothers Karamazov,* who felt overwhelming guilt for the murder of their licentious father.

That great French novelist Honoré de Balzac instinctively knew the value of the real thing. His character Inspector Vautrin in *Le Père Goriot* is drawn wholly from the life of François Eugène Vidocq, convict, police spy and later the founder of the French police organization, the Sûreté. (American mystery writer Edgar Allan Poe admitted under pressure from newsmen that his *Murders in the Rue Morgue* had been wholly influenced by Vidocq's *Memoirs* and the underworld of Vidocq's Paris.)

Some of the great English classics have been rooted to real, if gory, crime, criminals and detectives. Here are but a few:

• The best-known Elizabethan domestic tragedy, *Arden of Feversham* (attributed to William Shakespeare) was based upon the murder of Thomas Arden of Kent, England, who was also mayor of Feversham. Arden was killed by his wife's lover, a tailor named Thomas Morsby, who was hanged. Alice Arden was burned to death for her part of the murder conspiracy, as well as for being unfaithful, such was the prim and proper temper of the times.

• *A Warning for Fair Women,* a popular drama, found its plot in the killing of George Sanders of London in 1573. A Captain Browne, who coveted Sanders' wife, Anne, employed a fortuneteller, the Widow Drury, to persuade Mrs. Sanders to join the murder conspiracy. Browne and Anne killed Sanders in a wood near London, and, in the course of their careless clubbing, only knocked Sanders' servant, John Bean, senseless, instead of killing him. Bean testified against the lot, and Browne, Anne and the obliging soothsayer, the Widow Drury, were all hanged.

• The play *A Yorkshire Tragedy* was taken from Walter Caverley's murder of his two children while temporarily insane in 1580, brutal slayings for which he was pressed to death.

• *The Witch of Edmonton* is based upon the murder of a farmer's daughter named Susan by one Frank Thorney, who was executed in 1621.

• Probably the most used murder in providing grist for British writers was that of Ellen Scanlan by Stephen Sullivan on July 14, 1819, at the instigation of his employer, John Scanlan, Ellen's husband. This fairly tame homicide was profiled in Gerald Griffin's novel *The Collegians* (1829),

---

Bela Lugosi enacting the film version of Bram Stoker's *Dracula;* this all-time monster was based upon a human vampire of the real world.

Dion Boucicault's 1859 play *The Colleen Bawn,* and Julius Benedict's 1863 opera *Lily of Killarney.*

• The stage melodrama *Murder in the Red Barn* is based upon the murder of twenty-five-year-old Maria Marten by her paramour William Corder on May 18, 1827. Corder had gotten Maria pregnant and promised to take her from her Suffolk, England, farm to Ipswich and marry her. Instead, he walked the girl to a red barn on his property and killed her with a pickaxe. Corder cleverly covered up the murder by writing long letters to Maria's parents, telling them they were living on the Isle of Wight. Mrs. Marten's sleep was disturbed by a dream in which she saw her child killed and buried in the red barn. So vivid was this nightmare that Mrs. Marten nagged police into digging up the Corder property; her daughter was found buried in the red barn. Corder insisted he was innocent but Maria's younger brother testified that he saw Corder emerge from the barn with the bloodied pickaxe. Corder was convicted and sent to the gallows on August 11, 1828, but not before he wrote out a full confession.

• Even the venerable Charles Dickens could not resist the real-life rogues of his era, whom he chose to populate his dire novels, but one of his most powerful *roman à clef* selections was that of the intrepid Inspector Field, who became Inspector Bucket of Scotland Yard in his fiction.

• The Granddaddy of all Gothic horror fiction, *Dracula* by Bram Stoker, would seem to be an exclusive nightmare of the author's, yet a close look at fifteenth-century middle Europe reveals the real-life monster from whom Stoker drew his shuddering details, one Vlad Tepes, also known as Vlad the Impaler (1431?–77), a bloodthirsty Romanian prince who murdered with impunity and for pleasure over several decades until the residents at large put an end to Vlad's lethal career.

In Detective Fiction

The dark fiction of the detective genre, the sinister murder mystery, the hard-knuckled mobster story are also all rooted in reality.

The paragon of detectives, Sherlock Holmes, was not wholly the sleuthing genius of Arthur Conan Doyle's imagination, but was mightily drawn from the life of an astounding clairvoyant, Dr. Joseph Bell, professor of medicine at the University of Edinburgh, one of Conan Doyle's teachers, whose "deductive reasoning" brought all crime mysteries into the scope of the "elementary." Holmes's nemesis, the abstract-thinking super criminal Professor James Moriarty, is undoubtedly based upon the historical exploits of Jonathan Wild, born in England in 1682 and executed in 1725 as a receiver of stolen goods; Wild was known as the "Prince of Robbers." Other notable real-life portrayals in this genre include:

Arthur Conan Doyle, who based his unforgettable Sherlock Holmes upon one of his own college professors.

Munitions king and international intriguer Basil Zaharoff shown here being knighted at Westminster Abbey on May 21, 1924; he was certainly the real-life counterpart to Eric Ambler's evil genius in *A Coffin for Dimitrios*.

• America's first detective story, *The Gambler* by Charles Burdett, published in 1848 and based entirely on the murder of Mary Rogers.

• The insidious Jack the Ripper, who plagued London's Whitechapel in 1888 when he preyed upon prostitutes, killing at least five, caused a spate of books based upon his nefarious guessed-at activities, the most prominent and best written being *The Lodger* by Mrs. Belloc Lowndes in 1911. The Ripper later appears in Alban Berg's opera *Lulu,* emerging in the last act to slice up the fallen heroine, who has been reduced to streetwalking, in apparent retribution for her evil ways.

• Dimitrios Makropoulos in Eric Ambler's spy-mystery masterpiece *A Coffin for Dimitrios* was certainly based upon the early career of Basil Zaharoff, the conniving munitions millionaire.

• Dashiell Hammett's deep-thinking rogue Casper Gutman of the un-forgettable *Maltese Falcon* was undoubtedly based upon the life of A. Maundry Gregory, one-time British detective turned entrepreneur and highly paid associate intriguer of Basil Zaharoff. Like all good writers, Hammett employed any and all real-life characters for his work. It is plain that his character Nora Charles in *The Thin Man* was drawn wholly from Hammett's lover, playwright Lillian Hellman. The free-swinging, hard-drinking, joke-cracking Nick Charles is none other than Hammett himself, a once top-notch Pinkerton detective.

•The 1896 murders of Captain Charles Nash and his wife, Laura, and Second Mate August W. Blomberg on board the barkentine *Herbert Fuller* en route from Boston to the Argentine on the nights of July 13–14, were portrayed in Mary Roberts Rinehart's mystery novel *The After House* (1914), and served as the plot outline for many of the novels of Clark Russell.

• Even American western novelists were not immune from using the ac-tual badmen of frontier days to juice up their characters and plots. Zane Grey was no exception. He studied long and hard the life of Henry

Playwright Lillian Hellman turned into *The Thin Man's* Nora Charles.

Plummer, notorious outlaw of Idaho-Montana who forms the role model in Grey's rip-snorting Western *Border Legion*.

Events in latter-day gangsterdom and lone killer lore were widely used and described in gory detail by American novelists. The garroting of New York gangster Larry Gallo in a bar on August 20, 1961, was depicted in Mario Puzo's best-selling *Godfather* as the killing of the behemoth bodyguard Luca Brasi. Truman Capote's *In Cold Blood* fictionalized the slaughter of the Clutter family in Kansas by Richard E. Hickock and Perry E. Smith, both later hanged. Dorothy Uhnak's best-selling *The In-*

The great film director David Wark Griffith, who made the first gangster film in 1912, basing his story on real events and using actual gangsters in the film.

The shooting of New York gambler Herman Rosenthal in 1912, as depicted in this early-day newspaper montage, inspired Griffith's gangster film.

vestigation was probably based upon the sordid Alice Crimmins kidnapping-murder case of New York.

It is obvious from these samples that some of the most popular heady fiction in the world has been supplied by the true occupants of the underworld and their restive pursuers, the cop and the detective, without whose exploits even the most powerful novels would be left ineffectual and decidedly dull.

In Motion Pictures

The first gangster film was produced in 1912 by the industry's greatest director, D. W. Griffith, and was entitled *The Musketeers of Pig Alley*. Griffith got the idea for the picture from newspaper stories of the day, particularly the blatant murder of New York City gambler Herman "Beansie" Rosenthal on July 21, 1912. As the gambler stepped in the wee hours from the Metropole Cafe, four vicious hoodlums in the hire of a crooked cop, Lieutenant Charles Becker, shot Rosenthal down on the sidewalk. Quickly rounded up, the killers named Becker as their sponsor

Gang moll and Bugsy Siegel's flamboyant lover Virginia Hill was loosely portrayed by Joan Crawford in 1950.

—he had ordered Rosenthal "croaked" because the gambler had balked at paying kickbacks and informed on Becker—and all were executed.

Griffith's penchant for realism in depicting elements of the Rosenthal story went as far as hiring actual gangsters from New York's Lower East Side, Kid Brood and Harlem Tom Evans, to name two, to portray themselves in the film. This film established the genre which proved to be highly successful motion picture fare.

Real gangsters continued to be seen in Hollywood films. One character, Harry "Big Greenie" Greenberg ran out on his New York chums with a bagful of loot in the 1920s. Benjamin "Bugsy" Siegel and Louis "Lepke" Buchalter put orders out to find and kill the defector. One of their henchmen, Abe "Kid Twist" Reles of Murder, Inc., went to the movies and almost fell out of his seat when he spotted Big Greenie as a film mobster in the movie *The Racket* (1928). When Siegel moved to the West Coast to establish rackets for the newly born syndicate, one of his assignments was to murder the mobster-turned-movie-actor Greenberg, which he did in Los Angeles on November 22, 1939.

Siegel's own story was told with variations many times, but most fancifully, especially his liaison with mob girl Virginia Hill, in the 1950 Warner Brothers film *The Damned Don't Cry* with Joan Crawford playing a role typical of the tempestuous, ruthless Ms. Hill, and Steve Cochran snarling à la Siegel. Bugsy's close associate and the man who later ordered him murdered in 1947, syndicate czar Charles "Lucky" Luciano, received Hollywood's spotlight more than a decade earlier in *Marked Woman*, which was based upon Luciano's 1936 trial and conviction for wholesale white slavery and prostitution.

Chicago thugs were not overlooked. George "Bugs" Moran was played by miscast Spencer Tracy in *Quick Millions* (1931). Earl "Hymie" Weiss, who inherited the Dion O'Bannion gang of Chicago's North Side when his leader was shot to death by Capone henchmen in his flower shop in 1924, was the role model for the sinister lead in one of the first talking films, *The Lights of New York* (1928). In the film, the gang boss tells his boys to eliminate a rival, ordering them to "take him for a ride." Weiss was the inventive hoodlum who instituted the one-way ride in 1921.

Mark Hellinger's production *The Roaring Twenties* had James Cagney in the lead, his criminal career almost identical to that of New York rackets boss Larry Fay. Cagney was destined to play many a real-life gangster in his fabulous Hollywood heyday. In his first film in 1931, *The Public Enemy*, Cagney's Tom Powers was heavily based upon the career of Chicago gangster Charles Dion "Deanie" O'Bannion. In the same film Leslie Fenton plays "Nails" Nathan, who is killed when his horse throws him, kicking him to death. Nathan is avenged by Cagney, who promptly goes to the riding stable, buys the horse and shoots the animal in its stable. This is the same fate met by World War I hero Samuel J. "Nails" Norton, a confederate of O'Bannion's, who was kicked to death on the bridle path of Chicago's Lincoln Park in 1922. "Two-Gun" Louis Alterie, Morton's close friend and trigger finger for O'Bannion, responded by renting the same horse, taking it to the spot where the erstwhile Morton had been stomped and shooting it to death. After taking the horse "for a

ride," Alterie called the stable owner and yelled over the phone: "We taught that goddamn horse of yours a lesson! If you want the saddle, go and get it!"

Perhaps no other American gangster received as much attention from Hollywood cameras as did Al Capone, Chicago rackets kingpin. In addition to the aptly named *Scarface* (1932), Capone was portrayed by Louis Wolheim in *The Racket* (1928), and, of all people, by Clark Gable in *The Secret Six* (1931), twice by Edward G. Robinson in *Little Caesar* (1930) and in *Key Largo* (1948), by Lee J. Cobb in *Party Girl* (1959), most realistically by Rod Steiger in *Al Capone* (1960), by Jason Robards, Jr., in *The St. Valentine's Day Massacre* (1967), and Ben Gazzara in *Al Capone* (1976), with Neville Brand doing a convincing Scarface in the TV series "The Untouchables."

Perhaps moviedom's fascination with Capone has to do with an attempt to understand a real-life monster more sinister than Mary Shelley could ever conjure in her story of Frankenstein, one responsible for the deaths of more than 1,000 persons, mostly rival gangsters, in the days when he made $50,000,000 tax-free a year from his Prohibition empire even as syphilis ate his brain to pieces.

One of the biggest hits of the last decade, *The Sting,* was based upon the flamboyant careers of the Gondorff Brothers, two con men who reaped millions in various big store routines at the turn of the century, and were portrayed by Robert Redford and Paul Newman. One of the most effective and legendary of confidence men, Jefferson Randolph "Soapy" Smith, the virtual ruler of Skagway, Alaska, during the Gold Rush was played with a vengeance by John McIntire in *The Far Country.*

Bossism is another favorite in film cycles, one of the most devastating careers being that of Tom "Boss" Pendergast, whose rule of Kansas City, Missouri, politics during the 1920s and 1930s was absolute. It was Pendergast who sponsored a young Harry Truman in his first bid for public office. Pendergast's astounding life story was brought to the screen in 1956 in *Boss,* with John Payne in the leading role.

Of all the underworld bosses, millionaire gambler and Manhattan crime sachem Arnold Rothstein was a perennial favorite for film profile. Edward Arnold played Rothstein in *Unholy Alliance* and the gambler was also shown in *Manhattan Melodrama,* a 1934 gangster epic in which Rothstein, profiled under a fictional name, is gunned down by Clark Gable.

The indefatigable James Cagney (shown with Jean Harlow) in *Public Enemy* was enacting the crime career of Chicago bootlegger Dion O'Bannion.

Edward G. Robinson as Little Caesar (clutching the coat of a terrified William Collier, Jr.) gave an electrifying portrayal of Al Capone.

Killers have been Hollywood's top selection in crime movies. Head of New York's Murder, Inc., Louis "Lepke" Buchalter was portrayed as oozing evil by Everett Sloane in the 1951 production of *The Enforcer,* with Humphrey Bogart playing the role model of District Attorney Thomas E. Dewey, who helped to break up the killers-for-hire legion, and Ted De Corsia playing the role of Abe "Kid Twist" Reles, who served as Dewey's chief informant.

Other notable killers from real life in Hollywood films include:

• Hawley Harvey Crippen, the doctor who chopped up his wife and buried her in the basement of his home outside of London in 1910. (The only identifiable remains of Mrs. Crippen, part of her stomach showing an abdominal scar, were exhibited at Crippen's trial, passed from one queasy juror to another on a soup plate.) Charles Laughton played the cuckolded

Crippen in the 1944 film *The Suspect,* with Stanley Ridges portraying
Scotland Yard's indomitable Chief Inspector Walter Dew, who chased
Crippen across the Atlantic on an ocean liner, capturing the killer when
he landed in Canada.

• Mass murderer of women, the one and only "Bluebeard," Henri
Désiré Landru, who was found guilty of killing, dissecting and burning at
least ten Parisian females from 1914 to 1919, was later portrayed as a
philosophical Bluebeard by the comic genius Charlie Chaplin in *Monsieur
Verdoux* in 1947.

• Peter Kurten, who murdered at least two dozen men, women and children in Germany—he was known as "The Monster of Düsseldorf"—from
1913 to 1929 and who was beheaded in 1931, returned to life in Fritz
Lang's chilling 1931 German production, *M,* with Peter Lorre playing the
child-molesting Kurten. Director Lang had a penchant for taking crime
stories directly from the headlines and converting them into sensational
movies. The lynching of Thomas Thurmond and John Holmes, two kidnapping killers, in San Jose, California, by 15,000 irate residents in 1933
was used by Lang in his film study of mob violence, *Fury,* with Spencer
Tracy as the victim of the frenzied crowd. Lang also used the story of outlaws Bonnie Parker and Clyde Barrow, with Sylvia Sidney and Henry
Fonda in the roles for his 1937 production of *You Only Live Once.*

Charlie Chaplin with Martha Raye in one of the many disguises he used in his
offbeat performance in *Monsieur Verdoux,* contemplating another wife murder;
Chaplin's role was based upon Landru, the monstrous "Bluebeard."

• Charles "Kid" McCoy, former world's welterweight champion, who senselessly murdered his sweetheart, Mrs. Albert Mors, in 1924 in Los Angeles, provided the story for John Garfield's memorable performance in the 1939 production *They Made Me a Criminal*.

• Erwin Walker, World War II hero turned burglar and cop-killer in 1946 in Los Angeles, became the film menace in *He Walked by Night*.

• Frank Santana, ruthless and lethal leader of a teen-age gang in New York, undoubtedly served as the role model for the movie *The Young Savages*.

• Joe Majczek, imprisoned for a decade in Illinois for a murder he did not commit, his release brought about by dogged newspaperman Jim McGuire of the Chicago *Sun*, who unearthed evidence that set him free, was portrayed in 1948 by Richard Conte, the newsman played by James Stewart in *Call Northside 777*.

Hollywood, then, has kept as sharp an eye on the lives of criminals as have law enforcement agencies, filmdom's message consistently clear that crime doesn't pay, except at the box office.

DRUGS

THE HARD ROAD TO NIRVANA, A BRIEF HISTORY

Centuries before Columbus stumbled onto the hot white sands of the Bahamas, the trafficking in hard-line drugs was an everyday occurrence in the Middle East and the Orient. Inside the turbulent cradle of civilization, ancient use of drugs was rampant. A recently unearthed Egyptian papyrus details drug prescriptions at about 3700 B.C.

As emigrating tribes from the Levant spread north and west, opium in large quantities was packed and subsequently peddled in new lands. This drug was used in Cyprus, Crete, and Greece as a medical remedy at about 2000 B.C. Opium, cannabis ("kannabis" is Greek for hemp), mandrake, hashish and myriad other drugs were consumed by dedicated users throughout the known world with as much ease as gulping well water.

Points of interest:

• According to archaeological discoveries, the Sumerians, circa 3000 B.C., used opium in religious rituals to produce states of ecstacy in priests communicating with their gods in oracular divination. In Assyria, opium was sucked as a lozenge, taken in liquid form, sniffed, eaten and used in suppositories. The hemlock of Socrates' death drink was laced with opium. The Greeks, by 400 B.C., employed opium as a hypnotic and analgesic; it was, when mixed with hemlock, used to poison political enemies.

• Cannabis first appeared about 430 B.C., according to ancient records. In his *Histories,* Herodotus describes how the Scythians used wild hemp in a purification rite which followed the elaborate ceremonies at the burial of a king. Hot stones were placed in a cauldron within a tent (much like today's Finnish sauna) and hemp seeds were thrown on the stones. The bathing Scythians, deeply inhaling the vapors, "howled with joy." Cannabis was, no doubt, the "grass" (today's slang for marijuana) that King Nebuchadnezzar ate when he was described as being mad.

• The drug mandrake (*Mandragora,* a solanaceous plant) is described by Hippocrates as being used with wine to relieve depression and anxiety. During the Roman occupation of Israel, it was allegedly used by Sanhedrin women, who gave the drug to those crucified so that they might appear dead and who were revived after being taken from the cross. (Some scholars have speculated that Christ was given mandrake and that Christ's rising—living after death—was attributable to this drug.)

Mandrake, which was later to find extensive use in ceremonial witchcraft in medieval Europe, served early-day militarists well. Both Hannibal and Caesar used it to spike wine left in deserted camps, whereupon their enemies found it, drank it, were put to sleep and were subsequently captured.

• Drugs continued to be used by conquerors, both in the East and West, as emotional goads for their troops. Genghis Khan, whose conquests spanned most of his known world, ordered hashish to be distributed throughout the ranks of his armies to stimulate the fury of his Golden Horde in battle. The Khan, Tamerlane, Babur and other Mongol warrior leaders were partial to hemp sweetmeats and opium balls, consuming these as delicacies before and after meals. In one instance, drugs accidentally obliterated an entire army. Marc Antony's troops accidentally ate datura (*Datura stramonium*) on their retreat from Parthia in 38 B.C. Phalanxes fell en masse in stupor and were butchered by the pursuing enemy. Thousands went insane and thousands more died via the lethal drug.

With the discovery of the New World, explorers, traders, and settlers brought their drugs to bewildered natives, albeit the Indians of North and South America had employed their own homegrown plants to supply them for centuries with hallucinogens. Noteworthy historical uses include:

• Cannabis smoking was introduced into South America by the Spaniards in 1545; within two hundred years the habit was rampant throughout all Spanish territories in the New World.

• Opium and cannabis were smoked openly in lavishly styled "drugging houses" in New Orleans by the mid-1700s.

• By the eighteenth century, India was providing the greatest supply of opium to America, where it was primarily cultivated since the Chinese, through an edict of the emperor in 1729, had all but ceased growing opium crops under pain of death. (The emperor referred to the drug as "a devilish foreign substance.") At first, Portuguese, Dutch and British ships monopolized the opium trade to America. When the Chinese relaxed their laws governing opium, American "China Clippers," known in the trade as "Opium Clippers," took control of that drug traffic.

• Indian hemp (cannabis) was grown freely by the plantation rich of early America, both for fiber and medicinal purposes. It was also raised and smoked for pleasure by the landed gentry. One of these was George Washington, whose diary shows the following entries:

1765

May 12–13—Sowed Hemp at Muddy Hole by Swamp.
August 7—began to seperate [sic] the Male from the Female hemp at Do—
    rather too late."

It is interesting to note that the potency of the female plants decreases after they have been fertilized by the male plants, thus Washington's regret at having separated the male from the female plant too late—after fertilization—clearly indicates that he was cultivating the plant for smoking.

Red Man's Dream

Indians in the New World experimented with the drugs of the white foreigners but were partial to their own crude homegrown drugs which had been cultivated for centuries. Points of interest:

• The earliest known drug-taking Indians in the Americas were the Oaxacas of Mexico, who used mushrooms as hallucinogens as early as 1000 B.C., the drug employed for healing, divination and mystical experiences. The drug of the mushroom, known as teonanactl, was heavily used by the Aztecs, particularly in religious rites such as divination and human sacrifice, on the part of both priests and victims. The tribe used it en masse at the coronation of Montezuma. The drug was also employed to murder Montezuma's political foes; the king's foe Tozon was killed with an overdose of the mushroom drug.

At a later time, the Mazatecs, distant Aztec kin, used teonanactl for black magic and it was through this usage that the notion of the "evil eye" was given birth. The "toadstool habit," as it was later known, filtered down to many remote Central American and Mexican tribes.

• Among the ancient Inca and Chibchas of South America, datura (Jimsonweed, or thorn apple), a hallucinogen, was used widely. The Chibchas gave the drug to slaves to increase their productivity and to women who were to be buried alive with their dead masters (a form of Indian suttee), an act considered quite humane in that the drug provided a fear-deadening reaction—at least, the Chibchas thought so. Datura was known as tooache to the tribes along the California coast who used the drug for puberty rites which lasted several months. It was also used as a pain-killer. Children were given this drug in order that they conjure visions of a personal spirit who, according to the tribal belief, would become the child's protector. Braves took datura for endurance trials and combat.

• Coca, a drug stimulant, had been intensively cultivated in Peru since A.D. 1000. The Incas considered it a sacred emblem of endurance and fertility. At first, it was used only by the Inca court and nobility but soon became universally used throughout the kingdom.

Pizarro's conquest in 1532 gave the Spanish a monopoly in coca. Since the Indians were already addicted, the conquistadores paid off their slave laborers with the coca plant. Catholic prelates visiting the area attempted to stop such barbarous methods; one was quoted as saying: "The plant is only idolatry and the work of the devil . . . it shortens the life of many Indians . . . they should therefore not be compelled to labour and their health and lives should be preserved." The Spanish grandmasters ignored such pleas, continuing the slavery and the plant payment. (Pope Leo XIII, three centuries later, approved of coca after using it to "support his ascetic retirement.")

• The cactus peyote (*Lophophora Williamsii*) has been used extensively for centuries by southwestern American Indian tribes like the Navajos and Zuñis. The hallucinogen has been used by Zuñi priests who applied peyote buttons to the eyes to bring rain. The Navajos began to take peyote solely in ceremonial healing rites but then became cultists of the drug, making it integral with their culture and the center of religious-magical ceremonies. The peyote practice spread to the Plains Indians in the mid-1800s and they used it as freely as Caucasians later used aspirin. The drug is still used regularly in rituals practiced by the (Indian) Native American Church.

Many Comanche and Kiowa tribesmen of the Plains Indian nations used peyote. The Comanche chief Quanah Parker consumed peyote in liquid form prepared for him by a Mexican woman, a descendant of the Yaquis, when he grew ill in Texas in 1909. Cured, he all but venerated the drug and spread its use to his people.

• Cannabis was used by the Shoshoni and Chinookan tribes of the far West who were visited by Meriwether Lewis. They told Lewis that the Indian hemp was "silk grass."

The great Sioux chief Sitting Bull smoked Indian hemp at religious rituals, along with fellow chief Black Elk. Both wrote detailed accounts of their experiences while under the influence of cannabis.

Sitting Bull, the great Sioux chief, not only liberally smoked hemp but wrote an account of its effects. (Library of Congress)

General George Armstrong Custer's defeat at the Little Big Horn in 1876 was assured when he and his 7th Cavalry troopers inadvertently rode through the Indians' sacred hemp field. (Library of Congress)

The death of George Armstrong Custer and the destruction of the 7th Cavalry under his command at the battle of the Little Big Horn were, in a large way, attributable to cannabis. Unknown to Custer, he led his troops into the valley of the Little Big Horn via a ridge of sacred ritual to the Sioux. On this ridge the Indians had planted their hemp, which, when fully grown, would be used to produce the colorful puberty dreams of their apprentice braves. So incensed were the Sioux, some Indian tales relate, that Custer would so cavalierly desecrate their sacred hemp ridge by riding pell-mell through it, they killed his troopers to a man.

Drugs in Early America

With the development of western lands, drugs and their hard use by frontiersmen became a regular reality. Mexicans introduced marijuana to early settlers in the southwestern states; Mexican peasants rubbed marijuana on their sore joints as a healing agent and smoked it widely in the early 1880s. Opium arrived in San Francisco with Chinese coolies imported to work on the railroads in 1853.

The lusty denizens of San Francisco more than sampled the easily available drugs in the Chinese opium dens, which created, according to one lurid account, a population of "degenerate, drug-sodden, sex-crazed dope fiends" among artists looking for new experiences, distraught widows "for whom alcohol was taboo," gamblers, miners, prostitutes and soldiers of fortune.

The use of opium in the United States, then called "The Mongolian curse," afflicted the Chinese inhabitants of America first, before finding widespread use among whites.

Points of interest:

• By the 1850s, millions of men in China were addicted to smoking and eating opium (the latter termed a "stomach habit"); they considered the drug an aphrodisiac. By the time of the Chinese migration to the United States, chiefly to San Francisco and New York, most adult Chinese males were addicted. (Up to 1937, in a futile attempt to curb the habit, the Chinese Government meted out for centuries the death penalty for addicts who failed to be cured. Though thousands were executed in China, the opium party, akin to a cocktail party, continued to flourish in China as well as in the United States.)

• In the 1870s San Francisco's Chinatown became the fanciful hub of opium smoking and eating with at least two hundred opium dens operating around the clock. More than two dozen of these dens, lavishly decorated, were run exclusively for whites, especially women from High Soci-

A San Francisco opium den catering exclusively to whites in the 1870s.

ety. Opium addiction became a way of life for hundreds of San Francisco's leading society matrons and daughters of the rich.

• In 1885 a special committee for the Board of Supervisors found twenty-six opium dens solely patronized by whites. The committee counted 320 silk-encased bunks upon which the white womanhood of regal Society eased opium into their lungs.

• San Francisco's white addicts, both male and female, down on their luck after years of opium smoking, gathered at a dive near Chinatown called The Slaughterhouse (later rechristened The Morgue). From this headquarters, the hoppies, as they were then called, served as a small army of work slaves who ran errands for bordello keepers and prostitutes. They also collected wood and old boxes for Chinese merchants.

When tourists sauntered into the area, known as "The Devil's Acre," a host of hoppies would surround them, and, for a few pennies, proudly show the startled visitors the holes in their arms. The pathetic addicts, who could no longer afford the pleasures of opium, were reduced to using the cheaper cocaine and morphine. The hoppies who could not afford a hypodermic needle employed an ordinary medicine dropper, filling it with cocaine or morphine and forcing the point into their flesh. By 1885, an all-night drugstore on Grant Avenue supplied close to one thousand hoppies with cocaine and morphine. The cost of a full injection of either drug was from ten to fifteen cents.

• In New York City, the Chinese community settled in and about Pell

Opium king of New York's Chinatown, Tom Lee.

One of Tom Lee's low opium dens in New York's Chinatown.

and Doyer streets. By the late 1850s, dozens of opium dens were opened to white and Chinese patrons. The tongs, as in San Francisco, controlled the opium traffic in New York. The two most powerful tongs, the On Leongs led by Tom Lee and the Hip Sings (from which the drug slang "I'm hip" purportedly stems) headed by Mock Duck, conducted a long and bloody war for control of the lucrative opium dens in New York (which reaped owners tens of thousands of dollars each year). From 1900 to 1906 the war raged through Chinatown with hundreds slain. An odd treaty of peace between Lee and Duck was signed in 1906 in the home of Judge Warren W. Foster of the Court of General Sessions.

Opium smoking was so heavily practiced by whites by the turn of the century that the old Chinese Theater on Doyer Street became a drug haven. In the theater's cellar hundreds of hooks were affixed to the masonry and from these were hung bunks for the opium addicts.

The "Soldier's Disease"

Morphine and heroin were liberally used by doctors administering to the wounded during the Spanish–American War. Cannabis was so popular at that time that soldiers openly smoked the drug as one would cigarettes during the building of the Panama Canal. When Pershing led his punitive expedition against Pancho Villa into Mexico in 1916, his soldiers were liberally supplied with marijuana by natives. One lieutenant in this expedition who was particularly fond of the drug was George Patton.

Morphine became a cure-all, according to army physicians, who universally gave the drug to wounded soldiers through all the major wars of the twentieth century, this drug giving way to heroin, which was widely used by U.S. troops serving in Vietnam, a practice that created hundreds, if not thousands, of hardcore addicts.

The medical messiahs of the nineteenth and twentieth centuries, especially those working in the U. S. Army, thought morphine to be a cure for the opium habit. It was not. Heroin, first appearing in 1898, was thought to be a cure for morphine; its habit was even more deadly, far from being the "heroic" (thus the name) savior of those addicted by morphine.

Use Among Blacks

The use of drugs, particularly cannabis, by American Negroes is consistent with the historical social oppression exercised against them by whites, particularly its rampant development from slave trade days to and through the antebellum South.

Points of interest:

• Blacks in the Congo, notably Simba warriors, for centuries used

The use of heroin was widespread among the American troops in Vietnam.

hemp to rouse themselves for battle and magically guarantee immunity from harm.

• In the seventeenth century West African tribesmen traded slaves among themselves, then with the Arabs, and were, in turn, themselves traded. To endure the impossible hardships of the journey to the New World—first Brazil and the West Indies, then the Colonies—slaves consumed great quantities of cannabis. The drug desensitized the hapless slaves against disease, starvation, beatings and mutilation.

• In the American South, notably before the Civil War, slaves clandestinely grew small plots of hemp undetected by their white masters. It became a family ritual, even to the smallest of children, to smoke hemp in the evening as a synthetic escape from their plight.

• Cannabis became a pennant advertising belief in the black national movements of the 1920s, especially among the followers of Marcus Garvey's Back-to-Africa movement. It is still used on this basis by those Negroes involved in the Black Muslim, Afro-American and Black Power movements.

Jazzman's Junket

American jazz musicians have widely used drugs since about 1900, when the use of cannabis, cocaine and, to a lesser degree, heroin, began to be popular, chiefly in the jazz headquarters of New Orleans.

The types of drugs used by jazz musicians varied with the types of music played—blues, Dixieland, Chicago style, hot, cool, modern jazz—and, in the words of those who used drugs, from 1920s clarinetist Milton "Mezz" Mezzrow ("mezz" is now an official slang term for marijuana) to Gerry Mulligan, the motivation for drug use varied according to temperament.

Points of interest:

• Brothel madams sniffed cocaine in New Orleans and dispensed cocaine to their clients and girls. Many black jazz musicians who played in the more lavish bordellos around 1900 picked up the habit in these surroundings. The lyrics of an early New Orleans jazz song reported:

> *I was comin' down Canal Street*
> *Comin' down Main*
> *Looking for the woman*
> *That uses cocaine.*

Storyville became a leading center for marijuana use. Small Negro jazz joints were beehives of cannabis smoking and selling. Another lyric ran:

> *Gimme a pigfoot*
> *An' a bottle of beer.*
> *Send me gate—I don't care.*
> *Gimme a reefer*
> *An' a gang of gin,*
> *Slay me cause*
> *I'm in my sin.*

And yet another:

> *Did you ever hear about Cocaine Lil?*
> *She lived in a house on a cocaine hill.*
> *She had a cocaine dog and a cocaine rat.*
>
> *She had cocaine hair on her cocaine head.*
> *She had a cocaine dress that was poppy red.*
> *But the cocaine blues, they made her sad.*
> *Oh, the cocaine blues, they made her feel bad.*

• Black jazz musicians like Buddy Bolden were not alone in their drug habits. White musicians like Joseph Leon Rappolo, Dixieland clarinetist supreme (who first took lessons from Professor Carrie, a drug-addicted whorehouse piano player), began with marijuana in New Orleans, graduated to harder drugs, and, like the great Buddy Bolden, died in an insane asylum.

• Heroin addiction destroyed "cool" jazz musician Charlie "Bird" Parker and killed Fats Navarro in the early 1950s. (The same kind of addiction moved jazz great Stan Getz to attempt the armed robbery of a drugstore, which all but ruined his reputation and career.)

• The 1920s jazz musician and historian Mezz Mezzrow began smoking marijuana, which he and other jazz artists like Bix Biederbecke called "tea" and "muggles." He graduated to opium, a habit that took him five years to quit. According to Mezzrow, Detroit gangsters, all members of the Purple Mob, introduced him to opium smoking in 1925. He was given a fancy pipe with a diamond implanted in the stem and told to puff "in quick jerks." He described his reaction thusly:

. . . Before I finished one pill a heatwave heaved up out of my stomach and spread all through me, right down to my toes, the most intense and pleasant sensation I have ever felt in all my life. At first it tipped easy-like through my main line, then it surged and galloped down all my sidestreets; and every atom in my body began to shimmy in delight. That fiery little pill was toe-dancing up and down every single strand of my nervous system, plucking each one until it hummed a merry song, lighting up a million bulbs in my body that I never knew were there—I didn't even know there were any sockets for them. I glowed all over, like the sun was planted in my bread basket. Man, I was sent, and I didn't want to come back . . .

Contemporary jazzman Gerry Mulligan recalled:

In the late 1940s, just making a living was rough. I had my first hard stuff, heroin, in 1947 or 1948. It was a one or two time affair. A friend of mine thought I'd like to try it. The first time somebody tried to inject a needle in me, I jumped ten feet and felt that was the end of that. The next time was a muscle shot and I liked it pretty much. These were the days of widespread general use of junk around town [NYC]. I knew there were guys in bad shape, but I didn't associate their conditions with junk. I figured they were in bad shape anyway. There was a frustration everywhere with us. Nobody really seemed to know what they were doing or where they were going. Junk could provide a dream world. The daily process of living was dull, and you had to scrounge for an income when you just wanted to play your horn. Junk seemed to help in a bad time . . .

Literati Lighting Up

Writers, particularly those working with creative forms, have long experimented with drugs. The most sensational user of drugs, and the first to write openly in favor of them, was the noted British essayist Thomas De Quincey, who penned his *Confessions of an English Opium Eater* in 1821. He, Gautier, Hugo, Baudelaire, Balzac and others belonged to a strange pro-drug group which called itself the Club des Hashischins.

Other European writers using drugs, basically to stimulate their creative powers, include (cocaine) Arthur Conan Doyle, who has his most famous character, Sherlock Holmes, use cocaine in the story "The Sign of Four"; Sigmund Freud, who bought cocaine in the early 1880s for $1.27 a gram and who extolled the drug's medicinal virtues, especially for hangovers or indigestion, in his *Uber Coca;* Robert Louis Stevenson, whose use of cocaine undoubtedly produced *Dr. Jekyll and Mr. Hyde* (after taking massive doses of the drug, Stevenson reportedly wrote the manuscript inside of six days, revising the 60,000 words twice in what must be a record for a book's completion); Aleister Crowley, an eccentric writer of the 1920s, who preferred being called "The Great Beast"; and James Joyce; (cannabis) Stéphane Mallarmé, Friedrich Nietzsche and Guillaume Apollinaire.

American writers of repute have also experimented with one dangerous drug or another; these include Edgar Allan Poe, Mark Twain, Walt Whitman, Gertrude Stein and her friend Alice B. Toklas, Henry Miller, William Burroughs, and most of the "Beat" writers of the late 1950s.

The first major American writer to introduce knowledge of cannabis to America was the then extremely popular Bayard Taylor, who tried hashish first in Egypt and then in Damascus, where, as was the custom, he ate it. Taylor then wrote a book about his experiences with the drug which was published and widely read in 1855.

The first I-was-an-addict type of article in the United States was written by Fitzhugh Ludlow, who consumed cannabis in Poughkeepsie, New York, procuring the drug from a local pharmacist who had imported the resin for use in treating lockjaw. Ludlow's article, the first of its kind, appeared in *Scribner's Magazine* in 1856.

Cure or Kill?

As medicine, drug use in early America stemmed from the home remedies sold by early peddlers and so-called prescriptions advocated by physicians which created mass drug habits. Doctors administered drugs long after addiction to opium, cocaine and morphine had been medically determined.

Points of interest:

• From the colonial period through the greater part of the nineteenth century, peddlers of habit-forming drugs plied their trade along the fron-

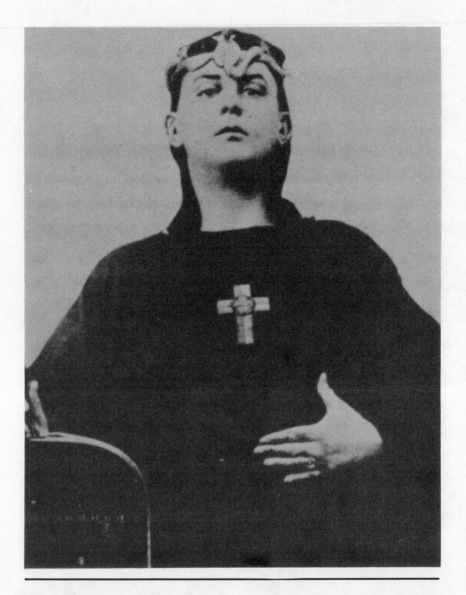

The eccentric English psalmist/hedonist Aleister Crowley, who spent his time and money on hideous orgies and preferred to be known as "The Great Beast," or "666," a number indicating the ancient legend of the evil beast, was a cocaine addict all his adult life.

tier and through the backwaters of America. The peddler assumed the role of doctor without any formal medical education, his drug-laden nostrums sold as cure-alls for any malady from gout to dysentery. The most popular remedies in America, bought and consumed in large quantities mostly by women, were Dover's Powders and Sydenham's Syrup, which were loaded with mind-altering opium and caused mass addiction.

• In the 1890s, the first soda fountain in a drugstore was opened in Georgia and with it came a concoction called "Dr. Pemberton's French Wine of Coca, the Ideal Tonic." This commercial folk medicine had a hefty cocaine base and its widespread popularity also caused mass addiction. Coca was featured in most home remedies and in soft drinks, particularly Coca-Cola, and was then highly addictive. The Pure Food and Drug Laws of 1906 caused the coca stimulant to be removed.

• Cocaine, isolated from coca in 1858 by Dr. K. Neimann, was first heralded (by Freud in 1884 among many) as a cure for morphinism. Physicians at large became cocainists, addicted like the famous American surgeon Dr. William Halsted, who discovered its use in nerve blocking but, in the process, himself became dependent on it.

• Doctors have recently found themselves under heavy criticism in the dispensing of drugs. For more than a century, physicians' unsupervised access to drugs has created, whether intentional or not, wholesale drug addiction. Most of this kind of drug usage is attributable to patients receiving opiates or their synthetic analogues in supervised medical treatment. (In one year, 1963, over a billion doses of true narcotics were administered or prescribed.) A large percentage of American drug addicts are sustained in their habits via sympathetic or larcenous physicians.

Under the Law

Governments throughout the world have, since the early part of this century, passed severe drug laws with equal punishments meted out to drug smugglers and pushers of hard-line drugs. In the United States, the first stringent federal law governing the use of hard drugs was the passing of the Harrison Act in 1914, which made it a federal offense, among others, for any physician to administer morphine except under special conditions.

Yet the smuggling of drugs into the United States, the country most plagued by hard-line drug addiction, due to the amount of money available for drugs, continued and increased. By 1920, $20 million in drugs

---

Intellectual American exiles in Paris Gertrude Stein and Alice B. Toklas experimented constantly with hard drugs as they did ideas.

was smuggled into the United States each year, the most popular drug at the time being opium. By 1923 there were one to four million users of smuggled dope in the country, and by 1928, experts claimed that 69 per cent of all violent crimes in New York City could be traced to the use of cocaine.

The Marijuana Tax Act of 1937, hotly debated by present-day drug users, made it illegal to use cannabis. Strict federal enforcement of this law was carried out by the Federal Bureau of Narcotics, which operated under the Treasury Department from 1930 to 1973, headed by the controversial and unorthodox Harry Anslinger.

It was Anslinger who was the first to announce the existence of a national crime syndicate, which now reaps, according to reliable estimates, as much as $3 billion in yearly profits from the sale of hard-line drugs.

The FBN drew great criticism for its colorful oft-times illegal methods, but Anslinger's retort to such criticism was to point out that the ruthlessness of organized crime could only be met by similar measures. (It was not uncommon, as the author discovered in interviews with ex-members of the FBN, for raids to be led by agents carrying baseball bats, which were used on dope smugglers and peddlers, guaranteeing hospitalization, if not conviction, of those arrested.)

The bureau's files are overflowing to this day, and they are replete with reports of violence, from mayhem to murder, originating with users of drugs.

A sample report from FBN files:

On August 4, 1930, in a hotel room in Spokane, Wash., Joseph Mines, 26 years of age, battered almost beyond recognition the body of 74-year-old John Karakinikas. Apparently Mines had never known Karakinikas before the moment he jumped through the window of his room and beat him to death. Mines had jumped from his own room 18 feet above, and after the crime jumped 30 feet to an alley without injury to himself. He said he felt as if he were flying, and he claimed to have no recollection of what he had done.

Mines alleged that he had been crazed by smoking two marijuana cigarettes. A small quantity of the drug was found in his room, and he had just been released a few days previously after serving a sentence for the possession of marijuana.

(Mines pleaded guilty to a manslaughter charge and was sentenced to serve twenty years in the state penitentiary.)

FEMALE CRIMINALS

THE TIDY METHODS OF WOMEN KILLERS

Seldom in history have female slayers resorted to messy means of dispatching their victims. Most murdering women are much more meticulous than men, preferring slow poison or the help of conspirators.

A flirty female named Bathsheba Spooner set the latter style during the American Revolution.

Bathsheba, the daughter of Tory General Timothy Ruggles, had no use for her revolutionary husband, Joshua Spooner. She attracted two deserting British soldiers to her Brookfield, Massachusetts, home and convinced them to bash in her husband's head on March 1, 1778. The soldiers were seen, and they, along with Bathsheba's lover, Ezra Ross, and the lady herself were hanged two years later.

Subtler methods appeal to the greater number of female death-dealers. The chief mode of such homicidal operations was best summed up by a Mrs. Fullam of Agra, India, who desired to eliminate her foreign officer husband. One day in 1913, Mrs. Fullam wrote on her memo pad: "So the only thing is to poison the soup."

Poison has been the most popular modus operandi with female killers for a simple reason—not until recent times have women been taught the use of sophisticated weapons. Many variations have been played on this poison theme. Miss Mary Blandy of Henley on Thames, England, found such methods useful in the 1750s.

Miss Blandy's crusty father objected to her proposed marriage to Captain William Cranstoun, mainly because the gentleman was already married. The daughter responded in June 1751 by repeatedly administering

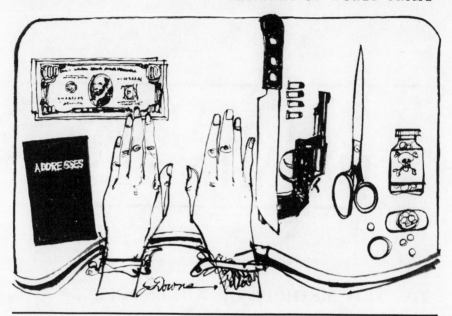

poison to the old man's tea and gruel, a diet which assured his slow and painful death, on August 14, 1751.

For this patricide, Miss Blandy was hanged at Oxford in 1752, but not before she told her executioners: "Gentlemen, do not hang me high, for the sake of decency!"

America's Lydia Sherman set this country's first records for poisoners when she fed arsenic to three husbands and eight children in the 1870s. She collected insurance from several of her victims, which some observers noted was one way of making a living.

At her trial, which resulted in a life sentence, Lydia told the judge she gave her victims poison so "they would be better off."

Sarah Jane Robinson of Cambridge, Massachusetts, also collected insurance on her husband, son and daughter after slipping arsenic into their food in the 1880s. However, Sarah was not content to confine the lethal meals to her immediate family. Apparently because she had become such a proficient poisoner, Sarah added a nephew, her brother-in-law and her landlord to her list before being trapped by the law and sent to prison for life.

Miss Cordelia Botkin of San Francisco, California, put great store in the use of poison, sending a box of homemade bonbons to the wife of her lover in 1897. The wife, Mrs. Elizabeth Dunning, munched on a few of the arsenic-ridden candies and soon died, along with a neighbor who also partook of the treat.

It is hard to beat the efforts of Belle Gunness, in the 1900s. This resident of LaPorte, Indiana, actually advertised for her victims, placing lovelorn notices in the Chicago, Illinois, papers for respectable suitors who were "looking for a good woman."

More than fourteen suitors applied over a period of several years. When they arrived at Belle's house, they were fed a rich meal and sent to bed. Before they retired, Belle insisted they drink a glass of warm milk. The poison in the milk did the rest and Belle scooped up the suitors' money.

LADIES WHO KEPT PACE WITH INCREASING CRIME

Opportunities for the female of the species to pathfind, let alone participate, in the world of crime have been limited to the poverty point in North America until recent history, much to the spiritual edification of law enforcement officers everywhere. Yet there have been infamous female exceptions who have left their zany and lethal marks upon each decade. When most women, out of a common virtue subscribed to by male and female alike under the dictates of Victorian and Edwardian morality, were compelled to hug the hearth and home, some rarities stepped into an underworld dominated by males.

Fredericka "Marm" Mandelbaum was one of the first of these, going into business as New York City's biggest fence of stolen goods in 1862 at age forty-four. For the next twenty years, "Marm" fenced everything from stolen horses, brought sheepishly to her by the notorious Loomis gang, to priceless jewelry burglarized by Banjo Pete Emerson and Mark Shinburn, who later retired to the Riviera as Baron Shindell before committing suicide. Marm herself retired with $12 million, dying peacefully in bed in 1894. She never served a day in jail, much to the disgust of New York's finest.

When it came to murderers, few men matched the ruthless extermination practiced by one Kate Bender, who made the alleged exploits of Lizzie Borden seem boring (Lizzie was acquitted at her trial and declared legally innocent of the hatchet murders of her parents). Kate, along with her father, mother and brother, robbed and murdered with sledgehammers at least fourteen travelers who stopped at her two-room inn on the barren plains outside of Cherryvale, Kansas, in 1872–73. Kate, a buxom, attractive type, took time from her slaughterhouse robberies to deliver spiritualistic lectures in neighboring towns. She and her family disappeared forever on May 5, 1873, only hours ahead of a suspicious sheriff (Kate had been tipped by a smitten swain; in return for his information, the murderess spared his life but stole his purse).

The West later boasted of its Calamity Janes and other harmless hellions but few women touched the horse reins in the days of the old outlaws. Etta Place, irrespective of her motion picture and television reincarnations, never shot a pistol, let alone knew how to hold one, and never robbed a soul of a dime. She was a lonely, albeit pretty schoolteacher who was attracted to Harry Longbaugh, alias the Sundance Kid, and simply became his mistress. Belle Starr was a hatchet-faced harridan who gussied herself up in velvet and six-guns for intrigued photographers, but she confined her "outlaw" career strictly to horse stealing.

Pearl Hart has an odd distinction in the inflated fame of the Old West. While in her early twenties and being romantically impressed with bandit tales devoured from dime novels, Pearl decided to rob a stagecoach. She convinced one Joseph Boot, the town drunk of Globe, Arizona, to accompany her. Both stopped the stage outside of Globe one day in 1899, taking $450 and then getting hopelessly lost before an unarmed posse arrested them. Pearl received five years in the Yuma Penitentiary and would be forgotten today had it not been for the fact that she was the last person to rob a stagecoach.

Lady con artists were exceptions until the liberated 1960s but Canadian-born-and-bred Cassie Chadwick and New Yorker Sophie Lyons more than made up for the deficiency. Cassie passed herself off to Cleveland society in 1894 as the illegitimate daughter of Andrew Carnegie through forged notes and lived like a queen until exposed. Sophie Lyons worked con games for forty years in New York before retiring; in the 1890s police estimated her overall flimflam take at $1 million. Cassie went to jail for ten years for her swindle. Sophie, always original, joined the staff of the New York *World* and became the first Society columnist in the United States.

As the twentieth century blossomed so did female criminals, only the number of killers in their midst grew to alarming proportions. The first mass murderer of the fairer sex in this period was the portly Belle Gunness of LaPorte, Indiana, who poisoned and then chopped up fourteen suitors who answered her marriage ads in Chicago newspapers. A blaze gutted Belle's rural home in 1908 and startled fire investigators found the pieces of bodies half buried in her pigpen. Belle disappeared after the fire.

The murderesses mounted in number during the 1920s and 1930s. Ruth Snyder murdered her husband with Judd Gray in 1927 in New York and was executed at Sing Sing, where a front-page-lusting newsman with a camera secretly tied to his leg shuttered her end, making Mrs. Snyder not only the first woman but the first person to be photographed while being electrocuted, an event that led to strict reforms in such press coverage.

Etta Place, companion of the Sundance Kid and Butch Cassidy. (Pinkerton, Inc.)

Con lady Cassie Chadwick.

A short while later a Brooklyn lady named Maria Tucci shot and killed her sister Angelina out of jealousy over a boyfriend. One of the more passionate prose writers of the decade portrayed Maria playing for public sympathy; Maria boldly lied, the writer stated, when she claimed to have killed Angelina because her sister had tried to force her into prostitution: "Society women and social workers, on the wrong track as usual, raised a fund for the defense and talked about gold medals. At the trial Maria Tucci outdid herself, Sarah Bernhardt, and Duse in the grand style. Her black weeds matched the sorrowful black of her eyes. She bridled with tragic indignation at every innuendo, let alone at what the district attorney had to say. She told her story on the witness stand with a thrilling accent of truth. And all the while she was tearful with repining for her unfortunate sister." Maria was convicted of manslaughter and got eight to fifteen years in prison.

After hearing the sentence, Maria was returned to the Tombs. Guards were thunderstruck as they heard her shriek with laughter. She tore her

Belle Starr, horse thief with an inflated legend. (Western History Collection, University of Oklahoma)

Sophie Lyons, from swindler to gossip columnist. (UPI)

funeral black dress away and donned her gayest gown. As the bug-eyed guards gathered in front of her cell, Maria lustily sang Sicilian songs, and danced the tarantella. "Manslaughter . . . manslaughter . . . manslaughter," she sang to the frenetic beat of her heels.

The names of females were forever attached to the types of crimes they committed as the years rolled forward. Winnie Ruth Judd would forever be "the trunk murderess" after being found guilty in 1932 of chopping up her two best friends in Phoenix, Arizona, and shipping the pieces by trunk to Los Angeles. Arizona Donnie Clark Barker would be universally known as the infamous "Ma" of the Barker boys after she was shot to pieces at Lake Weir, Florida, in 1935 as she dueled it out with FBI agents.

There were the women behind the men, like Kathryn Kelly, who bought her drunkard husband George a machine gun and taught him how to use it, even giving him the fearsome monicker "Machine Gun" Kelly (he was known as "Popgun" Kelly in the underworld). And there, too, was Bonnie Parker, the young psychopathic killer from Rowena, Texas, who stood side by side with her equally unbalanced boyfriend, Clyde Barrow, killing until killed in 1934.

From that time to this, a queasy pattern emerged, one where the so-called "weaker sex" amply demonstrated the ability to kill, rob and terrorize along with any much-vaunted male counterpart. Women have "arrived" in crime, lamentably, catching the last elevator. Going down.

NOTABLE PERSONALITIES: LIZZIE BORDEN

In 1927 an austere lady died a recluse at her elegant estate, Maplecroft, in Fall River, Massachusetts. From a fortune of more than $200,000, the deceased left $30,000 to a society to prevent cruelty to animals. She had been kind and gentle in life and her will expressed high-minded grace. This woman was Lizzie Borden, whose name is unjustly synonymous with murder.

Of all the circumstantial "evidence" mounted against Lizzie for the gruesome murders of her father and stepmother, none proved her guilt. In fact, most of the prosecution's case went to prove Lizzie's innocence.

It all began about 11:15 A.M. August 4, 1892, when Lizzie Borden

stood at the foot of the stairs in her home and shouted to the maid, Bridget Sullivan:

"Come quick! Father's dead! Somebody came in and killed him!"

Andrew Borden had died on the living room sofa. His head was caved in and his features obliterated, as if someone had taken an axe to him. (The three-and-a-half-inch penetrations into the skull determined the use of an axe, investigators said later.)

Lizzie's stepmother, the former Abby Gray, was found on the floor of the upstairs guest room about an hour later. Her head had also been bashed in.

Mr. Borden apparently had been napping when he was killed, and Mrs. Borden had obviously been making the bed when murdered.

Lizzie said she was in the barn loft looking for fish-line sinkers at the time of the killings. Bridget was in her attic room dozing through the intolerable heat of the day. Emma Borden, Lizzie's older sister, was away in Fairhaven, and John Vinnicum Morse, a visiting uncle, was out of the house on business when the murderer entered.

Lizzie came under suspicion within days of the murder and was subsequently indicted and tried in June of 1893. The prosecution strove mightily to affix guilt with strictly circumstantial evidence.

District Attorney Hosea Knowlton's case was all roar. He pointed out that Lizzie had admitted being near the house at the time of the murders. Both Lizzie and Emma ardently disliked their stepmother, Knowlton said, thereby casting suspicion on the other Borden sister. (It was later suggested that Emma Borden could have slipped unnoticed back into the house, murdered the Bordens, then returned to her friends and a concrete alibi.) Knowlton concluded that Lizzie was afraid of being disinherited in favor of her stepmother and therefore had reason to slay the couple.

The defense was conducted by George D. Robinson, a former Massachusetts governor. Robinson pointed out that though Lizzie was in and out of the house at the time of the murders, anyone could have entered the building through an unlocked side door. He stated that Andrew Borden had many enemies through his cagey banking tactics and one of these could have easily killed Mrs. Borden before slipping downstairs to murder the patriarch while Lizzie was in the barn.

The axe alleged to have been used on both Bordens was never produced, although the prosecution did unearth a broken hatchet in the basement. This tool was covered with ashes but was without a trace of blood. Also, anyone killing the Bordens would have been coated with gore, yet Lizzie had no blood on her.

(It was later claimed that she washed twice within an hour and a half—the estimated time between the two murders—and changed her dress. But, given the known movements of the thirty-two-year-old spinster, such actions would have been impossible.)

Lizzie Borden anxiously leaning forward at her trial. (*Leslie's Weekly*)

It was alleged that Lizzie burned a blood-spattered dress after the crime. She did burn a dress some days after the killings but it was covered with paint from decorating done the previous May. The dress was examined by both Bridget and Emma, and they said no blood was on it. Also, it was Emma who found the dress in a closet and urged Lizzie to burn it.

Few involved in the case then or the scores of detective writers who followed decades later remembered that the Borden house had been burglarized repeatedly only months before the murders and that several witnesses swore they had spotted men sneaking about the house before the double slaying.

After an hour's deliberation, the jury found Lizzie innocent. However, certain scandal-mongering reporters and slander-gulping gossips would have it otherwise, and Lizzie's guilt was established through innuendo and rumor. In place of convicting the real killer, Lizzie would do. What most damned Lizzie for the ages was the following bit of doggerel (sung to the tune of "Ta-ra-ra-boom-de-day") :

> *Lizzie Borden took an axe*
> *And gave her mother forty whacks.*
> *When she saw what she had done*
> *She gave her father forty-one.*

It did not matter that the actual number of "whacks" was twenty-nine or that Lizzie was apparently and legally innocent. The clever quatrain, which became universally accepted, insisted Lizzie was guilty and she is today in the minds of the uninformed.

A bit of charity is obviously due for Lizzie. The following verse was penned by A. L. Bixby during the agonizing trial.

> *You have borne up under all,*
> *Lizzie Borden*
> *With a mighty show of gall,*
> *Lizzie Borden.*
> *But because your nerve is stout*
> *Does not prove beyond a doubt*
> *That you knocked the old folks out,*
> *Lizzie Borden.*

FRAUD

THE MAIL HAS NO MERCY

Each year the American public drops millions of hard-earned dollars into the hands of those geniuses of crime, con men, especially those operating through the apparent sanctity of the U.S. mails.

In one recent year, fraud and misrepresentation in the mails levied $514 million (up $119 million over the previous year) against duped consumers, an amount that did not stagger experts who are painfully aware of the long and profitable history of mail-order cons.

In 1911, for instance, suckers mailed off $77 million for goods that never arrived, invested in oil lands as dry as the bleached earth of Death Valley, and bought miracle cures that promised everything from eliminating obesity to changing Negroes into white persons.

Nothing has changed, as Postmaster General Benjamin F. Bailar well knows, except the types of enticing offers. Today the accent of the confidence man is on stock and land investments.

Though postal inspectors and other law enforcement personnel have had about 17,650 convictions for mail fraud within recent years, and recovered $14.4 million, great fortunes are made each year by con men never apprehended.

It seems to be a losing battle as long as suckers continue to swallow the con man's bait, that furiously wiggling plastic worm of promise.

Perhaps the most absurd mail-order con on record began in 1946, when wild rumors abounded of Adolf Hitler's survival and subsequent escape to points unknown following the end of World War II. Spellbound by tales of Hitler smuggling himself out of Germany as his Third Reich collapsed in flames, a semiliterate miner, Will H. Johnson of Middlesboro, Kentucky, put in motion a mail-order scheme as bizzare as any within human memory.

Johnson, quite simply, decided to impersonate through the mails Hitler himself, stating in prose any educated person would dismiss as inane that he had not only fled the Führer bunker intact but had resettled with several of his erstwhile staff members in Kentucky, where plans were being made to take over the United States.

This fumbling con man's suckers were drawn from the far right-wing, fascist-leaning malcontents, mostly of German extraction, throughout the country and in Canada. The most durable mark Johnson mulcted was a former U.S. soldier of German descent who resided in Bristol, Virginia. From 1946 to 1956, Johnson and the Bristol resident carried on a ridiculous correspondence, with all the cash, more than $4,000 in postal money orders over a decade, flowing one way—to Johnson. (Johnson took in more than $15,000 during this period from several dupes, according to postal inspectors.)

In his rambling letters to the Bristol sucker, signed "Adolf Hitler," "Eva Hitler" and "Chief of Staff," Johnson spun incredible tales of his plans for space ships, invisible boats and underground ammunition centers that, of course, existed only in his childlike imagination. He referred to himself as the "Furrier" instead of Führer, but such blatant errors did not stanch the flow of money from suckers who were promised high power positions once the "furrier" and his minions took over the country.

Once Johnson wrote stating that he had to call off a top-level meeting because he had no shoes. "Please send size 11." The Bristol sucker sent the shoes and the money, confident that once the "furrier" took over he would assume the number two power position.

The farce might have gone on indefinitely but the Bristol sucker suddenly dropped dead in August 1956, and found among his effects were the canceled money orders and Western Union payments to Johnson. Postal inspectors closed in on Johnson and found him living with his family in Middlesboro, his delapidated shack near collapse.

Far more vicious was the mail-order con practiced by Charles Aycock, who marketed from 1918 to 1928 a useless drug called Tuberclecide, which Aycock claimed would completely cure tuberculosis, especially in children.

Aycock was arrested dozens of times and tried, but the indecision of testifying doctors and legal loopholes allowed the con man continually to evade conviction for fraud. Some deaths were attributed to the sole use of this drug but the charges were never completely proved.

A federal court in 1928 finally determined Tuberclecide was useless and Aycock was fined and put out of business.

Postmaster General Bailar knows that today such schemes as those perpetrated by Johnson and Aycock can still succeed. He was recently quoted as saying:

"There is always going to be an area where people for a moderate price

are going to take a chance that a miracle will be visited upon them. Genetically it will take a long time to breed gullibility out of the human race." Most likely, that time is forever.

THE YELLOW KID'S FIRST 100 YEARS

It's no secret that the ancient con games of the gold brick, three-card monte and salted diamonds have evaporated from the American scene. They have been replaced by sophisticated confidence games that are centered in phony corporations and bogus stock deals. Such paperwork grifting may make fortunes for the con man, but according to one old-time grifter, the adventure of fleecing the gullible has vanished.

"There's no class left," the late Jerry Wall, an experienced con man, told the author. "These new guys have no invention, no creativity. Ahh, there'll never be another Yellow Kid."

The reference was to the late Joseph "Yellow Kid" Weil, dean of American confidence men for more than eighty years.

Born in Chicago, Illinois, in 1875, the Kid learned the art of con early

The elegantly bearded Joseph "Yellow Kid" Weil disdainfully listening to charges of swindling in court in 1956.

in his father's saloon. By the time he was a teen-ager, Weil was selling useless "Meriweather's Elixir" to farmers as a cure-all for gout, consumption and just about every other ailment.

Weil was addicted to reading a comic strip popular at the turn of the century entitled "Hogan's Alley," in which his favorite character, the Yellow Kid, was portrayed as a lovable con man. John "Bathhouse" Coughlin, owner of a notorious Chicago saloon, once caught Weil chortling over the cartoon character and dubbed him the Yellow Kid.

Needless to say, the name stuck.

It was also in Coughlin's dive that the Kid met and merged talents with his erstwhile crony, Fred "The Deacon" Buckminster. Ironically, Buckminster was a plainclothes cop working on the vice and bunco squad who happened to arrest the Kid one day in 1908. The charge was contracting to paint City Hall with a "waterproof" covering that had washed off in the first rain.

As the Kid and Buckminster were walking to the precinct station, they paused on a street corner. Weil produced a wad of bills and placed it in the Deacon's hand.

"Here," the Kid said, "you've got my elixir, my phony sets of glasses [which he sold by the score to farsighted farmers]. You might as well have my dough."

Buckminster was flabbergasted. He counted more than $10,000 in the wad.

"How does a mug like you come by so much money?" he asked.

"Oh, that's just walk-about money," Weil replied, winking.

The temptation was too great for the Deacon. He removed his shield from his vest with one hand and weighed it against the money in the other hand. He pocketed both, shook the Kid's hand, and became his partner in scam.

Over the next few decades, the pair enacted some incredible schemes. In one, they rented an abandoned bank in Muncie, Indiana, populated it with other con artists pretending to be prosperous depositors and scammed shady financiers into investing in the bogus bank. In another, they sold mongrels as pedigreed dogs and netted themselves thousands of dollars a week.

Once, they even dressed as U. S. Army officers, contracted with western ranchers to buy horses for the government, paid the ranchers off with official-looking checks and awaited the ranchers' return of one fourth of the value of the phony checks for possible rejection of part of their herds.

Neither Weil nor Buckminster evaded the law forever. In fact, they served many prison sentences. During one of the Kid's terms at Leavenworth Prison, George "Machine Gun" Kelly approached him.

The "Yellow Kid's" companion in fraud, Fred "The Deacon" Buckminster. (UPI)

"You know," Kelly said, "I don't understand a guy like you. You go right up to people and let 'em see your face. You go back time and time again to the same guy. What kind of crook are you?"

"The kind who's doing a couple of years, George," the Kid shot back. "I understand you're doing life."

With Weil, it was all ego and warped ambition. He was brilliant enough to have been an enormous success in life without breaking the law, but his weakness was himself.

"I never could resist taking a sucker," he once told this writer. "Never. I had to scratch that itch."

When the Kid was over a hundred years old and living in a Chicago nursing home, the author visited him.

"If you could get out of that wheelchair," I asked him, "and go out to that street, would you still try for another con, Kid?"

His reply was instant. "Does a hungry dog like food?"

By his own estimate, the Yellow Kid scammed more than $12 million from suckers during the first hundred years of his life. The irony of that rich crime career was that he was penniless at death. The Yellow Kid was buried in an unmarked grave in Archer Woods on the far south side of Chicago in potter's field.

THOSE WHO PROFIT FROM
THEIR OWN DEATHS

Throughout the history of insurance, fraudulent death claims have caused premium prices to soar and worn down insurance investigators' heels. Yet these detectives invariably get their suspect—dead or alive.

Faking one's own death for huge insurance payments is a tricky affair. It is essentially a battle of wits between the "dead man" and the insurance sleuths. However, Sam Abrams of New York discovered that the best plan he could devise was no match for fate.

In the spring of 1928, Abrams went swimming on a beach at Rockaway, New York. His clothes were later found in a bathhouse and he was presumed drowned and carried out to sea. However, when investigators arrived at Mrs. Abrams' Manhattan home, they found her hysterical with grief *before* she had been informed of her husband's disappearance. The wife's strange actions led detectives to believe a fraud had been perpetrated, yet they could prove nothing without a body.

The insurance settlement was withheld pending a full-scale investigation. But two months later, just before the insurance firm was about to give in and make payment, destiny took a hand. Two cars collided in Montreal, Canada, and the driver of one auto was carried unconscious to a hospital.

Authorities searched the injured man's clothing to determine his identity. They found nothing but faded newspaper clippings describing the disappearance of Sam Abrams. The news stories provided a detailed description of Abrams, the very man unconscious in the hospital bed. By the time the "dead man" awoke, police were placing him under arrest for insurance fraud.

Occasionally, perpetrators of insurance frauds have selfless aims. One such person was Davis Rowland MacDonald, who was thought to have drowned himself on February 14, 1924. Along with his clothes, an apparent suicide note was found on an Allegheny River bank near Pittsburgh, Pennsylvania.

Clara MacDonald lost no time in having her husband declared dead. She then remarried and collected three large insurance policies on Mac-Donald's life. Fourteen years later, though, a man calling himself John Edgar Davis was arrested on a minor offense. As a matter of routine, police checked his fingerprints. He proved to be the missing MacDonald.

MacDonald explained that he knew his wife was unhappy and chose to enrich her life by faking his own death so Clara could remarry and get the insurance money. He was not prosecuted.

George F. Knoop of Las Vegas, Nevada, who had failed in business and marriage, prompted a death claim fraud that baffled investigators for years.

Because of their financial and marital problems, Knoop and his wife, Janice, decided to end his official life. Knoop, a well-known scuba diver, drove to Lake Mead, near Las Vegas, parked his auto at the water's edge, disrobed, piled his clothes on the beach and waded into the water. Instead of swimming out to his doom, though, Knoop methodically swam along the shoreline.

Some distance away, Knoop left the water and walked to another car and a new identity. He was now John L. Deviland, the name under which the car was registered. He drove to Los Angeles, California, and obtained a Social Security card, which permitted him to live and work as a machinist in El Segundo, California.

To complete his blissful new role, Knoop-Deviland married a pretty twenty-five-year-old divorcee with two children. Janice Knoop also remarried, but not before collecting $23,000 in insurance and Social Security payments for her "late" husband.

No one would have ever known the truth had it not been for an anonymous tip sent California authorities in January of 1967. John Deviland of El Segundo, the unnamed informer pointed out, was none other than the "late" George Knoop. Knoop-Deviland was arrested for failing to return the $150 worth of rented scuba equipment he used in his

1964 "death dive," a charge used only as an excuse to hold the man until his identity could be determined.

This was quickly established by Knoop's mother and sister, who visited the swindler in jail. The women's shock at seeing Knoop alive quickly turned to anger. How could you, George, they cried, not only pretend to be dead but move into a house only three miles from us without ever coming to visit? Knoop had no excuses. Neither did Janice Knoop. Both admitted to defrauding the government and were given suspended sentences.

THE BUREAU'S MOST INCREDIBLE AGENT

Although the late Federal Bureau of Investigation Director J. Edgar Hoover took pride in his policy of keeping agents out of the limelight, there was one G-man Hoover could never control.

Gaston Bullock Means, the agent in question, was never Hoover's responsibility, but he certainly was his headache. A large man, Means was a North Carolina gumshoe who joined the Burns Detective Agency in 1910, after having failed as a cotton broker, school superintendent and occasional lawyer.

William J. Burns, a great sleuth in his own right, viewed Means as Sherlock Holmes in the flesh, calling him "The greatest natural detective ever known." Means, however, was also one of this country's greatest con men.

In 1916, while still in the employ of the Burns Detective Agency, Means sought to increase his income by hiring himself out to Germany as a secret agent. As he later boasted to Hoover, his job was to "embarrass British commerce." Not one to overlook opportunities, Means also went to work for the British and collected huge spy funds as a double agent.

"Of course I quit the Germans," Means explained to Hoover some years later, "when America entered the war."

Means took delight in describing his alleged cloak-and-dagger jobs. He once claimed to have captured two trunkloads of secret documents vital to America's defense. As he was dragging the trunks down a Washington, D.C., alley en route to army intelligence, Means said he was jumped by the Kaiser's minions and the secret papers were stolen. Means never did explain, however, that the two trunks weighed the same when finally delivered empty to intelligence headquarters as they had when allegedly crammed with top-secret files.

Means's war work was interrupted in 1917 and his position as a special agent with the Bureau of Investigation (the precursor to the FBI) became

untenable after it was discovered that he had not only bilked Maude King, a wealthy, eccentric heiress, but was involved in her death.

Investigators proved that years earlier Means had staged a hold-up of King as she was walking down a Chicago, Illinois, street. Means interrupted the phony thief to save the damsel in distress and become her hero and self-appointed business manager. He then systematically milked King's considerable funds through fraudualent investments.

When the lady eventually became suspicious, Means suggested a trip to Concord, North Carolina. While on a walking picnic in the woods there, King borrowed the detective's service automatic "to play with it" and "accidentally" shot herself behind the left ear.

"Mrs. King," Means explained to a sympathetic corner's jury, "poor soul, was very light-headed." He was acquitted of any wrongdoing, but the publicity about the death caused Means's removal from the Bureau.

William Burns, the Bureau's new boss, by 1921 rehired Means as the Bureau's top informant. As such, the con man wheeled and dealed through the early years of the corrupt Harding administration, working exclusively for the less-than-reputable Attorney General Harry Daugherty and his shadowy aide Jess Smith.

At that time, Means headed what one newsman termed "a private, hole-in-the-corner goon squad for the attorney general. Its arts were the arts of snooping, bribery and blackmail." Hoover, who was then an assistant to Burns, was powerless to control Means, but did insist by formal letter that the man be ordered to stay out of his office.

When the Teapot Dome scandal wrecked the Harding administration, Means sauntered through the political ruins unscathed. His secret black books, in which he had recorded the indiscretions of almost everyone in Washington, undoubtedly prevented his own indictment.

Nothing was beneath or beyond Means. He stole the diary of an Ohio poetess named Nan Britton, an attractive lady who had been carrying on an affair with the President. With this document, Means tried to blackmail Harding and his wife for $50,000 but the President died before the sum was collected. Undaunted, Means then wrote a best-selling book, *The Strange Death of President Harding*. In it, he implied that Mrs. Harding had poisoned her husband in revenge for his affair with Britton!

For the next decade, Means went his wily way. Hoover, by then chief of the newly reorganized FBI, had his agents constantly checking on the super con man. Means was too smooth for them, however, although he was busily bilking dozens of wealthy persons in coast-to-coast schemes.

Means's final con involved the kidnapped Lindbergh baby. Means

Gaston B. Means, a federal agent with a knack for fraud.

Millionairess Evalyn Walsh McLean, wearing the Hope Diamond, who was adroitly swindled by the amazing Mr. Means. (UPI)

promised the wealthy Evalyn Walsh McLean, who was married to the publisher of the Washington *Post,* that he could deliver the stolen child intact from bootleggers he knew. He obtained $100,000 from McLean for the ransom, but it was all a ruse and Means was subsequently convicted of fraud.

Hoover beamed delight when "special agent" Means was sent to Leavenworth Prison for fifteen years. The con man suffered a heart attack in 1938, and as he lay dying in his cell, FBI agents visited him. They wanted to know where McLean's $100,000 had been buried. Means merely put a finger to his lips to seal the secret, blinked and died with a smile on his face. Hoover never recovered the money, and remembered that smile for the rest of his days.

KIDNAPPING

THE EGO AND MADNESS OF THE PIED PIPERS

The rash of brutal abduction-murders plaguing the Detroit suburbs in recent years has produced seven dead children and, at this writing, seemingly slim hope of catching the unbalanced person (or persons) responsible. Because of the modus operandi—suffocation in three instances—the police are convinced most of this heinous work stems from one man.

Yet the prospect of the killer being a woman or more than one man is quite possible. Jack the Ripper's London murders have been attributed to many persons, a small legion of lethal maniacs who took to the streets once the Whitechapel killing spree began.

The first sensational abduction in American history occurred on July 1, 1874, when two men stopped their buggy in front of a Germantown, Pennsylvania, mansion and induced four-year-old Charles Brewster "Charley" Ross to accompany them to nearby Philadelphia.

They promised little Charley firecrackers and a balloon for the upcoming Fourth of July celebration. He was never seen again, even though his kidnappers attempted an awkward ransom collection.

And, as is the pattern of such abductions, the identities of the kidnappers were revealed only by the culprits themselves. Six months later, Joseph Douglass and William Mosher, shot while burglarizing a Brooklyn home, admitted the abduction with their dying breaths. "We done it," gasped Mosher. "We did it for money," heaved Douglass.

The mastermind of this abduction, an ex-policeman in Manhattan, one William Westervelt, was convicted of the kidnapping on circumstantial evidence, and was sent to prison for seven years. Strangely enough, Westervelt, the underworld grapevine had it, was not at all eager to collect a ransom for little Charley. He had simply drowned the boy in a river for personal satisfaction or sexual gratification.

Stranger still were the exploits of Albert Fish, termed by the press of

Charles Brewster "Charley" Ross, America's first kidnap victim in 1874.

his day "the moon maniac." (Fish ate raw meat, his bizarre confession later detailed, by the light of the full moon before embarking upon his horrendous crimes.)

Examined and released many times by psychiatrists in New York's Bellevue Hospital as disturbed but sane, Fish, from about 1910 to 1934, abducted, killed, ravished and cannibalized many children, four hundred by his own raving account. Not once did he demand a ransom. His own ego led to his capture.

Albert Fish took to writing the parents of some of his victims, chiefly the mother of Grace Budd, a twelve-year-old he had abducted and dissected in 1928. Police traced the letter and were soon leading the killer to prison.

Fish appeared harmless to the world; he looked like everybody's kindly grandfather. But beneath his placid physical make-up lurked a wild killer who achieved sexual joy while slaughtering children. And he was not afraid of the electric chair, which brought about his end in 1936. He looked forward to his own execution as "the most supreme thrill of my life."

Fish's colossal ego and seething insanity found duplication in the terror of Düsseldorf, Germany, Peter Kurten, whose gruesome crimes and mental maladies were enacted by Peter Lorre in Fritz Lang's classic 1931 motion picture *M*.

Kurten, whose actions appear alarmingly identical to those of the Michigan murderer of the present day, preyed especially upon children, first killing and ravishing an eight-year-old girl on the night of May 25, 1913.

For seventeen years following that brutal assault, Kurten walked calmly through Düsseldorf's streets, murdering at will, and then sexually ravishing his victim. He was at heart a thief; he stole children to possess them, to rob their parents of their lives. He took immense pride in his ability to terrorize an entire city. In his tortured mind, the killings made him important, special.

Kurten was an ordinary-looking man who held the simple job of a molder. He lived quietly with his wife and kept regular hours, until he slipped into the night to commit the acts of a vampire. Often, he would visit the graves of his victims and, without remorse, converse with the dead.

In May 1930, Kurten's vanity in murder and escape backfired. He bungled a rape-murder, and the would-be victim, accompanied by scores of police, was soon hunting him in the streets. Kurten confessed all to his wife, who promptly turned him over to authorities. His identity discovered, the killer insisted he be credited with the nine deaths he had brought

Mosher and Douglass, abductors of Charley Ross, were fatally shot by police as they emerged from the basement of a Brooklyn home they had burglarized.

Child killer Peter Kurten, the terror of Düsseldorf, Germany, who was the essence of respectability to his neighbors.

about to assure his place among the arch fiends of criminal history.

The psychological profile of the Michigan murderer describes him as being "a fanatic of cleanliness"; likewise, Kurten's interrogators found him extremely fastidious. His clothes were always cleaned and pressed, like those worn by the Michigan murderer. He washed his hands repeatedly up to the time of his beheading.

And like Albert Fish, Kurten looked eagerly forward to his own death. He spoke words that should certainly echo inside the head of the Michigan murderer: "When I think about my deeds and in particular about the children, then I loathe myself so much that I am impatient for my own execution."

Other notable kidnappings include (it is significant to note that the "popularity" of kidnapping, particularly as a political weapon, starts only in the last decade, the year 1970 being an extraordinary year for kidnapping):

Richard I of England, 1192: Leader of the Third Crusade to free the Holy Land, the intrepid Richard Coeur de Lion was returning to England when, while traveling through Austria in 1192, he was kidnapped by

Duke Leopold and thrown into a fortress on the Danube. Emperor Henry VI, who had encouraged Leopold, demanded a ransom of 150,000 marks (about $15 million). In England, Richard's brother John delayed the payment, hoping to usurp the throne. The English subjects, however, chiefly the merchant class, feared John more than the roving Richard and collected the ransom, paying Henry in 1194, when Richard was released.

Atahualpa, King of Peru, 1532: When Spanish conqueror Francisco Pizarro entered Peru searching for riches, his ambitions were quickly realized when the Inca ruler, Atahualpa, paid him a state visit at his fortress, Cajamarca. Pizarro's soldiers quickly attacked and killed the several hundred natives accompanying the emperor and made Atahaulpa hostage, the first important kidnap victim in the New World. Pizarro demanded a fortune in gold from the king's subjects for Atahualpa's return. The Incas filled a hall twenty-two feet long, seventeen feet wide and seven feet high with gold, with another hall twice as large filled with silver. It took the Incas five months to meet the near impossible ransom, an equivalent of about $175 million. Pizarro did not release his prisoner, convicting Atahualpa in a mock trial for treason against the Spanish crown. The Inca emperor was executed on July 16, 1533.

Lord and Lady Muncaster, April 11, 1870: The Greek bandit Takos and a band of forty men kidnapped the British aristocratic family of Mun-

Richard the Lion-Hearted of England, kidnap victim.

caster while they were sightseeing near the battle site of Marathon in Greece, holding them for a ransom of one million drachmas ($500,000). The Greek Government and British diplomats completely mishandled the affair, sending troops to rescue the Muncasters, which caused the bandits to kill three of their companions before the main party was released. Takos was never apprehended.

Edward A. Cudahy, Jr., December 18, 1900: The fifteen-year-old son of millionaire meat packer Edward A. Cudahy, Sr., of Omaha, Nebraska, was abducted in the evening as he was collecting magazines on the street by two men who claimed to be detectives. Held for two days, Eddie Cudahy was released after his father paid the ransom, $25,000 in gold pieces, all in five sacks dumped at a remote spot outside of Omaha.

The kidnapper, an adventurer named Pat Crowe, escaped (his associate was never discovered) to South Africa, where he fought in the Boer War and grew rich. He returned to the United States in 1906, sending back the ransom money through an Omaha attorney before announcing to the press that he was Cudahy's kidnapper. Crowe was quickly acquitted, more for his beau geste and the fact that he had victimized a member of the Meat Trust than for any other reason.

Ion Perdicaris, June 1904: A wealthy American living in luxurious exile in a villa (which he called the Place of the Nightingales) outside of Tangier, Perdicaris was kidnapped by a local chief named Rassouli. No

Edward Cudahy, Jr.—his kidnapper sent him Christmas cards years later.

ransom was demanded; Rassouli's motive was to embarrass the sultan of Morocco in his already strained relations with the United States. Though Perdicaris was released within a few days, a cable from the State Department to the U. S. Consulate in Morocco was sent (not composed by the iron-willed President Theodore Roosevelt, as was popularly thought later, but written by John Hay, goaded by newsman E. M. "Eddie" Hood). The cable tersely read: "We want either Perdicaris alive or Rassouli dead!"

This demand gave rise to the belief throughout the world that the United States, or Teddy Roosevelt, the great Rough Rider, would go to war over the safety of one citizen, the kind of jingoism unfairly attributed to Roosevelt. A motion picture based upon this incident, *The Wind and the Lion,* is a complete fabrication of the events of this kidnapping.

Willie Whitla, March 1909: The eight-year-old son of a rich Sharon, Ohio, lawyer, James P. Whitla, who was related to steel tycoon Frank Buhl, was kidnapped from his school, told by his kidnappers that he would be visiting his parents. A ransom note demanding $10,000 followed and was promptly paid. The Whitla child was released in Cleveland. The kidnappers, Helen and James Bogle, were found drunk in a Cleveland bar with most of the ransom money. They were given long prison sentences.

Robert Franks, May 22, 1924: The fourteen-year-old Bobbie Franks was kidnapped in Chicago by two eccentric University of Chicago students, Nathan Leopold, Jr., and Richard Loeb. Though the abductors sent a $10,000 ransom note to Franks's wealthy father, they had no intention of releasing the boy, or collecting the ransom (a ruse to make the kidnapping appear to be the work of a professional criminal), but planned from the start to murder Franks, which they did, burying his body in a culvert. Their aim was to plan and commit the "perfect crime." Both were apprehended through their own mistakes. Defended by Clarence Darrow, Loeb and Leopold drew life sentences in Stateville Penitentiary. Loeb was killed in a homosexual argument in 1936, slashed to pieces by a fellow inmate, James Day. Leopold, through the help of Carl Sandburg and lawyer Elmer Gertz, was paroled in 1958. He died of a heart attack in Puerto Rico in 1971.

Marian Parker, December 15, 1927: Twelve-year-old Marian Parker, one of twin girls of successful Los Angeles lawyer Perry Parker, was kidnapped by William E. Hickman, who demanded $7,500 ransom (he later claimed that $1,500 was for his college tuition). When Parker paid the money to twenty-year-old Hickman, their cars parked on a lonely road, Hickman dropped the blanket-wrapped child on the road and sped off. The horrified father found his child not only strangled but with her legs cut off. Hickman was apprehended in Oregon and returned to California, where he was given a speedy trial and conviction, and hanged at San Quentin on October 19, 1928.

Charles A. Lindbergh, Jr., March 1, 1932: The twenty-month-old son of Charles A. Lindbergh, America's greatest aviator and hero, was taken from his crib in a second-story room of the Lindbergh home in Hopewell, New Jersey. A $70,000 ransom was demanded but only $50,000 was paid by a go-between (who held out the other $20,000, thinking to save the family money) to a man known only as Cemetery John. Two meetings took place in the Woodlawn Cemetery in the Bronx, New York, the last being on April 2, 1932. The meetings occurred in the dark so that the go-between, Dr. John F. Condon (known as Jafsie, a name representing his initials), did not get a good look at the kidnapper.

The Lindbergh child was found dead, murdered, on May 12, not far from his home, covered with leaves, just off the roadway, which bore witness to the fact that the kidnapper had killed the child only minutes after kidnapping him. The manhunt that ensued was nationwide, with thousands of state and federal police searching for the kidnapper; much of their efforts, from the beginning, were at cross purposes and were not only inept but helped to obliterate important clues.

About $20,000 of the ransom money had been paid in gold certificates. This currency was withdrawn from circulation in 1933. None of the market gold certificates given to the kidnapper surfaced until September 15, 1934, when thirty-five-year-old Bruno Richard Hauptmann paid for gas in a Bronx filling station with one of the ransom notes, which was identified by the attendant (it was his ritual to check any gold certificates against the list of Lindbergh notes posted in his station, from a widely circulated Treasury Department list). Hauptmann was arrested four days later, on September 19, 1934, by New York police. Found in the unemployed carpenter's garage was $14,000 of the ransom money. Hauptmann, who had smuggled himself illegally into the United States in 1923, had a long record of crime in his native Germany.

Hauptmann's trial in Flemington, New Jersey, was a sensation. He was identified by Condon as being Cemetery John and by others who saw him in the Hopewell area at the time of the kidnapping. Further, wood experts matched the homemade ladder used in the kidnapping to planks in Hauptmann's attic. The carpenter's fate was sealed. He was electrocuted on April 3, 1936, in Trenton, New Jersey.

William A. Hamm, Jr., June 15, 1933: Arthur "Doc" Barker, his brother Fred, Alvin Karpis, Fred "Shotgun Ziegler" Goetz, Monty Bolton and Charles J. Fitzgerald kidnapped the millionaire brewer in St. Paul, Minnesota, holding him for $100,000, which was paid and caused Hamm's release three days later. Karpis was sent to Alcatraz for life for this kidnapping in 1936; Doc Barker was already doing a life term on The Rock for this crime. Fred and Ma Barker were dead, killed in an FBI shootout at Lake Weir, Florida, in 1935. Karpis, paroled in 1969, died in Spain in 1979.

Charles F. Urschel, July 22, 1933: Millionaire oilman Charles Urschel was kidnapped from his home in Oklahoma City by George "Machine Gun" Kelly and Albert Bates—he was taken at gunpoint as he sat with friends on the front porch of his home—and held for $200,000 ransom. The money was paid in Kansas City and Urschel was released on July 31, 1933. Kelly and his wife, Kathryn, who was the real brains behind the kidnapping and her husband's inflated career, for that matter, were arrested in Memphis by local police. They and three others were sent to prison for life.

Kelly, who died in Leavenworth in 1954, wrote a pathetic letter to Urschel before his death in which he lamented the kidnapping, finishing the missive with: "These five words seem written in fire on the walls of my cell: Nothing can be worth this!"

Brooke Hart, November 9, 1933: Hart, the twenty-two-year-old son of a wealthy department store owner in San Jose, California, was kidnapped by two local youths, Thomas Harold Thurmond and John Maurice Holmes. They killed Hart on the same day of the abduction, dropping his body into San Francisco Bay. Thurmond was arrested on November 15 while arguing over the phone about the size of the ransom money to be paid. He and Holmes were placed in the San Jose, California, jail, pending trial. When Hart's body was fished out of the Bay, the citizens of San Jose went berserk, more than 15,000 of them storming the jail on the night of November 26, 1933, dragging out Thurmond and Holmes and lynching them.

Edward G. Bremer, January 17, 1934: The Barker gang struck again in St. Paul, Minnesota, taking Edward G. Bremer, president of the Commercial Bank, and demanding a $200,000 ransom (it was Ma Barker's idea). Bremer was released on February 7, following payment, but the ruthless Barkers were identified when Doc Barker left a fingerprint on a flashlight dropped at the site of the abduction, which led to the identification of the gang and the subsequent arrests and imprisonment of members.

Alice Speed Stoll, October 10, 1934: Mrs. Stoll was abducted in Louisville, Kentucky, by twenty-seven-year-old Thomas Robinson, Jr., a petty crook with a long history of mental disorders. The victim was returned to her family days later with no ransom paid.

George Weyerhaeuser, May 24, 1935: The nine-year-old Weyerhaeuser was abducted from the home of his wealthy family in Tacoma, Washington. He was returned home on June 1 after $200,000 was paid to kidnapper William Mahan. As in the Hauptmann case, a citizen was responsible for the capture of the kidnapper, when a department store clerk identified one of the marked bills cashed by Mahan and notified police. Mahan was given sixty years in prison.

Generalissimo Chiang Kai-shek, December 1936: The Chinese mili-

Nine-year-old George Weyerhaeuser, heir to a billion-dollar timber fortune, was kidnapped in Tacoma, Washington, in 1935.

tary leader visited Sian, China, in mid-December 1936 to encourage the ten army divisions under the command of warlord Chang Hsueh-liang to take the offense against Chinese Communists in North China. Chang Hsueh-liang kidnapped his nominal superior, holding Chiang incommunicado, thinking to kill him and thus end a military commitment his troops had no wish to fulfill.

Ironically, the Communists, even authorities in Moscow, intervened on Chiang Kai-shek's behalf, feeling he was the only unifying force that could rally the Chinese against the military aggressions of the Japanese. Not only was the generalissimo released, but his friendly captor, Chang, followed Chiang back to his headquarters and meekly submitted to house arrest which continued for the remainder of Chiang's life, even in exile in Taiwan. According to military historian Barbara Tuchman, writing in *Stilwell and the American Experience in China,* as of 1971, Chang "lives in Taiwan and is seen from time to time on Sundays in the same church attended by the Generalissimo."

Charles Mattson, December 27, 1936: The kidnapper asked for $28,000 in ransom after taking the ten-year-old Mattson boy from his Tacoma, Washington, home. The boy's body was found on January 11, 1937. The kidnapper, who failed to contact the Mattson family for delivery of the money before the child's remains were found, was never apprehended.

Charles S. Ross, September 25, 1937: The seventy-two-year-old Ross, a greeting-card tycoon, was stopped by John Henry Seadlund and James Atwood Gray as he and his secretary, Florence Freihage, were driving near Franklin Park, Illinois. It was the intention of Seadlund and Gray to rob the couple, picking an expensive-looking car. Ross signed his own death warrant as the two men approached his car, guns in hand, saying to them through the open window rather whimsically: "I've often thought of being kidnapped." With that, Seadlund got the idea of a kidnapping and altered his plan from robbery to abduction, ordering Ross from his car.

Seadlund, Gray and Ross then drove to Wisconsin. A $50,000 ransom demand, written by Ross himself, was sent to one of Ross's friends. This amount was finally paid in mid-October 1937. A motorcyclist, George Kukovac, dressed all in white—his cycle painted white, too, as per Seadlund's instructions—dropped the ransom money, packed in a satchel, after seeing an auto's lights blink three times on a lonely road near Rockford, Illinois, the prearranged signal for the drop.

Ross did not appear. The money, all marked, began to show up in a half dozen places, from East Coast cities to Denver, mostly at racetracks. With this pattern established, the FBI concluded the kidnapper was working his way toward Santa Anita racetrack in Los Angeles and stationed men at the betting windows there. The hunch was accurate. Seadlund walked up to the ten-dollar window to place a bet on January 14, 1938.

The bill he shoved forward was immediately identified as part of the Ross ransom money. Agents closed in quickly, arresting Seadlund. The twenty-eight-year-old kidnapper only sneered when he was asked about Ross's whereabouts: "Dead, of course. I shot him," he told startled FBI men. "I also killed a fellow with me, a punk named James Atwood Gray. They're dead in a hole up in Wisconsin."

Following the brazen kidnapper's directions, the bodies were dug up near Spooner, Wisconsin. As Seadlund awaited trial, he asked his wardens jokingly: "Will I get hanged or fried?"

Convicted, Seadlund got his answer on July 14, 1938, when he was strapped into the electric chair in the Cook County, Illinois, jail. J. Edgar Hoover, who personally directed the dragnet for Seadlund, told reporters that the kidnapper was "the most vicious cold-blooded killer I ever knew."

Peter Levine, February 24, 1938: The twelve-year-old Levine boy was kidnapped from his New Rochelle, New York, home but no ransom was made. His dismembered body was discovered on May 29, 1938, his kidnapper never found.

Suzanne Degnan, January 7, 1946: The six-year-old Degnan child was dragged from her bedroom in a second-floor Chicago apartment by William Heirens, a seventeen-year-old incorrigible who had already committed several burglaries in 1945, killing two women in the process. Heirens, who left a ransom demand of $20,000 for the return of the Degnan child, carried the girl down a homemade ladder, took her to a basement nearby, killed her and then, inexplicably, like the mutilation practiced by William Hickman in 1927, dissected the body. The remains Heirens shoved down several sewers. He was caught in the act of burglarizing another apartment by police on June 26, 1946.

The kidnapper was given a life term, thought to be unbalanced. It was Heirens who had written to police on the bathroom mirror of one of his victim's apartments: "For heaven's sake catch me before I kill more. I cannot control myself."

Robert C. Greenlease, Jr., September 28, 1953: On the ruse that the six-year-old boy's mother was ill, Mrs. Bonnie Brown Heady convinced authorities at Bobby Greenlease's private school to allow her to accompany the child to the hospital (she claimed she was the boy's aunt). Heady, with Carl Austin Hall, an alcoholic with a long criminal record, then took the boy out of Kansas City, Missouri, across the Kansas state line, and murdered him. They buried the body in the garden of Mrs. Heady's St. Joseph, Missouri, home, and then demanded $600,000 for the boy's safe return.

After several botched attempts to deliver the money, the ransom was finally collected. Two days later Hall and Heady went on a binge. A suspicious cabdriver turned them in. They quickly confessed. Both were sent to the gas chamber simultaneously on December 18, 1953.

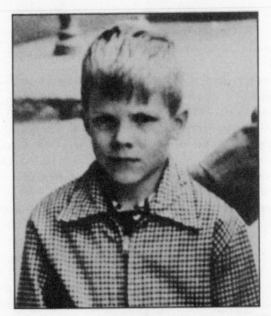

Bobby Greenlease, Jr., who was kidnapped from his private school in Kansas City in 1953.

Mrs. Bonnie Heady and her lover co-kidnapper of the Greenlease child, Carl Austin Hall, following their arrest.

Evelyn Smith, June 9, 1954: The twenty-three-year-old woman was kidnapped in Phoenix, Arizona, and released unharmed on June 10, 1954, after a $75,000 ransom was paid; her kidnapper was never apprehended.

Peter Weinberger, July 4, 1956: Only thirty-two days old, the Weinberger child was taken from his baby carriage on the front porch of his Westbury, Long Island, New York, home by Angelo John LeMarca, a thirty-one-year-old bootlegger down on his luck. He left a ransom note demanding $2,000 for the child. The child was later found dead. LeMarca was traced by the FBI when his handwriting on a 1954 liquor case was matched to that of the kidnap note. He was arrested on August 22, 1956 and electrocuted at Sing Sing, August 8, 1958.

Lee Crary, September 22, 1957: The eight-year-old child was abducted from his Everett, Washington, home by George E. Collins, Jr., who demanded $10,000 for his return. Three days later, before the ransom could be paid, the child escaped, returning to the kidnapper's hideout with police. Collins was given a life term.

Eric Peugeot, April 12, 1960: The four-year-old son of the French auto manufacturer was grabbed while romping in a playground at the golf course of St. Cloud in Paris. The kidnappers demanded $300,000 for the child's return. This was paid and the child was released three days later. Two of the kidnappers were later sent to prison.

Frank Sinatra, Jr., December 8, 1963: Son of the popular singer, Frank Sinatra, Jr., then nineteen, was kidnapped from a Lake Tahoe, California, hotel room. He was released on December 11, 1963, after his father paid a ransom of $240,000. Most of this money was recovered and the kidnappers shortly apprehended. Joseph C. Amsler, John W. Irwin and Barry W. Keenan were given long prison terms.

Mrs. Betty Hill, January 6, 1967: Mrs. Hill was held prisoner in her own Boulder, Colorado, home by an intruder who collected $50,000 ransom from her husband; the forty-two-year-old woman was released unharmed a few days later.

Kenneth King, April 3, 1967: The eleven-year-old boy was taken from his Beverly Hills, California, home by kidnappers who demanded a ransom of $250,000, which was paid. The boy was released on April 6, 1967.

Barbara Jane Mackle, December 17, 1968: Daughter of a wealthy building contractor, Robert F. Mackle of Miami, Florida (friend of President Richard Nixon), twenty-year-old Barbara Mackle was roused from her sleep at the Roadway Inn outside Emory University in Atlanta, Georgia, by a kidnapper who chloroformed the student and her mother, taking only the girl with him in his car. Barbara was told that she would be put underground while the kidnapper awaited the ransom money, $500,000.

Outside of Atlanta, Barbara was placed into a crudely made capsule, a

Kenneth King, kidnapped and held for a ransom of a quarter of a million dollars in Beverly Hills, California, in 1967, shown reunited with his parents.

photo with a sign reading "KIDNAPPED" was taken of her, and then she was sealed inside. The kidnappers had made provisions for air, light, food and water, leaving elaborate instructions inside the box for the girl to follow, saying that they were staying in a house nearby and that they would check on her every few hours until her father paid the ransom and she would be released.

The photo and the ransom demand were delivered to Robert Mackle, who hurriedly assembled the ransom money. The $500,000 was paid in Miami but local police frightened the kidnappers into deserting their car. Inside the auto, some of the ransom money was discovered, along with photos of Barbara in her coffin, and photos of a man and woman who, authorities soon learned, were Ruth Eisemann-Schier, a resident of Honduras who had once studied at the University of Miami, and an itinerant named Gary Steven Krist.

On December 20, at 12:47 P.M., the FBI office in Atlanta, Georgia, received a phone call (undoubtedly from Krist), directing agents to the

Gary Steven Krist, kidnapper of Barbara Jane Mackle in 1968.

spot where Barbara Mackle had been buried. The agents found the site
that day and dug furiously, breaking open the capsule. Staring up at them,
after eighty-three hours of being buried alive, Barbara Mackle smiled and
said: "You're the handsomest men I've ever seen."

Eisemann-Schier and Krist were tracked down. Krist attempted to flee
by boat but abandoned his craft on Hog Island, west of Florida, leaving a
duffel bag stuffed with $479,000 in twenty-dollar bills. He was taken
alive, shouting to agents: "You might as well shoot me! I'm a dead man
anyway!" He was sent to prison for life; Ruth Eisemann-Schier was given
a seven-year prison sentence.

Anne Katherine Jenkins, May 10, 1969: $10,000 ransom was paid by the father of the twenty-two-year-old woman after she was kidnapped from her Baltimore apartment. She was released unharmed three days later. The crime was attributed to Marie Calvert and Edward Lee Hull.

Mrs. Roy Fuchs and family, May 14, 1969: A gang of men held Mrs. Fuchs and her three children until her husband, a bank manager, turned over $129,000 in bank money to them. The ransom was recovered and the gang captured shortly after the payment.

C. Burke Elbrick, September 4, 1969: The U.S. ambassador to Brazil was kidnapped by local revolutionaries in Rio de Janeiro, who demanded that the Brazilian Government publish a manifesto of the terrorists and release fifteen political prisoners, which was done. Elbrick was released on September 7, 1969.

Mrs. Mary Nelles, September 7, 1969: Mrs. Nelles was kidnapped by a gang outside of Toronto, Canada, and released some days later when $200,000 ransom was paid. The money was recovered and the five kidnappers caught and given each ten to fifteen years in prison.

Sean M. Holly, March 6, 1970: Terrorists seized the U.S. diplomat in Guatemala, demanding the release of three terrorists from prison. When the prisoners were set free three days later, Holly was released unharmed.

Lieutenant Colonel Donald J. Crowley, March 24, 1970: Crowley, a U.S. air attaché in the Dominican Republic, was released after twenty prisoners were allowed to leave the country.

Count Karl von Spreti, March 31, 1970: When Guatemala refused to pay the $700,000 ransom for the release of the West German ambassador to that country, along with releasing twenty-two political prisoners, Spreti was found dead some days later.

Pedro Eugenio Arambaru, May 29, 1970: The former Argentine president was killed after terrorist demands were not met in Argentina.

Ehrenfried von Holleben, June 11, 1970: The West German ambassador to Brazil was released unharmed after forty prisoners were set free.

Fernando Londone y Londone, July 9, 1970: Colombian terrorists seized the former Colombian foreign minister, holding him until his family paid a ransom of $200,000.

Daniel A. Mitrone, July 31, 1970: Kidnapped by Uruguayan terrorists, Mitrone was held until all political prisoners would be released from prison. When the demand was rejected by the government of Uruguay, the U.S. diplomat was killed, his body found outside of Montevideo, on August 10, 1970.

Aloysio Dias Gomide, July 31, 1970: The Brazilian vice-consul was released by political terrorists on February 21, 1971, in Montevideo, after his wife paid a reported $250,000 ransom.

Claude L. Fly, August 7, 1970: The U.S. agronomist was kidnapped in Montevideo, Uruguay, terrorists demanding political concessions, but was released on March 2, 1971, because of illness.

James R. Cross, October 5, 1970: Four armed men abducted the British trade commissioner at his home in Montreal, Canada. The kidnappers, all members of the FLQ (Front de Libération Québec), a fanatical separatist group, demanded that more than twenty of their number in prison be released and flown out of the country and about $4 million be paid to them.

In this first of political kidnappings in Canada, the government was adamant in refusing the demands. Prime Minister Trudeau stated: "You can't let a minority impose its view upon the majority by violence. . . . It is a difficult decision when you have to weigh a man's life in the balance, but certainly our commitment to society is greater than anything else." Government officials, however, continued to negotiate.

The kidnappers insisted that a manifesto be broadcast to the province; it was. This did not satisfy the separatists. On October 10, 1970, armed members of the FLQ, wearing masks, kidnapped the Quebec minister of labor, Pierre Laporte. A photo of Cross playing solitaire in captivity was released by the kidnappers to prove he was still alive. Laporte was allowed to send a letter to the premier of Quebec, which asked that police stop looking for him. He added: "We are confronted by a well-organized escalation which will only end with the freeing of the political prisoners. After me it will be a third and then a fourth and then a fifth. If all the politicians are protected they will strike elsewhere—against other classes of society. Better to act quickly and thus avoid a useless bloodbath and panic."

The Canadian Government's answer was to offer to free five FLQ prisoners, but no more. Laporte was then murdered by the kidnappers, his body stuffed into the trunk of an auto which was found October 18, 1970, in the parking lot of St. Hubert's Airport outside Montreal. (The kidnappers called police and told them where to look.)

Admitting defeat, the government allowed three kidnappers and four other members of the FLQ to leave the country. They flew to Cuba, and Cross was released on December 3, 1970.

Eugene Beihl, December 1, 1970: Basque separatists seized the West German businessman in San Sebastián, Spain, for political sanctions. He was released December 25, 1970.

Giovanni E. Bucher, December 7, 1970: The Swiss ambassador to Brazil was kidnapped by revolutionaries in Rio de Janeiro. After the government released seventy political prisoners, Bucher was set free unharmed on January 16, 1971.

Geoffrey Jackson, January 8, 1971: Tupamaro area terrorists kidnapped the British ambassador to Uruguay in Montevideo, demanding that political prisoners be released. When these terrorists were set free, Jackson was released on September 9, 1971.

Ephraim Elrom, May 17, 1971: The Israel consul general was kidnapped in Istanbul and held for ransom of other terrorists in Turkish prisons, who were not released. Elrom was murdered, his body found on May 23, 1971.

Mrs. Virginia Piper, July 27, 1972: Kidnapped from her home in a suburb of Minneapolis, Minnesota, Mrs. Piper was held for two days until her husband paid $1 million ransom. Mrs. Piper was found alive, tied to a tree in a remote spot near Minneapolis.

J. Paul Getty III, June 10, 1973: Known as "The Golden Hippie," Getty was the grandson of J. Paul Getty, the richest man in the world, according to most reports, including his own. The sixteen-year-old Getty, on June 10, 1973, got drunk, bought a newspaper and a comic book and headed for his residence in Rome, Italy. Four men seized him, driving him to a distant hideout in Calabria.

The heir to the world's largest fortune was held for months as the kidnappers attempted to negotiate a staggering ransom. J. Paul Getty appeared reluctant to pay. It was thought that the enire affair was a hoax, a trick engineered by the grandson himself to obtain more money to fund his free-and-easy life-style.

On October 21, 1973, the kidnappers devised a method which, they felt, would convince one and all that the kidnapping was genuine. They

J. Paul Getty III with his mother, Mrs. Gail Harris, in Rome just minutes after his release in 1973. (UPI)

J. Paul Getty, the richest man in the world, who paid a reported $2.9 million ransom, the largest in modern times, for the return of his grandson.

cut off the boy's ear and took a photo of his mutilated head. The ear was mailed to a newspaper in Rome, received in early November, followed by the photo. The kidnappers further stated that other parts of the boy's body—fingers, toes, etc.—would arrive shortly if their ransom demands went unanswered.

J. Paul Getty paid, shipping three billion lire, about $2.9 million, by truck to Calabria. The grandson was released. It was later determined that the kidnapping scheme, gleaning the largest ransom in modern times, was the result of a plot by the Mafia.

Heiress Patricia Hearst; her kidnapping plight was always in doubt.

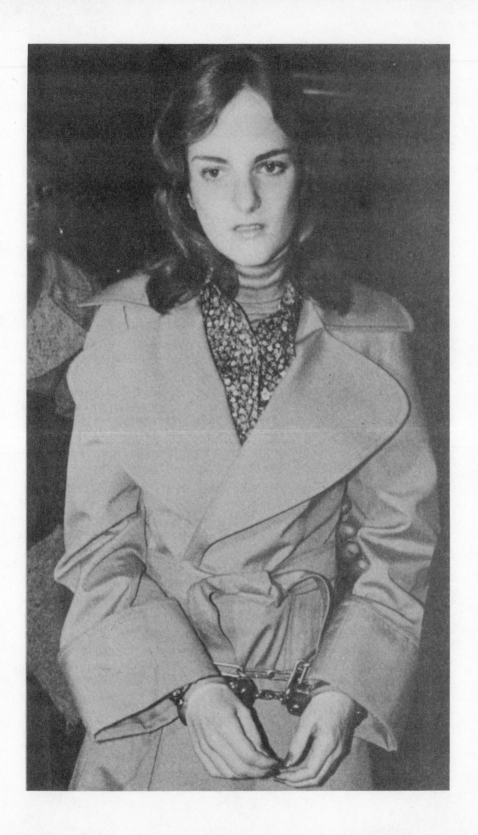

Patricia Campbell Hearst, February 4, 1974: Taken from her Berkeley, California, apartment she shared with her lover Steven A. Weed by members of the fanatical political sect the SLA (Symbionese Liberation Army), Ms. Hearst was in the hands of a psychopathic professional criminal, Donald DeFreeze, an escaped convict, who ordered her father, newspaper magnate Randolph Hearst, at the threat of her death, to distribute $400 million in food to needy Californians.

Hearst began the delivery of these foodstuffs, much to the objection of most authorities, including then California Governor Ronald Reagan, who said he hoped that all who ate the food would get botulism. Tapes were released of Ms. Hearst in which she claimed that her father was shortchanging the food program. Many came to believe that Patty Hearst was not only co-operating with her kidnappers but had been part of a conspiracy to repudiate the Hearst newspapers and help the SLA cause.

The Hearst handouts resumed, with boxes containing turkey, frozen fish, chicken and steaks, each box worth about $25, more than $2 million handed out to those in need (and many not in need). Patty Hearst's messages on tape took on a new accent, one that endorsed the SLA kidnapping and their lunatic cause. The naïve girl was suddenly happy to become a propaganda tool in DeFreeze's hands.

Shock after shock in the kidnapping case unfolded. Patty Hearst participated in the robbing of the Hibernia Bank of California of $10,900 (albeit it appeared on the TV monitors recording the robbery, that DeFreeze and another of the SLA thugs were holding guns on Ms. Hearst as a way of compelling her to aid in the robbery). DeFreeze and five of his fanatical followers were subsequently killed in a police battle in a Los Angeles suburb. Patty Hearst was eventually freed, then arrested and imprisoned for aiding the SLA in their activities, then pardoned by President Ford, a sad and sorry victim and/or accomplice to a lunatic kidnapping.

James Hoffa, July 30, 1975: The volatile Teamsters Union boss disappeared outside a restaurant in a suburb of Detroit, the obvious victim of a kidnapping; he was never found again.

Twenty-six children, July 15, 1976: A school bus carrying twenty-six children near Chowchilla, California, was curbed by three kidnappers who, according to their careful planning, directed the driver, Ed Ray, to drive the bus to a spot where a large hole had been dug, driving the bus down into it. The kidnappers then buried the bus, driver, children and all, making meager provisions for air to be carried into the entombed bus. They next demanded a $5 million ransom for the return of the children but were apprehended before this sum was paid. The kidnappers pinpointed the spot of the buried bus and the driver and children were rescued unharmed after being buried alive for thirty hours. Kidnappers James and Richard Schoenfeld and Fred Woods were sent to prison for life.

Achilleas Kyprianou, December 14, 1977: The son of the president of Cyprus, a lieutenant in the Cypriot National Guard, was seized by terrorists and released unharmed four days later after political sanctions were granted to them.

Aldo Moro, March 16, 1978: The former Prime Minister of Italy was seized by Red Guard terrorists. Their demands of releasing political terrorists from prison were denied by the government. Moro's bullet-ridden body was found fifty-five days after his abduction.

Tammy Wynette, October 4, 1978: The thirty-six-year-old popular country singer was abducted, beaten and held in her car for two hours by a kidnapper wearing a ski mask. His only utterance to her was: "Drive!" The kidnapper held a gun on Ms. Wynette for two hours, terrorizing her as she drove ninety miles from Nashville, Tennessee. She was then released. The kidnapper is still sought at this writing.

Teamster tyrant James Hoffa shortly before his 1975 disappearance, an obvious kidnapping and murder.

LAW ENFORCEMENT

DETECTION METHODS—THE AMERICAN SHERLOCK HOLMES

Although no official policy governs policemen who gingerly step into the limelight, the consensus attitude of the nation's police departments is one of anonymity. The sentiment that "the days of the grandstanders are out and gone" is supported by many law enforcement officers.

Teamwork and unity of effort on all levels are the hallmarks of most police work today. Though such a philosophy produces the great body of "solved" cases, it eliminates the spectacular sleuth of old who relied upon his investigative prowess to track down elusive criminals.

Such a man was Edward Oscar Heinrich, a legend in police annals, marvelous pioneer in scientific crime investigation known as "the wizard of Berkeley." A chemist from Clintonville, Wisconsin, Heinrich was a master of many sciences—botany, geology and ballistics. In July 1919, the thirty-eight-year-old Heinrich set up the first modern laboratory devoted to crime detection in San Francisco, California. Later, he moved the operation to Berkeley.

At first, Heinrich's detractors were legion. Most lawmen scoffed at his "mysterious behavior." Some even labeled him a crackpot. Yet this man was responsible for solving some of America's most baffling crimes, including the Hindu-Gahdr revolutionary plots and the Roscoe "Fatty" Arbuckle case.

Heinrich's wizardry was at its zenith when police officers came to him for help in 1923. Southern Pacific Railroad train No. 13 had been stopped October 11 near Siskiyou, Oregon. Three bandits had killed four members of the train crew while attempting to rob the mail car. The identities of the killers remained a mystery. Daniel O'Connell, chief of the Southern Pacific's train police, was given only two items left at the scene —a pair of overalls (all three bandits wore overalls as part of their disguises) and a Colt pistol with the serial numbers filed away. Several police departments threw up their hands. Impossible clues, officers carped, and told O'Connell to mark this one "Unknown."

As a last resort, O'Connell took the overalls and pistol to Heinrich. The quiet, withdrawn criminologist told O'Connell he would need two days in his laboratory.

At the end of forty-eight hours, Heinrich appeared in O'Connell's office. He announced: "These overalls were worn by a left-handed lumberjack who has worked around fir trees in the Pacific Northwest."

The criminologist went on to explain that the suspect was a white man between the ages of twenty-one and twenty-five, possessed medium-light brown hair, was not taller than five feet ten inches, weighed about 125 pounds and was "very definitely fastidious in his habits."

It was all very simple, Heinrich told O'Connell. The fir pitch staining the overalls and tiny Douglas fir needles found in the pockets (indigenous to the Northwest), which Heinrich examined under a powerful microscope, along with small tree chips found in the right-hand pocket of the overalls pointed to the fact that the suspect was a left-handed lumberjack.

"A left-handed lumberjack, you know," said Heinrich, "stands with his right side to the tree he's cutting, and chips fly to the right, not to the left."

Heinrich determined the man's size by measuring the overalls. The fact that he was "fastidious" was established when Heinrich found some neatly cut fingernail slivers in the seam of a pocket. The man's age, hair color and race were determined by examining a hair caught in the button of the overalls.

"The pistol is easy," Heinrich said. Although the first three serial numbers had been filed away, another set of serial numbers was hidden inside the weapon. Heinrich merely dismantled the pistol and found the number. (Firearms manufacturers had been doing this for a number of years for the purpose of establishing ownership, but this process had been little publicized.)

Tucked into the bib pocket of the overalls was a tiny, faded mail receipt, which Heinrich had examined under his microscope. He could make out the number 236 L. Armed with this information, the police tracked down three brothers, Hugh, Roy and Ray D'Autremont. These lumberjacks in rural Oregon had decided to "hit it rich" by imitating Jesse James's long-dead act of train robbery.

The brothers were sent to prison for life, but Hugh was paroled in 1958

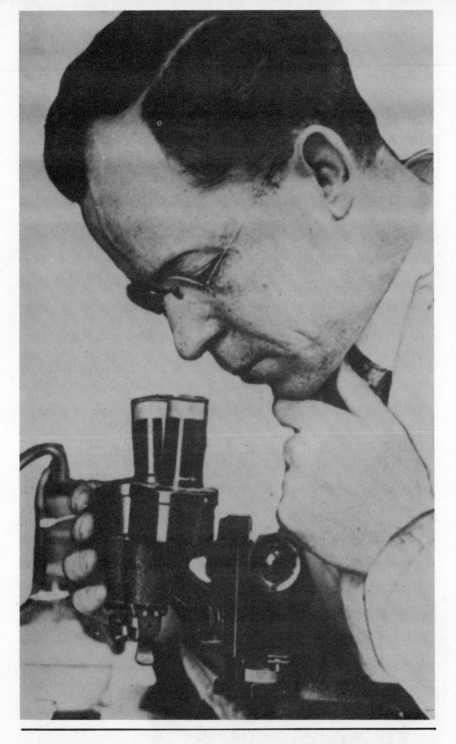

One of America's foremost scientific detectives, Edward Oscar Heinrich, who solved scores of cases that baffled the best of police departments.

and Ray in 1961. Roy D'Autremont, whose overalls betrayed him to America's Sherlock Holmes, died in a mental institution.

DETECTION METHODS—THE LOT OF THE POLICE INFORMANT

Estimates vary but probably 50 to 60 per cent of all major crime is solved through the activities of police informants, a fact of law enforcement that hasn't changed in centuries. The role of the informant is prompted by myriad reasons—revenge, self-preservation, sometimes the wish to be a good citizen, a fast diminishing compunction in the light of today's lightning retaliation, especially on the part of organized crime.

Informants were as populous in the Old West as they were in the people-clotted cities of the East during the nineteenth century. Most sheriffs relied very heavily on information supplied by informants to track down outlaws; the informants generally were rewarded with money or continued freedom as their own crimes, usually of a lesser nature than those of the

outlaws being sought, were ignored.

One such informant was the notorious "Black Jack" McCall, who was every lawman's snitch in a dozen cow towns during the 1870s. McCall operated petty western rackets such as running guns to the Indians and selling watered-down booze to the cowboy bars. He was permitted to operate as long as he provided information on gunmen and desperadoes.

This tentative immunity went to McCall's head on August 2, 1876, in Deadwood (Dakota Territory). Strolling into a saloon, the cross-eyed, broken-nosed McCall proceeded to get knee-wobbling drunk. From the bar, he blearily saw the deadliest gunfighter of them all, James Butler "Wild Bill" Hickok, sitting at a card table with three other men.

It was the first time McCall had known Hickok to sit with his back exposed instead of against a wall. That fact in and of itself apparently motivated the drunken informer to draw his pistol and blow out Wild Bill's brains. Hickok slumped over his card hand, aces and eights, which forever after was known in poker as the "dead man's hand."

McCall was tried in Yankton for the murder, found guilty and hanged. His reasons for killing "the prince of pistoleers" were obscure, but many thought McCall shot the lawman because he would not overlook McCall's petty rackets in exchange for information on more infamous outlaws.

The informant system also was responsible for eliminating the majority of high law offenders in the early years of this century.

Corrupt police officers such as NYPD's Lieutenant Charles Becker, whose brutal career was exposed by gambler Herman "Beansie" Rosenthal, were deposed. Informant Rosenthal was murdered for his pains in 1912; Becker was electrocuted for having the gambler killed in 1915.

Crime kingpins Al Capone, Lucky Luciano, Louis "Lepke" Buchalter, Vito Genovese all toppled as a result of informants such as Abe Reles and the non-stop gravel-voiced Joe Valachi, whose motivations were clearly in the realm of the mobster's revenge.

The upright citizen who turns informant out of civic responsibility is undoubtedly the most courageous of the lot, but the path he treads is the most dangerous. Arnold Schuster, a Brooklyn resident, spotted bank robber Willie "The Actor" Sutton and informed police, who quickly captured Sutton. Mafia killer Albert Anastasia saw Schuster interviewed on TV and erupted before gang members, screaming: "I can't stand squealers! Hit that guy!" Schuster was promptly killed by mobsters. Anastasia acted on whim; he had no association with Sutton, as Willie confided to the author.

As of late, informants have fared poorly. Dozens of informants either have been beaten up or killed. One of the most important was Frank Chin, a wire-tapping wizard who was murdered recently for his spying-informant activities against organized crime.

In the last few years, the FBI has lost more than thirty top informants

Top killer of Murder, Inc., Abe "Kid Twist" Reles, whose information sent Louis "Lepke" Buchalter to the electric chair in 1944. (UPI)

who feel that their identities might be made public. (The Bureau is thought to have more than 1,500 political informants in this country.)

All in all, the informant business is hazardous duty that may not always lead to the grave but certainly leads to the house of fear.

THE TWEEDLEDUM AND TWEEDLEDEE OF PROHIBITION

In the 1920s, no other Prohibition agents created as much fear in the marrow of bootleggers and speakeasy owners as did Izzy Einstein and Moe Smith. Each man tipped the scales at more than 240 pounds, yet after being hired to enforce the Prohibition laws of New York City, they became the greatest bloodhounds the government let loose to sniff out breweries and stills. Izzy and Moe were more than detectives. They were natural comics possessing acting abilities that trapped their gullible bootlegging prey and caught the fancy of the public through a bemused press.

Einstein thought the direct approach was most effective. On his first assignment, the agent waddled up to a speakeasy door and told the man peering from inside, "I'm Izzy Einstein. I want a drink!"

"Oh yeah?" asked the bouncer. "Who sent you?"

"My boss sent me," Einstein replied. "I'm a Prohibition agent."

"That's a hot one, fella." The bouncer laughed while throwing open the door. "So you're a Prohibition agent, huh? Where's your badge?" he asked as Izzy bounded inside.

Einstein brought out his badge and placed it on the bar. He then motioned the bartender over.

"That's the best one I've seen yet," howled the bartender. "Looks like the real thing. Here, have one on me."

The roly-poly agent belted down the drink, but the joke went sour when he lunged for the bottle. The bartender got there first and broke it. Einstein went to court without the evidence and the arrest was thrown out.

Because of that experience, Izzy and Moe devised an "evidence collector," which consisted of a small funnel nestled in a vest pocket. The funnel was connected to a tube which ran to a flat flask in the back pocket. The agents simply poured their drinks into this contraption and collected enough evidence to make any arrest stick.

To get into speakeasies, the portly men took to wearing disguises. They pretended to be college students, rabbis, fishermen—even bootleggers. Once, they wore long black coats and carried violin cases to enter a speakeasy that catered strictly to musicians.

As the Jazz Age wore on, Izzy and Moe became more elaborate with their ruses. During a raid in the Bronx one evening, they appeared before a speakeasy door dressed as football players.

"We won the game!" they shouted. "Let us in! We want to celebrate with a pint!"

They were ushered inside by a congratulating speakeasy owner, whose smile turned to a frown when Izzy and Moe handed him a summons.

The pair's exploits became so well publicized that the "Tweedledum and Tweedledee of Booze," as they were dubbed, became celebrities. Fame brought Izzy an introduction to Professor Albert Einstein.

"I discover stars in the sky," said the professor.

"I'm a discoverer, too," replied the agent. "Only I discover in the basement."

Izzy and Moe's discoveries led to 4,392 arrests, with the confiscation of more than five million bottles of bootleg swill. But the fame also created problems for the two agents, especially Einstein.

Toward the end of his career as a Prohibition agent, Izzy sauntered into a speakeasy, only to see his photo above the bar. Around it, the bartender

had hung black crepe. When Izzy ordered a drink the bartender shook his head.

"I don't know you," the man said.

"Sure you do," Einstein replied. "I'm Izzy Epstein, the famous Prohibition agent." He flashed his badge for good measure.

"Look, mug," smirked the bartender. "You could at least get the name right. The jerk's name is Einstein."

"Epstein!" Izzy replied. "I know my own name all right!"

"Listen," said the bartender. "The bum's name is Einstein. E-I-N-S-T-E-I-N."

"Okay," Izzy said, "I'll bet you drinks on it."

"You're on, wise guy," yelled the bartender, who poured the drinks. Einstein promptly arrested him and everyone in the speakeasy.

NOTABLE PERSONALITIES: J. EDGAR HOOVER AND ORGANIZED CRIME

For all of his much-vaunted law enforcement acumen as a "gangbuster" and "racket-buster," FBI Chief J. Edgar Hoover proved to be the crime syndicate's inadvertent ally throughout his controversial career. Despite overwhelming evidence, Hoover refused to recognize the existence of organized crime almost until the time of his death.

Hoover's disbelief in the syndicate was long-established. In 1938, for example, he wrote that the "boy down the block" was the only criminal menace in America.

"The names [of most U.S. criminals] are monotonously of a type we have come to classify as 'American' against the Latin or north of Europe 'foreigners,'" Hoover wrote.

One can little wonder then that the Director, as Hoover was known, ignored the records of such persons as Charles "Lucky" Luciano, Meyer Lansky, Vito Genovese and Louis "Lepke" Buchalter, who had set up a nationwide criminal cartel several years before Hoover had penned his thoughts.

Ironically, when Buchalter surrendered personally to Hoover a few years later, the Director regarded him as nothing more than a common felon, although Buchalter headed up the mob's strong-arm division, Murder, Inc. Hoover may have been the only law enforcement official in the nation who failed to recognize that Buchalter's 1944 execution was the only time a syndicate boss paid the supreme penalty for his crimes.

When it was widely reported in 1957 that over a hundred ranking hoodlums were meeting in Apalachin, New York, Hoover made no com-

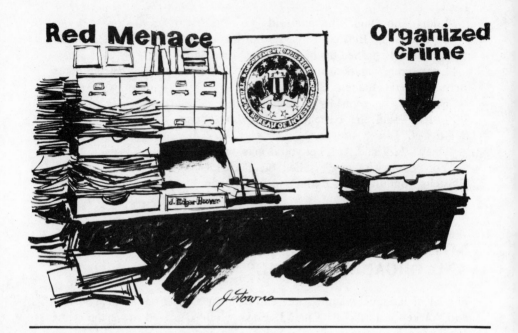

ment. As a result of this meeting, an FBI report which documented the existence of the Mafia was sent to twenty-five top government law enforcement officials in the fall of 1958. Hoover knew nothing of the report, but had the numbered copies recalled the next day. His only comment about the paper was, "Baloney!"

Hoover reported to Attorney General Robert Kennedy in 1962 that "No single individual or coalition of racketeers dominated organized crime across the country." The Director failed, though, to explain how crime across the nation could, therefore, be "organized."

When one looks at Hoover's amazing career, such conclusions on his part were not startling. The Director was preoccupied with combating the "Red Menace," which he thought was a greater peril to the security of the United States than some obscure thing called organized crime.

Following the attempted bombings of thirty-eight government officials and businessmen in 1919, Hoover put together one of the country's first white papers detailing the Communist conspiracy. The threat was then real and terrifying, but fear of the Red Menace seemed to grip Hoover more than it did most people.

Aside from the momentary respites of combating gangsters in the 1930s and Nazi agents in the 1940s, Hoover seldom flagged from the pursuit of Communists. He supported Senator Joseph McCarthy's witch-hunts in the early 1950s and confidently told the senator that he would provide charts listing Communists in the State Department. Like McCarthy's charges, however, those charts remained mythical.

Though it was certain some very real Communist agents were operating in the United States (and undoubtedly still are), Hoover saw the Red Menace in America as endless armies gathering down every street.

A decade following McCarthy's demise, Hoover still employed much of the FBI's manpower in seeking out suspected Reds. One Chicago, Illinois, agent said he was assigned solely to watch three Greek men, all in their seventies and long retired from radical activities.

"I watched them for months on end and all they did all day long was play dominoes. It was ridiculous," the agent said.

But, according to the Director, anything that moved was suspect. Except, of course, the organization that did not exist—the organization that is today second in power only to the federal government.

J. Edgar Hoover when he took over the FBI in 1924; he spent most of his time rooting out the Red Menace.

Hoover at the end of his long reign over the FBI, when he still insisted that no national crime syndicate existed. (UPI)

PROCEDURES: MINORITIES AND THE FBI

The FBI formally announced in recent times that the Bureau intends to hire more minority group members as agents. Of the almost 8,000 agents today, 150 are black, 163 Hispanic, 96 female (eight of whom are black), 34 Asian-American and 14 American Indian. These avowed intentions were a far cry from the rigid ideas of J. Edgar Hoover, who must be spinning in his much troubled grave at the mere thought of such liberal policies.

Oddly enough, the percentage increase of blacks has not been drastically altered since 1972, when this writer authored a book entitled *Citizen Hoover* (a critical study of the life and times of J. Edgar Hoover and his FBI). Nine years ago there were nearly 8,000 special agents in the Bureau, as today, 108 of them being black.

Years earlier, Hoover had had a terrific battle with his boss, Attorney General Robert Kennedy. "He," growled Hoover about Bobby Kennedy, "wanted me to lower our qualifications and hire more Negro agents . . . I said, 'Bobby, that's not going to be done as long as I'm director of this bureau.' He said, 'I don't think you're being very co-operative.' And I said, 'Why don't you get a new director?' "

Of course, Kennedy had no choice but to keep J. Edgar in his entrenched position, especially since Hoover went over his superior's head to President Johnson, who drawled to the director: "Stick to your guns."

Hoover stuck, as usual, keeping the role of minorities in the Bureau at a minimum. Most of the director's black agents, if not all, were nothing more than domestic servants or, as one white agent sarcastically put it, "house niggers."

The first token black in the Bureau was Jim Amos, who had once guarded President Theodore Roosevelt and had been appointed to the Bureau in 1921, three years before J. Edgar assumed command. Hoover kept him on the rolls until he died at age seventy-four in 1953, twelve years beyond his retirement age. Two more aging black agents served Hoover through his long directorship, one as his chauffeur, the other, Sam Noisette, as his receptionist, a front man who never failed to impress visiting dignitaries from the NAACP and the Urban League.

Robert Kennedy, however, was relentless in his demand to have Hoover hire more agents from the minority ranks. As a result, J. Edgar, ever the showman, hired Aubrey C. Lewis, a black All-American football star, who played for Notre Dame and the Chicago Bears. Hoover made sure that Lewis was photographed often, his picture appearing in many national publications, especially those specializing in Negro readership.

When pressure became too great from Kennedy to hire more blacks, the word went out from Hoover's Washington office to his local bureaus to hire Negroes and fast. In Chicago, the response was prompt, albeit unorthodox. A black man who had worked primarily in a janitorial capacity inside the Chicago bureau was ushered in front of the agent in charge of the Chicago office.

"Would you like to be a special agent of the FBI?" the man was asked.

"What's that?" the thunderstruck black janitor stammered.

"Your beginning salary will be more than eleven thousand dollars a year," the Chicago chief told him.

"I'll take it," nodded the janitor.

He was handed a badge, credentials, and was ordered to buy a new, conservative suit. The next day, the new black special agent of the FBI became the Chicago chief's chauffeur.

None of this ridiculous maneuvering was surprising in Hoover's heyday, since it was widely known in his powerhouse circles that the fearless director always considered blacks (and Orientals) as "all right . . . in their places." (It was also not surprising that Hoover's favorite radio program was "Amos 'n' Andy.")

But blacks weren't the only ones who received Hoover's lashing disdain. He fired one agent, a war hero whose plastic surgery left him with a

F.B.I. HIRING PRACTICES

MINORITIES

President Johnson, shown here with President Kennedy, was a firm supporter of Hoover's hiring practices at the FBI; Johnson was annoyed when Hoover failed to send him daily reports on the sexual activities of Washington politicians, reports Johnson delighted in as bedtime reading.

yellowish pallor, because he didn't "look right." He fired another because "he looked like a truck driver." Another one was fired because Hoover learned the agent had married "a woman of Arabian extraction." Another agent was kicked out of the Bureau for wearing a tie with loud colors. And there were many agents who were summarily dismissed after shaking the hand of J. Edgar Hoover; the rock-ribbed G-man had felt sweat in their palms!

LOOTING

THE PUBLIC CRIME OF DISASTER

Inherent with almost all known natural and man-made disasters has been the sordid crime of looting, ghouls filching valuables of all sorts from the hapless dead. Paradoxically, such despicable acts have been committed by those of all classes, albeit the poor and criminally bent were and are most prone to looting.

It has been claimed that such acts are in keeping with the searing trauma of disaster, irrational and unreasonable extensions of the calamity, committed by many as a sort of assurance of survival. Authorities in any era, however, have considered looting as a high and repugnant crime and have dealt with such offenders (until recent permissive times) with on-the-spot executions.

Here are but a few of the major instances in history when looting was rampant following catastrophe:

Vesuvius, A.D. 79: The volcano Vesuvius towering 4,000 feet above Naples today, in its first recorded eruption in historic times, obliterated the Italian cities of Herculaneum, Stabiae and Pompeii, killing more than 16,000 persons with great showers of ash, steam, water, sand and noxious vapors. Centuries later, archaeologists excavating Pompeii discovered hundreds of completely preserved humans, many of whom appear in the act of looting, frozen in their crime by volcanic material. Several bodies were discovered near the old prison of the dead city clutching handfuls of silver coins stolen only moments after the massive eruption.

England, 1069: Looting was widespread in the northern counties of England during the great famine of 1069, three years after the devastation left by the Norman Conquest. Countless bands of looters plucked valuables and foodstuffs from the bodies and homes of the 50,000 dead.

Petrified bodies from the eruption of Vesuvius. in A.D. 79. Many of these corpses preserved in volcanic lava and ash were frozen in the act of looting the houses of the rich.

World, 1348–1666: The more than 300-year reign of the nightmarish Black Death (bubonic plague), which ravished Asia, Africa and Europe, killing an estimated 22 million people, brought with it uncontrollable looting in every city, county and nation. Tens of thousands of looters roamed the countryside and city streets, taking what they wanted at will, officials as powerless to stop them as they were to remedy a disease unknown to the medical world.

Lisbon, Portugal, 1755: Almost immediately following the titanic earthquake (coupled to a gigantic seismic sea wave and fire) which leveled Lisbon on November 1, 1755, hundreds of hardened criminals fled through the crumbling walls of the prison and busied themselves with looting. To aid themselves in their work, the looters set fires to further confuse home dwellers and authorities.

Youthful Dom Joseph, the king, acted swiftly, ordering dozens of gallows erected on the hilltops surrounding the city. From these, several hundred captured looters were hanged and left dangling as a warning to all.

Chicago, Illinois, 1871: The great fire that wiped out almost all of the city of Chicago killed between 250 to 300 persons and left 90,000 homeless with damage soaring to more than $200 million. Looting went unchecked in the downtown business area and the notorious red-light district known as Conley's Patch, where hundreds of thieves, prostitutes and murderers helped themselves to whiskey, dry goods and cash (most of whom being so drunk they were oblivious to the fire raging about them and perished, making up the bulk of the fatalities). Several businessmen were murdered by the raging, half-mad bands of looters crashing into their fire-swept stores. Jacob Klein, a dry goods store owner, had his skull crushed by looters wielding shovels—for two bolts of cloth.

The ruins of Lisbon, Portugal, where looters from the prison were hanged in pairs.

Kentish Knock, England, 1875: The huge iron passenger liner *Deutschland* slammed into the Kentish Knock shoals near the Thames River, England, on December 6, 1875, during a gale. Stranded and sinking on the rocks, the ship lingered for several hours, allowing the large tug *Liverpool* to come alongside and rescue 136 of the 155 survivors. Most of the 157 who drowned on board the ship or froze to death while awaiting rescue on the main deck were immigrants sailing for the United States.

Also coming alongside the stricken ship were fourteen fishing smacks, their callous crew members clambering aboard the *Deutschland* to strip the bodies of the frozen dead of wedding rings, watches and what little money the impoverished travelers carried. These looters also tore away every salable item the ship boasted, from lamps and paintings to wall fixtures and teakwood paneling; many of these items were being hawked by the looters only hours later in the streets of Harwich. Many of these looters were arrested and sent to prison.

One of the safest oceangoing ships of its time, the *Deutschland* sank slowly after striking the reefs off Kentish Knock, England, in 1875. Most of the ships hovering about the stricken liner did not take off the 157 dead or dying passengers and crew members but were loaded with ghouls who stripped the disaster victims. (*Illustrated London News*)

Johnstown, Pennsylvania, 1889: The 100-foot-high earthen dam broke containing the South Fork Reservoir above Johnstown and four other towns on May 31, 1889. From 2,500 to 7,000 persons were swept away to eternity by 4.5 billion gallons of rushing water weighing 20 million tons. No sooner had the waters begun to settle than scores of looters crawled over the floating debris, stealing from the dead wedding rings, watches, cash and anything valuable that could be carried to high ground.

One survivor, a Miss Wayne from Altoona, found herself swept off a small ferryboat by the raging waters and deposited upon a beach unconscious. She awoke, according to her later claims, to find herself stripped naked by bands of looters clawing at the dead on the beach, describing them as "foul-smelling, grunting Hungarians." She pretended to be dead, but through a squint saw the looters "slice off with wicked knives" the fingers of women in order to obtain their wedding rings. Miss Wayne's hair-curling story so enraged a Johnstown mob that when one looter was discovered with a severed finger encircled with a wedding ring in his pocket, he was beaten unconscious and drowned on the spot. At least a dozen citizens were arrested by the militia for looting, most of them normally upstanding citizens, and sent to prison.

Galveston, Texas, 1900: Scores of looters descended upon the city of Galveston after it was devastated by a hurricane on September 8, 1900, that left in its wake more than 6,000 dead, one fourth of the city's population. Even while the two billion tons of rain engulfed the city, energetic looters dashed into stores and homes, plundering at will.

Most of these looters were from the criminal element of black communities surrounding the helpless city. To combat the hundreds of rampaging Negroes, two regiments of infantry from Houston arrived under the command of a Major Faylings. He assembled his troops and barked: "Shoot them [the looters] in their tracks, boys! We want no prisoners!"

What ensued was the harshest campaign against looters in any disaster in modern times. A day after the storm had passed, ninety blacks had been caught looting and were summarily shot by troopers. When Major Faylings heard that a gang of black looters were stripping a home at Nineteenth and Beach streets he rushed out to a platoon of troopers and simply shouted: "Plant them!" The men raced to the site and shot all twenty loot-clutching blacks to death on the spot.

Citizen soldiers, local militia, spent hours shooting the looters, killing scores of them. According to one account, a black looter "was searched and $700 found, together with four diamond rings and two water-soaked gold watches. The finger of a white woman with a gold band around it was clutched in his hands." Another report had it that "one Negro had twenty-three human fingers with rings on them in his pocket."

The shooting went on for two more days. In one instance, fifty looters,

including several white women, professional whores who had traveled from New Orleans upon hearing of the disaster, were found looting a huge apartment building. All fifty were lined up against a brick wall and shot to death. About 500 looters were apprehended in the Galveston disaster and dispatched by execution squads.

Martinique, 1902: When the volcano Pelée on the island of Martinique literally blew itself to pieces on May 8, 1902, the city of St. Pierre and several small towns and villages were utterly destroyed, annihilating from 30,000 to 36,000 people, with only thirty surviving, one only in Martinique, Raoul Sarteret, a black murderer languishing deep in the dungeon of the local prison. (Sarteret was later released and, because of his experience, became a missionary.) The French cruiser *Suchet,* in waters nearby, received an urgent cable from Fort-de-France, stating: "St. Pierre is infested with pillagers who are forcing safes and stealing money, and valuable books and papers." Well-armed French sailors were landed from the cruiser only three and a half hours after the eruption to find dozens of flesh-caked ghouls (all from distant towns on the island) racing madly about while clutching loot. They arrested twenty-seven and killed two men who were found rifling the pockets of the dead.

Laurel Run, Pennsylvania, 1903: The Duquesne Limited rounded a bend on December 23, 1903, near Laurel Run and slammed into a pile of timbers which had fallen from a freight train that had passed the spot fifteen minutes earlier. The collision caused the train to derail with sixty-four persons killed. Number 49, approaching on the single track from the opposite direction was flagged down before it crashed into the debris of the Limited. Trainmen and detectives from Number 49 raced forward to aid the injured, who were strewn about for 500 yards. They found several men looting the bodies of the dead and promptly arrested them. One looter was caught in the act of taking the shoes from a small dead child, an act that so enraged one of the detectives that he broke the looter's jaw before dragging him away to jail.

San Francisco, California, 1906: The massive earthquake (8.3 on the Richter scale) and subsequent fire that destroyed San Francisco on April 18, 1906, caused the deaths of more than 700 persons and created damage of $500 million. Though Mayor Eugene E. Schmitz ordered execution squads to move immediately against the hordes of criminals from the Barbary Coast who were ravaging the stricken city, it was Brigadier General Frederick Funston who issued to his troops the hard-line "shoot-on-sight"

Troopers guarding a captured looter during the Johnstown flood of 1889 against incensed citizens.

Troops with guns at the ready shot more than 500 looters in Galveston, Texas, in 1900 after that city was devastated by a monster hurricane. (UPI)

order that quelled the riotous looters. Funston declared martial law without civil approval, an unconstitutional act for which he was never rebuked.

Everywhere in burning San Francisco, the scenes of looters and soldiers shooting them at will met the eyes of those fleeing before the creeping fires. R. F. Lund of Canal Dover, Ohio, staggered from his crumbling hotel down a narrow alleyway behind the Emporium, where he witnessed "a rough fellow, evidently a south of Market Street thug. He was bending over the unconscious form of a woman. She was clothed in a kimono and lay upon the sidewalk near the curb. His back was toward me. He was trying to wrench a ring from her finger, and he held her right wrist in his left hand. A soldier suddenly approached. He held a rifle thrust forward, and his eyes were on the wretch.

"I remember only this, that it seemed in that moment a good thing to me to take a life. The soldier's rifle came to his shoulder. There was a sharp report, and I saw the smoke spurt from the muzzle. The thug straightened up with a wrench, he shot his right arm above his head and pitched forward across the body of the woman. He died with her wrist in his grasp. It may sound murderous, but the feeling I experienced was one of disappointment. I wanted to kill him myself."

Jack Spencer from Los Angeles approached Third and Market streets to see a man trying to cut away a woman's finger to obtain her wedding ring. Three soldiers rushed forward. The ghoul turned and drew a pistol, shooting at the soldiers. "The three soldiers," Spencer later remembered, "reinforced by a half-dozen uniformed patrolmen, raised their rifles to their shoulders and fired. With the first shots the man fell, and when the soldiers went to the body to dump it into an alley, eleven bullets were found to have entered it."

On his way to the ferry, one of the few avenues of escape from the flames, J. C. Gill was "sickened" at the sight of "scores of men, wharf rats, who had looted wholesale liquor houses and were maudlin drunk

After the city of St. Pierre was destroyed by the 1902 eruption of Pelée, an army of looters raced through banks and private homes.

. . . [They] were burned to death without being the wiser, because of their condition."

Standing outside the once resplendent Palace Hotel, Oliver Posey, Jr., saw a looter dragged from the ruins; he had been caught taking the jewelry from some of the dead guests. He was promptly hanged to a beam in front of the Palace. "No sooner had he been hoisted up and a hitch taken in the rope than one of his fellow criminals was captured. Stopping only to secure a few yards of hemp, a knot was quickly tied and the wretch was soon adorning the hotel entrance by the side of the other dastard."

Of the overall fatalities in this most celebrated disaster, easily 100 were made up of those killed for looting.

More than 100 looters such as these picking through the rubble of a bank, were executed during the catastrophic earthquake-fire that destroyed San Francisco in 1906. (California Historical Society)

An artist's rendering of the devastation of Messina, Sicily, in 1908 after the city was demolished by a seismic sea wave and quake; scores of looters pillaged the town at will.

Messina, Sicily, 1908: The Strait of Messina was shaken by a massive underwater earthquake (7.5 on the Richter scale) on December 28, 1908, leaving 80,000 dead in Messina and 25,000 fatalities in Reggio di Calabria; including surrounding communities the total death tally was a staggering 160,000. Looters by the hundreds swept over the stricken towns tumbled to rubble by more than thirty shocks. At first the looters, mostly criminals, concerned themselves with valuables. Constantine Dorsea witnessed the havoc in Messina and lunging through it "panic-stricken fugitives and escaped prisoners, the latter looting. I saw wretches hacking off the fingers of the dead to get their rings." Fascinated, Dorsea followed one drunken cluster of convicts, watched them smash the windows of a women's dress shop, dive inside and emerge adorned with the latest Paris creations crazily draped about their bodies.

Hours later the rampaging looters forgot jewels and money and sought only something to eat. "Bands of famished individuals were groping among the debris in the hope of discovering food. The first of the searchers who were successful were attacked by others with revolvers and knives, and were obliged to defend their finds literally with their lives . . . The struggle was fierce. The famished men threw themselves upon each other like wolves, and several fell disemboweled in defending a handful of dry beans or a few ounces of flour. One of the unfortunates was pinned to a plank with a knife, while clinging to his hand was a little child for whom he had sought food."

The few policemen who survived attempted to stop the looters but they were overwhelmed by the berserk bands and shot to death. Not until the next day, when three battleships of the Russian Navy arrived, were the looters suppressed. More than 600 armed Russian sailors landed and began rounding up looters, shooting them by the dozen. An estimated 500 looters were thus dispatched.

China, 1911: Roaring floodwaters from the Yangtze River swamped the city of Shanghai and four provinces in China in early September 1911, an area of about 700 square miles in which at least 100,000 persons (out of a population of two million) were drowned. Starving men by the hundreds pillaged the area, murdering for food. Hardest hit by the looters was the town of Quisan, which had been completely submerged only an hour after the river broke its banks. No reprisals were enacted by local authorities, who were obviously powerless to prevent the wholesale pilferage and killing.

Omaha, Nebraska, 1913: When the city of Omaha was struck by the most devastating tornado in its history, on March 23, 1913, 115 persons were killed with more than 1,500 homes destroyed and damaged. Looting was not widespread, thanks to the prompt order of Governor J. H. Morehead, who sent troops to patrol the shattered city. Some looters were discovered rummaging through homes for valuables and quickly arrested. Troopers had been cautioned not to display the kind of Wild West antics employed in the Galveston disaster thirteen years earlier. When one soldier was called over to the ruins of a house by a politician who had spotted a looter, he lowered his rifle.

"Fire a shot at that man," the politician ordered the soldier. "An obvious ghoul. We want none of that here. This is no Galveston."

"That's right, sir," replied the trooper. He shouted at the looter, a feeble old man, who hobbled off into the darkness.

Japan, 1923: The Great Kwanto Earthquake which devastated the entire Eastern Plain—obliterating the Tokyo–Yokohama megalopolis (8.2 on the Richter scale), killing more than 143,000 people, saw no real looting among the well-disciplined Japanese, but massive pillaging was reported for political reasons. To eliminate political foes against the Japanese war machine and find a scapegoat for the blameless destruction, the militaristic Black Dragon Society publicly accused Koreans of looting (a claim tacitly endorsed by Emperor Hirohito, who, contrary to Western wisdom to this day, wholeheartedly backed Japan's imperial aims of conquest from the early 1920s). More than 4,000 Koreans were rounded up only hours after the disaster by the police and military and, following mock street trials, were sentenced to death for looting none of them had committed. By the score the Koreans were then beheaded in full view of cheering thousands, all victims to Hirohito's political pogrom.

Lorain, Ohio, 1924: Hit by a vicious tornado on June 28, 1924, the city of Lorain suffered seventy-eight deaths. The devastation left by the twister was enormous, with more than 700 office buildings and homes smashed to pieces. Looters were on the scene before the police could take action. The chief of police rushed to the town's main square and shouted to one and all of the dazed citizens nearby: "We've found some men robbing bodies. From now on I'm giving orders to shoot to kill anybody found looting the dead." Though several ghouls were arrested, no one was shot.

Ava, Ohio, 1925: When the U.S. dirigible *Shenandoah* broke up in a storm over Ava, Ohio, on September 3, 1925, fourteen of its crew members were killed, twenty-eight surviving. Looters on this occasion were ostensibly souvenir hunters who swarmed to the peaceful glen where the ripped sky behemoth was crumpled. An armed detachment of the Ohio American Legion was sent to guard the wreckage and those bodies inside. Eager memento hunters, however, dashed into the debris to pluck loot, causing the guards to drive them off with gunfire. No one was injured. Said the Chicago *Evening Post* in a later editorial: "The sole complaint that we lodge against the legionnaires is that they did not shoot straight."

Chicago, Illinois, 1946: Chicago's twenty-two-story LaSalle Hotel (built in 1909), located in the heart of the Loop's financial district at LaSalle and Madison streets, caught fire on June 5, 1946, gutting the building and killing sixty-one guests, most of whom died by anoxia and carbon monoxide poisoning in the country's worst hotel fire to that time. Hotel looters were busy during the holocaust, going from one room to another, taking wallets and jewelry. Hotel detectives arrested several of these ghouls; two men were found carrying suitcases full of loot valued at close to $200,000.

Caracas, Venezuela, 1953: A looter of sorts actually began the Caracas calamity on April 14, 1953. A pickpocket attending a Caracas church ceremony at the beginning of Holy Week resorted to standard criminal procedures. He shouted: "Fire! Fire!" which panicked the great throng. The resulting stampede to the doorways caused fifty-three persons to be trampled to death, twenty-two of them children. The pickpocket was then seen to filch the valuables and cash of the dead; he disappeared, never to be apprehended.

Nagoya, Japan, 1959: More than 5,000 persons were killed on September 26–27 when hurricane Vera slammed into Nagoya, Japan's third largest city. Looters by the hundreds scavenged the ruins with such boldness that they entered partially wrecked homes with the occupants still inside. It took a special armed police force of 1,100 men to drive off the ghouls, with as many as 100 looters shot.

Chile, 1960: The earthquakes that ravaged central Chile on May 21–30, 1960, also set off eruptions from many onetime dormant volcanoes, all of which resulted in the death of close to 6,000 persons. More than 100,000 homeless victims of these titanic calamities roamed hunger-crazed through dozens of towns and villages, looting what food could be found. Men fought duels with knives to the death over a can of beans. To stop the plundering, picked troops were compelled to fire into mobs of looters, killing scores.

San Diego, California, 1978: On September 25, 1978, a Pacific Southwest Airlines jetliner, with 135 persons aboard, collided with a small private plane over the residential North Park district of San Diego. All 135 persons on the passenger plane, two in the Cessna and seven in homes on the ground, were killed. The entire crash was witnessed by Emilio Olivetas, a San Diego resident, horrified at not only the death and destruction exploding before his eyes, but the instant looting he saw practiced by the good, upstanding citizens of San Diego. Said Olivetas: "The people from the jetliner were falling into the trees and onto the rooftops and into the streets, and when I got there a lot of people were running around on fire and screaming. It was terrible, but even more terrible were the people who came like vultures and began robbing the dead.

"There were maybe twenty people and they had come and they were picking through the pieces of airplane and burned-out homes. They removed rings and watches from the hands and arms that they found lying in the trees and bushes and on the grass and they took the wallets from the pieces of bodies, which were lying all over . . . All I could think of was, 'What has happened to people? How could they do such a thing?' I am ashamed of being a human being today."

Fifteen minutes after the looters swarmed into the area, the police arrived and arrested fifteen persons, who were charged with minor offenses and subsequently released.

MURDER

THE MASS MURDERER—A BRIEF HISTORY

Within human memory the mass murderer has leaped from the shadows of his own madness to slaughter his fellow beings on a grand scale. These horrendous incidents of the past were nevertheless isolated events producing authentic shock in a public that thought of such mass killings as nightmares, eruptions of the medieval era, monstrous acts far distant from the realm of modern man.

Gilles de Rais in France and Sawney Bean in Scotland left their grotesque scars as mass murderers in other centuries. Remote now is America's most prolific murderer, Herman Webster Mudgett, alias H. H. Holmes, whose strictly female victims topped two hundred in Chicago during the fair of 1893. Up to the 1970s, this century had seen the mass killer only in rare instances.

The mass killer is not the kind of slayer who takes lives for gain. The profit, if any, is not known, the purposes are dark.

No one, for instance, ever explained why the Bible-reading Earle Leonard Nelson strangled twenty landladies from coast to coast in 1926–27.

Perhaps the reason had to do with the trolley car that snared him on its cowcatcher when he was a boy playing ball in a Philadelphia street, dragged him fifty feet and caused head injuries that may have permanently damaged his mind. Maybe the cause was a kindly aunt, a landlady by profession, who raised the boy and indulged his strange habits without ever seeking outside help. Nelson himself never explained, crying out his innocence "before God and man" as he was hanged in Canada in 1928. And he was without remorse at the end.

Howard Unruh, alive today in a New Jersey mental hospital, inexplicably stepped out onto the streets of his hometown, Camden, New Jersey, and shot and killed thirteen people inside of twelve minutes on September

6, 1949. Cornered in his home by police, Unruh calmly answered his phone when a newspaperman called to interview the mass slayer before he surrendered.

"Why are you killing people, Howard?" asked the editor.

"I don't know," Unruh replied.

Upon his capture, Unruh told police: "I'm no psycho. I have a good mind." He later shouted at a psychiatrist: "I'd have killed a thousand if I'd had bullets enough!"

The tempo of the mass murderer increased a decade later. Charles Starkweather killed ten persons in two days in and about Lincoln, Nebraska, in 1958. Charles Schmid murdered three near Tucson, Arizona, in 1964–65. In July of the following year, a staggering number of victims fell to two mass murderers—eight student nurses slain by Richard Speck in Chicago, and sixteen residents of Austin, Texas, by sniper Charles Whitman. Neither man gave reasons for the slaughter; Speck reportedly confessed his murders recently to Chicago columnist Bob Greene.

Whitman, who died in a campus tower as the police closed in, oddly enough had been to see a psychiatrist shortly before his murder spree. He told Dr. Maurice Heatly he had been feeling hostile, and had thought, as the psychiatrist recorded, "about going up to the tower with a deer rifle and start shooting people." That is exactly what Whitman did nine days later.

By 1969 mass murder went into dumbfounding acceleration with the Manson Murder Family claiming seven Los Angeles victims inside of two days. Perhaps no other mass murderers received so much attention in present times, and, with the recent granting of a new trial to Leslie Van Houton, one of Manson's minions, that type of heinous criminal is still in sharp focus.

Since the Manson mayhem, literally scores of persons have fallen prey to but a few mass slayers.

Juan Corona was convicted in 1973 as California's top killer, murdering twenty-five migrant workers in 1971. Also in 1973 Dean Allen Corll and Elmer Wayne Henley were found to have murdered at least twenty-seven teen-age boys in a three-year period in and about Houston, Texas.

The year 1971 witnessed a hallmark of mass killings in Europe when one-time monk Frans Hooijaijers of the Netherlands embarked on murdering patients in the nursing home where he worked, injecting them with overdoses of insulin. He was convicted of five killings and given thirteen years in prison. Prosecutors estimated that, over a five-year period, Hooijaijers may have killed as many as 259 other patients in his care.

In 1976 six mass murder sprees of epic proportions took place in the United States, and in 1977 three separate slaying sprees occurred. No one has yet to put forward an intelligent explanation for the incredible increase of such bizarre outbreaks.

Herman Webster Mudgett, alias H. H. Holmes, who murdered more than two hundred people, mostly women, inside of two years in Chicago.

Some authorities argue in a blasé way that it has to do with our population explosion since 1930. Others state that the killers are seeking self-esteem, attention. Still others merely shrug and point to the easy access of sophisticated weapons.

Whatever, the mass killer is no longer a rare species but a norm in the world of the criminal, a devastating day-to-day trend spiraling horribly upward.

Notable mass murderers include:

Sawney Bean: Born outside Edinburgh, Scotland, in the fifteenth century, Bean was the son of a sheep herder. Little is known of his early life other than that he was an illiterate and knew nothing of manners or morals. According to an early-day criminal scholar, John Nicholson,

Bean met a woman, as hardscrabble a person as himself, and ran away with her, "and these two took up their habitation in a cave by the seaside on the shore of the county of Galloway; where they lived upward of twenty-five years without going into any city, town or village."

During these years, Bean and his wife and his many offspring, some through incest—eight sons, six daughters and thirty-two grandchildren—lived by murdering travelers going and coming from Edinburgh. They not only murdered men, women and children, stripping their victims of everything, but cannibalized these hapless persons, an estimated fifty persons a year for a total of 1,500 murder victims.

One victim escaped while his wife was dragged down from her mount, her throat cut and instantly cannibalized by the insensitive Bean family. The man fled to Glasgow, telling his story to the king. The king instantly proceeded to the lonely stretch of Scottish coast with 400 men and scores of bloodhounds. The dogs led the army into the giant cave where the Bean family, surrounded by the limbs and torsos of their victims which "were hung up in rows, like dried beef," were captured after a prolonged battle. The family members were taken to Leith, where they were executed without trial, burned at the stake. "They all in general died without the least sign of repentance," wrote Nicholson, "but continued cursing and venting the most dreadful imprecations to the very last gasp of life."

Gilles de Rais (or de Retz): Born in 1404, the Baron de Rais proved to be the most ardent supporter of Joan of Arc, following her blindly into battle while believing wholly in her inspired crusade against the British. As the richest landowner in France, De Rais also financed her armies and expeditions. He had, under Charles VII, shown himself to be an exemplary militarist, becoming a Marshal of France at the age of twenty-five. When the Maid of Orleans was burned to death by the British in 1431, De Rais, who had shown signs of sadism as a youth, gave himself over to debauchery of all kinds, including mass murder. (It was later claimed that he was so crestfallen by the death of Joan of Arc that his character altered from goodness to the personification of evil.)

"His ego had a Jekyll and Hyde variability," claimed one of his many biographers, "now urging him to depravity, now propelling him on to self-fulfillment through the use of his undoubted gifts." At his worst, De Rais, who had years earlier turned many of his castles into theaters, having a love of drama, directed his agents and servants to round up young orphan boys and bring them to his court. He would then order them tortured, mutilated and killed for his amusement and he watched the horrid killings as one would a dramatic performance. More than 800 such deaths are attributed to the sadistic baron.

Learning of these killings, the bishop of Nantes ordered De Rais to appear before a tribunal on charges of child murder, heresy and sorcery. Under threat of torture, De Rais confessed to all charges. He and a score of his servants were hanged, some burned while still alive in October 1440.

Elizabeth Báthory: Born in 1560 in Hungary, Báthory married Count Ferencz Nadasy, a man of immense wealth. Unbalanced since childhood, the Countess Báthory tortured the servant girls of her castle at will. Following the death of her husband in 1600, Báthory suddenly got the notion that human blood would make her appear youthful. One story had it that a young maid combing Elizabeth's hair one day cut her hand, the blood spurting onto Elizabeth's arm. The mad countess thought the blood made her own flesh look younger. Her servants Thorko, Johannes and Ilona Joo, all practitioners of black magic, rounded up young maidens from the countryside at her orders. Báthory had their throats slit, their bodies drained of blood into a large vat and in this murderous brew took long baths to improve her complexion.

As was the case of De Rais before her, one of Elizabeth's victims escaped to blurt her horrid story to the authorities. Soldiers were sent to inspect the Báthory castle and they found much evidence of murder, particularly human corpses stacked and awaiting burial in the castle's dungeons.

Put on trial on January 2, 1611, Elizabeth Báthory was accused of murdering 610 persons (this number was corroborated by a witness who told of seeing a ledger in which the total was made by Elizabeth's own hand). Her servants were found guilty and hanged. Elizabeth, too, was convicted, but was spared execution through the intervention of the Prime Minister, who was her cousin.

The arch-murderess was walled up in her room at Csejthe Castle, with only a small opening in the wall, through which her food and toilet was passed. She died three and a half years later on August 21, 1614. The room became her tomb.

Marie de Brinvilliers: Born July 22, 1630, as Marie Madeleine d'Aubray to an aristocratic family, Marie had all the advantages of life. When she married the Marquis Antoine Gobelin de Brinvilliers, her sizable fortune was doubled. She tired of her husband early and took on a lover, Godin de Sainte-Croix. Sainte-Croix was thrown into the Bastille on orders of Marie's father. There he met a master poisoner named Exili, who taught him the subtleties of murder by poison. This knowledge Sainte-Croix passed on to his mistress, Marie. They both consulted Christopher Glaser, chief chemist of Paris, who gave them more invaluable information about undetectable poisons.

Marie experimented with these drugs at the Hôtel-Dieu, the great public hospital, administering to the sick her deadly poisons. Scores died, the method of their deaths going undetected in scrupulous autopsies. De Brinvilliers thought it then easy to poison her father, Dreux d'Aubray, who was much hated by her lover Sainte-Croix. She poisoned her father's soup in 1666, thus inheriting his fortune, which she soon dissipated. Next she poisoned her two brothers to obtain their wealth.

De Brinvilliers then took on several other lovers, but her devotion to Sainte-Croix, her accomplice, was almost total. Madame de Sévigné, one of her chroniclers, wrote later that "Madame de Brinvilliers wanted to marry Sainte-Croix. With that intention, she often gave her husband poison. Sainte-Croix, not desiring so wicked a woman for his wife, gave antidotes to the poor husband with the result that, shuttlecocked about in this manner five or six times, now poisoned, now unpoisoned, he still remained alive." The experience, however, left the husband permanently ill.

Others, scores of them, were not so fortunate. Marie poisoned almost total strangers at random. A woman made a remark at a reception she attended, one Marie did not like. She poisoned her coffee and the woman died within the hour. Another spilled a drink on her gown; she too died of poison days later.

Her lover Sainte-Croix was kept so busy making up new poisons in his laboratory he forgot through exhaustion to wear the glass mask he commonly used when mixing the lethal drugs. The fumes overcame him and he died of the deadly gas. When he was found dead in his laboratory, authorities began to investigate. A valet named La Chaussée, who had helped Marie and Sainte-Croix to murder her brothers, was picked up and he quickly confessed, implicating Marie. He was executed, broken at the wheel.

Before police arrived to arrest her, the arch-poisoner fled, remaining in hiding for three years. She finally found a home in a convent in Liége, where she was arrested on March 29, 1676. One hundred cavalry officers escorted her to Paris for trial; en route she attempted to commit suicide three times, once by swallowing broken glass.

Marie refused to admit her guilt. Dozens of witnesses, from servants to friends, testified against her, saying they saw her administering suspicious drugs to the hospitalized, her own servants, her family members. She was condemned on July 16, 1676, but tortured first to exact a confession. Once on the rack, the poisoner admitted her guilt, screaming: "I cannot remember the composition of the poisons. Only toad's venom."

She was next driven in an open cart wearing only a light shift to the Cathedral of Notre Dame. She knelt in front of the church and made her public confession as thousands craned to listen: "I confess that wickedly and for revenge and to secure possession of their fortunes, I poisoned my father and two brothers, and tried to destroy my sister. I now ask pardon of God, the King, and the Law of my country."

As all Paris lined up to watch, the mass murderess—her victims numbering almost 100—was driven to the Place de la Grève, where she was beheaded. Her body was then burned. Peasants in the crowd raced forward after the fires died and plucked her bones for souvenirs, believing that the remains of those committing murder brought good fortune.

Andreas Bichel: A native of Bavaria, Bichel, born in 1770, set himself up as a "reader of the future," in the Bavarian town of Regendorf in the early 1800s. Many superstitious persons came to him to learn of their future, paying him in silver. Normally a mild-mannered person—he never smoked, drank or quarreled—Bichel shrewdly picked his victims, knowing that he could not murder anyone from the local town. They would be missed and dangerous inquiries would be made. He preyed upon travelers wandering into his lodgings, strangers who could conveniently disappear, chiefly young girls with traveling money.

Bichel convinced these young women that he could not fully read their futures unless they were absolutely motionless. He would be required to bind them securely to a chair. Such was their naïveté that the young women readily agreed. Once she was bound, Bichel would step behind the woman, cut the spinal cord with one movement of his sharp blade, then plunge the blade into a lung. He stripped the bodies, secretly burying them in the woodshed behind his house. Bichel also kept the meager jewelry and threadbare clothing of these working girls.

The slayer's undoing came when a sister of one of his victims, Catherine Seidel, appeared in Regendorf, searching for the girl. By accident she spotted a garment worn by her sister being sewn in the local tailor's shop. The tailor told her that Bichel had sold the garment to him. The sister went to the police, who, in turn, scurried to Bichel's home. A quick search uncovered piles of women's clothes and a box of jewelry. The bodies were found later in the woodshed.

Bichel was found guilty and sentenced to death in 1808. He was broken at the wheel, specifically tied to a wheel so tightly that the cords broke his flesh. His bones were then broken one by one by an executioner wielding a sledgehammer. He was then beheaded. Only moments before his execution, this killer of at least fifty young girls was visited by a priest, who asked Bichel if he was sorry for his horrible crimes.

Sneered Andreas Bichel: "Do not tell me of repentance, but tell me if the dead can tear and injure."

Anna Maria Zwanziger: Born in Nuremberg in 1760, Anna Zwanziger grew up in her father's inn, her homelife stable and decent. She married early, but her husband was a hopeless drunkard. Anna left him and took odd jobs, working throughout Germany as a housekeeper and cook.

Nearing fifty, Anna took the job of cook and housekeeper in the home of a Judge Glaser in Pegnitz near Bayreuth. She schemed to become Glaser's wife by slipping large amounts of arsenic into Mrs. Glaser's coffee and wine. The woman died inside of three days. When Glaser showed no signs of interest in her, Anna left, becoming the housekeeper of another judge named Grohmann.

Learning that Grohmann, upon whom she had made marital designs, had no interest in her and was engaged to be married, Anna decided to kill him. She systematically poisoned his tea with arsenic. He soon died in agony.

A magistrate named Gebhard soon asked Anna to be a nurse to his wife and newly born child. She accepted with alacrity, poisoning Mrs. Gebhard in record time, thinking in her deluded way that the magistrate was interested in her. When the magistrate showed no indications of passion toward the dumpy, plain Anna, she sought revenge through wholesale murder, murdering anyone she could with arsenic.

She poisoned visitors and servants alike in the Gebhard household. When these victims were seized with paroxysms of pain, Anna glibly told her employer it was due to indigestion, or that she had put too much spice into the food, or used the wrong ingredient. Gebhard asked her to leave, stating that he could not continue to employ such an inept cook.

Anna departed but not before heavily dosing all the kitchen canisters containing coffee, salt and sugar with arsenic. Bidding farewell at the front door of the Gebhard home, she kissed the baby in her employer's arms, and in what appeared to be an act of love, popped a poisoned sweet into the child's mouth. The Gebhards grew violently ill only hours after her departure. Police were called and they quickly found the poison in the kitchen canisters, but they failed to arrest Anna until they dug up the bodies of the Glaser and Grohmann families. When they discovered the presence of arsenic, police arrested Anna in Nuremberg on October 18, 1809.

As was the custom then in Bavaria, the presiding judge at Anna's trial also served as the prosecuting attorney. Anna proved a clever court foe, sidestepping questions with ease. She denied all accusations of murder, even stating that Glaser had murdered his own wife. The trial sluggishly churned on for two years.

Finally, one day in the dock, Anna's resistance collapsed. Her body began to quake. She suddenly screamed: "Yes I killed them all, and would have killed more if I had had the chance!"

Anna Zwanziger was beheaded in July 1811.

Gesina Gottfried: Like Anna Zwanziger, Gesina was a middle-aged housekeeper and cook who poisoned to death with arsenic at least twenty persons, all in the German households she served. Unlike Zwanziger, who murdered out of a sense of sexual rejection, Gottfried poisoned her victims merely because it gave her a feeling of ecstacy to witness the agonizing death she could bring about. She was executed in Bremen in 1828.

William Burke: Born in Ireland in 1792, Burke was a common laborer whose miserable lot in life improved vastly when he became, along with his shifty-eyed friend William Hare, a "resurrectionist," meaning a body snatcher, a well-paying occupation at the turn of the nineteenth century in that anatomists were in dire need of human corpses for study. Though it was then illegal, dissection was privately sanctioned for medical research.

Burke and Hare serviced Dr. Robert Knox, a famous Edinburgh anatomist. Instead of digging up bodies fresh enough for study, they found it easier to waylay derelicts, taking them to their seedy quarters, getting them drunk and then killing them. They allegedly killed thirty-two persons, mostly males, in this fashion before Hare, who had aroused police suspicion, informed on his friend Burke. Hare was pardoned, left Scotland and vanished forever. Knox was cleared of any complicity in the murders; neither he nor his associates knew that the bodies supplied to them were murder victims. His career, however, was ruined by the publicity.

William Burke was hanged in Edinburgh before a great crowd on January 28, 1829. The author Sir Walter Scott was in attendance. Commemorating Burke's departure via the rope, an enterprising wag wrote a song which is still sung on macabre occasions in England today:

> Up the close and down the stair,
> But and ben with Burke and Hare,
> Burke's the butcher, Hare's the thief,
> Knox the boy that buys the beef.

Charles Gibbs: Born in Rhode Island, Charles Gibbs went to sea early, participating in many mutinies and committing, by his own count, more than four hundred murders, a doubtful figure, but it is quite possible that half that number was real. Gibbs and a black cook, Thomas G. Wansley, mutinied on board the *Vineyard* sailing from New Orleans to Philadelphia in November 1830, killing Captain William Thornby and first mate William Roberts. Shipmates informed on them after they beached the vessel and both were arrested. They were hanged on Ellis Island, N.Y., April 22, 1831.

Buhram: A member of the dreaded Indian secret murder cult, Thuggee, Buhram, it was established at his trial, had murdered 931 persons between 1790 and 1840, in the Oudh district, all strangled with his *ruhmal*, a waistcloth. Thugs also used the pickaxe and knife to dispatch their victims, the weapons of their weird ritual. Thuggee, which existed from 1550 until 1852, when it was eradicated by the British raj, was a strange sect, in that both Muslim and Hindu made up its membership, and that the members worshiped the Hindu goddess of death, Kali. It was for Kali, and the loot they could gather from victims, that the Thugs (*burtotes*) murdered more than two million people, mostly wealthy travelers during their three-hundred-year-reign, the deaths conceived of as human sacrifices to their goddess. The Thug Buhram was executed in 1840.

Hélène Jegado: A cook, Jegado delighted in poisoning the food she prepared for her employers, merely for the sake of the suffering she could induce. In one house, seven persons died of her poisoning, including her own sister. She moved on, stating that "wherever I go, people die."

Jegado retired to a convent, becoming the cook. When many of the sisters got sick over her meals, she was asked to leave. She was hired by M. Bidard at Rennes in Brittany in 1851. When the Bidard household grew ill, authorities were called and poison was found. Jegado's past was explored with horrifying revelations. The woman had murdered more than sixty people over a twenty-year period. Hélène Jegado was executed at Rennes in 1851.

Charles Avinain: A killer for profit, this French mass murderer, a butcher by trade, operated from 1833 to the 1860s. His routine was unvaried and prosaic. Avinain would pretend to buy hay from farmers, saying he could beat anyone else's price. The farmer would accompany Avinain to his broken-down farm near Clichy, where Avinain would kill him with a hammer, throw the body into the river, then sell the hay, horse and wagon. Police were led to Avinain's door when two of his victims, Désiré Daguet and Isidore Vincent washed ashore. When asked if he had any last words as he stood upon the scaffold awaiting the guillotine's blade, Avinain shouted: "Never confess!"

Joseph Phillipe: The known victims of prostitute killer Phillipe number eight but the real number is probably eighteen. Phillipe, whose background and motives are shady at best, cut the throats of prostitutes in 1861, 1862 and in 1864, a year in which he murdered six prostitutes on dark Paris streets, and also a child. As he was attacking another victim on January 11, 1866, a policeman interrupted him and he fled. The victim remembered seeing a tattoo on Phillipe's arm which read: "Born under an unlucky star," a clue that allowed police to track him down. Phillipe was executed in July 1866. (Another mass murderer, Richard Speck, a century later, had a similar tattoo reading "Born to raise hell.")

Pierre Voirbo: A killer for profit, Voirbo was brutalized as a child, his father refusing to give him his name. He committed murders in Aubervilliers and other areas, perhaps a murder total of ten, before killing Désiré Bodasse in January 1869 in his Paris apartment. Bodasse had loaned Voirbo 10,000 francs and, knowing he had no way to repay the old man, Voirbo asked him to have a cup of coffee in his rooms, where he murdered him, then dissected his body, throwing everything but the head down a well. Into the skull, Voirbo poured molten lead. He took the head to the Seine and threw it into the river while standing on the Pont de Concorde.

When the torso and limbs were discovered in the well, a young detective, Gustave Macé, investigated. (Macé was later to become a master sleuth for the French police.) He tracked down Voirbo, learning from the killer's landlady that Voirbo, a normally sloppy lodger, had cleaned his rooms immaculately. Voirbo had claimed to have spilled a bottle of cleaning fluid and therefore decided to clean his entire apartment. This, as Macé later learned, was to explain why the floor was scrubbed clean of bloodstains.

Macé confronted Voirbo and the killer made a spectacular confession. He was jailed pending trial but committed suicide, cutting his own throat with a knife smuggled to him inside a loaf of bread.

Jean-Baptiste Troppmann: The youthful Troppmann, born in 1848, befriended the wealthy Jean Kinck, a resident of Roubaix, outside of Lille, France. Troppmann told Kinck that he had discovered a gold mine in the Vosges Mountains and that he needed funds to develop his find. Kinck, a gullible sort, not only advanced the young Troppmann money, but was easily talked into giving Troppmann power of attorney to act in his name. Both men then went off to inspect the mythical gold mine. Troppmann poisoned Kinck by dosing his wine with prussic acid as he and his benefactor strolled through a meadow outside of Paris in September 1869. Troppmann next dissected the body and tossed the remains carelessly about a farmer's field. These were found on September 20, but by then Troppmann had lured Kinck's family, Mrs. Kinck and her six children, to Paris, using Kinck's name to send for her. When they arrived at Troppmann's rural rented house, he killed them all, stabbing, strangling and battering all seven to death (Mrs. Kinck's body was found with thirty stab wounds). These bodies were buried in shallow graves but found by September 23, 1869.

Troppmann's plan of escape was incomplete. He went to Le Havre immediately after the murders and attempted to book passage for America. He aroused the suspicion of the local police when he appeared without the proper papers and passport. As he was being taken to the police station for questioning, Troppmann dove into the harbor in an attempted suicide, but an intrepid sailor pulled him from the water. On his person police found 250 francs, several watches and a woman's ring, and papers that identified him as Jean Kinck.

Police quickly associated Troppmann with the mass slaying of the Kinck family. He was escorted with fanfare to Paris. Crowds, hearing of the mass killing, gathered at railroad stations to catch a look at the youth. Troppmann, riding inside a railcar, covered his face with a handkerchief.

Admitting his true identity, Troppmann at first blamed the mass killing on Gustave Kinck, the oldest boy in the family. When Gustave's body was found, Troppmann was rushed to the morgue. He was shown the body of Gustave. Troppmann was startled. Then he put his handkerchief on his face, saying, "Ah, the poor fellow."

"Take down that handkerchief," said a magistrate. "You needn't pretend to cry. Look at this body! Do you recognize it?"

"Yes, it is Gustave."

"And you killed him?"

At this point Troppmann stammered that the father, Jean Kinck, was responsible for all the murders. Before he was led away, Troppmann sighed, "Ah, I wish I was in Gustave's place."

Troppmann was kept in jail pending trial. The waiting apparently unnerved him. Only days before his court appearance, on November 13, 1869, Troppmann made a full confession, admitting that he had killed the entire Kinck family for their money and small possessions.

The killer was quickly condemned, sent to the guillotine on January 19, 1870. Great numbers of celebrities, from aristocrats to millionaire merchants, attended the execution, including the Russian novelist Turgenev, gathering in the Place de la Roquette. One and all took notice of Troppmann's short stature—he was only five feet tall—and his odd-looking thumbs, which were as long as his forefingers. Turgenev, who was to write of Troppmann later, was impressed by his self-possession and dignity; to him, the mass slayer's appearance was wholly unlike that of a fiend.

Vincenz Verzeni: A native of Rome, Verzeni came from a low-life, bigoted family. Early-day phrenologists (a discarded science in which the criminal type is ascertained through strictly physical characteristics) such as Cesare Lombroso studied his body, and came to the conclusion that

Mass killer Jean-Baptiste Troppmann, shortly before his execution in 1870.

John Bender and his daughter Kate, killers without compassion, who turned their Kansas wayside inn into a slaughterhouse.

though Verzeni appeared to be sane, he was an hereditary criminal in that his "cranium was of more than average size," and that he was "bullnecked . . . both ears defective in the inferior half of the helix . . . enormous development of the cheek bone and inferior jaw bone; penis greatly developed . . ." Krafft-Ebing, writing in *Psychopathia Sexualis* seemed to endorse this archaic analysis by adding that "Verzeni had a bad ancestry—two uncles were cretins; a third, microcephalic, beardless, one testicle missing, the other atrophic. The father shows traces of pellagrous degeneration and had an attack of pellagrous hypochondria. A cousin suffered from cerebral hyperaemia; another was a confirmed thief."

None of this academic addenda properly explained why Verzeni, born in 1849, attacked several young women outside of Rome from 1871 to 1872, strangling them, disemboweling them and drinking their blood. Two known murders led to his being imprisoned for life in 1873 as unbalanced, but his victims undoubtedly numbered at least twelve. The acts of murder, Verzeni himself confessed, gave him sexual pleasure and release. "I am not crazy," he insisted at his trial, "but in the moment of strangling my victims I saw nothing else."

The Benders: Led by John Bender and his daughter Kate, the Bender family set up a murder inn outside of Cherryvale, Kansas, in 1872. This was a one-room affair divided by a canvas wall. Travelers were seated with their backs to this canvas while being served dinner. John Bender and his son would then strike the unsuspecting guests on their heads with sledgehammers as they rested against the canvas. More than fourteen victims of the Benders were found buried near their inn in late 1873. By then, hearing that lawmen were growing suspicious, the Benders left the area and were never seen again.

Jesse Pomeroy: A Boston street waif, born in 1860, Pomeroy's physical appearance made him a pariah among his own set. He had a harelip and one eye was entirely white. He was tall for his age, which allowed him to bully other children, practicing his antisocial cruelty, as it were, to appease his own misfortune. At age thirteen Pomeroy was sent to the Westboro Reformatory for beating a boy almost to death. Released, Pomeroy worked in his father's Boston shop for about a year. During this time a great number of youngsters began to disappear. Jesse Pomeroy, it was later learned, was systematically killing children for no other reason, it appeared, than because it gave him pleasure. He waylaid nine-year-old Katie Curran, burying her body in the basement of a shop near his father's. Using his twelve-year-old brother, Harry Pomeroy, as a decoy, Jesse enticed a twelve-year-old boy named Albert Pratt from his school. The mutilated body of the Pratt boy was discovered the next day near the Bigelow School.

On April 22, 1874, Pomeroy took Horace Millen, a four-year-old, to Dorchester Bay. When alone with the child on the beach, Pomeroy knocked out his victim's eye, then stabbed him fifteen times. He left the body on the beach for police to find. So blatant had Pomeroy become that he grabbed William Barton on the street in broad daylight, dragging him into an alley and tying him to a telegraph pole, telling the youngster he was going to kill him slowly.

The Barton boy, however, managed to break his binds and ran to the police, describing his attacker in detail. Pomeroy's unusual appearance left no doubt in the minds of detectives who hurried to his father's shop, where the killer was arrested. Digging in the rubbish heap behind the Pomeroy shop, police unearthed twenty-seven bodies in various states of decomposition, some merely skeletons.

Pomeroy was tried and, in 1881, sentenced to death. The governor refused to sign the death warrant or commute his sentence. For two years Pomeroy lingered in jail. A new governor changed the sentence to life imprisonment.

When Pomeroy was imprisoned he vowed he would escape. His warden had little doubt that he would try, stating at the time of his imprisonment that Pomeroy "seems to emanate a concentrated ferocity of mind and purpose." Using tools smuggled to him in the Old Charlestown Jail, Pomeroy tried to chisel, chop and saw his way to freedom on two separate occasions but was discovered.

In 1890, Pomeroy felt he had devised a foolproof plan. Removing a stone in his cell, he found a gas pipe. Piercing the pipe, Pomeroy held his breath, letting the gas escape. Then he struck a stolen match. As he had planned, the resulting explosion blew him right out of the cell and into a corridor, but he was slammed into a wall and knocked unconscious. Further, the explosion created a fire in the jail which took the lives of three prisoners.

The attempt earned Pomeroy continued solitary confinement until 1916, when he was allowed at age fifty-five to mingle with other prisoners of the New Charlestown Jail, where he had been placed after the 1890 explosion. Pomeroy wrote several accounts of his life during the next ten years, but these remained unpublished. All of Pomeroy's many appeals for parole were denied. He was finally moved to the Bridgewater State Farm for the Criminally Insane, where he died on September 29, 1932.

Alfred Deeming: A swindler by trade, Deeming murdered his wife and four children at Rainhill near Liverpool, England, some time in the late 1880s, merely because he was tired of them. He then moved about the globe, enacting elaborate swindles while he posed as a millionaire, a scientist, a member of the British aristocracy in Montevideo, Antwerp and Johannesburg.

Deeming, using the alias Williams, moved to Australia, married again and murdered his second wife, this time for insurance money. As with his first wife and family, the second wife was buried in cement, Deeming's favorite method of hiding corpses. In Perth, Deeming became a baron, attempting to woo a wealthy young lady, Kate Rounsville. She grew suspicious when he began to pressure her for a will made out to him before their marriage. When police arrived to question him, Deeming attempted to flee. He was captured and his past was revealed. Deeming was condemned, no less than twenty murders attributed to him. He was hanged on May 23, 1892, at Swanston Jail in Melbourne.

Joseph Vacher: Born in 1869, Vacher came from an average home in France but early displayed laziness and boredom. He took up the life of a tramp in his youth, committing his first murder in 1894, when he attacked and killed a young woman, mutilating her corpse and then performing sex with the body, the same method he employed with his next known nine victims. (Vacher's total may have exceeded twenty.) The French Ripper murdered women young and old, as well as young boys. When arrested for murder in 1897 Vacher calmly told police that he had murdered out cf insanity.

Vacher was at first studied by "alienists" before being placed on trial. He told his keepers that he was not responsible for the deaths and showed no remorse. Wrote one medico after examining him: "Vacher is neither an epileptic nor subject to an impulsive disease. He is an immoral, passionate man, who once temporarily suffered from a depressing persecution mania, coupled with an impulse to suicide. Of this he was cured, and thereafter became responsible for his actions. His crimes are those of an anti-social, sadistic, blood-thirsty being, who considers himself privileged to commit these atrocities because he was once upon a time treated in an asylum for insanity, and thereby escaped well merited punishment. He is a common criminal and there are no ameliorating circumstances to be found in his favor." Vacher was executed on December 31, 1898.

Ludwig Tessov: A traveling carpenter, Tessov preyed upon children, boys and girls, throughout Germany from 1898 to 1901, killing an estimated thirty youngsters. He abducted two young schoolgirls on September 9, 1898, from the village of Lechtingen near Osnabrück. He strangled them, then chopped up their bodies and scattered the remains in the woods. Tessov performed the same kind of murders on two young brothers on the island of Rügen in the Baltic in July 1901.

Residents had seen Tessov talking to the boys shortly before the murders and he was questioned. He claimed that the stains on his clothes were wood stains, not blood. His clothes were sent to the noted forensic scientist Paul Uhlenhuth whose newly developed methods of testing bloodstains proved Tessov a liar. Tessov was quickly tried, convicted and executed.

George Chapman: The Polish-born Chapman (real name Severin Klosowski), gave arsenic to his wife, Maud, in 1902, but his suspicious mother-in-law called in police. When they checked into Chapman's back-

Mass murderer Joseph Vacher, known as "The French Ripper."

ground, they easily determined that the thirty-six-year-old tavern keeper had murdered many women: an alcoholic mistress, Mary Spinks; a previous wife, Bessie Taylor, who had been his one-time barmaid; and Maud Marsh.

At one time it was seriously thought by members of Scotland Yard that Chapman was a likely candidate for the role of Jack the Ripper. Born in Nargornak, Poland, on December 14, 1865, Chapman was a surgical student, later becoming a barber surgeon removing warts and treating skin ailments. He immigrated to England in 1888, living in the Whitechapel area. This was just before the Ripper murders in that area, mutilation killings of prostitutes that might fit Chapman's low skill with a surgical knife. Another barber surgeon operated in the same Whitechapel area during the time of the Ripper murders, a mystery man known as Alexander Pedachenko. Many believe that, for arcane reasons, Chapman and Pedachenko were one in the same. When Chapman was arrested for mass murder in 1902 by Chief Inspector Godley, the venerable Detective Inspector Frederick Abberline of New Scotland Yard, who had worked on the Whitechapel murders in 1888, remarked to Godley: "You've got Jack the Ripper at last!"

Yet everything in Chapman's modus operandi refuted his being the Ripper. Chapman's whole demeanor was that of a poisoner; all of his known victims were poisoned, not butchered in the Ripper style. Further, he was secretly trying to obtain poison from underworld sources in Whitechapel at the very time of the Ripper murders. Clearly, Chapman was not a man to resort to the knife.

The mass poisoner was found guilty of the Maud Marsh killing and he was hanged at Wandsworth Prison on April 7, 1903.

Johann Otto Hoch: Emigrating from Germany in the late 1870s to the United States, Hoch had a long career in murder for profit. He had married many women in Europe for their money, slowly poisoned them to death, then departed when obtaining his inheritance. Hoch practiced the same way in the United States, killing gullible females in West Virginia, Ohio, the West Coast and in Chicago. He was captured in New York after pressuring his landlady to marry him; the suspicious woman turned him into police, who found vials of poison on him. Hoch, returned to Chicago for one of his murders there, was found guilty and hanged in 1906. This marrying murderer is credited with more than fifty victims.

Belle Gunness: A widow with several children, Belle Gunness ran a broken-down hog farm outside of LaPorte, Indiana. To supplement her meager income, Belle placed countless ads in the lovelorn columns, blatantly advertising for a wealthy husband, a not uncommon practice of the day. She always ended her ad with the words: "Triflers need not apply."

To this middle-aged woman flocked more than fourteen suitors—the number has never been firmly fixed. After obtaining what money and property these lonely men had to offer, Belle poisoned them and, with the aid of her farm helper, Ray Lamphere, who was devoted to her, she chopped up their bodies, feeding the flesh to her hogs and burying the bones in her hog pens.

Belle's last known suitor was Andrew Helglien from South Dakota. Shortly after his arrival and disappearance at the Gunness farm, a fire broke out on April 28, 1908, which gutted the main house. The bodies of Belle's children were found but no trace of Belle could be discovered.

Police picked up Lamphere, who was in a drunken stupor. He told them everything, including the grim facts that Belle murdered her husband and at least fourteen of her suitors, and probably had set the fire to rid herself of the three children.

The farm was dug up and dozens of human bones were unearthed, perhaps the remains of thirty men, not fourteen, but it was difficult to determine. Lamphere was sent to prison for life, where he died dreaming of his lusty Belle. Mrs. Gunness never surfaced, most experts believing she escaped to live comfortably on the money she stole from those who loved her.

Béla Kiss: A Hungarian, born in 1878, Kiss was a well-liked tinsmith who murdered his wife, Maria, and her lover, Paul Bihari (Maria was about fifteen years younger than Kiss), in 1912. Then, either out of revenge on all women or as a way of getting more money, he advertised for new wives, killing twenty-one responding women in a fifteen-year period, all inside his Budapest apartment, where he lived under an alias. Kiss removed these bodies to his native town of Czinkota, keeping them for long periods of time in his cellar, stuffed into drums and floating in alcohol, until he could secretly bury them on his property.

One crime author thought Kiss lived only to have sex with women, stating, "Kiss was obviously a man of very strong sexual appetites, verging on satyriasis. It was his main preoccupation, and he needed a woman every day, if not several times a day. His potency must have been quite unusual; his entire life centered on the pursuit of feminine flesh."

Kiss visited the many brothels of Budapest during his undetected career in murder. In one such place he was observed to be "a man of great physical strength . . . and almost finicky habits, washing his hands frequently, brushing his clothes, wiping his shoes as if being immaculate was the most important thing in his life . . . He knew some poetry by heart and had a pleasant voice in which he sang snatches of ballads or sentimental hits."

The crimes of Béla Kiss were discovered just as World War I broke out, for Kiss a convenient chaos. During the war, he vanished completely.

Henri Désiré Landru: France's counterpart to Belle Gunness was Landru, the notorious "Bluebeard." Born in 1869, Landru led a simple, uneventful life in Paris as a used furniture dealer, dabbling in petty swindles. At the age of thirty-one he was convicted of fraud and sent to prison for two years. On and off, he spent an additional nine years in prison for confidence games.

In 1914, at the eve of World War I, the titanic events of which certainly clouded his activities in and around Paris, Landru, using many aliases (Dupont, Guillet, Fremyat, Cuchet), placed ads in the matrimonial columns of papers, stating that he was a considerate widower with a handsome income and was ready to marry.

The "Lonely Hearts Killer" found more applicants than he could juggle in his murder scheme. Police later found, along with his damning notebooks and love letters to his victims, 283 replies to his advertisements. Landru filed them in separate groups, labeling each group:

1. To be answered *poste restante.*
2. Without money.
3. Without furniture.
4. No reply.
5. To be answered to initials *poste restante.*
6. Possible fortune.
7. In reserve. For further investigation.

Landru, on the promise of marriage, would take his homely brides-to-be, mostly washerwomen types in their desperate fifties, to a ramshackle villa, the Villa Tric at Gambais outside of Paris, where he murdered them, then spent hours chopping up the bodies into small pieces and burning them in his furnace. Though the neighbors complained to local police about the awful smell at the villa, nothing was done.

Landru was tripped up quite by accident on April 12, 1919, after almost five years of nonstop mass murder, when a sister of one of his victims recognized him while he was buying a gift for another victim on the Rue de Rivoli. This woman led police to his door.

Detectives found his notebooks, which the meticulous, penny-pinching Landru had filled with damning information, including the names of his victims, the dates of their deaths, the exact amount of money he had spent on them and the value of their possessions. When arrested, Landru cried out: "Oh! Fancy accusing me of being an assassin. That's too much. For it could mean a man's head!"

In court, Landru played the innocent. The women—he was finally convicted of killing ten females and a young boy, but the score might easily have been ten times that number—had simply disappeared, he claimed, and insisted the prosecution furnish proof. The broken-down furniture Landru had seized from his hapless victims was brought into court, cluttering the entire room.

As the trial dragged on, Landru became France's blackest *cause célèbre.* Songs were sung about him; he was caricatured in music halls.

Dozens of international reporters wrote thousands of pages describing the stoop-shouldered, bald, heavily bearded little man in the dock. Artists set up easels in the courtroom, painting him. Photographers with heavy equipment photographed his every move.

His defense counsel Moro-Giafieri had little with which to protect his client. He suggested to the court that Landru was not a murderer but a white slaver who had shipped his victims to South America, where they were working hard in brothels.

"What?" roared prosecutor Robert Godefroy. "Women of over fifty? Women whose false hair, false teeth, false bosoms, as well as identity papers, you, Landru, have kept and we captured?"

"Produce your corpses!" Landru screamed back excitedly from the dock.

Landru's great wit served the newsmen well. When the judge once said to him: "You are a habitual liar, are you not, Landru?" the defendant thinly smiled and retorted: "I am not a lawyer, monsieur!"

He would not comment on his so-called affairs, saying that he was a man of honor and as such would never reveal such delicate information. He did remark that "the ladies whom you call my fiancées knew what they were doing, seeing that they were all—of age."

Landru was defiant to the end. Shown his notebooks, he sneered: "Perhaps the police would have preferred to find on page one an entry in these words, 'I, the undersigned, confess that I have murdered the women whose names are set out herein.'"

Nothing daunted Landru. When reminded how his neighbors complained of the smell emanating from the chimney of his villa, he laughed, stating: "Is every smoking chimney and every bad smell proof that a body is being burned?"

It was true that police combed through Landru's villa, sifting the ashes, and found no concrete evidence. Yet Landru's own writings served as proof enough for a jury to convict him almost three years after he had been arrested. As Landru entered the court for the last time to hear the verdict, he looked about at the jam-packed spectators, most of them women, their faces running sweat, their clothes rumpled. He bowed to his anxious female audience and said: "I wonder if there is any lady present who would care to take my seat?"

Landru was convicted and sentenced to die by the guillotine. On the day of his execution, February 25, 1922, a priest entered his cell with the guards who were to escort him to the scaffold. Landru waved away the priest's offer to receive his confession, pointing indifferently to the guards and uttering his last words: "I am very sorry, but I must not keep these gentlemen waiting."

Only members of the press and favored dignitaries were allowed to watch the execution. The noted journalist William Bolitho was present.

He recorded Landru's last moments with these words: "At the appointed hour, before it was light, the door [of the Versailles prison leading to the courtyard and the guillotine] opened, and with tied feet, his chest bared by the executioner's shears, and ghastly rags of shirt hanging over his bound arms, Landru was jostled to the towering machine that in a flash ended him and all his secrets."

Carl Denke: A resident of Münsterberg, Silesia, (now Ziebice, Poland), Denke ran a rooming house from 1918 to 1924 and, as the landlord, found easy prey among his boarders. Denke, known to his unsuspecting roomers as "papa," was an out-and-out cannibal, killing an estimated thirty persons from 1921 to 1924, men and women, whose bodies he chopped up and ate piecemeal, pickling the remains in large vats, preserved in brine for later consumption. He was arrested on December 21, 1924 but committed suicide by hanging himself with his suspenders in his cell.

Fritz Haarmann: Known as the "Ogre of Hanover," born in 1879, Haarmann was a product of the ruinous Weimar Republic following World War I, when Germany was overrun with the drifting homeless, starving, penniless, a social condition conducive to the lethal operations of creatures like Haarmann and Peter Kurten.

Haarmann's homelife was miserable as a child. His father beat him. His three sisters went into prostitution at an early age (as a boy Fritz delighted in dressing in his sisters' clothing). At age seventeen Haarmann sexually attacked several small children, was caught in the act and sent to a mental institution. He escaped and joined the Army but was released as an undesirable. Following that he committed many burglaries and sex offenses.

A flagrant homosexual, Haarmann secured a position in Hanover as a police informant. He was given a badge and a small salary. What the police actually did was to give him a license to commit mass murder.

Haarmann preyed upon the homeless youths streaming into Hanover, spilling into the main train station by the hundreds to loiter and beg. Here Haarmann picked them up, from 1918 to 1924, usually flashing his police badge and telling the youth he desired to murder that he wanted to question him. The young boy would accompany Haarmann to his grubby apartment, which he shared with his homosexual lover, twenty-year-old Hans Grans, at the Rote Reihe (Red Row) in Hanover's crumbling Jewish ghetto, his third-floor walk-up overlooking the river Leine. Once inside the apartment, Haarmann would sexually attack the boy, strangle him to death, then cart his body to the attic, where he kept a room for his side business—that of a black-market butcher. Here Haarmann labored long, chopping and slicing up the bodies (the walls of this room were solid with crusted blood when police finally discovered it). The mass slayer would next carry the remains of the bodies in small lots inside pails to the open market in Hanover, where he sold the hacked up bodies as horsemeat to starving citizens. He and Grans, who often participated in the murders, lived off the proceeds of these "meat" sales along with selling the meager clothes and property of the slain boys.

Disposing of the bones and skulls of his victims became difficult for Haarmann. At first he gave the bones to neighbors, who used them to make soup, thinking they were animal bones. When some grew suspicious because of the whiteness of the bones, Haarmann merely dumped the skeletal remains out his window and into the river Leine.

When some of these bones, particularly human skulls, were found by boys fishing in the river on May 17, 1924, the police investigated. They dragged the river and uncovered hundreds of human bones. On June 22, a boy in the railway station rushed up to police officers, complaining that a man had taken indecent liberties with him. He pointed to Haarmann, prowling among the sleeping boys.

While Haarmann was taken in for questioning, detectives visited his rooms, finding the heaps of clothing and other shabby belongings the monster had taken from his youthful victims. Next, they found the blood-splattered attic room. Haarmann, given the "third degree," confessed to the mass slayings, implicating his lover Hans Grans, who was also arrested.

Both were tried together in a long-winded trial, rather a last show for Haarmann, who reveled in his guilt, conducting the trial himself at times, making lewd statements to Grans, who stood passively at his side without uttering a word throughout the trial. Pressed for the number of his victims, Haarmann shrugged at the judges: "It might have been thirty, it might have been forty, I don't remember."

Of the twenty-seven charges of murder brought against him, Haarmann denied only three. Arrogantly, he told the court that he was a "selective" killer, one who would not pick just anyone to butcher. A father of a missing youngster came forward in court, offering a photo of his son, Herman Wolf, and claiming that Haarmann had murdered him.

The fiend grew indignant. "I have my tastes after all," he carped, upbraiding the father in court. "Such an ugly creature as, according to his photographs, your son must have been, I would never have taken to. You say that your boy had not even a shirt to his name, and his socks were tied on to his feet with a string. Pfui Deibel! You ought to have been ashamed to have let him go about like that. Poor stuff like him there's plenty. Just think what you are saying. Such a youngster was much beneath my notice!"

Finally convicted of twenty-four murders, Haarmann was sentenced to death. He took joy from the announcement, agreed most newsmen covering the trial. His body quivered with excitement as he blurted to the court: "I want to be executed on the market place [where he had sold his

Germany's mass murderer of young boys, Fritz Haarmann.

human flesh]. On my tombstone must be put this inscription: 'Here Lies Mass-Murderer Haarmann.' On my birthday Hans Grans must come and lay a wreath upon it."

Grans was given life imprisonment (this sentence was later reduced to twelve years; after serving this time Grans was quietly released and vanished).

Haarmann, who was beheaded in January 1925, had several last requests. He wanted to "pass one merry evening in the condemned cell" with his lover Grans. With his last meal he insisted upon "coffee, hard cheese, and a cigar." At the moment of death, Haarmann vowed he would curse his father and "regard his execution as his wedding."

Susi Olah: A Hungarian seeress, Olah convinced the native citizens of her village, Nagzrev, that she could predict the deaths of all unwanted persons in the neighborhood, from straying husbands to crippled children. To fulfill these prophecies, from 1909 until her ultimate exposure as a mass murderess, Olah poisoned more than one hundred persons with arsenic, having extensive help from three "spiritual aides." Well paid for these predictions, the seeress was informed on by an employee in 1929 but before she could be tried, Susi Olah committed suicide. Her three aides were executed.

Adolf Seefeld: A traveling watchmaker, Seefeld, born in 1879, was a homosexual killer in Germany who, from 1908 to 1935, murdered twelve young boys after raping them. There was no indication of mutilation in any of the murders. Seefeld was executed on May 23, 1936.

Franz Wagner: Born in 1874, Wagner had an unstable homelife in Germany. Following his father's death, his mother displayed wildly promiscuous behavior; so did his sister. His brother became a drunkard early in life. Though Wagner was a bright pupil, he was, as he later stated, "haunted." He became a teacher in Radelstetten and married. His wife then bore one child after another, five in all. Wrote Wagner in his diary: "All these children are coming against my wishes!"

For years Wagner thought of suicide. He bought several guns in 1908, secretly practicing his marksmanship in the woods. He became even more morose in 1912, when he was transferred to Degerloch, outside of Stuttgart.

Then, without any apparent provocation, on the night of September 3, 1913, he exploded into a homicidal maniac (much like Howard Unruh in New Jersey thirty-six years later). He murdered his wife and children with a razor-sharp knife, then rushed into the streets, where he shot and killed nine more persons, all picked at random. Running out of victims in his wild spree, Wagner lit a torch and ran from building to building, setting houses afire. He shot cattle and horses as they raced from burning barns.

Police arrived to subdue the madman. It took a squad of men to beat him unconscious with clubs to stop his outburst. Wagner was adjudged a hopeless paranoiac and, although he insisted he be executed, he was sent to a mental asylum for life, where he died in 1938.

Bruno Ludke: Born in 1909 in Germany, Ludke was a sex criminal all his life. When the Nazis took over the German Government, Ludke's extensive file was examined along with those of all others the Nazis termed mental defectives. He was sterilized as part of the eugenics plan. Ludke, however, went on with his sexual offenses, moving to Berlin during World War II. On January 29, 1943, police interrupted Ludke as he was having coitus with the body of a young woman he had just murdered. Hauled before a police court, Ludke confessed that he had murdered eighty-five women from 1929 to 1943, and that he was a confirmed necrophiliac, raping most of his victims after they were dead. Ludke was bright enough to point out to his Nazi captors that Nazi law prohibited the indictment for murder of mental defectives, which they themselves had earlier judged him to be.

The Nazis agreed with the arch killer, and, without a trial, he was sent to a hospital in Vienna for "further experimentation." This consisted of a fatal injection which killed Ludke on April 8, 1944.

Ernest Ingenito: A malcontent most of his life, Ingenito got into a family argument in Gloucester, New Jersey, shooting his wife, Theresa, and eight of the Mazzoli family, his in-laws, who died of wounds on the night of November 17, 1950. Ingenito was confined to the New Jersey State Hospital for the Criminally Insane for life.

Melvin David Rees: An unbalanced musician, Rees stopped cars in Maryland and in Virginia, in order to rape women. He killed Margaret Harold on June 26, 1957, and, in 1959, an entire family: Carroll Jackson, his wife and two children. FBI agents tracked Rees to a West Memphis, Arkansas, store where he was selling pianos. He was executed for the Jackson murders in Virginia in 1961.

Charles Starkweather: Born on November 24, 1938, Charles Starkweather lived the life of an itinerant, working as a garbage man in Lincoln, Nebraska, a job he detested. Bandy-legged, myopic, always the subject of ridicule, Starkweather struck back with murder, killing a gas station attendant who made fun of his appearance on December 1, 1957, robbing the Crest Service Station in the process. Then, when the parents of his girl friend, fourteen-year-old Caril Fugate, told him he could not see her again, Starkweather, with Caril at his side, on January 28, 1958, went on a murder spree, killing Caril's parents, her thirty-month-old half sister, and six others, until police overpowered him on the road as he was attempting to flee the Lincoln area. He was sent to the electric chair on June 25, 1959.

Teófilo "Sparks" Rojas: Colombia, racked with civil disorder in a period called La Violencia, from 1945 to 1962, produced an incredible murder rate, an estimated 300,000 homicides, or forty-eight murders a day, each day, for seventeen years. Chief killer during this bloody period was Teófilo Rojas, a bandit leader who was credited with murdering 592 persons between 1948 and January 22, 1963, when he was killed in an ambush near Armenia. As many as 3,500 murders have been attributed to Rojas, which would make him the greatest mass slayer in all history.

Richard Franklin Speck: Born in 1941, Speck devoted himself to crime at an early age, specializing in burglary. He was arrested thirty-seven times before moving to Chicago in 1966, where, on the night of July 13–14, 1966, he raped and murdered eight nurses in their dormitory. A surviving nurse identified him at his trial. He was given several life sentences, making parole impossible.

Robert Benjamin Smith: A high school student with a good record, eighteen-year-old Robert Smith entered a beauty parlor in Mesa, Arizona, on November 12, 1966, forcing at gunpoint five women and two children to lie on the floor, forming the spokes of a wheel. He shot all seven to death, then walked outside into the arms of the police, telling them he "wanted to be known." When Richard Speck heard of this mass slaying, the multiple murderer said: "Boy, I'd like to get my hands on that guy— I'd kill him." Smith was imprisoned for life.

Klaus Gossmann: A cold and calculating murderer, Gossmann lived in Hersbruck, close to Nuremberg, Germany, a student with a high average who thought of himself as a superman. He was enamored of the stories told by his father about how the elder Gossmann, as a German soldier, had shot American GIs during World War II.

At age nineteen in 1960, Gossmann, waiting for the bells to toll at midday to drown out any cries for help, calmly shot two strangers, Ernst Hering and his fiancée, Valeska Eder, when they opened their apartment door to him. Following these murders, Gossmann returned to his studies. Later that day he recorded the double murder in detail.

In 1962, Gossmann, again picking the midday so that his murder would be shielded by the sounds of bells (he came to be known as the "Midday Murderer"), walked into the Deutsches Bank in Ochenbruch, shot Erich Hallbauer, the bank director, and left, taking more than 3,000 marks. In that same year Gossmann robbed another bank, killing a porter.

On March 29, 1963, Gossmann shot down a widow who ran a gun shop in Nuremberg, also killing her son. Three years later he shot and killed a businessman in a department store, also in Nuremberg, but was captured. On the handle of one of his guns, Gossmann had scratched the name Elke. He admitted it was a reference to the actress Elke Sommer, whom he planned to kidnap or kill when she next visited Nuremberg to see her family.

Gossmann received his sentence of life imprisonment without any show of emotion, telling the judge on July 4, 1967: "People are no more than inanimate things to me . . . I am a pragmatist."

Herbert Mullin: In late 1972 and early 1973 Mullin murdered thirteen men, women and teen-age boys. His motives were hazy. A member of the hippie-drug culture set in San Francisco's Haight-Ashbury district, Mullin mumbled something about killing people as a sacrifice to the gods so that major earthquakes would be prevented. He was sent to prison for life in 1973.

Dean Corll, Elmer Henley: Corll, a thirty-three-year-old electrician in Houston, Texas, with the help of teen-agers Elmer Henley and David Brooks, killed twenty-seven young boys over a period of many months, all homosexual killings done to appease Corll's appetite. Henley and Brooks served as procurers of the youths, given five and ten dollars by Corll for each youth brought to him. Corll raped, strangled, then mutilated the youths, burying most of the bodies in a boat shed near his house. On the night of August 8, 1973, Henley shot and killed Corll as the sadist turned on him. Henley was given 594 years in prison. Brooks was sent to prison for life.

John Wayne Gacy: A Chicago area building contractor, John Wayne Gacy preyed upon homosexual whores in the Newberry Library district of the city (a notorious homosexual area known earlier as "Bughouse

Square"), picking up youths and returning with them to his Norwood Park Township home, where he reportedly paid them for sexual favors, then drugged and killed them, burying most of his thirty-two victims in the crawl space beneath his home.

Gacy's mass murders were discovered in late 1978, when local police were investigating the disappearance of some of his victims. Gacy not only confessed the murders but directed police to the areas where the bodies were hidden. He was found guilty and sentenced to death.

THE MANY JACK THE RIPPERS

To this day in the East End of London, England, schoolchildren can be heard chanting:

> *Jack the Ripper's dead,*
> *And lying on his bed.*
> *He cut his throat*
> *With Sunlight Soap.*
> *Jack the Ripper's dead.*

Jack's death, however, has long baffled sleuths the world over. His identity has been a subject of controversy to the present.

The notorious killer began his slaughter of prostitutes in the slums of Whitechapel on August 31, 1888, and continued until November 9 of that year. During the period, five prostitutes were definitely killed by Jack.

The killer was a megalomaniac, delighting in not only sending missives to inspectors about his murders, but telling authorities in advance of the killings he would commit.

True to style, Jack the Ripper vanished as abruptly as he had appeared. And strangely, the quest for his identity has intensified with each passing decade.

Suspects during that gaslight era were seemingly endless. A strong argument was made for a deranged doctor M. J. Druitt, who disappeared shortly after the last killings and who was found a suicide victim a month later floating in the Thames River. Druitt was undoubtedly sexually insane, and his own family believed him to be the Ripper.

Other maniacs were said to be the killer. A man named Kominski, who hated prostitutes and displayed strong homicidal tendencies, was nominated. So was a Russian doctor, Michael Ostrog. (Doctors were favorite candidates due to the Ripper's obvious surgical talents.) Both Kominski and Ostrog were sent to lunatic asylums.

A notorious sexual sadist, Thomas Cutbush, and a poisoner of some note, George Chapman, were also strong suspects. They, along with sev-

eral other persons, however, were eventually dismissed as Ripper nominees.

As late as 1970, a strong case was made by an academic writer against Edward, the Duke of Clarence. Edward was Queen Victoria's grandson and an heir to the throne of England. Another "expert" proposed that Edward's tutor, Cambridge-educated J. K. Stephen, was the likely killer.

Some people have said Jack might have been a woman (a Jackie?). Sir Arthur Conan Doyle, who created the fictional Sherlock Holmes, suggested the murderer was an unhinged midwife. He based his idea on the killer's knowledge of anatomy and skill in dissecting the victims.

At first glance at this puzzling case, one of the most likely selections for the Ripper role appeared to be the bragging killer Dr. Thomas Neill Cream. After obtaining his medical degree from McGill University, Cream moved to Chicago, Illinois, to practice a weird brand of medicine. He poisoned a patient named Stott in 1881 while having an affair with the victim's young wife.

Cream was sent to the Illinois State Prison at Joliet on a second-degree murder charge, but officials there later released him on the grounds he had been "rehabilitated." Returning to London, Cream began to poison prostitutes in 1891, killing several before being apprehended, convicted and hanged on November 15, 1892.

It is known, however, that Cream could not have committed the Ripper slayings since he was imprisoned in Joliet at the time of those slayings. After an earlier arrest on bigamy charges, Cream claimed that he was in an Australian prison during the time of his alleged illegal marriage and he was released on information to that effect from Australian prison officials.

According to some theories, there were actually two Thomas Neill Creams, and one of them was the likeliest Ripper. As one official put it, "Neill Cream had a double in the underworld and they went by the same name and used each other's terms of imprisonment as alibis for each other."

It is quite possible, argue some theorists, that while one Neill Cream was serving his life sentence in Joliet, the other Cream was slaughtering women in Whitechapel. The erstwhile doppelgänger had provided Cream with an alibi on the bigamy charge. Cream, at the moment of death on the scaffold, attempted to repay the debt to his dedicated double. His last baffling words, heard by the hangman, were shouted just as the trap was sprung:

"I am Jack—"

UNSOLVED: THE PUBLIC MURDER OF JOSEPH ELWELL

Of all the unsolved murders on the New York Police Department's books, no case nags the homicide division as doggedly as the strange demise of Joseph P. Elwell, a millionaire, ladies' man, horse owner and card wizard. In addition to baffling sleuths and criminal historians alike, his slaying was one of the most public crimes in the annals of murder.

As a young man, Elwell was a genius with pasteboards. Elwell also was lucky in love, marrying wealthy Helen Darby in 1904. This patient lady took great pains not only to teach Joe table manners and polish, but ghosted two books for him, *Elwell on Bridge,* and *Elwell's Advanced Bridge.* The books sold in the millions, making the cardsman famous across the country. Bridge table arguments were universally settled with "Elwell says . . ."

With the fame came more money than Elwell ever imagined he could earn from occasional lectures and lessons. He lavished himself with comfort, purchasing five autos, a twenty-racehorse stable in Kentucky and mansions in Palm Beach, Saratoga and Manhattan. There were also women, phalanxes of showgirls with whom Elwell dallied.

His wife suffered through Elwell's pulchritudinous pleasures for ten years before leaving him. The playboy shrugged his indifference to this loss and retired to his yacht with an entire chorus line to celebrate.

Dapper, handsome, with wavy hair and pearly teeth, Elwell at forty-five was at the zenith of life. Yet an unknown enemy had marked him for death.

On the night of June 10, 1920, the card genius dined at the Ritz with Mr. and Mrs. Walter Lewisohn and Viola Kraus, whose divorce decree had been granted that day. Ironically, Miss Kraus's ex-husband, Victor von Schlegell, dined at the next table with an elegant lady named Emily Anderson. Elwell and his party adjourned to the New Amsterdam Roof to enjoy a frothy musical entitled *Midnight Frolic*. By 2 A.M., Elwell went home alone to his mansion at 244 W. Seventieth Street.

Miss Kraus called at two-thirty to apologize for a small misunderstanding but Elwell didn't mind. He was an insomniac and spent most nights wandering about his mansion. This night was no exception. Worried about some of his horses, the millionaire called his trainer in Far Rockaway. He also placed a call at 6 A.M. to somebody in Garden City.

The milkman arrived at Elwell's place at 6:30 A.M. and deposited two bottles. These were gone an hour later when the postman left mail, indicating to sleuths later that Elwell never went to bed that last dawn of his life.

A little after 8 A.M., Mrs. Marie Larsen, Elwell's housekeeper, arrived to find the front door ajar. She stepped inside, took one look into the living room and screamed for the police.

What Mrs. Larsen saw was a mystery to her. An old man she had never seen before sat slumped in a chair. He was bald, toothless and blood trickled from an ugly bullet hole in the middle of his forehead as he breathed his last. An hour later, Mrs. Larsen learned the victim had died in a hospital and that he had been none other than her employer, Joseph P. Elwell.

In no time, the press discovered Elwell had kept his lost youth a desperately guarded secret. He had forty wigs combed and waiting in a secret closet, along with several sets of teeth. More devastating was a secret file kept by Elwell which newsmen subsequently dubbed "a love index"—hundreds of names and addresses of ravishing females.

None of the women proved to be likely suspects, though. All ardently claimed they were bridge pupils.

Elwell's murder baffled police all the more because it was so public. His front door was open and his shades were raised. Since Elwell was found with a letter delivered that morning in his hand, it was concluded the killer entered the mansion after the postman's stop at seven-thirty and before Mrs. Larsen's arrival at eight.

During that period, the street outside was bustling with thousands of passersby. If only one had looked up and into Elwell's window, he would have certainly seen the killer send a .45 slug into the millionaire's head. (The heavy caliber weapon, police contended, ruled out a female slayer.) But no witness was ever found.

UNSOLVED—THE MURDER THAT KILLED HOLLYWOOD CAREERS

One of the oddest unsolved murders in America was that of movie director William Desmond Taylor, who was found in his Hollywood, California, bungalow February 2, 1922, with a bullet in his heart. The death of Taylor, who had earned more than $100,000 a year for Famous Players-Lasky Studio, brought down a scandal that made the Fatty Arbuckle case look like a low-life melodrama in comparison.

The murder involved the most revered female stars in Hollywood—Mary Pickford, Mary Miles Minter and Mabel Normand. When detectives investigated Taylor's residence, they found astonishing keepsakes abounding. There was a photo of Pickford occupying a special place in the house. Although "America's Sweetheart" knew nothing of the killing, her name was linked to the strange case for months.

Normand, the brightest star in Mack Sennett's comedy films, did not fare as well as Pickford—she was the last person to see Taylor alive. The actress told police she had dropped by to see the director about seven o'clock on the night of the murder. What occupied their time? Oh, they talked about Normand's next picture, good books and the actress' French lessons.

Normand insisted that Taylor had escorted her to her car at 9 P.M. She illustrated the director's thoughtfulness by telling police that Taylor spotted some trashy magazines in the auto, chided her about her reading habits and then raced inside the bungalow to return with a book by Sigmund Freud.

Detectives ransacked Hollywood for clues leading to Taylor's killer, but found nothing. This did not, however, prevent a bevy of women's groups from loudly lobbying for Normand's scalp. The actress was all but ruined by the murder. Her following in the films dwindled and two years later she was involved in another scandal and that closed her career. Her chauffeur shot another man in a dispute over her favors. She was then named as a corespondent in a divorce action. Hounded from Hollywood, Normand was spared further trouble when she died of tuberculosis in 1930.

One who was not spared at all was actress Mary Miles Minter, whose

love for Taylor apparently transcended the grave. Police found her perfume-scented stationery bedecked with gushing love messages fluttering from the pages of Taylor's books.

In one letter, Minter's fans learned that the actress was nothing less than tempestuous, the note ending with "I love you—I love you—I love you . . . XXXXXXXX." The last X in the row was two inches high so that Taylor would not miss Mary's point.

Minter did not deny her ardor for the slain director. "I did love William Desmond Taylor," she told detectives. "I loved him deeply and tenderly, with all the admiration a young girl gives a man with the poise and position of Mr. Taylor."

Minter proved her feelings at Taylor's funeral. At the height of the ceremonies, the actress swept onto the scene, dashed to the open coffin and tenderly kissed the corpse.

She later told reporters that Taylor had whispered from death as she kissed him, saying something like, "I shall love you always, Mary." The tabloids went berserk with that story as women's clubs and religious groups tore apart the career of the naïve Minter.

Police never closed the case, which became more and more bizarre as the months passed. It seemed that an army of attractive females were enamored with Taylor, but none were selected as suspects.

All that really mattered was that Taylor was very much dead and his slayer was never found. One movie mogul summed up the entire affair with one sentence:

"That case was one of the greatest scripts ever produced in Hollywood."

MURDER UNSOLVED

It will come as no surprise to any law enforcement official to learn that most murder cases are never solved. The public is less conscious of this grim fact as it is told how Karen Kupcinet (actress daughter of Irv Kupcinet, Chicago columnist) dies mysteriously in the seedy center of California's movie colony, how actor Bob Crane is battered lifeless, the headlines evaporating to back-page stories of police dilemma, no suspects, then silence.

In a given year as much as 80 per cent of the murders committed across the country go unsolved, the killer or killers still free and dwelling among us. It has been so, lamentably, throughout history.

Here are some of the most notable unsolved murders since the records were begun:

Amy Robsart, September 8, 1560: Amy, the beautiful daughter of the wealthy knight Sir John Robsart of Norfolk, was married on June 4, 1550, at age eighteen, to Sir Robert Dudley, later Earl of Leicester, who was only one year older than she. Dudley was much hated at court; a born intriguer, he became Queen Elizabeth's lover and remained so for eight years. The queen intended Dudley to be her prince consort but his wife, Countess Amy, stood in the way of the marriage. This auburn-haired, fair-complected, one-wife-too-many was eliminated on September 8, 1560, when she was found dead, her spine snapped, her skull fractured, at the foot of the stairs in her manor place, Cumnor House, remotely situated in Oxfordshire.

It was blatantly obvious to all investigating the matter that Amy did not die accidentally, as the bribed coroner and his carefully selected jury later decreed. Such a fate was near impossible; the Elizabethan staircases of the day were wide and low-treaded. The twenty-eight-year-old victim was in excellent health. Mysteriously, on the day of her death, all the servants at Cumnor House had been dismissed and the guests were highly suspect. Queen Elizabeth had been so bold as to utter prior knowledge of the murder, informing the Spanish ambassador Álvarez de Quadra, the bishop of Aquila, of Amy's death on September 3, 1560, five days before her actual end came.

The killing, later attributed to Dudley's servant, Richard Verney, and another henchman, aroused so much furor at court that Elizabeth thought to quash the scandal by publicly discarding Dudley, though he was to receive handsome lands and titles from her in the coming decades. (Verney was also rewarded, being made a knight.)

Christopher Marlowe, May 30, 1593: The twenty-nine-year-old playwright was dining in Eleanor Bulls's tavern in Deptford, later a London suburb, when he became involved in a violent argument with his three companions, Nicholas Skeres, Ingram Frizer and Robert Poley. After consuming much drink, Marlowe, according to the three others present, inexplicably lunged for Frizer's dagger, cutting him on the head. Frizer tore the weapon from Marlowe's grasp and then drove it into the writer's head, killing him with one wound above the eye. The claim of Frizer, Skeres and Poley of self-defense was accepted, but the murder of Marlowe was never fully solved, if, indeed, it was Marlowe who was killed in the first place.

Many later claimed that Marlowe had been killed by Frizer over Marlowe's homosexual advances. Another theory is that Frizer was under orders from his master, Sir Thomas Walsingham, to get rid of his lover Marlowe, having tired of him and preferring Frizer as the poet's replacement. The most astounding story has it that the entire affair was a plot designed to allow Marlowe to effect a permanent escape to the Continent. (Shades of the motion picture *Bullitt*.)

Marlowe had recently been arrested and imprisoned for atheist attitudes, an Elizabethan offense that could have resulted in his execution. When he was released on bail, it was thought, his "murder" was contrived by his sponsor and lover Walsingham. Another body was substituted and Marlowe sailed for France, where he lived comfortably and wrote the plays later attributed to Shakespeare. For the investigative mind, this claim may not be unthinkable.

William Shakespeare of Stratford was a businessman and actor who was never known in his own town to have been a writer. His parents, as well as his children, were illiterate and there is every reason to believe he was barely beyond that intellectual state. None of his manuscripts or copies of his plays survive and none are mentioned in Shakespeare's will.

It is conceivable that Marlowe did write the Immortal Bard's plays; Shakespeare's first publication, *Venus and Adonis,* appeared four months *after* Marlowe's alleged murder. Most Shakespearean experts agree that his plays are so like Marlowe as to be Marlowe's, and Thomas Corwin Meadenhall, the foremost authority on "thumb prints" (an early-day identification system in which writers were identified by the frequency of letters and words they used), reported that Marlowe's and Shakespeare's work were one and the same.

The theory was advanced that Shakespeare secretly sold the use of his name to guise the brilliant work of Marlowe, a not uncommon practice in that era.

Sir Edmund Berry Godfrey, October 12, 1678: A well-respected,

fair-minded magistrate, Godfrey, weeks before his strange murder, had
been plagued by a virulent anti-Catholic gadfly, Titus Oates, who claimed
that all England was afoot with a popish plot to seize the government, kill
King Charles II and re-establish the Catholic Church, which had been os-
tracized by Henry VIII, he of the many wives. Such anti-Catholic scan-
dalmongering was not new in England; Catholics were energetically per-
secuted—none could hold office or even enter London, except vital
tradesmen. (Such a climate had forced Charles II to become a Catholic in
secret.)

Godfrey was not at all receptive to the wild claims of ex-Jesuit priest
Oates, claiming Oates had perjured himself in identifying high-stationed
persons as part of the so-called Catholic plot. Godfrey had even stated his
fear of being killed one night on a London street. Upon leaving his home
on Hartshorn Lane on the night of October 12, Godfrey vanished. His
body was found the following week in a ditch at Primrose Hill. He had
been strangled, his neck broken and a sword blade had been run through
his body. A man named Miles Praunce soon confessed under torture, saying that Godfrey had been murdered by three servants, all secret Catholics, Robert Green, Henry Berry and Lawrence Hill.

With Titus Oates screaming for their heads, a kangaroo court soon sent
the hapless trio to the chopping block. A bloody persecution of Catholics
followed. It was later discovered that Oates and others had created the
murder of Godfrey to make it appear that the Catholic plot was real. The
magistrate's true killers were never apprehended (although a few gifted
historians have pointed to the alcoholic, sadistic Earl of Pembroke, who
once stamped a man to death and was convicted of manslaughter before
Magistrate Godfrey, an all too willing and revengeful pawn of the conniving Oates).

Oates did pay the penalty for his slander. After boldly accusing the
queen of plotting to murder her husband, Charles, on the Pope's behalf,
the vicious Oates was convicted of libel, and sent to prison for life, with
regular whippings while tied to a cart-tail as part of his official punishment.

Sellis, manservant to the Duke of Cumberland, May 31, 1810: The
red brick St. James's Palace in London, then the residence of the strange
Duke of Cumberland, echoed screams and scampering feet at three
o'clock in the morning, Thursday, May 31, 1810. The duke had appeared
in a hallway, severely cut about the head and chest, bleeding through a
nightshirt and shouting the alarm.

The duke called for Sellis, one of three valets attending him; servants
ran to the valet's room but found the door locked and were forced to
break it down. Sellis was found lying in bed, covered with blood, his body
slashed to ribbons, his throat cut.

An inquest and subsequent investigation left the obvious murder unsolved, the case concluded with the theory that Sellis had inexplicably attacked his master and then committed suicide. Discrepancies were rampant. The valet could not have caused many of the wounds found on his body, especially the knife cuts on his back. Further, the Duke of Cumberland, George III's quirkish son, was himself suspect, a pariah at court due to his sadistic temper, his ugly countenance (he was near blind, with one eye that rolled uncontrollably), and his notorious sex affairs.

Not until 1832 was more light shed upon this haunting murder. At that time Josiah Phillipps, publisher of the *Satirist,* printed an article in which it was alleged that the duke and his vallet Neale had murdered Sellis and then made it appear that Sellis had attempted to kill the duke, all because Sellis intended to make public the homosexual affair between the duke and Neale.

For his efforts, Phillipps was charged with slander by the duke and was given a prison sentence. The Sellis killing to this day haunts British royalty.

Mary Ashford, May 27, 1817: The death by drowning of attractive twenty-year-old Mary Ashford is a hallmark case of unsolved murder in England. Mary was a resident of Erdington (near Birmingham, England) who attended a dance on May 27 in the company of a friend, Hannah Cox. The Ashford girl was much in demand at the dance, especially by Abraham Thornton, who confided to a friend during the festivities that he "would have her" before the night was out. Thornton and Mary left the dance at midnight. The girl returned to Hannah Cox's house at 4 A.M., changing back into her regular clothes, and departed for home carrying her dance frock, appearing happy. An hour and a half later a man discovered Mary's bonnet, neatly folded dress and shoes at the edge of a pond, which was immediately dragged; her body was quickly recovered.

Thornton was the only suspect in the case and was brought to trial with dispatch. He not only admitted being with Mary Ashford until 4 A.M., but that he had, indeed, seduced her, which explained the large amount of blood covering her skirt and stockings, she being a virgin. He insisted, however, that he did not murder the girl (he was not charged with rape as it could not be determined whether or not Mary had voluntarily submitted to Thornton).

Thornton was seen walking home some miles from the pond at about the time Mary was murdered—if she had not fallen into the pond and drowned accidentally—and there was no direct evidence to link him with the girl's death. He was acquitted by a jury in a six-minute deliberation. Thornton was not yet out of danger. Mary's brother demanded an "appeal of murder," lobbying the courts to try Thornton a second time, the law of double jeopardy not then a reality. As Thornton was once more brought before the court, the judge intoned: "Are you guilty or not guilty?"

Thornton drew himself up with rage and shouted: "Not guilty, and I

Abraham Thornton in the dock at his trial, claiming the "wager of battle" to prove his innocence.

am ready to defend the same with my body." With that, he held a buckskin glove over one hand and threw its mate to the feet of Mary's brother, challenging his accuser to a duel to the death. The brother was restrained from retrieving the glove. Thornton was judged not guilty for a second time.

As for Mary Ashford's questionable demise, the drowning is debated by mystery aficionados to this day.

Mary Rogers, July 28, 1841: Known as the "Beautiful Cigar Girl," Mary Cecilia Rogers, who worked the counter at John Anderson's cigar stand at 319 Broadway in New York City, was a stunning twenty-two-year-old who captured the heart of every customer, including such famous writers as James Fenimore Cooper, Washington Irving and Edgar Allan Poe (who was later to write the first thriller ever published based on Mary Rogers).

Mary appeared a proper lady to one and all. She was engaged to Daniel Payne, a roomer at her mother's boardinghouse on Nassau Street. She was last seen on July 25, 1841, talking to Payne, telling him that she was going to visit an aunt and to pick her up on Jane Street at 6 P.M. When

Payne arrived, Mary was not with her aunt; she was nowhere to be found. For three days an intensive but futile search was conducted. Then, on July 28, three fishermen plucked the girl's body from the Hudson River. She had been strangled to death with a piece of her own petticoat.

Police investigators unearthed nothing in the case. It was discovered that Mary had many lovers beside Payne, but all were cleared. This mystery remains baffling today, even though later evidence pointed to a secret lover, a naval officer who later became an admiral. It was theorized that this socially prominent officer discovered that Mary was pregnant and murdered her rather than face disgrace; he was, however, cleared by police.

Carpetbag Mystery, 1857: Similar to the gruesome discovery by Manhattan fishermen in the Rogers case was the startling find of two youths rowing on the Thames in 1857. The boys spotted a carpetbag on one of the abutments of Waterloo Bridge (coincidentally near the spot where young Eliza Grimwood was slain in the 1840s after being seen with a mysterious stranger, her murder never solved).

Retrieving the bag, the boys opened it and fell back in horror; it contained fragments of a human body and bloodstained garments that appeared to have been slashed with a dagger. Scotland Yard worked feverishly on the case for years and then gave up. They could not identify the body fragments, let alone the possible killer.

A neat little fairy tale relating to the Carpetbag Mystery was concocted years later by Sir Robert Anderson, Assistant Commissioner of the Metropolitan Police. He wrote in *Blackwood's Magazine* that the body fragments belonged to an Italian spy who had been identified and murdered by confederates fearing they would be linked to his secret affairs.

The most probable explanation dealt with a man named Butterfield, who wrote penny dreadful stories for the newspapers. It was thought that the pulp writer prepared the bag himself, from morgue leavings, in order to write about the awful discovery. Said one acquaintance of Butterfield's: "He was the most audacious and enterprising penny-a-liner of his day . . . an impudent boaster of his exploits . . . truth was not familiar with him."

Scotland Yard, however, believed strongly that the Carpetbag Mystery was not a hoax, for its files on this inexplicable murder are marked "unsolved" to this day.

Dr. Harvey Burdell, January 29, 1857: Wealthy Dr. Burdell was slain in the middle of a word moments after he entered his mansion at 31 Bond Street, New York City. The forty-six-year-old Burdell, a tall, heavyset man, was seen by no less than four persons to enter his building at about a quarter to eleven that night. Wearing a shawl over his shoulders, the doctor was observed by a man named Ross to walk up the stairs, unlock the front door and enter.

Mrs. Cunningham, the likeliest suspect in the Dr. Burdell murder. (*Harper's Weekly*)

The ubiquitous John L. Eckel of the Burdell mystery. (*Harper's Weekly*)

Ross kept walking. "When I got about a house and a half or two houses on," Ross later told police, "I heard the cry of 'Murd—' short like that, the word wasn't finished."

Another man, named Strangman, also walking on Bond Street, heard the cry, "loud . . . like that of a person in agony." And across the street at Number 36 dwelled the neighborhood snoop, Mr. Brooks. "The first syllable *Mur* was distinct," he later reported, "but the *der* was prolonged and guttural . . . I was going to bed . . . I instantly sprang on a chest of drawers and through the venetian blinds which were shut I could distinctly see the house [No. 31] . . . I looked up the street to see if garotters were around; I saw nothing further."

Another man, named Farrell, was sitting on a stoop some doors away; he, too, heard the cry. Police answering the alarm found Dr. Burdell in his first-floor single room, his horribly disfigured body in the proverbial pool of blood. He had been knifed fifteen times, several wounds in the heart. The killer made sure of his prey by also strangling him. There was

The opening of Mrs. Cunningham's trial. (*Harper's Weekly*)

no murder weapon and no signs of forced entry into the house, which was heavily locked. No money or valuables were taken, and no one was seen to flee by the witnesses strolling on Bond Street.

Utterly baffled, the police turned their suspicions to those occupying rooms which Burdell rented in his mansion. (He was much disliked, a miser, mean-tempered and taciturn, working as a dentist in a single room where he also slept on the couch, eating his meals out in cheap restaurants.) The doctor's Irish maid was not present at the time and all other roomers had acceptable alibis.

However, a Mrs. Cunningham, who lived on the second floor with her two daughters, some weeks later claimed to be Burdell's secret wife, filing for a sizable inheritance. She claimed that the odd Burdell had married her wearing false whiskers. After weeks of investigation, police learned that Mrs. Cunningham did marry a man in such a disguise but that the imposter was probably John L. Eckel, a butcher who also roomed in Burdell's spacious house. Eckel, it was assumed, disguised himself so that Mrs. Cunningham could later claim her strange-looking groom was the quirkish Burdell, who was then murdered by the scheming pair for an inheritance he never bequeathed. Mrs. Cunningham was arrested and tried but she was freed for lack of evidence. Determined, she pressed for the inheritance, borrowing an infant and attempting to pass the child off as Burdell's offspring. She was imprisoned briefly for this fraud. The child and her real mother became an instant hit at Barnum's Museum, where they were put up as living exhibits, a farcical show undoubtedly enjoyed by Dr. Burdell's real killer, who was never apprehended.

Benjamin Nathan, July 29, 1870: An almost identical mystery to that of Burdell was the killing of Wall Street broker Benjamin Nathan, murdered in his West Twenty-third Street mansion a little after midnight on July 29, 1870. Nathan, worth a fortune, was found battered to death by an iron bar found inside the entrance of his house. His sons Frederick and Washington were the only other persons in the house, discovering the body the next morning. They were cleared of suspicion. Though Nathan's small safe had been opened with keys taken from his night-robe, only a few household dollars were taken. Police labeled the case unsolved, even though a notorious burglar, John T. Irving, later "confessed" that he and others broke into the house and a man named "Kelly" killed Nathan. Irving was serving a long prison term at the time of his revelation. His story (later dismissed) was obviously concocted to effect his release, the tactic of myriad convicts.

James Maybrick, May 11, 1889: Another real whodunit rocked England almost twenty years later when James Maybrick, a Liverpool cotton broker, died on May 11, 1889. It was quickly asserted that his wife, the former Florence Chandler, an American southern belle, had poisoned him

Wealthy New York businessman Benjamin Nathan, whose mysterious murder in 1870 remains unsolved to this day. (*Leslie's Weekly*)

with arsenic, which was found in great quantities about his mansion. Though it was later determined that Maybrick's cause of death was gastroenteritis, and that he was a chronic arsenic-eater (to flavor his food), Mrs. Maybrick was sentenced to be hanged on the flimsiest of evidence. Her sentence was later commuted to life; she served fifteen years and was released in 1904, thanks largely to the persistent efforts of her lawyer, the brilliant Sir Charles Russell.

As for Mr. Maybrick, arsenic-eater, his end is still labeled as murder by English police, the case yet unsolved, irrespective of the nagging question: Was Maybrick murdered? That is one query not politely entertained in Liverpool drawing rooms to this day.

Marion Gilchrist, December 21, 1908: An eighty-three-year-old spinster, Miss Gilchrist was found in her Glasgow, Scotland, flat, her head battered faceless. Her maid, Helen Lambie, and a downstairs neighbor, Arthur Montague Adams, entered the flat to see a well-dressed man casually emerge from a spare room, leave the flat and race down the stairs. They later identified, with police coaching, one Oscar Slater (real name Leschzinger) as the escaping man. Slater was convicted of killing Miss Gilchrist and sentenced to hang on May 27, 1909, but was reprieved two days before the execution, his sentence commuted to a life term.

Slater would have, no doubt, died in prison had it not been for the tireless efforts of Sir Arthur Conan Doyle, the creator of Sherlock Holmes, who, after studying the case, realized Slater had been wrongly identified and imprisoned. Doyle's battle with Scottish authorities raged until 1928, when he managed to have Slater retried; he was found innocent and given a 6,000-pound payment by the crown (he lived until 1948, dying at age seventy-five). Miss Gilchrist's cool-minded killer was never found.

Annie Bella Wright, July 5, 1919: While riding her bicycle on a visit to the hamlet of Gaulby, near Leicester, England, twenty-one-year-old Annie Bella Wright was shot through the head. A mysterious young man seen to accompany Miss Wright was sought as the murderer for six months, parts of his green bicycle accidentally fished from the Leicester canal six months later, traced to a Cheltenham mathematics teacher, Ronald Vivian Light.

The wounded World War I veteran at first denied ever meeting Miss Wright on her bicycle trip, that he owned a green bicycle and that he had been in the Gaulby district at the time. Charged and brought to trial, he then reversed himself and admitted all, saying he tried to destroy his bicycle out of fear when reading of the murder. He was acquitted. Miss Wright's killer was never apprehended, her death theorized by some to have been caused by a stray bullet from the gun of a hunter.

Father Hubert Dahme, February 4, 1924: One of the most sensational murders in America occurred on Main Street, Bridgeport, Connecticut, just before 8 P.M. when elderly Rev. Hubert Dahme was approached by a young man and shot in front of several witnesses. His murder was later attributed to one Harold Israel, a jobless drifter who, after intense police grilling and the shaky identification of several witnesses, confessed.

In a step-by-step examination of the killing, State's Attorney Homer Cummings, who had been appointed to prosecute Israel, proved the man innocent, and that Israel's confession had been blurted out of hunger and exhaustion. (Cummings' conscionable conduct later resulted in his being appointed U. S. Attorney General, the youngest at that time ever to hold the office, by President Roosevelt.) Israel was freed; Father Dahme's bold killer was never apprehended, many critics insisting that the police should have investigated malcontents in the priest's congregation, rather than yielding to public pressure in arresting too obvious a suspect.

Patrolman Frank Lundy, December 9, 1932: When Chicago police officer Lundy, whose beat was the notorious stockyard district, entered a seedy restaurant-speakeasy, he interrupted two holdup men and was shot to death. One of his killers was, on shabby testimony, named as Joseph Majczek, a machinist living nearby. He was sent to prison for ninety-nine years in 1933. Not until his scrubwoman mother took out a newspaper ad, on October 10, 1944, offering a $5,000 reward for the real cop-killer, was new interest shown in the case. A conscientious reporter, James McGuire of the *Sun,* through agonizing months of research, exposed the Majczek conviction as a farce; the machinist was released, but Lundy's killer was never found.

Elizabeth Short, January 15, 1947: The twenty-two-year-old Hollywood drifter known later to the world as "The Black Dahlia," was viciously murdered and bisected at the waist in an open Los Angeles field on South Norton Avenue, near Thirty-ninth Street, a killing so brutal, so senseless that it shocked L.A. police and stunned the nation. More than fifty persons, from limelight-seeking crackpots to genuinely disturbed individuals, have "confessed" to the horrid crime since 1947; to this day they are still swinging through precinct doors to make the lurid claim. Yet no positive suspects or clues ever emerged and the Dahlia's killer—who even had the audacity to send her personal belongings to police—was never pinpointed, perhaps living still in the "golden" state.

Undaunted, police are ever optimistic, no matter how many years intervene, in ultimately discovering long-sought killers, from San Francisco's "Zodiac" slayer to the Michigan child-killer of recent times. With L.A. Police Sergeant Harry Leslie Hansen, who stayed with the Dahlia case for decades, it's a matter of patience. "Unsolved murders have a way of clearing themselves up," he stated recently, "if you wait long enough and keep your files up-to-date."

THE LEGEND OF A ONE-ARMED MURDERER

Seeking to pacify their restless slaves, plantation owners dwelling about New Orleans turned run-down Circus Square into a once-a-week (4–6 P.M.) gathering place for their wretched, living chatel. Blacks danced wildly here from 1817 to the Civil War every Sunday, gyrating to the beat of the calinda, a derivative of a voodoo stomp, and the bamboula, a tribal African rite. One of the greatest dancers in Circus Square—renamed Congo Square for obvious reasons—was the giant, massive Bras Coupé, who would become one of the most feared outlaws ever to murder his way through New Orleans and down the Natchez Trace.

Bras Coupé, who was then known as Squier, was at least six foot six, bone-hard and the loudest, highest-jumping dancer who ever shouted "Badoum! Badoum!" in Congo Square. (It was said that he was the first to affix small bells to his ankles when stomping the bamboula.) He was owned by an extremely tolerant plantation master, General William de Buys, who coddled his prize Negro with education and free time, rare acts in that oppressive Deep South era which did not endear the general to his white peers. (No doubt, Bras Coupé served as a model for Rau-Ru in Robert Penn Warren's *Band of Angels*.)

De Buys taught Squier how to shoot, loaned him his rifle and encouraged him to hunt alone through the forests about New Orleans. He became an expert marksman with both hands, telling friends that he once dreamed of losing an arm and knew he would need the other. This is exactly what occurred in 1834, when several whites, thinking him a runaway, wounded him in the arm as he stalked game in a swamp. The arm was amputated.

The loss of his arm embittered Bras Coupé and he began running away. When he was caught several times, General de Buys refused to have him whipped, relying upon grandfatherly sermons to alter Squier's errant ways. The troubled Negro only shrugged and then fled permanently into the swamps, where he organized a band of outlaws and adopted the sobriquet Bras Coupé (he was also then known as the Brigand of the Swamp).

For three years, Bras Coupé and his renegades, whose number included some white criminals, led sallies into New Orleans' thickly residential districts, robbing and murdering—the count varies between thirty and fifty deaths—until driven back into the swamps by armies of vigilantes. He would then reappear in small villages along the Natchez Trace, terrorizing and robbing the inhabitants. He became the most famous black outlaw in the United States. (Nat Turner had already been captured and hanged for his slayings in 1831.)

To the whites of New Orleans, Bras Coupé's mere name served to chastise unruly children—"You'll be trimmed by Bras Coupé unless you behave"—much the same way the names of Jesse James and John Dillinger were later employed by frustrated parents.

For the blacks, Bras Coupé, outlaw or not, became a folk hero about whom elaborate tales of invincibility were woven. No bullets could penetrate his skin, it was said. He could not burn since he coated his magnificent body with herbs, it was told. Creoles related how detachments of soldiers vanished in mystical fogs when in pursuit of the outlaw. He could also wither and kill anyone with his stony stare. Hunters recalled that, at night, deep in the swamps, they heard his booming laughter; one said he watched the murderer in his camp devour the flesh of four soldiers whom he had killed with his bare hands after they had attempted to capture him.

Mayor of New Orleans Dennis Prieur placed a $2,000 reward for the capture (dead) of Bras Coupé in 1837, following several bombastic newspaper editorials denouncing the government's inability to cope with the brigand. The New Orleans *Picayune* was to describe him as a "Semi-devil and a fiend in human shape whose life was one of crime and depravity."

The legend came to an end on July 18, 1837, when Francisco Garcia, a fisherman, sat angling in a boat in the Bayou St. John. Bras Coupé saw him and fired at him, missing. Garcia went ashore, he later claimed, and attacked the large outlaw, who was weak from a wound he had received on April 6, 1837, from two bounty hunters. Using a club, Garcia beat out Bras Coupé's brains, then wrapped his body in sacks and took it by cart to New Orleans to claim the reward. (Another account states that Garcia invited the desperate outlaw to sleep in his hut while he was on the run and then murdered him as he slumbered.)

After traversing the streets of New Orleans with his grisly cargo, viewed by thousands of wailing, weeping slaves, Garcia stopped before City Hall, raced inside and demanded the $2,000 from Mayor Prieur. They haggled and Garcia went away with $250.

Bras Coupé's shattered body was displayed for several days on the water fountain at the Place d'Armes, a fate similar to that which would befall the remains of the great Mexican patriot Emiliano Zapata after his betrayal when Zapata's body was exhibited in his native state of Morelos. Ten thousand slaves, some brought a hundred miles by their masters to New Orleans, were force marched past the body, a move to caution all blacks that whites were supreme in the South.

But, like the peasants of Morelos in Mexico who were compelled to stare at the blood-caked corpse of their magnificent leader Zapata, the slaves murmured in their ranks that the body was not that of Bras Coupé. It was the corpse of some other hapless black and the white man lied, as usual. Everyone knew, was noddingly sure, Bras Coupé could not die.

DOCTORS WHO MURDERED

Technically, doctors who murder are almost unbeatable; their word is law with patients and, more than any other type of murderer, the physician is highly trained in administering death, the method invariably used by this type of killer being poisons, although some notable murdering doctors of the past have departed from that technique when carefully laid plans went awry. (Today's medical slayer employs sophisticated drugs and poisons; the traditional "secret deaths" of the past involved morphine, aconite, arsenic, antimony, cyanide and strychnine.)

That doctors do fail at murder can only be attributed to human, not professional, weakness. Only after the murder has been committed does the doctor join the ranks of the common killer, compounding his guilt by the typical suspicious behavior, incriminating remarks and gross errors in judgment as he is hounded by ordinary conscience and fears. It is in this area where the doctor falls prey to his own crime, albeit it is the belief of the author that a greater percentage of physicians do get away with murder than in any other professional group.

Since the earliest of times, poison was the safest murder method, there being no way to detect its presence until the popes authorized pathological dissections in the fifteenth century. Not until 1814 did Matthieu Joseph Orfila, the father of modern toxicology, show how poisons were absorbed and accumulated in certain tissues and could thereby be detected in organs other than the stomach. The medical murderer, however, had the edge for decades as new alkaloids were discovered and subtle murder weapons increased (morphine in 1803, strychnine in 1818, brucine in 1819, codeine in 1832, aconite, 1833, many of these being rediscoveries).

One of the earliest users of morphine as a poison was an avaricious French doctor Edmé Castaing, who, at age twenty-seven, decided to become a millionaire overnight. He learned in 1823 that one of his patients, a wealthy young man named Hippolyte Ballet, had not included his younger brother Auguste in his will. He proposed to Auguste that he eliminate Hippolyte for a handsome fee. Castaing, with the brother's approval, promptly dosed Hippolyte's food; his death was attributed to a strange vegetable poison.

Not content with the large payment from Auguste Ballet, the doctor resolved to snare the entire fortune. First, he insisted that the surviving brother make out a new will naming him as the sole heir. This Ballet did, no doubt at the urging of Castaing's blackmail, certainly not out of gratitude.

Castaing then invited his naïve patient to dine with him at the Blackamoor's Head pub in St. Cloud, near Paris. The doctor ordered mulled wine but told the innkeeper not to bring sugar since he had his own. When the wine was served, Dr. Castaing put in the sugar. Auguste found the wine bitter, then he took ill and was immediately put to bed in a room at the inn.

At 4 A.M. the next morning, the good doctor woke up a chemist, and purchased a packet of morphine. He took this back to the inn and served it to his moaning patient in a glass of milk, which immediately produced vomiting and diarrhea. Local doctors were called at Ballet's insistence but they could do nothing but watch the young man die, a Dr. Pellatan noticing that the pupils of the dead man's eyes were extremely contracted (later determined to be a telltale sign of morphine poisoning).

Suspicion was immediately shed on Castaing when it was learned that he had not only treated Ballet but was his only legatee under his will. He was arrested and tried for the murders of both brothers. He was acquitted of killing Hippolyte since no adequate autopsy revealed poison, but morphine was found in Auguste's body. The doctor was found guilty and was executed, claiming innocence to the last breath. Castaing's undoing was that he relied upon the ignorance of the medical world regarding morphine, but he did not count on Professor Orfila, who testified in the case, revealing his findings through his newly developed toxicology experiments.

In America, Dr. Valorus P. Coolidge attempted to poison a creditor, Edward Matthews, on September 30, 1847, while the man sat sipping brandy in Coolidge's Waterville, Maine, offices. The poison, however, was too slow for the impatient doctor, so Coolidge "thumped" Matthews on the head, dashing out his brains. Incredibly, Coolidge performed, as the town's leading physician, the autopsy on the same man he had murdered. Had it not been for the curiosity of another doctor, who found prussic acid in the dead man's stomach, Coolidge might have succeeded. As it was, Coolidge was sentenced to the gallows, which he escaped by committing suicide, swallowing prussic acid which had been smuggled into his cell.

Harvard-trained Dr. John White Webster was also a physician living beyond his means and beset by creditors, chiefly Dr. George Parkman, a wealthy loan-shark and cranky skinflint. On November 23, 1849, Parkman entered Webster's Boston offices and screamed for his money. Webster's murderous response was not in keeping with tradition. Instead of reaching for the poison, he grabbed a chunk of firewood and bashed in Dr. Parkman's head. He then dissected the corpse and attempted to burn it in his laboratory. A nosy janitor discovered the remains. Webster confessed at his trial before being hanged on August 30, 1850.

Dr. Webster killing his creditor Dr. Parkman in his Harvard laboratory in 1849.

Before going to the gallows, the cherubic-looking Webster did, indeed, turn his thoughts to poison, somehow procuring strychnine, which he gulped from a vial in his cell. The suicide attempt failed. The strain of the trial had caused Webster to develop a nervous stomach, which threw back the poison, thereby bungling the physician's own remedy for the rope.

Of all the medical murderers in the past, Dr. William Palmer of Rugeley, Staffordshire, England, was the most determined in killing for profit. He had no equal in the nineteenth century.

Born to wealth, Palmer was motivated by greed, treachery for its own sake and cruelty for pleasure, yet English authorities considered him sane. Sir James Stephens, who was to pen *The History of the Criminal Law*, remarked of Palmer: "His career supplied one of the proofs of a fact which many kind-hearted people seem to doubt, namely the fact that such a thing as atrocious wickedness is consistent with good education, perfect sanity, and everything in a word which deprives men of all excuse for crime."

William Palmer simply enjoyed crime. Even though his father left him a great fortune of 70,000 pounds, Palmer squandered his inheritance through wild gambling on horses. As an apprentice in a chemical firm, Palmer was found to be stealing money from company coffers and was fired. He went to London and studied to become a doctor in St. Bartholomew's Hospital in 1842. Four years later Palmer reportedly poisoned a man named Abley, drugging his brandy; Abley, Palmer thought, had learned of his affair with Mrs. Abley.

Marrying an heiress, Annie Brooks, Palmer quickly took out insurance policies on her and his own brother. Both died after he poisoned them, leaving him 26,000 pounds, money he used to pay off his bookmaker. So great were Palmer's losses that he began to poison his bookmakers, killing a man named Bladon, to whom he owed 800 pounds, in 1850.

Palmer's next victim was his mother-in-law, whose life was also heavily insured by him. Sometimes the doctor murdered merely for convenience, poisoning one of his children when the youth became a nuisance.

His gambling debts mounting, Palmer sought to eliminate his most pressing debts by killing one of his closest friends, John Parsons Cook, in 1855. Over a period of several days, Palmer administered doses of strychnine to his fellow gambler Cook, who had won a substantial amount at Shrewsbury on a horse named Polestar. During the time he was slowly poisoning his friend, Palmer, by forging Cook's signature, collected his victim's winnings to pay off his gambling debts.

After Cook's death, public suspicion was thrown upon Palmer for the first time; he had blatantly purchased heavy doses of strychnine from a druggist, who later testified that the doctor had asked him: "If I poison a dog with strychnine will there be any traces left in the stomach?" (The druggist had said no, the poison would not be apparent.)

Incredible as it may seem, Palmer, like Dr. Coolidge in America before him, was allowed to assist in the autopsy of his own victim, Cook. He was caught trying to steal the dead man's stomach from the laboratory and later tried to bribe a courier taking the organ to London for analysis to drop the container carrying it. Dr. Alfred Swayne Taylor sealed Dr. Palmer's fate when the poisoner was brought to trial in May 1856. Taylor was one of the first authorities on the symptoms of strychnine poisoning, his testimony positively linking the death of Cook to such poison by pointing out that strychnine would not remain in the stomach but be absorbed by the nervous system. Palmer, with six known victims on his grim list, perhaps a half dozen more murders not proved, was sent to the gallows. He showed no remorse, eating a hearty breakfast and then going wordlessly to the rope on June 14, 1856.

A caricature of Dr. William Palmer, mass poisoner, at the track.

Dr. Edmond de la Pommerais, who settled his debts with murder.

Other notable medical murderers of this era include:

Dr. Edmond de la Pommerais, 1863: Like Palmer, De la Pommerais, a young physician from Orleans who had set up a Paris practice for the aristocracy, was a heavy gambler. To cover his financial ruin, he poisoned his ex-mistress and mother-in-law with digitalin, a vegetable poison, to gain inheritances, for which he was executed.

Dr. Edward William Pritchard, 1865: A vain, flamboyant English physician, Dr. Pritchard, at age thirty-five, though he later insisted he loved her (insisting that the lid of her coffin be lifted so he could kiss her lips), dosed his wife with aconite and antimony, killing her; he also poisoned his mother-in-law, thinking she suspected him. His motive was never made clear but most believe Pritchard, like the megalomaniacs Loeb and Leopold after him, committed the murders to prove that he could get away with them. He didn't. On the night before he went to the scaffold, Pritchard confessed to both murders. When asked why he murdered, he only smiled.

Dr. Edward Pritchard.

Dr. Alfred Warder, 1866: Warder, an esteemed British lecturer and physician, was a much marrying man, wedding three times and losing his wives under suspicious circumstances. The death of his third spouse, Ellen Vivian Warder, caused authorities to examine the body. Again the noted toxicologist Dr. Alfred Taylor diagnosed death by poisoning; Warder had given his wife small doses of aconite over a prolonged period. The killer escaped the gallows by swallowing prussic acid in his home just before the police came to arrest him.

Dr. Thomas Neill Cream, 1881–92: The latter part of the nineteenth century was crowded with medical murderers, it seemed, beginning with Dr. Neill Cream, a Scottish-born, American-raised creature who dosed a half dozen women to death on a transcontinental basis, from 1881 to 1892. Cream's first victims were in Canada and Chicago, women he butchered in horrible abortions.

He was convicted of murdering one Daniel Stott, a Chicago area man; Cream was having an affair with Stott's wife, Julia, when he dosed the epileptic Stott's medicine with strychnine. He was sent to Joliet prison in Illinois, where he remained until his life sentence was commuted in 1891.

Cream lost no time in traveling to London, where, following the bloody footsteps of Jack the Ripper four years before him, he proceeded to poison four prostitutes over the course of a year. Cream was hanged for his diabolical murders, puzzling the world with his last words. A moment before he shot through the gallows trap, he yelled: "I am Jack—" The rope cut off his claim of being the Ripper, an impossible one at that since Cream was inside Joliet's walls when the Whitechapel murderer was busy at his own quasi-medical murdering.

Dr. George Lamson, 1882: Broke, Lamson decided to enrich his coffers by cleverly administering aconite, a vegetable poison, to his youthful brother-in-law, Percy Malcolm, from whose death he would benefit by 1,500 pounds. The British physician simply fed Percy a piece of cake, pre-sliced, which contained a currant containing aconite. Lamson confessed the murder before being hanged.

Dr. Lauren Eustachy, 1884: The patriarchal physician of the town of Pertuis in southern France, Eustachy felt threatened by the arrival of another doctor, young Dr. Tournatoire. He first libeled his rival (for which he paid a handsome settlement) and then attempted to murder him by sending Tournatoire six thrushes, a delicacy, having these delivered as if from an anonymous grateful patient. Tournatoire's wife and cook ate the thrushes and became violently ill but survived. The doctor examined the thrushes and found they contained lethal doses of atropine, a derivative of belladonna. Eustachy, the only suspect, quickly admitted at his trial that he indeed tried to kill his medical adversary. He spent eight years in prison for his crafty efforts.

Dr. Philip Cross, 1887: A retired army surgeon of sixty-two, Cross retired to rural County Cork, Ireland, with his wife, Laura, forty-six, and his four children. When a Miss Skinner, a twenty-year-old governess, came to live with the family, the doctor played the proverbial old lecher,

Dr. George Henry Lamson in 1882.

pursuing the young woman, who was apparently not offended by his advances. Mrs. Cross told her husband to discharge the hussy, but Cross instead procured large amounts of arsenic, dosing his wife's food. To make sure, Dr. Cross added some strychnine. Only days after his wife died in agony, Cross ran away with the alluring Miss Skinner.

Authorities exhumed and examined Mrs. Cross's body. They found 3.2 grains of arsenic. Cross was found guilty of murder in a four-day trial. He was hanged. Miss Skinner did not attend the ceremonies.

Dr. Thomas Thatcher Graves, 1891: Dr. Graves's bedside manner endeared him to Mrs. Josephine Barnaby, a wealthy Providence, Rhode Island, heiress, so much so that Mrs. Barnaby gave Graves her power of attorney. Graves promptly began to manipulate her estate after convincing Mrs. Barnaby to travel. Graves somehow had Mrs. Barnaby's will changed so that he became the beneficiary of her huge estate. This done, he promptly sent an anonymous gift, a poisoned bottle of whiskey, to Mrs. Barnaby, who was staying in Denver. The heiress and a friend, Mrs. Worrell, downed several shots and became violently ill, dying six days later on April 19, 1891.

Graves was trapped by his own cleverness. After doctors found poison in the victims, Dr. Graves was put on trial. The prosecution produced a witness Graves never expected to see again, Joseph M. Breslyn. Dr. Graves had stopped Breslyn in the Boston train station and had asked him to write a note to a friend, saying he could not write. The note was the same one delivered with the whiskey to the hapless Mrs. Barnaby.

Graves was found guilty but escaped legal execution. He took some of his own poison and died in his cell in April 1893.

Dr. Robert Buckanan, 1892: An egotist who thought himself the intellectual superior to most men, Dr. Buckanan was after money. He divorced his young wife and married Anna Sutherland, the rich madam of a New Jersey whorehouse. Shortly after the couple moved to New York, Buckanan began to tell friends his wife was terminally ill. She died on April 23, 1892, and Buckanan immediately departed to Nova Scotia, where he remarried his first wife, collecting Anna Sutherland's $50,000 savings in the bargain.

Authorities, suspicious of Dr. Buckanan's activities, examined Anna's body and discovered, after painstaking work, that Buckanan had poisoned his wife with morphine. To cover the symptoms, the contraction of the pupils of the eyes, he had dropped belladonna into Anna's eyes shortly before death, an agent which enlarged the pupils.

Buckanan was convicted and electrocuted at Sing Sing July 2, 1895, a man who thought himself able to commit the perfect murder, but one who proved to be just another medical bungler in the end.

Dr. Bennett Clarke Hyde, 1909: The medical murderer of the twenti-

Dr. Bennett Clarke Hyde, who tried to kill an entire family to inherit the Swope fortune.

eth century enthusiastically pursued his grim goals, often, as in the case of the amazing Dr. Bennett Clarke Hyde in 1909, exceeding with murderous industry the exploits of his nineteenth-century counterparts.

Dr. Hyde, a prominent physician in Kansas City, Missouri, age forty, had already achieved the goals he set in life by marrying a wealthy woman and having the city's upper crust as his patients. Yet pure greed led him to attempt wholesale murder.

Hyde's uncle-in-law, Thomas Swope, one of the founders of Kansas City, had drawn a will in which his daughter and other relatives were to share his fortune of more than $2 million upon his death. The will served as a mighty goad to Hyde, who promptly poisoned old man Swope and his executor and constant companion James Hunton, dosing both with cyanide and strychnine, a truly sinister plan in that the poisons counteracted each other to conceal symptoms, strychnine agitating the nerves of the heart and producing convulsions, cyanide slowing down the heart and congealing the blood.

In order to make his wife the sole inheritor of the great fortune, and thinking himself to be named as the executor, Hyde next attempted to poison six more family members, dosing all with typhoid cultures he had borrowed from a laboratory. Fortunately, only one, Christian Swope, died of the disease before authorities grew suspicious and exhumed Thomas Swope and Hunton, discovering poison in their bodies.

In April 1910 Hyde was tried for the mass murders; he was convicted and given a life term, but his wife, who refused to believe her husband guilty of such monstrous acts, threw her support and considerable fortune behind him. Three more trials ensued, dragging on over the years, the second declared a mistrial because a jury member became ill. The jury failed to agree in the third trial. At the beginning of the fourth trial, Hyde's well-paid lawyers insisted that their client had already been tried three times without conviction and demanded charges against him be dismissed. They were and Dr. Hyde, mass murderer, went free.

Dr. Hawley Harvey Crippen, 1910: Dr. Crippen, a much henpecked creature, poisoned his obnoxious wife, Cora, with hyoscine, chopped up her body, burying some of the remains in the cellar of his North London home, and then fled to America with his secretary and lover, Ethel Le Neve. He was tracked down by Scotland Yard's dogged Inspector Walter Dew, who arrested him as his ship docked in Canada and returned him for trial in England. Crippen was found guilty and was hanged on November 23, 1910. A photo of Miss Le Neve was placed in his coffin at his request.

Dr. John MacGregor, 1909–11: MacGregor, a married rural physician in Bad Axe, Michigan, took up with Mrs. Carrie Sparling on the pretense of doctoring a persistent eye infection. It was claimed that MacGregor first poisoned her husband, farmer John Wesley Sparling, then three of her sons to obtain insurance money on their lives, which, through Carrie Sparling's generosity, he did. MacGregor was found guilty of administering arsenic to all the Sparlings and was given a life term in 1912, only to be released by Governor Ferris in 1916, a scandal-ridden pardon, whereupon he was appointed prison physician to the Jackson penitentiary, where he had been an inmate, a post he held until his death in 1928.

Dr. Demitri Panchenko, 1911: This Russian physician had a reputation of being for hire to kill off unwanted relatives in the St. Petersburg area; knowing this, an impoverished noble of Grodno, Patrick O'Brien de Lacy, employed Panchenko to poison his brother-in-law and mother-in-law and father-in-law so that his wife could inherit the family fortune, agreeing to pay the doctor 620,000 rubles. Panchenko was delighted at the prospect; his mistress, Madame Muraviora, was expensive. The doctor borrowed cholera and diphtheria cultures from a laboratory and inserted these into the brother-in-law's caviar; he promptly died. Authorities, however, examined the body and found the poisons. Further, Panchenko had been overheard telling his mistress about the plot. He was given fifteen years in prison; his employer, De Lacy, got life.

Dr. Tom Dreher, 1927: Dreher fell in love with one of his patients,

Dr. Hawley Harvey Crippen grew so annoyed with his henpecking wife he poisoned her and fled to Canada.

Ada Le Bouef of Mason City, Louisiana. Ada was married to Dreher's best friend, but that didn't prevent him from shooting Jim Le Bouef. He confessed to police upon his arrest; both Ada, who plotted to kill her husband, and Dreher were hanged together on February 1, 1929.

Dr. Pierre Bougrat, 1927: Dr. Bougrat, to obtain money for his mistress, murdered his patient Jacques Rumebe by injecting an overdose of arsenobenzol. He was sent to Cayenne in French Guiana for life but he escaped to Venezuela in October 1928, one of the few ever to do so.

Dr. Buck Ruxton, 1935: A resident of Moffat, Scotland, Dr. Ruxton (real name Hakim, born 1899, a native of Bombay, India) went berserk and strangled his common-law wife, Isabella, and then strangled her maid, Mary Rogerson, who had inadvertently witnessed the killing on September 14, 1935. He surgically dissected both victims and threw them into the river Annan. The bodies were later found and identified. Ruxton was executed on May 21, 1936, at Strangeways Jail in Manchester.

Dr. Marcel Petiot, 1941–45: Petiot's criminal career was a long one; born in 1897, he began trafficking in drugs as an army surgeon in 1916. He robbed his patients and burglarized their shops and homes. He became mayor of the town of Villeneuve-sur-Yonne, where he looted municipal stores. During the Nazi occupation of Paris, Petiot murdered sixty-three persons, mostly Jews who were attempting to flee the country. He had promised he could smuggle them out. Instead, he injected them with poison, watched them die in agony, took their possessions and dropped them into a secret quicklime pit constructed in his sprawling home. He was beheaded on May 25, 1946.

Dr. Marcel Petiot, the inhuman mass murderer of Paris.

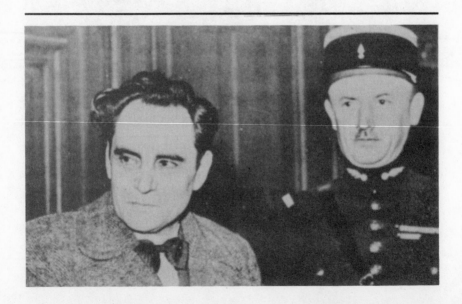

Dr. Robert George Clements, 1920–47: Clements was a marrying murderer, from all reports. The British physician was fond of wedding rich women, who conveniently perished to leave their wealth to him. The first, Edyth Anna Mercier, died in 1920; Clements signed her death certificate, listing the cause as sleeping sickness. Mary McCleery was next, dying after a four-year marriage, Clements having gone through her fortune. Again he signed the death certificate. The cause, he said, was endocarditis. His third wife, Katherine Burke, died of cancer, he said, in 1939. The fourth and final Mrs. Clements, Victoria Burnett, was the daughter of a wealthy industrialist and twenty years Clements' junior. She perished in May 1947, but this time another doctor was brought in and noticed that the pupils of the eyes of the deceased had contracted to pinpoint size, a symptom of morphine poisoning, which was confirmed by an autopsy. Before police could arrest him, Clements killed himself with an overdose of morphine.

Dr. Sam Sheppard, 1954: One of the most celebrated murder cases in American history involved Dr. Sheppard's killing of his wife, Marilyn, his boyhood sweetheart, on July 4, 1954. Sheppard, in love with another woman, apparently struck his wife twenty-seven times on the head with a blunt surgical instrument while she was sleeping, and then called for help, blaming the murder on a "bushy-haired" intruder who stole only Sheppard's tee shirt from their suburban Cleveland home. (This, Sheppard surmised, was done to replace the killer's own bloodstained shirt; he claimed he was knocked unconscious by the killer.) The story seemed bogus to a jury, who convicted Sheppard of second-degree murder, which resulted in life in prison.

Dr. Bernard Finch, 1959: Finch, a Los Angeles doctor long involved in love triangles, divorced his first wife to marry his best friend's wife, Barbara Daugherty (her husband married Finch's ex-wife). He soon tired of her and, having fallen in love with Mrs. Carole Tregoff, a married woman, Finch decided to murder Barbara, who knew of the doctor's latest trysting and reportedly threatened to shoot the physician and Mrs. Tregoff unless the affair was halted. On the night of July 18, 1959, Barbara Finch was shot by Finch in front of her home while Mrs. Tregoff hid in nearby bushes. The doctor was seen standing over his wife with the pistol in his hand. Both Finch and Mrs. Tregoff received life terms after being convicted of second-degree murder. Carole was paroled in 1969, not once having replied to Finch's letters to her in prison. The romance-glutted doctor was released in 1971.

Dr. Geza De Kaplany, 1962: A Hungarian anesthesiologist living in San Jose, California, Dr. De Kaplany had married a twenty-five-year-old beauty queen. The thirty-six-year-old doctor was insanely jealous and when he realized he could not consummate the marriage, De Kaplany resolved that his wife Hajne would never appeal to any other man. He tied

Dr. Bernard Finch, who murdered for love.

her to a bed in their honeymoon cottage, and, with a hi-fi blaring, made deep surgical slashes in her face and body, pouring nitric acid into the wounds, then dousing her privates with the acid.

No atrocity by any medical murderer in history equaled the torture killing performed by the "acid doctor." Though she looked like she had been placed in an incinerator, Hajne lived for twenty-one days, her mother praying at her hospital bed for her to die. De Kaplany later explained that he only intended to spoil her looks, not to kill her. "It was my one-hour crack-up," he quipped with a sneer.

This monster was given a life term, but the Adult Authority inexcusably

released him after thirteen years in 1975, actually smuggling him out of
the United States to Taiwan six months before his official release date.
The explanation given was that he was sorely needed as a heart specialist
in Taiwan, even though De Kaplany had no medical experience in this
field. Before he could be interviewed, the head of De Kaplany's parole
board, Ray Procunier, resigned, which has since aroused suspicion as to
the board's true motivations in releasing such a maniac, but lamentably
reflects the tragic, true state of gross irresponsibility on the part of many
of today's parole board members, an attitude that ignores the victim and
paradoxically rewards the killer, sending to the streets the dedicated enemies of humanity.

Dr. Geza de Kaplany, shown walking before his jurors, who found him guilty,
murdered out of insane jealousy.

ORGANIZED CRIME

METHODS OF MURDER BY CONTRACT

The current price of murder, according to some sources, ranges in the United States from $250 to $500. But to break legs and arms might cost as much as $1,000 or more. The economic philosophy of the hired assassin is simple: People with broken legs can talk, can identify an attacker. Dead men, as Captain Kidd was wont to say, tell no tales.

Killing in America without motive other than collecting cash became widespread in the 1870s in New York with Manhattan's most devastating street mob on record, the old Whyos gang, which dominated the Lower East Side. Members of the Whyos—the name of the gang has no definite origin—committed armed robbery in the middle of streets during broad daylight. They raided other sections of the town at will. From rival gangster to policeman or average citizen, anyone who got in the way of the Whyos was murdered.

Men like Big Josh Hines, Red Rocks Farrell, Piker Ryan and Slops Connolly became so proficient at murdering competing mobsters that they soon offered their services to anyone who could afford their price. If a businessman wanted his partner eliminated, all he had to do was saunter into a drinking hellhole aptly called The Morgue, which was the Whyos' headquarters.

The customer merely ordered whatever savagery he had in mind, paid the price in cash, and the deed was carried out within hours, providing the victim was easily located. It was strictly business. Officers who arrested Piker Ryan in 1884 found in his pocket a printed list of the services offered by the enterprising Whyos, and the cost of each. It read:

Punching	$ 2
Both eyes blackened	$ 4
Nose and jaw broke	$ 10
Jacked out [knocked out with a blackjack]	$ 15
Ear chawed off	$ 15
Leg or arm broke	$ 19
Shot in leg	$ 25
Stab	$ 25
Doing the big job [murder]	$100 up.

The price of the most grotesque hit man on the Black Hand payroll in New York some two decades later was even cheaper.

Ignazio "Lupo the Wolf" Saietta was employed as a Black Hand enforcer in New York for thirty years. If a Black Hand victim refused to pay the extortion demanded, Saietta, for twenty-five dollars, murdered the truculent one. The Wolf charged Black Handers another ten dollars if he was compelled to dispose of the corpse. In such instances he merely threw the body into his horse-drawn wagon, drove to his home and burned the remains in his basement furnace. (Saietta was finally sent to prison for thirty years for counterfeiting, an endeavor for which his peculiar talents were less pronounced.)

Murder for profit went into high gear with the establishment of Murder, Inc., by Louis "Lepke" Buchalter in the early 1930s. New York-based, the savage killers that made up Lepke's troop would go anywhere in the United States and kill anyone for as little as $500, whether the victim was a mob-connected person or just an average citizen someone wanted dead. Murder, Inc., had its own undertaker as well as "cemeteries" about the country—swamps and quicksand pits where bodies would never be recovered. That service cost extra.

There is no way of telling how many victims fell to the knives, guns and brickbats of Murder, Inc., but certainly it was hundreds, according to Abe "Kid Twist" Reles, one of several Murder, Inc., members who turned informant before being murdered. Lepke went to the electric chair in 1944 on the basis of testimony by Reles and others, the only syndicate crime chieftain ever to pay the supreme penalty.

One of Lepke's most trusted murder merchants was a dapper fellow named Charles "The Bug" Workman, who, on orders from the heads of the syndicate, singlehandedly wiped out the Dutch Schultz mob in 1935. Schultz, always an unreasonable type, insisted on murdering New York

Special Prosecutor Thomas E. Dewey, but was voted down by Meyer Lansky, Lucky Luciano, Lepke and others.

Schultz stormed out of the crime cartel meeting shouting that he would kill Dewey anyway. The crime kingpins voted to kill Schultz instead to prevent the avalanche of police pressure that would surely occur should Dewey die.

Lepke chose Workman for the job. The Bug entered the Palace Chophouse in Newark, New Jersey, some days later and, with two automatics blazing, killed three of Schultz's men and mortally wounded the Dutchman. He was so methodical in his work that he checked the pockets of each victim to make sure he had murdered the right people. Workman, identified by several witnesses, was later arrested and sent to the New Jersey State Prison. He was released twenty-three years later.

The hit man's fee for this quadruple slaying was reportedly disregarded at the killer's request; he was merely doing a "business" favor for Lepke.

Such favors have continued over the years for professional hit men who roam far, free and wide across the land, few ever arrested, let alone convicted. The most important hit man to be convicted in recent times was Robert "Bobby Darrow" Bongiovi, an enforcer for the once feared Gallo Mafia family of New York, who was sent to prison for life for killing a Times Square bar manager. Such legal triumphs are rare these days.

THE RISE OF A MAFIA KING

In that terrible tangle that makes up today's Mafia hierarchy, one man emerged as the so-called "boss of bosses." But New York's Mafia king, Carmine Galante, gunned down in 1979 in a New York restaurant, a cigar clenched in his teeth, was not always the imperial "Godfather" dispensing favors and managing a hoodlum empire that gleans and circulates $50 billion annually in "washed" money.

He began, as did his mentors Lucky Luciano, Vito Genovese and Joseph "Joe Bananas" Bonanno, by finding lucrative employment in the streets of New York.

Known early as "Lillo" and "The Cigar," Galante, born in East Harlem on February 21, 1910, had his first brush with the law in 1921, serving time for assault and robbery.

In late 1930 he was one of four young men who tried to hold up a delivery truck on a Williamsburg, New York, street.

Detective Joseph Meenahan, riding by on a trolley, spotted them robbing the truck driver. As he approached the group, Meenahan saw one of the thugs, a pistol in either hand, turn toward him. It was Carmine Galante, the leader of the gang, who opened fire, advancing just as

Meenahan threw open his coat to reach for his own weapon.

Five bullets passed through the detective's coat. The other three gangsters leaped aboard the commandeered truck and sped off. Galante tried to hold on to the tailgate of the truck but lost his grip and fell.

With Meenahan in pursuit, Galante raced off. He fired four more bullets at the pursuing officer, hitting him once in the thigh. One of the gangster's stray bullets struck a six-year-old girl in the leg. The dogged Meenahan limped after his prey for several blocks, catching up to him and leaping upon him. The detective wrested Galante's pistol from his hand and with the gun butt he knocked the gangster unconscious.

For this bit of criminal caprice, Carmine Galante was sent to prison for twelve and a half years, being paroled in 1939. By then "The Cigar" was considered to be one of the top enforcers for madman Vito Genovese, who fled to Italy in 1934 to escape a murder charge.

Galante was essentially Genovese's representative in the United States. As such he was responsible for the murder of Carlo Tresca, the volatile anti-fascist editor of *Il Martèllo* (*The Hammer*), a New York-based newspaper dedicated to the elimination of dictator Benito Mussolini.

The Duce was quite cozy with the exiled Genovese, who remained in Italy under Benito's personal protection and who contributed heavily to the dictator's Black Shirt party. Mussolini gave Genovese $500,000 to

Carmine Galante, shown in 1930, who rose from street thug to king of the Mafia.

Mafia leader Joseph "Joe Bananas" Bonanno, one-time Galante sponsor.

have Tresca murdered in New York. (Half of this money Genovese cleverly kicked back to the Duce in the form of a new fascist headquarters in Nola, Italy.)

Throughout the next two decades, Galante, rising to the rank of Joe Bananas' underboss, flitted about this country and Canada, along with traveling to Italy to visit the deported Lucky Luciano. It was his job to establish a powerful network of hard drug smuggling, only a small segment of which involved the real French Connection.

Not until 1960 was Galante again convicted, this time for dope smuggling, which earned him a twenty-year prison term. Paroled again on January 23, 1974, Galante immediately set about the task of taking over the entire U.S. Mafia. At the time most of the top bosses of the ruling families had either died or were in retirement. Just so there would be no misunderstanding, forty-eight hours after Galante's release, the bronze doors of Frank Costello's tomb were blown to pieces by a time bomb; Costello and Galante had not been friendly.

At sixty-eight, the wiry little don was considered to be the most powerful, dangerous and wealthy Mafia king of them all, a man who had gone from thug to throne while spending half of his adult life behind bars.

When comparing the now dead Galante with competing Mafia members of his day, Lieutenant Remo Franceschini, head of the organized crime intelligence section of the NYPD, stated: "The rest of them are copper; he is pure steel." Steel, he might have added, that could not stop a bullet.

FEDERATIONS: THE BLACK LEGION

The fiery horrors of the Ku Klux Klan had subsided in the late 1920s to motley bands in the rural South, yet the progressive northern state of Michigan was to witness years later an even stranger secret brotherhood bent upon purity of race and religion through purges of blood. Its members wore, in lieu of the KKK's traditional white sheets, black robes and hoods. The brotherhood thugs carried every conceivable weapon, from blackjack to pistol, from knife to axe. Its leaders called the organization the Black Legion.

Michigan police, particularly the homicide squad in Detroit, were perplexed and helpless in early 1935, when a rash of fatal floggings occurred. In May of that year a Detroit Negro named Silas Coleman was found in a swamp forty miles from Detroit. His body was riddled with bullets. The hacked-up remains of a union organizer, one John Bielak, were discovered a short time later outside of Monroe. Edward Armour was shot to pieces as he walked down a Detroit street, by a carload of shotgun-toting men. Though he lived, Armour could not reason why he had been

blasted. None of the crimes were related to the underworld; the authorities had long since smashed the fearsome Purple Mob.

Then, in May 1936, a shot-up corpse was found at the wheel of a car run into a ditch off Gulley Road on Detroit's far West Side. Police found a number of spent cigarettes crushed all about the car and some empty .38 shells nearby. The murdered man, who had five bullets in him, yielded fingerprints that subsequently identified him as Charles Poole, who had once been arrested for vagrancy in Dodge City, Kansas. Why Mr. Poole would be executed was anybody's guess.

Coincidence intervened. A couple coming into the Detroit morgue to identify a traffic accident victim, stopped short when they spied Poole's uncovered body. "I know that man," said the woman. "He was a friend of my brother's. We called him Chap, but none of us have seen him in a good long while. People say he's been running around with a man named Tennessee Slim."

More citizens came forward. Mrs. Robert White and Mrs. Harvey Burke told authorities that Poole's wife was in the hospital, about to have a baby. Detectives waded through a bevy of relatives and neighbors who had known the Pooles. Tennessee Slim was finally identified as Harvey Davis, an employee of the Public Lighting Commission; he was arrested on suspicion of murder.

Detective Havrill tracked down Owen and Marcia Rushing, friends of the slain Poole. He told them of Davis' arrest. The couple walked nervously about their home. Mrs. Rushing seemed on the verge of collapse. "What's your wife hiding, Owen?" Havrill challenged. "See, she's eating her heart out . . . Come on, fella, don't let her go on like that."

Suddenly Mrs. Rushing burst out with: "We can't tell you. You don't know those people!"

"People? What people?"

"That . . . that organization! They kill people that talk. They carry guns and there are thousands and thousands of them—like the Ku Klux Klan, only bigger and more awful!"

The grim story of the Black Legion unraveled. Police began to pick up members. Erwin Lee was found with a .38 and a blackjack; John Bannerman's home was piled high with the legion's robes, all of black satin with white trim and a skull and crossbones insignia. When Detroit police arrested Dayton Dean, they possessed the key to the legion's murder sprees. Dean talked endlessly (and fearlessly) about the organization and "Colonel" Harvey Davis, the leader. Posing under its pseudonym, the Wolverine Republican League, the Black Legion, detailed Dean, stood for 100 per cent Americanism—white, native-born and Protestant. This secret vigilante brotherhood existed to defend decency in the United States, their primary function to protect American womanhood.

Through Dayton Dean, police learned that "Colonel" Davis had decreed Poole's death, claiming that Poole had so severely beaten his wife that his unborn baby had died. Seven of the Legion, wearing their black robes, took Poole for a ride and all took turns shooting him. Dean, who had inveigled Poole to the killing spot, where Davis barked the death sentence, was told that the Poole child had lived. He was "shocked," but he added in the tone that Nazi leaders would later take at the Nuremberg trials: "A horrible mistake, but I was just following the orders of my superiors."

Dean, who had been a member of the KKK in 1922, joined the Michigan Black Legion in 1933 at about the time of its establishment by Davis and others. It was out to eradicate all Jews, Catholics, Negroes, communists and anarchists in the name of American freedom. Initiation rites were written in terror, new members forced to kneel in a circle while black-robed members stood behind them with pistols to their heads. They chanted a long, rambling oath in quaking unison which in part read: "In the name of God and the Devil, one to reward, the other to punish, here under the black arch of Heaven's avenging symbol . . . I will exert every possible means in my power for the extermination of the anarchist, communist, the Roman Hierarchy and their abettors . . . I will show no mercy, but strike with an avenging arm as long as my breath remains . . . I pledge . . . never to betray a comrade, and that I will submit to all the tortures mankind can inflict, rather than reveal a single word of this, my oath."

The Legion boasted 20,000 members in Michigan, stated Dean (who would be portrayed by Humphrey Bogart in the later Warner Brothers film *Black Legion*), and he placed the murder of Negro Silas Coleman at

Davis' feet. The "Colonel" wanted "a nigger to shoot" and killed the hapless Coleman with a .38 after telling him to run for it through a swamp. Bielak, Armour and scores more were marked for death as racial and political foes.

The Legion, under tremendous pressure from the law and publicity, broke to pieces. Davis and his chief cohorts received life sentences. Following their trial, thousands of black robes were found in garbage cans and city dumps all over Michigan.

FEDERATIONS: THE TONGS

The lights are not only low in Chinatowns across the country but almost extinguished as Chinese-American communities await the next onslaught of marauding robber bands who have brought horror and homicide to ordinarily tranquil havens.

In the last few years every major city in the United States with a sizable Chinatown has been under attack by a criminal element not unlike the homegrown hatchet men of yesteryear. Scores of Chinese felons have been filtering into the country from Hong Kong and other Far East areas, first settling in New York, then going on to Chicago and San Francisco.

The gun battles raging in New York's Chinatown have involved hundreds of foreign hoodlums establishing massive extortion rackets, with separate gangs vying for territories. The Flying Dragons and the Ghost Shadows are the most ferocious of the new tong-like criminal bands. In the last two years, forty Chinese gangsters have been shot in New York's Chinatown disputes and of these, fourteen died.

No less active are the Chinese gangs in Chicago, the Gray Shadows, the Ghost Shadows and the Black Ghost Shadows. In lieu of extortion, armed robbery is the order of the day in Chicago's Chinatown, with more than $20,000 being taken from Chinese elders within the last two years.

Since the first tong was organized in the gold fields near Marysville, California, about 1860 and tongs spread as mutual benefit associations to the populous Chinese settlements along the Pacific Coast, fear stalked the streets of Chinatown.

Like chop suey, the tongs were strictly an American invention. Hop Sings, Suey Sings, Kwong Ducks, Sum Yops and Sue Yops, twenty fierce tongs in all, warred to the death for decades in San Francisco.

The tongs controlled all illegal activities, from gambling dives to opium dens, from brothels to the slave trade. Each tong maintained a fighting force of hatchet men known as the boo how doy, a company of soldiers whose job it was to defend territorial rights and murder interlopers.

In the spring of 1875, San Francisco's Low Sing of the Suey Sings and

Early-day San Francisco tong members and their weapons. (San Francisco *Examiner*)

Ming Long, a Kwong Duck killer of at least fifty men, argued over the favors of a slave girl named Kim Kum Ho. Ming settled the debate by splitting Low's cranium with a hatchet. This set off the first bloody tong war in America.

Unlike the gang raids of today, it was all quite formal. The Suey Sings posted a challenge to the Kwong Ducks to avenge Low's murder. The Kwong Ducks accepted, also via a posted notice. Twenty-five men of each tong met at Waverly Place, hooted insults at each other, then pitched into battle, wielding knives, hatchets and clubs. Four men died, the Kwong Ducks taking the worst of it and formally apologizing for Ming Long's transgression.

Of all the San Francisco hatchet men, Fung Jing Toy reigned supreme for more than twenty years. He was known as "Little Pete," and, as head of the Sum Yops he vigorously murdered a dozen opponents until all the tongs except the stubborn Sue Yops were under his command.

Little Pete's counterpart in New York was a strange tong leader named Mock Duck, who first appeared in 1900 to terrorize shopkeepers. In leading the Hip Sings (a branch of which was later established in Chicago) against the powerful On Leong tong, Mock Duck would face his enemies in the street, then suddenly squat, close his eyes and fire his pistol in all directions. His blind aim incredibly found dozens of victims and he was soon the most feared hatchet man in New York's Chinatown.

The tong war was halted in the court of Judge Warren W. Foster, who arbitrated a truce early in this century, but the battles flared up again in the 1920s, with automatics and even submachine guns replacing the hatchet men's cleavers and knives. From the 1940s to the 1960s there was relative peace in most of America's Chinatowns and it was thought that tong warfare was a thing of ancient history.

Then, in the late 1960s, the tongs jumped back into action in San Francisco, and the murders began all over again for control of drug traffic and kickbacks from the all too silent and honest Chinese majority. The terror has now spread East to Chicago and New York and even Newark, New Jersey, which boasts a large Chinatown.

Tradition was being broken, however, by Chinese victims who were beginning to talk to authorities in the late 1970s, to identify the new tong terrorists who brandish exotic new gang names but operate under the old principles of extortion, robbery and murder.

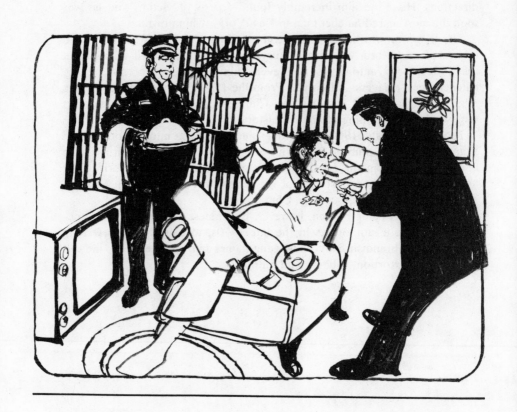

PRISONS

SPECIAL TREATMENT FOR SPECIAL PRISONERS

Special treatment of prisoners in the past has resulted in prison caste systems breeding hate, unrest and sometimes riot.

Prison was "a piece of cake" in the instance of Harry K. Thaw, the Pittsburgh millionaire murderer of architect Stanford White. Thaw killed the celebrated White in full view of an entire audience watching a musical on the roof of Madison Square Garden on June 25, 1906. The wealth-pampered egomaniac insisted he had shot White to avenge his wife, showgirl Evelyn Nesbit, who claimed White seduced her.

While awaiting trial in the New York Tombs, Thaw lived according to the style his money could purchase, sleeping in a special bed in his cell and having all his meals catered by Delmonico's Restaurant. This preferential treatment resulted in many violent outbreaks among other prisoners. (Thaw was eventually judged insane, a victim of what his lawyers termed "dementia Americana," a neurosis indigenous to American males who thought every wife sexually sacred; the killer was released from an asylum a few years later.)

Richard Loeb and Nathan Leopold, slaughterers of fourteen-year-old Bobbie Franks in Chicago in 1924, emulated Mr. Thaw's prison life-style while serving life sentences at Stateville, Illinois. The great wealth of their families allowed the homosexual "fun killers" to enjoy themselves as had few convicts in history. Loeb had in his cell a private library, expensive filing cases, a large glass-top desk. Both men had special toilet articles, dined privately in the officers' mess (their meals were prepared to their own specifications), kept their own hours and visited each other at will, their cell doors seldom locked.

Both killers were permitted to wash in the officers' shower room and to

Pittsburgh millionaire murderer Harry K. Thaw dined on catered meals from Delmonico's while awaiting trial in the New York Tombs prison.

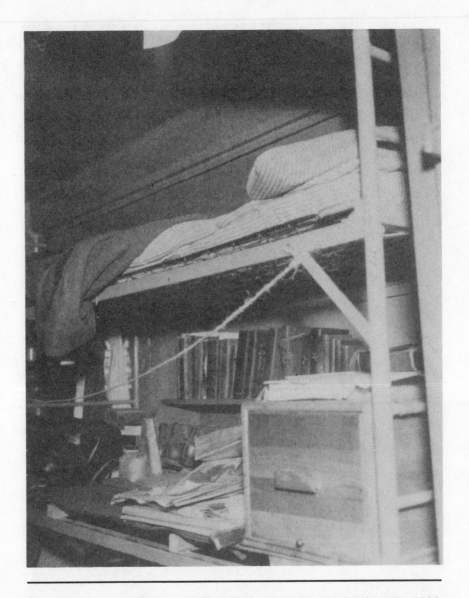

The interior of Nathan Leopold's cell at Stateville Penitentiary in 1936; Leopold's typewriter, library and "desk," took up the space of one bunk in the heavily overcrowded prison.

Where Richard Loeb, wealthy murderer of Bobbie Franks, made his home in Stateville Penitentiary; Loeb occupied the cell alone (photo taken in 1936), having a desk, library and two canaries.

roam about outside the prison walls, where they visited Leopold's garden. From outside sources they purchased bootleg booze and narcotics at a dollar a shot. They saw friends and family almost any time they desired and made phone calls at all hours from the prison storeroom.

Both men, especially Loeb, sauntered about the penitentiary as if it were a private estate, a condition which did not endear the convict population either to the two killers or the prison officials catering to their almost every whim. Such treatment, in fact, indirectly led to Loeb's own murder at the hands of another inmate.

While in prison, Mafia don and arch killer Vito Genovese lived in high style, his Mafia money and power assuring him of every comfort and convenience. Through a relaxed system of mail and other forms of communication, Genovese ordered the murder of dozens of men from inside his cell in order to protect his criminal interests.

But for special treatment of convicts, nothing ever beat the administration of Sheriff John F. Dowd, who in the late 1930s ran the Suffolk County Jail like a country estate for Boston criminals.

Job security was purchased directly from Dowd by prisoners. Those with the best jobs received the top dollar, kicking back to Dowd a percentage of their pay. The wealthiest prisoners, however, were given Ping-Pong tables, radios, books, a solarium with easy chairs. Special prisoners with money and political clout partook of Dowd's ample supply of booze from the private bar he had in his office; the bar never closed.

Champagne parties, when groups of call girls were allowed into the prison, were afforded special prisoners with Dowd collecting his toll. Many of Dowd's paying guests were allowed to travel by closed limousine to golf courses for some sunny exercise, at a cost, of course. Before his corrupt regime was exposed, Dowd pocketed more than $100,000 from convicts for his favors. The sheriff, fleeing in a boozy haze, was committed eventually to Bellevue as a hopeless alcoholic.

ESCAPES—DEPARTING THE "ROCK"

America's "escapeproof" penitentiary, Alcatraz, was the site of twenty-six authentic escape attempts. The Rock, squatting in the shark-filled waters of San Francisco Bay with its treacherous, dark, unpredictable currents, certainly must have offered by its mere location enough deterrent to would-be escape artists. Yet, one decade after another, prisoners made the attempt. The most notable attempt occurred on the night of December 16, 1937.

A record fog enshrouded the entire Bay area during that day. Inmates

Ralph Roe and Theodore "Sunny Boy" Cole determined to take advantage of the dense gray clouds billowing just above the choppy waters, fog so thick that guards pacing the catwalks on the Rock's walls could not see their own feet.

Both Roe and Cole had planned diligently to escape ever since arriving at Alcatraz in October 1935. Both schemers worked in the mat shop, which was at the north tip of the island. From its steel-barred windows it was a mere twenty-foot drop onto an area littered with old tires and other discarded mat shop material which, Roe and Cole reasoned, would cushion their falls.

The only other barrier was a ten-foot-high prison fence almost at the lapping water's edge.

At 1 P.M. that fog-filled December day a guard checked the mat shop and saw Roe and Cole hard at work (the inmates were checked here and in the machine shop every thirty minutes). A moment later, Cole slipped into the adjoining machine shop and grabbed a stillson wrench which he had secreted weeks earlier.

By the time he rushed back to the mat shop, Roe had used his heavy shoes to bash out the glass of the window overlooking the drop zone. Roe then clasped an eighteen-inch iron pipe in the wrench and, using his great strength, managed to break one of the bars on the window with this awkward tool. Both men wriggled through the opening. The guards never saw them leap twenty feet into foggy space to the spot where the rubber discards pillowed their bodies, a landing spot both men had obviously memorized.

No one ever saw the pair again. Experts speculated that the men tied the ends of their pants into crude water wings and then made a swim for it.

Most concluded that Roe and Cole had died in the water, yet reports of the pair being seen in and around San Francisco filtered back for weeks. It was thought that the two could have easily faded into obscurity, using Roe's unrecovered $200,000 bank loot to assure a comfortable future.

Three other Alcatraz prisoners over the years followed the path of Roe and Cole, their bodies never found, their fates undetermined.

Other notable prison escapes in America include:

1788: Thirty-three experienced highwaymen, all members of the Doane

Theodore "Sonny Boy" Cole, who, with Ralph Roe, may have escaped Alcatraz by swimming the treacherous San Francisco waters in 1937.

gang, escaped the Walnut Street Prison in Philadelphia. It took a battalion of infantry to track most of the escapees down.

1789: In March, convicts used as slaves, six in number, broke out of Philadelphia's Walnut Street Prison, stealing the keys from a drunken warden. They were all recaptured in a short time. Five more men escaped the jail in September. These, too, were rounded up. The use of convict labor ended with these breaks.

1808: At least sixteen men, on March 14, overpowered their jailers, killing one in the process, broke through a door of the old Baltimore jail, and made good their escape. Four of the inmates were recaptured and hanged for the guard's murder; the remaining twelve men were never found.

1835: Ten inmates of the old Baltimore jail jumped their guards, tied them up and smashed down a single door before making their way to freedom on December 6, 1835.

1838: Tunneling out of the newly built prison at Alton, Illinois, six convicts made good their escape in December. One of them, a horse thief, galloped off on the horse belonging to John R. Woods, superintendent of the prison.

1864: In April, the badly mistreated prisoners of the infant prison San Quentin in California, grabbed the sadistic warden, T. N. Machin, and put razor-sharp knives to his throat, forcing the guards not only to open the gates but also to flee. The entire prison population escaped, only to be decimated in a pitched battle with an army of farmers who met and overwhelmed them two miles away from the prison at Ross Landing. Dozens did escape into the hills; at least fifty were gunned down by the terrified citizens. The remainder were dragged back to the prison and tortured.

1874: Noted cannibal and thief Alfred (or Alferd) Packer escaped from the Los Pinos Indian Agency in Colorado, where he was being detained pending trial on murder charges. Packer went to Salt Lake City and then vanished, not recaptured until 1883.

1881: William H. Bonney, better known as "Billy the Kid," escaped the Mesilla, New Mexico, jail on April 28, 1881, using a gun that was either smuggled to him by an admiring Mexican girl or taken away from one of his keepers, deputy J. W. Bell, while Bell was helping him (he was shackled hand and foot) to the outside latrine from his second-floor cell in the makeshift jail above Murphy's Store. The Kid shot Bell dead, then broke into Sheriff Pat Garrett's gun room, took out a shotgun and waited for the other guard, deputy Bob Ollinger, to come running from the local bar where he had been drinking beer.

That is exactly what Ollinger did once he heard the shot that killed Bell. Ollinger had taunted the Kid ceaselessly while he was in his cell, prodding him with a gun and telling him to make a break so he could

A painting depicting the posse, led by Sheriff Pat Garrett (on white horse) that brought in Billy the Kid to the Mesilla, New Mexico, jail in 1881; the man on horseback at extreme left is deputy Bob Ollinger, whom the Kid killed a few days later in his spectacular escape.

shoot him in the back. When Ollinger approached the jail, he heard a voice behind him softly say: "Hello, Bob." Ollinger turned and the Kid let him have both barrels from the shotgun, blowing him into the street. The Kid then ordered a handyman to get him an axe. With this he chopped off his shackles, then stole a horse, guns and supplies, and rode out of Mesilla waving his hat at petrified townspeople and shouting: "*Adiós, compadres!*" He had less than three months to live before Sheriff Pat Garrett shot him dead.

1895: Train robber Oliver Curtis Perry, one of the most daring bandits of his day, sawed his way out of his cell in the State Hospital for the Criminally Insane at Matteawan, New York, on April 10, the saw sent to him in a food parcel by a lady who had fallen in love with him during his last trial.

Once in the outer corridor of the heavily barred cellblock, Perry stole a set of keys and let out other prisoners, knowing they would create a loud diversion, all being raving lunatics. He then opened a window. Perry saw a drainpipe running down the outside wall of the building. An excellent athlete, Perry dove for the pipe, grappled it in midair and slid down its entire length of eighty feet to the ground and freedom.

Inside Perry's cell, his startled keepers found a note reading:

I don't intend to serve this out,
Or even let despair,
Deprive me of my liberty
Or give me one gray hair.

Perry was captured a short time later, removed to the maximum security prison at Dannemora, and kept in solitary confinement for the next twenty-five years. At Clinton Prison, in New York, he blinded himself by his own hands; he died in his cell on September 10, 1932.

1902: The most feared member of Butch Cassidy's Wild Bunch, the psychopathic Harry Tracy, sent to the Colorado State Prison for murder, broke from his cell on June 9, 1902. Tracy somehow stole a guard's rifle and shot other guards off the prison wall, grabbing one of these wounded men and using him as a shield. Tracy and another inmate, Dave Merrill, broke through a gate and made a successful getaway, traveling to Oregon, where Tracy murdered Merrill, thinking his companion had informed on him some years earlier.

Tracy was hunted by dozens of posses through Oregon and Washington. He was finally cornered, shooting it out with a hundred men on August 3, 1902. Realizing his situation, Tracy waited until dusk. Possemen heard a single shot. The last of the Wild Bunch had sent a bullet into his own head.

1910: A spectacular prison break occurred at Leavenworth in 1910 when dozens of inmates took control of the small locomotive that was then used to haul supplies in and out of the prison. The prisoners got up a good head of steam, then raced the train through the yard and crashed it through the train gate, the guards firing a hailstorm of bullets at them. All were recaptured within days.

1913: The son of a wealthy San Francisco couple, Herbert Repsold, who had been sent to San Quentin for burglary, engineered a clever break in January. Repsold, a wealthy man in his own right, paid someone to leave a boat for him on the shore of San Francisco Bay. Waiting for a rainy night, Repsold, who worked in the power station, pulled the main switches, taking with him all the fuses.

With the entire prison pitched into darkness, Repsold managed to get over the wall, jump into the boat and row out into the Bay. His escape was short-lived. Apparently Repsold struck an object in the Bay or accidentally overturned the boat. His body washed ashore the next morning. Repsold's bloated corpse was put on display in the prison's reception room for two days as a warning to other prisoners scheming to escape.

Oliver Curtis Perry escaped from the Matteawan prison hospital in New York leaving a bit of whimsy behind. (Pinkerton, Inc.)

(Of all the major prisons in the United States, the most inventive, sometimes downright zany, escape attempts have occurred at San Quentin. An inmate named Martin hid in an incinerator, trying to find the right air shaft to freedom; he was finally talked out of the place before roasting to death. A convict named Edison stole some women's clothes from a guard's house and walked wobbly legged out the front gate on high heels, using a falsetto voice to convince a new guard he was a she, only to be caught a few blocks away.

Ernest Booth, who made considerable money writing from his San Quentin cell about prison life, lowered himself out of a prison hospital window, but a vindictive inmate leaned out of another window and cut the rope, dropping Booth to the concrete below, where he broke both legs. Ad Arkeley simply dove into San Francisco Bay and began to swim away. Every time the guards on the wall and in the towers ordered him to return, their guns leveled at him, Arkeley, trying psychology, gave them a cheery wave and a laugh. He was finally run down with speedboats and returned. The most bizarre escape on record at San Quentin was that made by a convict named Davis, who slipped into the tank of a milk truck making deliveries to the prison. He was forced to swim around in the milk. Though the truck got him out of the prison, he was heard to thump loudly on its sides as the truck came to a roadblock. He almost drowned.)

1921: Thomas "Terrible Tommy" O'Connor, Chicago cop-killer, escaped from the Criminal Courts Building in Chicago only a few days before he was sentenced to be hanged for murder, using a guard's gun to break out into the prison yard. O'Connor and another inmate scaled the twenty-foot wall by standing on the shoulders of other prisoners, dropped to the sidewalk on the other side, commandeered one car after another and lost themselves in the city. O'Connor is missing to this day but a court order has retained the gallows on which he is still scheduled to hang, the last person in Illinois who was sentenced to die on the gallows, the electric chair having been adopted as the new method of execution. The scaffold is stacked in the Criminal Courts Building at Twenty-sixth and California streets at this writing and will be kept until O'Connor's fate has been determined.

1926: Using homemade explosives, rioting inmates of Washington's Walla Walla State Penitentiary blew open the main gates of the prison; more than nine hundred convicts dashed to freedom, only to be driven back by hundreds of troopers within the hour.

1926: Bernard Roa, an inmate of Illinois' Stateville Prison, along with five others, managed to get out of the cell house and into the office of Deputy Warden Peter Klein. Roa and the others threatened Klein that unless he ordered a delivery gate opened, they would kill him. When Klein refused, he was stabbed to death with homemade knives. The prisoners ran to the yard, grabbed a guard and made the same threat. The guard agreed and the prisoners went free. All except James D. Price were later captured. Roa escaped again from a jail in Will County, Illinois, making his way back to his native land of Mexico. When the FBI discovered Roa was in a Mexican jail in 1939, they requested that he be returned to stand trial for the Klein murder but the Mexican Government refused, stating Roa must serve out a term for drug trafficking. Over the years, though Roa was released from jail, Mexico has adamantly refused to turn him over. His whereabouts at this writing, if he is still alive, is unknown.

All of the other inmates escaping from Stateville with Roa were executed for the Klein killing. James D. Price was discovered some years later to be an inmate of the Clinton State Prison serving a ten-year term under the alias of Frank Meadows. He was returned to Stateville in 1936. After pleading guilty to the killing, he was given a 150-year term.

1931: One of the most dramatic prison breaks in American history took place on December 11, 1931, when seven of the toughest convicts in Leavenworth broke out. Financed by bank robber Frank Nash, himself an escapee, recently paroled inmate Monk Fountain purchased a number of arms and explosives and shipped these into Leavenworth inside a box of shoe paste which was delivered to the prison's shoe factory.

It was the habit of inspecting guards not to open the boxes of shoe paste, which the convicts planning to escape knew full well, in that, once exposed to the air, the paste would harden and be useless. The box containing five pistols, a .30-30 Winchester rifle, a sawed-off shotgun (the rifle and shotgun were in a dismantled state to allow for packaging), and some dynamite bombs, was marked by Fountain, a mark which the inmates waiting for the guns easily identified.

On the morning of December 11, 1931, seven of the prisoners, armed with this smuggled arsenal, broke into the prison's administration office, took Warden Tom White and staff members hostage, and, threatening to kill these hostages, were let through a series of guarded, locked gates to the front entrance.

The convicts, taking only Warden White with them, commandeered a car in front of the prison and escaped. White struggled with the men once in the car and was shot in the left arm and chest (the arm was later amputated and White was removed from his position).

Within hours, an army of police and militia were searching for the convicts. Whitey Lewis was killed running across an open field. Surrounded by a hundred shotgun-carrying deputies, Grover Durrel and Bill Green, who had vowed never to go back to prison, shot and killed themselves.

Tom Underwood, Charles Berta and Stanley Brown, the nominal leader of the escape, were rounded up before the day was over. Only Earl Thayer, an old man who had robbed banks on horseback in the days of Al Spencer and Sam Starr, and was serving a twenty-five-year term for train robbery, doggedly stayed ahead of bloodhound-led posses. Finally, after four days on foot through the countryside, his body wracked with pneumonia, both his feet frozen, Thayer cursed his pursuers, threw down his pistol and surrendered.

1932: On December 12, after four days using a hacksaw smuggled to him by another prisoner, bank robber Willie "The Actor" Sutton, sawed through the bars of his cell in Sing Sing, wriggled into the corridor and, with John Eagan, picked two locks on corridor steel doors and got into the prison's dining hall.

Willie then picked the lock on the door to the cellar and Sutton and Eagan retrieved two ladders, lashing them together with wire. In the shadows of the prison yard, both men used the ladders to scale the wall, then dropped to the ground and ran to a spot where a confederate had left a waiting auto. This was one of many spectacular prison escapes by the wily Willie Sutton.

1933: Kidnapping the warden and two guards, whom they used for hostages and shields, eleven of the toughest bank robbers of the Southwest, led by old pro Harvey Bailey, crashed through the front gates of the Kansas State Penitentiary on May 31, 1933. Others in the mass breakout—the convicts wielded guns smuggled to them by Frank Nash, the mastermind of the 1931 Leavenworth break—included the notorious Wilbur Un-

Author Jay Robert Nash interviewing Willie "The Actor" Sutton, who detailed his many prison escapes. (Photo by James Patrick Agnew)

derhill, the Tri-State Terror; Big Bob Brady; Frank Sawyer; Ed Davis; Jim Clark; and five others.

James Henry "Blackie" Audett, who worked as an underground liaison man for Boss Tom Pendergast of Kansas City, met the escapees in a woods near the prison, driving a large touring car to a rendezvous which had been arranged earlier. Underhill, a vicious killer, wanted to murder the warden but Audett joked him out of it. The desperadoes left the warden and guards naked in the woods and sped off.

Bailey struck out on his own, heading for Mexico. He was later recaptured at the Shannon Ranch in Texas, operated by the "Machine Gun" Kelly gang, and locked up in the Dallas Jail. Bailey bribed a deputy guard, Thomas L. Manion, into smuggling to him a hacksaw, using it to escape on September 4, 1933. The obliging Manion helped Bailey saw through his bars when the outlaw tired, then gave him his pistol to use to cow a half dozen guards in the escape. Bailey was captured by a large posse a short while later outside of Ardmore, Oklahoma. His only comment to arresting officers was: "Well, I got out, didn't I?" Bailey was sent to Leavenworth for life, mistakenly convicted of the Charles Urschel kidnapping. He was paroled in 1965, retiring as a cabinetmaker in Joplin, Missouri. He died at age ninety-one in 1979.

Of the original eleven in the breakout, all were recaptured within a year. Underhill was shot and killed in Shawnee, Oklahoma, when he was on his honeymoon in early 1934. Big Bob Brady, who went on a bank-robbing spree with Blackie Audett after his escape, was ambushed and killed by a large posse outside of Paola, Kansas, on January 19, 1934.

1933: Taking a leaf out of Frank Nash's prison break schemes, John Dillinger, recently paroled from the Michigan City, Indiana, State Prison, bribed the foreman of a thread-making firm to "fix up" a box of thread being sent to the Michigan City Prison shirt shop. Dillinger placed several guns inside the box, marked it with a red X and this box was received by his waiting confederates in the prison on September 26. Ten men, the most professional bank robbers in the nation, four of whom later formed Dillinger's super bank robbery gang, escaped through the prison's front door, while holding the smuggled guns on guards. These included Harry Pierpont, Charles Makley, Russell Clark, John "Three-Fingered" Hamilton, Ed Shouse, Joseph Fox, Jim "Oklahoma Jack" Clark, Joseph Burns, James Jenkins and Walter Dietrich.

Jenkins was killed only hours later by farmers firing shotguns at him after he accidentally fell out of the jam-packed escape car at Bean Blossom, Indiana. Hamilton, Makley, Pierpont and Russell Clark went on to join Dillinger. The rest were recaptured in a short time.

1933: To repay Dillinger, who had been captured and placed in the Lima, Ohio, jail for bank robbery, Makley, Clark, Pierpont and Hamilton broke him out of jail on October 12, 1933, killing Sheriff Jess Sarber in the process.

1934: On January 16, three desperate bank robbers, Raymond Hamilton, Joe Palmer and Henry Methvin escaped the Eastham Prison in Texas with guns smuggled to them by Clyde Barrow. It was Methvin who would later set up the police ambush outside of Gibsland, Louisiana, on May 23, 1934, which slaughtered Bonnie and Clyde as they were driving down the road.

1934: Dillinger, captured in Tucson earlier in the year, was flown back to Indiana under heavy guard to face bank robbery and murder charges. He was placed inside the Crown Point, Indiana, Jail, the so-called "escapeproof" jail, and surrounded by hundreds of deputies and militia guards. Yet, on March 3, 1934, Dillinger escaped. He had carved a pistol from the top of a wooden washboard, blackened it with boot polish and bluffed his way into the jail's garage with Herbert Youngblood, a Negro

murderer. Dillinger escaped in the fastest car in Crown Point, the one belonging to Sheriff Lillian Holley. Youngblood was trapped by three deputy sheriffs in a candy store in Port Huron, Michigan, on March 16. He shot it out with them, killing one and wounding the other two before dying of six bullet wounds. Dillinger, as this author has written extensively about in an earlier book, and based on irrefutable evidence, was not killed at the Biograph Theater on July 22, 1934, as the FBI later claimed. Another man died in his place. (The autopsy of the slain man, along with a host of other documentation establishes this as a fact.) Dillinger, as far as the author is able to reconstruct events, escaped to Oregon following the shooting. James Henry "Blackie" Audett confided to the author in 1979 that he, Audett, witnessed the shooting outside of the Biograph Theater, then reported the event to Dillinger in Aurora, Illinois, where both men were in hiding in a rooming house. Dillinger and Audett left for the West Coast three days later, driving the "northern route" through Wisconsin, Minnesota, South Dakota and on to Oregon, where, according to Audett, Dillinger married an Indian woman and settled briefly on an Indian reservation near Klamath Falls, Oregon, before moving on in the early 1940s to disappear.

1935: Victor "The Count" Lustig, the most infamous confidence man then operating next to Joseph "Yellow Kid" Weil, escaped from the FBI federal detention center in Washington, D.C. on September 1, 1935. Treasury agents, who had captured Lustig in the first place and had turned him over to the FBI, captured the con man again on September 29 near Pittsburgh, all of which proved to be highly embarrassing for FBI Director J. Edgar Hoover.

1942: On October 9, Roger Touhy, Basil "The Owl" Banghart and five others escaped Stateville Prison in Illinois. Climbing the inside wall to a guard's tower, the seven men crept down the inside stairs of the tower and left by a steel door—to which they had the key—leading to the outside. A car was waiting for them, as prearranged with an outside contact. The convicts drove to Chicago and stayed in hiding until their apartment building was surrounded by police who received a tip on the hideout in December. All were recaptured, except Eugene O'Connor and St. Clair

John Dillinger standing outside his father's farmhouse near Mooresville, Indiana, a few days after his spectacular prison break from the so-called "escapeproof" Crown Point (Indiana) Jail; he holds in his right hand the wooden gun he carved from the top of a washboard in his cell and blackened with boot polish which he used to bluff his way out of the jail; the machine gun in his left hand is real.

Con man Victor "The Count" Lustig, who escaped from the FBI detention
center in Washington, D.C., in 1935.

McInerney, who shouted to FBI agents that they would never surrender.
Both men were killed in the ensuing gun battle.

This was the fourth major escape by Basil Banghart. He had escaped
the federal penitentiary in Atlanta in 1927. In a South Bend, Indiana, jail
in 1932, Banghart had thrown pepper in a guard's face, grabbed a machine gun and shot his way to freedom. In 1935 Banghart escaped
Menard Illinois Prison by driving a laundry truck through the main gates.
The 1942 break was his last.

1943: In late December four convicts, in an early morning dense fog and
under the pretext of attending Sunday church services, slipped through a
small hole in an inner wall of San Quentin where repairmen had been
working, then raced to the outer wall and scaled it with a crude scaffold
and ropes. Austin Redford was captured in northern California. The
remaining three—Lawrence Motari, Roy Drake and Ralph Wood—armed
with stolen guns and driving stolen autos, made it to Mississippi, where
they committed several holdups and were finally recaptured after a terrific
gun battle with local police.

1945: In his second spectacular escape, Willie Sutton and seven others
briefly escaped after tunneling beneath the walls of Pennsylvania's Eastern
State Penitentiary in Philadelphia (also known as Holmesburg) from

June 6, 1944 to May 7, 1945. Sutton was apprehended by two beat cops who accidentally happened to be converging upon the site just as Sutton jumped out of the hole and began to run away.

1946: William McManus escaped from the San Quentin prison farm on a June night, hiding in the hills until the next evening, when he tried hitchhiking out of the area. A driver picked him up, saying to him: "Nice night for a walk, huh, Mac?" McManus stared at the driver of the car in disbelief. The man at the wheel was an administrative aide at San Quentin. "Ah, hell," sighed McManus, "take me back to the prison."

1947: In his third big prison break, Willie Sutton, in what he called in his autobiography his "masterpiece" of escape, broke out of the Holmesburg Prison in Philadelphia on February 9, 1947, the first successful prison break from this institution in the fifty-three years since its construction in 1894. Using a smuggled gun, Sutton and four others ordered two guards to open vital lockup doors for them, obtaining the master key to the basement, where the convicts gathered up the forty-foot extension ladders, carried these into the outer yard in a blinding snowstorm, and scaled the twenty-eight-inch-thick wall, dropping to freedom on the other side.

Sutton was not apprehended until 1952, when a citizen, one Arnold Schuster, recognized him on a Manhattan subway and called police. Watching Schuster being interviewed on TV, Mafia enforcer Albert Anastasia screamed to some of his thugs: "I can't stand squealers! Hit that guy!" Schuster was shot to death on March 8, 1952, by Anastasia's goons. Sutton apparently had nothing to do with the killing, the murder being a typically insane whim of the lethal Anastasia.

1949: Fifteen prisoners of the Moundsville State Penitentiary in West Virginia, using homemade hacksaws, sawed the bars of six cells, overpowered a guard, and then made a ten-by-eighteen-inch hole in the prison's outer wall, escaping to freedom. All were apprehended within thirty-three hours.

1951: Joseph Holmes, a convict in the Maryland State Penitentiary, spent months digging a twenty-six-foot tunnel from his cell to the prison's outer wall using scraps of iron stolen from the prison workshop. He completely disappeared after emerging on the outside of the main wall, escaping into the surrounding city streets of Baltimore.

1951: In October, six hardened convicts of Rock Quarry Prison near Buford, Georgia, hopped into a truck while doing roadwork and escaped as guards emptied their shotguns of buckshot in their direction. The six were back in custody within fifty-two hours. Four of them, including the leaders of the break, Joe and Ray Mauldin, were tracked down by perhaps the most famous prison bloodhound in history, a tracker called Old Lady, who, in a period of almost ten years, had sniffed down 824 escaped prisoners.

1955: Ten prisoners dug their way to freedom in November, emerging outside the walls of Walla Walla State Penitentiary in Washington. All were recaptured within a week, in spite of the fact that they had prepared elaborate identification papers in the prison print shop, including driver's licenses, draft cards, birth certificates, even credit cards.

1959: In December, Charles "Yank" Stewart, fifty-two, led nineteen convicts out of the so-called "escapeproof" Ivy Bluff Prison in North Carolina, the modern institution then only four years old. Stewart, who had six escapes on his record (he had broken out of Raleigh's Central Prison only weeks before being sent to Ivy Bluff), vowed that he would escape the new prison. Stewart's father and brother had been sent to the electric chair in 1925 after killing two Prohibition agents raiding their moonshining still. Stewart had followed the criminal path ever since that event and had been imprisoned for armed robbery.

Using hacksaws Stewart arranged to have smuggled to him, the twenty men broke into a corridor, then subdued three guards and armed themselves with twenty-two weapons, including eight revolvers, eight rifles and a submachine gun, all taken from the guards' arsenal. They rounded up every guard in the prison, including those in the towers, stripped them and placed them in cells. The entire prison population, small at the time, was given the option of escape. Twenty-nine prisoners with short sentences yet to serve declined the offer.

Stewart then led the others through the main gate and to freedom. When news of the mass break of heavily armed prisoners was spread, many neighboring small towns were in terror for days, thousands of farmers and townspeople patrolling the streets and roads in posses, armed to the teeth. Helicopters swooped through the countryside. Hundreds of bloodhounds raced through rural areas. Gas station owner Wallace Burke in Yanceyville served customers while wearing a pistol in his belt. Leroy Jones, a farmer living near Pelham, sold his prize cow to buy an automatic weapon to protect his family.

The desperate precautions were for nothing. Stewart and the others were rounded up within a few days by state police. Three of the prison guards were fired for lax behavior.

1962: On June 12, after months of elaborate preparation, three of Alcatraz's most hardened convicts, Frank Lee Morris (whose IQ was 133, a genius rating being at 140) and the brothers Joseph and Clarence Anglin, escaped through the air vents of their cells. Using spoons stolen in the mess hall, the three men spent months chipping away at the walls inside the air vents, disposing of the rubble during their prison yard exercises. They carefully collected the scraps of hair in the prison barber shop and made plaster dummy heads with believable sleeping faces. These were placed on pillows at the ends of bunched-up blankets to make it appear that the prisoners were asleep in their bunks at the time of the break.

After nine-thirty bed check on the night of the break, Morris and the Anglins squeezed through the ten-by-fourteen-inch air vents (covering the openings with cardboard grates painted with a metallic gray), wriggling down the air shafts to the holes made in the walls of the shafts and into a rarely used utility corridor behind the wall of their cells. Inside this corridor (Morris, who planned the break, had somehow gotten the blueprints of Alcatraz and studied its architectural design), the convicts shinnied up a thirty-foot drainpipe to an air-conditioning vent. They broke through this vent and pulled themselves onto the roof.

Though the guards in Tower Number One at the northern end of the prison compound had a full view of the roof at this point, the three prisoners were not seen as they crawled the length of the 100-foot roof to slide down a forty-foot drainpipe. Racing to a fifteen-foot "control fence," the three scaled the wire, dropped to the other side and ran to the island's northeast extremity before letting themselves into the icy waters of San Francisco Bay. They were not missed until morning roll call at 7:15 A.M.

All authorities ever found of Morris and the Anglins was a crudely made paddle floating near Angel Island some distance from Alcatraz. A woman reported seeing three men paddling a raft at dawn of that day.

The possibility of a successful escape was real, more so, it was felt by federal authorities, than the break by Roe and Cole in 1937. Alcatraz's impregnable security had been breached. This escape led to the closing of Alcatraz and the removal of the prisoners to the maximum security prison at Marion, Illinois. It was later stated that the crumbling state of Alcatraz, used as a prison since 1935, would have cost many millions of dollars to repair, a price tag thought too high, but the overriding factor that closed the prison was the escape of Morris and the Anglins, who are considered still at large. (The motion picture *Escape from Alcatraz* is based on this break.)

1967: Albert DeSalvo, "The Boston Strangler," and two others escaped from the Bridgewater State Mental Prison in Massachusetts in February. George Harrison and Fred Erickson immediately got drunk in a Boston saloon and turned themselves in the next day. DeSalvo, some days later, entered a sporting goods store in Lynn, Massachusetts, asking if he could phone his lawyer, F. Lee Bailey, which tipped the manager as to his identity. DeSalvo called Bailey, the manager called the police. DeSalvo, who had confessed to the rape-strangulation of thirteen women in the Boston area, and the rapes of hundreds more, was returned to the institute without incident. He sat sipping coffee in the store, allowed the manager to "frisk" him and went meekly with the police when they arrived.

1967: James Earl Ray, later the confessed killer of Martin Luther King, Jr., escaped the Missouri State Penitentiary on April 23 by hiding in a bread crate inside a delivery truck. Ray, called "the mole" by other con-

victs, was recaptured within days. This was Ray's fourth escape attempt
from prisons; he was then serving time for robbery.

1972: Mass murderer Charles Howard Schmid, Jr., and Raymond Hudgens, killer of three, escaped the Arizona State Prison on November 11.
After holding four hostages near Tempe, Arizona, Schmid, wearing a
blond wig, attempted to flee on a passing freight train but was picked up
at a train stop. Hudgens was also captured a short time later.

1975: In one of the most startling prison breaks in American history,
forger and con man Dale Otto Remling actually flew over the high prison
walls of the Southern Michigan State Prison at Jackson. Morris Colosky,
a colleague of Remling's hired a helicopter and forced the pilot to fly him
inside the prison, landing on the athletic field near a red handkerchief
placed by Remling. Remling hopped into the copter and was whisked to
freedom.

The pilot was ordered to land near a roadway where two cars were
waiting. Remling and Colosky, after spraying the pilot, Richard Jackson,
with mace to disable him, ran to the cars and escaped. Remling was
picked up in a bar outside of Jackson a week later. He had gotten the idea

Mass murderer Charles Howard Schmid, Jr. (center), called "The Pied Piper"
of Tucson, Arizona—he had killed several teenagers—who escaped the Arizona State Prison in 1972. (Wide World)

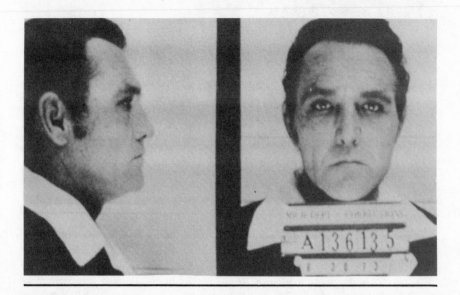

Dale Remling, who engineered the most outlandish prison escape in modern times in 1975.

Newspaper sketch depicts how the helicopter escape of Dale Remling from the world's largest walled prison was executed. (Detroit *Free Press*)

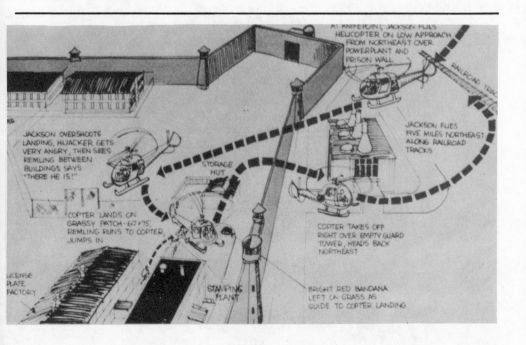

AT KNIFEPOINT, JACKSON FLIES HELICOPTER ON LOW APPROACH FROM NORTHEAST OVER POWER PLANT AND PRISON WALL

RAILROAD TRACK

JACKSON FLIES FIVE MILES NORTHEAST ALONG RAILROAD TRACKS

JACKSON OVERSHOOTS LANDING, HIJACKER GETS VERY ANGRY, THEN SEES REMLING BETWEEN BUILDINGS SAYS "THERE HE IS!"

STORAGE HUT

COPTER LANDS ON GRASSY PATCH· 60'×75' REMLING RUNS TO COPTER, JUMPS IN

COPTER TAKES OFF RIGHT OVER EMPTY GUARD TOWER, HEADS BACK NORTHEAST

LICENSE PLATE FACTORY

STAMPING PLANT

BRIGHT RED BANDANA LEFT ON GRASS AS GUIDE TO COPTER LANDING

Hijacked copter pilot Richard Jackson explains to police how he was compelled to free Remling at knifepoint.

A scene from the motion picture *Breakout;* Remling watched advertisements for this film on the prison TV and then copied to the letter the helicopter escape some weeks later.

for the break after watching commercials on the prison television which advertised a Charles Bronson movie, *Breakout,* in which a helicopter is employed.

1977: James Earl Ray and six others escaped the Brushy Mountain State Prison in rural Tennessee on June 15, using a homemade ladder to scale a wall at the end of the prison yard. Ray and the others were captured a short while later.

1979: On August 9, three convicts in San Quentin, all working outside the walls on an honor system, slipped into a warehouse, where they had made a kayak of Formica, wood and plastic; one of the convicts had been a boatmaker. The three men, Forest Tucker, John Waller and William McGirk, then pushed their blue kayak into the waters of San Francisco Bay and paddled away, right beneath the walls of San Quentin. Guards watched them paddling by, not recognizing the convicts' blue denim work clothes. They waved to the escapees, who waved cheerily back.

When the kayak appeared to be leaking, one of the guards shouted: "Do you need any help?"

"No, no," one of the convicts replied in a happy voice, "we're doing just fine!"

The three escaped convicts are still at large at this writing.

PROSTITUTION

THE CITY WHERE PROSTITUTION WAS QUEEN

Recent statistics indicate that prostitution is on the rise across the country. Every major city is teeming with ladies of the evening, and much of their activity gleans enormous profits for organized crime. However, one city still stands apart as the historical front-runner of trollop turnover.

For all its romantic allure and gift of American jazz, New Orleans is best known as the city of prostitutes. Storyville and the Red Light District are gone now, but in their heydays, these quarters were the most notorious scarlet patches in the country.

In the early 1870s, more than eight thousand professional prostitutes roamed the streets. In fact, in 1872 the New Orleans police superintendent told the governor of Louisiana that the hordes of harlots were "lost to all sense of shame and self-respect," and that they made the "night hideous with their drunken orgies, and [annoyed] the respectable residents of the neighborhood with their indecent behavior."

For almost forty years, beat cops ignored their supervisors' wrath and collected nickles and dimes left on the front stoops of bordellos. When business fell off and the small-change kickbacks narrowed, however, police would raid the brothels.

Although the city was inundated with ghettolike structures, New Orleans boasted the most opulent bagnios in the nation.

Inside these pleasure palaces, men wore tuxedos and women sported evening dresses. Only the best wines and champagnes were offered, and full-piece bands played the music of the era. Manners were so stressed that the business of sex was never mentioned, except obliquely by the proprietress, who usually billed her clients on a monthly basis.

One such madam was Kate Townsend, whose lavish house offered resplendent tapestries, damask and black walnut furniture. The New Orleans *Picayune* once reported of Townsend's bedroom that, "The hang-

Two of Kate Townsend's girls at work on champagne-soaked customers.

ings of the bed, even the mosquito bar, were of lace, and an exquisite basket of flowers hung suspended from the tester of the bed. Around the walls were suspended chaste and costly oil paintings."

Despite her beauty, fame and money, Townsend ran afoul of her "fancy man," Treville Egbert Sykes, the son of a wealthy New Orleans merchant. In a fit of rage over one of Sykes's indiscretions with another girl, Townsend almost slashed him to death while he slept. Sykes, however, wrested the knife from Kate and killed her. New Orleans courts ruled that Sykes acted out of self-defense.

Although Kate left an estate of $100,000, Sykes, after battling for the money for five years in court, was awarded $34. Complained the fancy man, "It ain't much for the love of your life."

One madam, Minnie Haha, was ever considerate. She made sure that free apples were fed to the horses of the waiting carriages outside her bagnio and their owners' suits were pressed and shoes shined before they departed for home.

Although few wives objected to their husbands visiting such establishments, one southern belle marched into Leila Barton's stylish bordello, kicked open the door of a bedroom, and, finding her husband in the arms of Blanche Rusell, began banging away with a pistol. The wild shots destroyed an expensive vase while Rusell hid under the sheets and the husband crashed through a window to escape in the street below.

As Storyville blossomed into the center of New Orleans prostitution, publishers began issuing "blue book" editions listing the prices charged by the most enterprising slatterns. These publications also carried advertisements from the better brothels which described their waiting delights in a more sophisticated way than the sleazy promotions of present-day Nevada bordellos.

The queen of all the New Orleans harlots was unquestionably the flam-

Madam Minnie Haha looks on as one of her harlots stops a potential customer outside of her bordello.

The card of T. C. Anderson, Josie Arlington's financial backer and protector.

boyant Josie Arlington, whose sex emporium cost several hundred thousand dollars to build. Arlington made untold fortunes, but she grew morose long before Storyville closed down and bought an expensive tomb in the Metairie Cemetery.

After Arlington's death and entombment, the city erected a red traffic warning light just outside the cemetery. Its glow at night freakishly reflected off the tomb, suggesting that New Orleans was honoring its most celebrated madam. As years went by, until embarrassed authorities removed the light, visitors stood gazing as the red light blinked on and off above the tomb.

Other notable events and personalities in prostitution include:

China, 650 B.C.: Chinese statesman Kuang Chung, according to earliest reports known, established prostitution in the mid-seventh century B.C. throughout China, possibly licensing prostitutes for the first time in history. The first known madam, or female proprietor of a house of prostitution was allegedly a beautiful courtesan called Hung Yai.

Rome, 240 B.C.: The most famous of Roman concubines, Flora, died in Rome, leaving a vast estate gleaned from her sexual trafficking with Roman aristocrats. In her will, the story was later told, Flora insisted that most of her ungainly wealth be spent on lavish festivals in honor of the goddess Flora, her namesake.

Rome, A.D. 89: The superstitious emperor Domitian, more to vex his enemies in the Senate than to serve any concept of morality, decreed that

Roman prostitutes could no longer travel in public on litters. He also denied them the right of inheritance or the receiving of legacies. Senators, according to Domitian's orders, were prohibited from marrying any woman who ever earned a living as a whore or any female whose past showed an ancestor who earned a living as a prostitute.

Constantinople, 560: Empress Theodora, one-time dancer (her lascivious dances are the first recorded which compare with latter-day burlesque in that she stripped before all-male audiences), then high court prostitute who married Justinian I, emperor of the Roman Empire of the East, aided young prostitutes sold into white slavery, particularly in Constantinople, by opening a haven for them in a deserted castle on the Buxine Sea. Hundreds of women were rehabilitated through Theodora's efforts.

Holy Land, 1097: During the First Crusade to free the Holy Land from Moslem tyranny, the ranks of the crusaders were swollen with prostitutes who had accompanied the knights from Europe. Many of these women, fervently supporting the crusade, sold their bodies in towns along the route of the crusade to raise money for food and equipment needed by the armies. Once in the Holy Land, priests drove thousands of these harlots from the encampments, leaving them to die in desolate areas or be captured by Moslems and either be killed or dragged into white slavery.

Italy, 1158: Frederick Barbarossa, the Holy Roman Emperor of Germany, who was later to lead the Third Crusade, became so enraged at the thousands of whores accompanying his soldiers while his armies moved through Italy that he ordered all soldiers whipped if caught with a prostitute. The woman thus caught had her nose sliced off, according to Frederick's decree.

Spain, 1220: King Alfonso IX of Castile laid down the first severe laws against prostitution in Europe. Any white slavers caught selling whores were banished from Spain. Landlords renting rooms to whores were heavily fined and their houses forfeited to the crown. Those found guilty of keeping a brothel were compelled to free their prostitutes, most of whom were sex slaves, and also find them husbands within a short period of time or be beheaded. Any husband who compelled his wife to acts of prostitution was quickly executed. Those found guilty of being pimps at the first offense were whipped. If a second offense was proved, the pimp was made a permanent galley slave. Women found guilty of turning wages over to a pimp were stripped naked, whipped and their clothes burned.

France, 1254: King Louis IX of France, to curb the rampant prostitution, chiefly in Paris, made all involved in prostitution outlaws by royal decree, their possessions to be turned over to the state. When decent women began to be raped by ruffians who called them whores, Louis modified his edict to less drastic regulations.

China, 1280: Marco Polo, according to his later dictated writings, reported that the Chinese capital city of Peking was overrun with prostitutes, with more than 20,000 earning their living from the practice. Twice that number operated in Hangchow.

France, 1347: In an effort to keep prostitutes off the streets of Avignon and other French cities, a state-run brothel was established at the design of Queen Joanna of Naples, who virtually owned Avignon. Women in this public brothel, built close to a convent, were ordered to wear a red knot on their shoulder. If they refused to wear this knot, they were led down the main streets with the symbol identifying them as prostitutes and then whipped in the public square. The doors of this house were always locked. An abbess had to approve of any male wishing to enter. If an abbess allowed any male to enter the house of prostitution on certain holy days, she was to be whipped and then fired from her position. No Jews were allowed to enter this house; if any Jews entered, as one did in 1498, they were publicly whipped. Prostitutes inside the house were regularly checked by doctors to determine if they had contracted venereal disease or were pregnant. If the latter, the women were restrained from having abortions, their children turned over to the state.

England, 1300s: Prostitutes were compelled to wear identifying trademarks such as striped robes, and, in London, whores could only parade in certain restricted districts. If found soliciting in any of the "respectable" districts, these women were driven from the city and into permanent exile.

Italy, late 1300s: Pope Gregory XI, according to religious historian G. G. Coulton, complained that many convents were nothing more than brothels with nuns having sex with priests and monks, many of these nuns giving birth to illegitimate children.

Italy, 1495: The first record of the disease of syphilis (then known as the "French Sickness"), and commonly referred to as the "whore's disease," was pinpointed by many historians to Naples, Italy, where the French King Charles VIII had brought an invading army made up of many nationalities. When these troops disbanded and returned to France, Italy, Switzerland and Germany, they carried the disease back to their homelands. Others hotly argued that the disease was brought back by Columbus' followers from the Americas in the late 1490s.

Rome, 1500s: Pope Alexander VI (Rodrigo Borgia, who was not a priest of the Church but a layman pope) proved to be the most corrupt of any papal leader in history. Four children were born to Alexander and his mistress, Vannozza dei Cattanei, including the conniving Cesare and Lucretia Borgia of the many poisons. Lascivious and obscene, Alexander often held private sex orgies, making him notorious, the most offensive being the so-called "chestnut supper," in 1501, at which fifty naked whores slithered on marble floors before Alexander and his then mistress, Giulia Farnese, a teen-age harlot. The prostitutes, recruited for the orgy from the slums of Rome, reportedly snaked their ways around burning candles, picking up hot chestnuts at the commands of Alexander and Guilia with their labia.

Europe, 1500s: Public outrage against blatant prostitution caused wholesale reforms across Europe. Those apprehended in the company of a whore in Frankfurt were heavily fined, according to a 1530 law. In 1546, all brothels in London were closed by government order. Fourteen years later, Paris officials ordered the closing of its many whorehouses.

France, 1540s: Francis I encouraged promiscuity at his court, stating that every reasonable French aristocrat should have a mistress (thus founding a French tradition). He himself had two courtesans in attendance on him, the beautiful Françoise de Châteaubriand and Anne, Duchess d'Étampes, the latter selected to act as a royal whore by Francis' wife, Queen Eleanor. Both women wielded enormous power in the French court, often dictating royal policy through the womanizing Francis. When the king died, Madame de Châteaubriand returned to her native Brittany and to her long-neglected husband, who murdered her.

Rome, 1566: Pope Pius V, enraged at the widespread prostitution plaguing Rome, ordered all involved in the practice to leave the Eternal City and never return. When Pius was told that half the city was packing, he withdrew the papal edict.

Florence, Italy, 1569: An official edict classified various types of prostitutes based upon their income. Those who possessed great wealth were to be listed as courtesans and entitled to all rights under the law. Those who were poor were classified as common whores and these hapless creatures were severely restricted in their activities.

Spain, 1601: Authorities made a rare head count of prostitutes overrunning the city of Seville in 1601, discovering more than 3,000 whores working the streets alone with perhaps half that number operating inside hundreds of brothels.

Boston, Massachusetts, 1672: The first notorious brothel madam in the colonies was Alice Thomas, who in 1672 was found guilty of keeping a whorehouse, for which she was whipped through the streets of Boston. Alice, according to the charges, was guilty of "giving frequent secret and unseasonable entertainment in her house to lewd lascivious and notorious persons of both sexes, giving them opportunity to commit carnall wickedness, and that by common fame she is a common baud."

Paris, France, late 1700s: The most notorious brothel on the European continent was undoubtedly that of Madame Gourdan, located on the Rue des Deux Portes. Here, men of wealth and royal blood gathered to select whores who posed in lascivious positions. The brothel, as elegant as any palace in style and comfort, served as a finishing school for successful prostitutes, and a training center for young farm girls entering Paris to establish themselves. One story had it that Madame Jeanne Bécu du Barry, last mistress to the French king Louis XV, guillotined in 1793 during the French Revolution, was trained by Madame Gourdan personally.

England, late 1700s: Emma Hart, a beautiful young woman born in London under cloudy and poor circumstances, became the mistress of several influential British military men, including Charles Greville, who, to eliminate a heavy debt to his uncle, turned his mistress over to that uncle, Sir William Hamilton, who later married her. As Lady Hamilton, Emma took many lovers, including the naval hero Admiral Horatio Nelson, having a child by him. Nelson, who was married, lived with Lady Hamilton until his death, at which time he left almost his entire estate to her. However, Emma Hamilton died in poverty in 1815.

Berlin, Germany, 1792: All prostitutes were required to live on specified streets and be the responsibility of their landlords, who were also responsible for any crime committed on their premises. Before opening a bordello, madams had to get the permission of the police.

Paris, France, 1796: Prostitutes, according to French law, had to register with the police. Two years later physicians were ordered to inspect all public prostitutes for venereal disease and treat them accordingly.

New York City, 1812: A black madam known only as "Big Sue" operated the first around-the-clock brothel in New York City in Arch Block in the city's fourth ward. Sue was also known as "The Turtle," a gigantic madam weighing more than 350 pounds who preferred to drag her customers in from the street, literally tossing them to her waiting girls.

Paris, France, 1828: According to law, a weekly medical inspection was required of all prostitutes of licensed brothels, a rule kept in force for decades.

New York City, 1838: The first prostitute booked and imprisoned in the city's new mammoth prison, the Tombs, was Catherine Hagerman, who was given six months on June 15.

Munich, Bavaria, 1848: Lola Montez, daughter of an English army officer and a Spanish woman (real name Marie Dolores Eliza Rosanna Gilbert), after marrying then leaving her husband in India to become a dancer and highly paid prostitute, traveled in 1846 to Bavaria, where she became the mistress to King Ludwig I. So enamored of Lola was Ludwig that he dismissed churchmen from his court at her whim and adopted whatever policies she fancied. More than any other reason, Lola was the cause of Ludwig's forced abdication in 1848.

Lola went on to other sexual adventures with high- and low-class patrons, traveling in Spain and then in the United States as an actress appearing in a play called *Lola Montez in Bavaria*. She danced in the hellholes of California during the Gold Rush of 1848–52, then settled down for a while with a San Francisco newspaper publisher. After a sojourn in Australia, Lola returned to the United States, devoting her time

The prostitute who toppled a kingdom, Lola Montez, shown here in a painting entitled *The Treacherous Water* by Franz Xavier Winterhalter.

to down-and-out prostitutes in New York City until her death in 1861.

San Francisco, California, 1849: Dozens of ships arrived in San Francisco during the Gold Rush loaded with hundreds of whores, who made up, at one time, half of the city's population.

Paris, France, 1867: British-born Cora Pearl (née Eliza Elizabeth Crouch), after several affairs in England, traveled to Paris, where she became a *cause célèbre* in prostitution, giving lavish parties and having her liveried butlers serving her naked on a huge platter to her guests as dessert. In 1867, Cora so charmed Prince Jérôme Bonaparte, cousin of Napoleon III, that he made her his mistress, installing her in a palace. When Bonaparte fled to England after his country's collapse following the Franco-Prussian War, Cora became the mistress to a wealthy French heir, Alexander Duval, whom she bled of millions. When the youth tried to commit suicide, Duval's parents influenced authorities to deport Cora back to her native England.

Shunned by her former lover, Bonaparte, Cora moved through the Continent, a courtesan available to the highest bidder. Cora finally returned to Paris. Contracting cancer, she died in 1886, her luminous career all but forgotten.

San Francisco, 1869: Hundreds of Chinese women arrived in San Francisco from their homeland, imported by Chinese merchants as one would import herring, these women to be sold as either wives or prostitutes, usually the latter.

Washington, D.C., 1874: President Grant, enraged at the flagrant shipments of Chinese prostitutes to the United States, chiefly those entering the port of San Francisco, urged Congress to enact laws prohibiting the migration of these women. In the following year Congress prohibited the migration of any women sent to this country "for the purposes of prostitution," the first in a long series of laws instituted to curb prostitution in the United States.

New Orleans, Louisiana, 1880: Brothels in New Orleans became so crowded with whores that the thousands flocking to the city found no home and were reduced to selling themselves on the streets. For ten cents, a customer could purchase a ten-minute trick from these women, most of them diseased harlots.

Belgium, 1890s: The center of white slavery in Europe became Brussels, where the local police had been corrupted almost to the last man. Setting the example was the king of Belgium, who imported for his own pleasure British virgins by the score, allowing a budget for that purpose which reportedly came to about 1,800 pounds a year.

Los Angeles, California, 1897: Prostitution in Los Angeles had become big business with many elegantly styled bordellos established by 1897, one of the most popular being owned by Ella Rorich, who appeared in a regularly published guide to bordellos in the city called *The Souvenir*

Cora Pearl, one of the most successful courtesans in Paris during the late 1860s.

Sporting Guide. In most American cities by this time similar booklets were published. In New Orleans, the guide was called *The Blue Book,* which took an ironic leaf from New York's publication of those in high society.

New York City, 1900s: Gangster Paul Kelly (née Antonio Vaccarelli) became king of the pimps in Manhattan. Like Big Jim Colosimo in Chicago (and after him Johnny Torrio and Al Capone), Kelly founded his underworld wealth on prostitution.

Kelly, early in the 1900s, imported more than 1,000 impoverished young girls from Italy, sending them into the street since his dozens of brothels were already filled. These pathetic streetwalkers serviced the lowest type of customers for fifty cents a trick, half of this amount being returned to Kelly by his "collection" agents, who waited on the spot for the money.

Europe, 1904: Mostly due to the tireless efforts of British reformer and newspaperman W. T. Stead, vigilance committees against white slavery sprang up all over the Continent, which resulted in the formation of the International Congress on the White Slave Traffic. This organization of thirteen nations led by England (the United States later became a member) on May 18, 1904, ratified an agreement to stop the white slavers, subsequently co-ordinating all information about international white slaving and enacting laws to prevent this traffic.

New York City, 1909: The political machine Tammany served as the overall protector of hordes of prostitutes in the city. In a five-month period in 1909, police records show, 3,145 whores were arrested for street prostitution but only 13 per cent of this number were given small prison sentences. Most received laughable fines of one to ten dollars, and these were paid by Tammany operatives.

Washington, D.C., 1910: The most severe federal law to date was enacted with the passage of the Mann Act, which provided for stringent penalties for any person found guilty of transporting or helping to transport any woman across a state line for immoral purposes.

Philadelphia, 1913: The Rockefeller Report, an extensive investigation into prostitution in the city, revealed that 372 brothels were openly operating in the city and that half of the 3,311 known prostitutes working in the city plied their trade exclusively on the street. The vice, according to the report, was a $6-million-a-year business.

Denver, Colorado, 1919: Big Time Charlie Allen, after numerous adventures—with Pancho Villa in the Mexican revolutions, and the Alaskan gold strikes—settled in Denver, becoming the richest pimp in the city. Allen imported his girls from the West Coast, scoffing at the Mann Act, and collected *all* the earnings of his hordes of whores, paying off his women in heroin. Once addicted, the girls became his virtual slaves. This method of payment boomeranged on Big Time Charlie. His home was raided in 1919 and heroin and cocaine in great quantities were discovered. Allen was sent to Leavenworth for five years for trafficking in drugs.

New York City, 1920: One of the most infamous madams of America, Polly Adler (born in Russia as Pearl Adler), rented a two-room apartment on Riverside Drive in early 1920, setting up her first of many successful brothels.

Chicago, Illinois, 1927: Al Capone's thousands of whores contributed most of the $5 million used as a campaign chest to re-elect William Hale Thompson as mayor of the city in 1927. Thompson, Capone's man, who had run on "a wide-open city" ticket, was re-elected in a landslide. In the first year of Thompson's term, 1928, more than 2,000 vice parlors of all

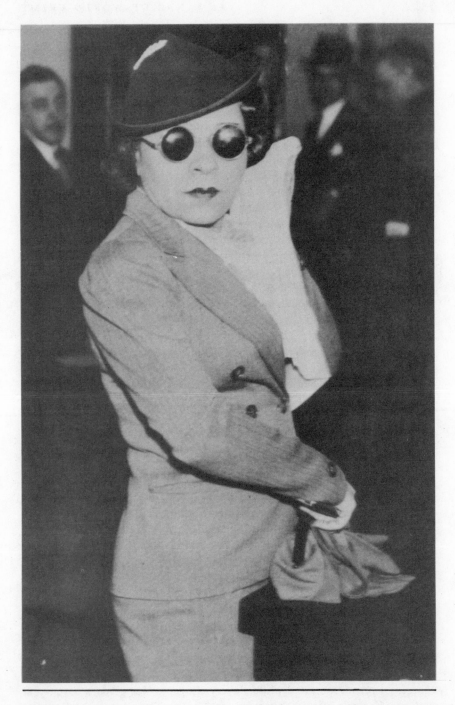

The notorious New York madam Polly Adler in one of her court appearances.

sorts were operating around the clock, most of the police force in league with the brothels, which kicked back from $250 to $1,000 a week to the police to continue operations. It became common knowledge that if a customer sought the whereabouts of any whorehouse, it was best "to ask a cop."

New York City, 1935: Charles "Lucky" Luciano, one of the founders of the national crime syndicate, had in his employ by 1935 more than 1,200 prostitutes working directly for him in his bordellos from coast to coast, returning a $10 million gross to him each year.

Vice detectives attempting to build a case against Luciano interviewed many of his prostitutes, who refused to provide information. When told of the investigation, Luciano snorted to newsmen that his employees were "gutless whores." This statement as quoted so enraged some of his prostitutes—they later claimed their pride had been hurt—that Florence "Cokey Flo" Brown, Nancy Presser and Mildred Harris readily testified against the country's leading pimp. Luciano was found guilty on sixty-two counts of prostitution and sent to prison for from thirty to fifty years. (He was released shortly after World War II, allegedly because of his help in convincing partisans to co-operate with the Allies during the invasion of Sicily.)

New Haven, Connecticut, 1936: Morris "Motzie" de Nicola, vice overlord of New England, whose brothels brought him a $2 million profit each year, was convicted on ten counts of prostitution and sent to Lewisburg Penitentiary.

London, 1940s–50s: The largest vice ring in Europe was operated by the brothers Carmelo and Eugenio Messina, who had immigrated to England in 1934 from Sicily. Renting hundreds of flats in London, the Messinas imported girls from Italy, Greece, France and Belgium, arranging phony marriages for them to enable these prostitutes to obtain British citizenship. The "husbands" were never seen again after the five-minute wedding ceremonies. The girls were then moved into Messina flats and worked as common white slaves, their actions totally controlled by pimps who collected immediately after a customer departed. One girl, who escaped her guarded flat to write an autobiography, stated that she had taken on forty-nine customers in one night, which was slightly above average for a Messina whore.

Any prostitute on the Messina payroll, which included most in London, who protested working conditions was beaten. Those who tried to escape or hold out payments were slashed with razors, disfigured so they could never again work the trade with any success.

The Messina brothers were finally tripped up in Belgium in 1956 on charges of prostitution and white slavery. Eugenio was given a seven-year sentence, Carmelo was sent away for ten months. The ring was broken up.

Bombay, India, 1957: Authorities became alarmed when swarms of prostitutes began openly soliciting near public buildings. By this time an estimated 40,000 prostitutes were operating in the city. (Prostitution was never stamped as an illegal act in India.) Officials decreed that whores must stay away from public buildings, particularly public shrines.

London, 1960s: Following the Street Offences Act in England, which compelled prostitutes to quit street soliciting under severe penalties, whores took to advertising their services on thousands of notice boards outside of motion picture theaters, newsstands and tobacco shops, a practice still in use today.

Nevada, 1971: Joe Conforte's Mustang Ranch brothel in Storey County reaped so much profit that Conforte became the county's largest taxpayer. He applied for a license to legalize his operation. This was granted by local commissioners. Conforte was given the exclusive prostitution franchise in the country, despite suits by other brothel owners wanting to set up operations.

Washington, D.C., 1976: A major scandal dealing with Elizabeth Ray and other so-called "secretaries" of federal officials made it apparent that vice rings operated at a high level among government personalities.

Las Vegas, Nevada, 1977: More than 7,000 prostitutes were recorded as working in Las Vegas, half of this number working almost around the clock and with the loose sponsorship of the casinos.

United States, 1970s: Rather than lead oppressive campaigns against vice operations across the country, most of which are controlled by the national crime syndicate, which reaps perhaps $1 to $2 billion in profits each year, most city governments take a posture of tolerance toward prostitution today, as long as the operations are confined to one area of a city.

These sections of cities are invariably the most run-down, dangerous areas where prostitution, robbery, and drug trafficking flourish. In New York City, the pesthole is the once-glamorous Broadway and Forty-second Street area. In Los Angeles, the whole of Hollywood is overrun with whores and pimps, particularly along Sunset Boulevard, so crowded at night that male and female prostitutes have a difficult time finding an advantageous place to stand to solicit passing motorists. In Chicago, the Bughouse Square neighborhood on the near North Side is a haven for male prostitutes (the area in which homosexual mass murderer John Wayne Gacy operated.) In Boston, the Liberty Tree district has been sanctioned by city fathers as the place of prostitution, commonly referred to as the Combat Zone, an area, like those previously mentioned, of murder and robbery that holds out terror rather than visions of pleasure to the eternal customer of the prostitute.

PUBLIC REACTION

THE OBSESSION OF COLLECTING CRIME MEMORABILIA IN AMERICA

A quirkish compulsion to collect mementos of American criminals and crimes afflicts many a citizen in the United States. The estate of Candace Mossler, Houston heiress who was once accused of murdering her husband, was auctioned in 1977, and hundreds of ardent souvenir hunters arrived to pay exorbitant amounts for the dead woman's possessions.

From diamonds to statues, the artifacts owned by suspect Candace were scooped up as soon as they went on the block, including the Mossler mailbox, which a Houston clothier purchased for fifty-five dollars. The haberdasher gave the mailbox to his girl friend to use as a planter.

The desire to own something, almost anything, once in the possession of a notorious criminal or connected to an infamous crime has flourished since our beginnings as a nation. Perfectly normal, law-abiding people have been demonstrating their fascination with miscreants and mayhem for centuries by squandering hard-earned money on this unusual memorabilia.

Just after the American Revolution collectors were in hot pursuit of tangible reminders of wild outlaws such as the Harpe brothers, who plundered and murdered their way through the wilderness of the Ohio Valley.

When Micajah "Big" Harpe was finally tracked down and slain by a posse in 1799 his head was severed from his carcass and carried in a sack toward civilization. The lawmen, however, ran out of food, and were compelled to boil Micajah's head for sustenance. The skull was nailed to a tree. Upon hearing this, an angry merchant who had offered ten dollars for the outlaw's skull (to adorn the portal of his store), chastised the gluttonous possemen and then upped the bid to twenty dollars if anyone would return to retrieve the gruesome trophy. There were no takers.

There were plenty of takers in St. Joseph, Missouri, on April 3, 1882, when Jesse Woodson James was shot and killed by Bob Ford in his small hilltop home. No sooner had "the dirty little coward" (Ford) raced into the streets shouting "I killed Jesse James!" than half the town poured into the outlaw's home.

Jesse's wife, Zerelda, was still cradling her murdered husband as scores of good townsfolk ambled through her parlor and kitchen pocketing photos, bric-a-brac, and even lugging chairs away with them as mementos.

Another outlaw, "Flat Nose" George Curry (née George Parrott), found the residents of Castle Gate, Utah, more impatient than the collectors of St. Joseph.

Curry, who had helped to develop Butch Cassidy's Wild Bunch, was being chased in a running gunfight by a sheriff who had caught him rustling horses. A lucky shot by the sheriff knocked Curry from his galloping horse and, as he sprawled bleeding to death on the open plain, the citizens of Castle Gate rushed out to look over a real outlaw. So impressed were some that they withdrew knives and began to skin Curry.

One of the townsfolk made a pair of shoes from Curry's chest, another made macabre watch fobs from other sections of the outlaw's anatomy. A Professor Reed of Wyoming University proudly carried one of these skin watch fobs in his vest for decades until turning it over to a museum.

In 1908 Chester Gillette was waiting to be electrocuted for drowning his sweetheart, Grace Brown, in Big Moose Lake, New York. The handsome youth, whose case inspired Theodore Dresier to write *An American Tragedy,* capitalized on the American lust of crime collecting and sold his own photo to many admiring females. With the profits, Gillette ordered catered meals brought to his cell. By the time of his execution on March 30, 1908, Gillette was considerably overweight.

Perhaps the most preposterous criminal artifact collected involved America's most successful safecracker, Morris "Red" Rudensky, who escaped from Leavenworth by squeezing himself into a tiny magazine box shipped out of the prison's print shop.

Rudensky had marked the box "This Side Up" but a freight handler had ignored the directive and Red was placed upside down on a jiggling, jostling freight car. He hemorrhaged. An alert freight guard spotted the blood and took Rudensky back into custody.

The box, bloodstained as it was, found its way to the Philadelphia Sesquicentennial International Exposition of 1926, where it was displayed to thousands of gaping visitors. (Red, who became totally rehabilitated in prison, and who now lives as a respected citizen of Minneapolis, put his

Outlaw "Flat Nose" George Curry, whose fate at the hands of fascinated citizens was the most ignoble in the Old West.

safecracking expertise to better uses. He became the chief locksmith for the 3-M Company.)

Savagery in American crime seems to stimulate the public's fantasies, which is, no doubt, why so many Chicagoans desperately vied for the bricks that made up the wall of the garage at 2122 North Clark Street. Before it was torn down this shabby edifice was the living memory of the 1929 St. Valentine's Day Massacre of seven gangsters.

Perhaps this urge to "see the beast" compelled men, women and children to dip their handkerchiefs into the pool of blood seeping from the man identified as John Dillinger by the FBI and killed on the sultry night of July 22, 1934, outside a Chicago theater.

More than morbidity has caused art collectors to bid for the sketches of the executed Gary Gilmore, a murderer who screamed impatiently for his own death. Self-identification with our own times might explain it, this public penchant to own symbols of lawlessness.

Ann Matthews of Beaumont, Texas, who attended the 1977 Mossler auction, may have summed it all up: "I just wanted something exciting that was hers to show my grandchildren when I'm a dull, old grandmother."

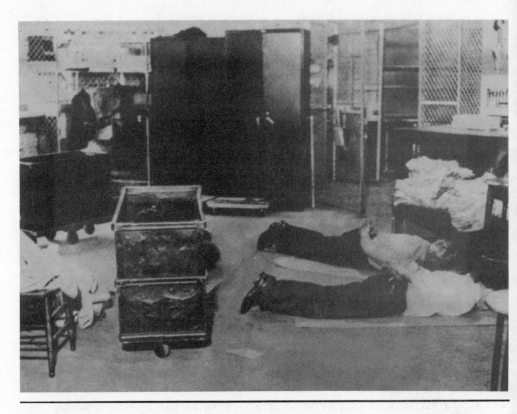

Site of the Brink's robbery in Boston with guards re-enacting the positions they were forced to take by the thieves. (UPI)

ROBBERY

THE NEAR PERFECT HEIST AT BRINK'S

Criminals the world over have, in their warped logic and lust, dreamed of committing the perfect robbery, so thoroughly planned and executed that not a single clue is left to lead to the guilty. This was the great ambition of Joseph F. "Big Joe" McGinnis, a Boston liquor dealer with a long rap sheet for robbery and narcotics, and one of his patrons, Anthony "Fats" Pino, whose record dated back to 1928, when he was charged with molesting a young girl. Nothing was too small for Pino; once he was arrested for stealing a dozen golf balls. But he, like the garrulous McGinnis, longed to commit the super crime. Pino and McGinnis began to share this great dark dream in the summer of 1948.

The two men drooled with desire at the thought of the Brink's armored car service office in Boston, a conduit, they knew, for every major payroll in the area, offices where as much as $10 million was processed daily. McGinnis and Pino began to recruit a small army of professional gunmen and thieves to commit "the robbery of the century."

Joining the ranks were nine other men: Vincent J. Costa, an expert wheelman; lock specialist Henry J. Baker; James Ignatius Flaherty, bartender, burglar and escape artist; gunmen and experienced robbers Adolph "Jazz" Maffie, Thomas F. Richardson, Michael V. Geagan, Stanley H. Gusciora, John S. Banfield and the redoubtable Joseph James "Specs" O'Keefe. (O'Keefe's face was afloat with freckles in youth, when he was dubbed "Specky"; the name "Specs" clung to him as an adult, a name he hated.)

For eighteen long, grueling months, McGinnis and Pino perfected their robbery plan, drilling the others as top sergeants might drive Marine trainees. The North Terminal Garage, which was the Brink's headquarters, was cased daily. The thieves systematically noted schedules and shipments of money, figured escape routes and discovered the exact times when the "big money" would be on hand and where.

Nothing matched the gall of these men. They took turns entering Brink's at night, knowing the routines of the night watchmen. In stocking feet, in twos and threes, the robbers entered, usually around midnight, when most of the money was in the main vault and vigilance was relaxed. Five locked doors between the street and the money had to be gotten through. Locksmith Baker and the others removed each lock, one during each nightly sortie. Baker then left the building, made a key for the lock and the lock was replaced that same night.

Security and caution, McGinnis and Pino declared to gang members, were the watchwords. More than twenty times, the gang practiced the robbery, from entry to departure, seven men entering, led by O'Keefe, one at the wheel of a truck to carry them and the loot away and two as lookouts on top of neighboring buildings with binoculars and a powerful telescope. Every man entering Brink's was to look identical; the seven robbers were selected because they were all the same weight and height, about five feet nine inches tall, 170–80 pounds. They would all wear navy pea jackets, grotesque Halloween masks, visored caps, gloves and rubber-soled shoes.

Finally, on the cold and drizzling night of January 17, 1950—the

Mastermind of the Brink's robbery, Joseph F. "Big Joe" McGinnis.

The happy-go-lucky thief and co-designer of the Brink's caper, Anthony Pino.

weather keeping everyone off the streets—the gang struck, going into Brink's a little before 7 P.M. The seven masked men crept forward through the five doors to the main counting room on their rubber-soled shoes, unlocking each door as they went. At exactly 7:10 P.M., O'Keefe, the others in Indian file behind him, stood in front of the wire mesh door to the main room, a door to which the robbers had no key.

Head cashier Thomas B. Lloyd was just emerging from the vault when he heard O'Keefe growl: "This is a stickup. Open the gate and don't give us any trouble."

Of the five men inside the cage, only Charlie Grell was armed. The weapons belonging to the other four Brink's men were resting in a nearby gun rack. Grell did not go for his gun. "It would have been sure death for him to reach for it," Lloyd later informed Boston's Police Commissioner Thomas F. Sullivan. Grell opened the cage door at Lloyd's order. The assistant cashier, James Allen, came out of the dispatcher's office just as the seven robbers poured into the counting room. He paused momentarily next to the gun rack and then dismissed the thought, joining the other Brink's men on the floor, where they had been ordered by O'Keefe to lie face down. Their hands were tied behind their backs, their feet were tied, and adhesive tape was slapped over their lips.

The thieves went to work, each knowing his job; one packed the large bills, one handed these in sacks to the others, who dragged them out. Of the $4 or $5 million on hand at the Brink's office, the gang scooped up $2,775,395 ($1,218,211.29 in bills and coins and $1,557,183.83 in money orders and checks, the total weight about 1,200 pounds). For a moment, gang members stared at a large metal security box which was locked. They debated whether or not to take it along. They left it; the box contained more than $1 million in cash. They were gone at exactly 7:27 P.M. accomplishing the robbery in seventeen minutes without interruption (a guard from the garage did ring the bell inside the money room but he went away after getting no reply).

The money was loaded into the truck and the robbers quickly drove to the home of Adolph "Jazz" Maffie in Roxbury. Here the negotiables and more than $90,000 in new money, all traceable, was destroyed. The remaining $1,100,000 was not divided, but left with Maffie.

Each man returned calmly to his home and family, punctually resuming whatever jobs each had the following morning while Boston and state police, plus the FBI, turned the city over many times looking for traces of the thieves. Aside from thirty-two pieces of white cotton line and a visored cap with the label torn from it, there was not a single clue.

Discipline still held the gang together and members waited patiently for

The man who blew the whistle on the Brink's thieves, Joseph "Specs" O'Keefe.

a month before dividing up the loot, about $100,000 for each. They went their ways to spend piecemeal through the years of the gang's anonymity and freedom loot they had so carefully stolen. Specs O'Keefe, however, made the one mistake not covered by the gang's exacting plan; he trusted another gang member with safekeeping most of his split, about $90,000, he later said. He was stalled for years whenever he tried to collect it.

O'Keefe grew exasperated and threatened to tell all. In retaliation, the gang hired madman Elmer "Trigger" Burke to machine-gun Specs to death. Burke missed but Specs became so rattled by the attack and so despondent over another hefty sentence, that he broke the whole story, carping for a finale: "I got gypped!" Dramatically, Specs waited until the last five days before the Massachusetts statute of limitations on the robbery expired.

Ten of the thieves were arrested (Banfield had died of natural causes in 1955), tried and given long sentences. Seven are now dead, according to a recent count of the Boston *Globe*. Costa was returned to prison in 1976 for counterfeiting. Richardson is a longshoreman; Geagan worked at that job until 1975; Maffie is still somewhere in Boston. None of the Brink's robbers are in the money. The dream McGinnis and Pino first shared turned into an endless nightmare.

Perhaps the surviving gang members find some grim irony in the fact that veteran Boston *Globe* crime reporter Joseph F. Dinneen, who practically dedicated his life to the Brink's story, made more money from the gang's exploits than any of them. Dinneen wrote a book and gleaned a movie sale (*Six Bridges to Cross*) for a reported $150,000 . . . and without the Halloween mask.

THE GIANT HAUL OF THE WHITE GLOVE GANG

On August 14, 1962, a mail van driven by Patrick R. Schena, and William F. Barrett ambled along Route 3, a divided highway stretching from Cape Cod northward to Boston. The drivers had been making a few stops at Cape Cod banks in the late afternoon and were driving sixteen mail sacks toward the Federal Reserve Bank of Boston. Inside the bags were huge amounts of small, old bills, destined for destruction. Little of the currency was traceable.

About 8 P.M. the truck was puttering along a lonely stretch of road near Plymouth. Seconds after it passed the Clark Road cutoff, a following Oldsmobile stopped and a fellow in a policeman's uniform got out and placed detour signs, traffic cones and an electric flasher across the Boston-bound lanes. Meanwhile, another man blocked southbound lanes several miles north on the highway.

The Oldsmobile then sped down Route 3 after the mail truck and passed it at ninety miles per hour. Neither Schena nor Barrett took notice. A minute later the mail van turned a corner and Schena had barely enough time to slam on the brakes to avoid hitting two cars parked across the road.

A policeman wearing glasses and carrying a submachine gun walked casually over to the truck. He jammed the weapon into Schena's face as another man wielding a submachine gun came up from the other side of the truck. Meekly, Barrett and Schena surrendered.

Using Schena's keys, the robbers opened the rear of the truck and forced the mail guards to lie down while their hands and feet were tied. The truck then rolled away with one of the robbers at the wheel.

Three times in an hour and a half the truck stopped along a lonely side road as several bags were tossed out to waiting confederates. During the trip, Schena overheard the names "Tony" and "Buster" spoken.

The truck was finally halted on Boston's Route 128. The man called Tony told the mail guards to "lie still or you're dead. Don't move for ten minutes." The thieves then apparently left. A minute later Schena stood up inside the truck, but a door opened and "Tony" yelled, "Lie down or I'll blow your head off! I mean it." Schena hit the deck.

A few minutes later, the guard tried again. He staggered outside and hailed a young fellow on a motor scooter, screaming to him, "Robbed of millions of dollars. Call the police!"

Ricardo G. Unda-Freire, a premedical student from Ecuador, gunned his scooter to the nearest phone booth and called police. The officer at the other end of the line demanded the student to spell his name and accused him of hoaxing the law. Undaunted, Ricardo hopped on his scooter and raced to a Stoughton police station.

The Stoughton police were skeptical, though, and it was almost two hours before they were convinced a robbery had taken place. By the time a search got underway, the robbers had utterly vanished.

Not a clue was found. The robbers had worn white gloves and left no prints, earning them the sobriquet of the "White Glove Gang." Although the thieves wore no masks, the police sketches drawn from the mail guards' memories produced no suspects. The case withered.

Few officers doubted the robbery was engineered from inside the postal and bank systems, but it was impossible to weed out suspects from hundreds of employees. Someone in the robbery gang, however, had known the post office had recently terminated a contract with an armored car service that had normally made the bank deliveries accompanied by state police.

At this writing, the White Glove Gang is still at large and the robbery swag of $1,551,277 in small bills has not been recovered. Amazingly, the vast amount taken was not made known to the public for some time. A reporter quizzing Hyannis postmaster G. Frank Swansey inquired if the stolen loot exceeded five hundred dollars. Swansey almost swooned. All he could utter was: "Oh, gracious, yes!"

AMERICA'S MASTER BANK ROBBER

It was long thought that bank robbery, particularly in the United States, was a thing of the past. Stringent laws, coupled with modern equipment and police techniques apparently made the "super heist" too risky. However, a rash of bank robberies in the past few years have police around the world scratching frantically.

The more than $8 million taken in 1976 in Nice, France, in what is now termed "the bank robbery of the century," continues to baffle international officers. In 1979, one professional bank robbery team has taken $150,000 from nine Buffalo, New York, banks alone.

Nothing like it has been seen since the American Depression, when bank robbery was a thriving business. And although he's little known today, one man more than any other was responsible for the torrent of

bank robberies in that era. Edward Wilhelm Bentz was an unusual pioneer of high crime whose penchant for detail and obscurity has undoubtedly become the credo of the modern bank robber.

Despite Bentz being the calculating master planner of almost every
significant bank robbery in America for a quarter of a century, few knew
his name or ever saw his face.

Bentz's childhood in Tacoma, Washington, never suggested his future
career. Studious, withdrawn, an avid book reader, Bentz grew to a strap-
ping size. He had a sharp taste for high culture. His affable personality
and intellectual pursuits beyond his high school graduation (he was first
in his class) gave him the confident image of solidity and honesty.

That image, Bentz was shrewdly aware, insulated him against suspicion
and countless times prevented his arrest.

"I'm a big farmerish-looking sort of fellow," he once remarked to federal officers, "sort of easygoing, like to laugh and talk and be chummy
with people, and that doesn't often match up with ideas about criminals.
And I always liked nice things—went to good shows, stayed at the good
hotels, ate at the best places, and was always quiet and gentlemanly about
it. People think crooks hide in cellars."

When Bentz decided on a crime career, he aimed higher than the average crook.

"I decided to become a yegg," he once admitted. "A bank robber, you
know. They're the aristocracy of the criminal profession."

At first, Bentz burglarized several small-town midwestern banks at
night. However, his keen sense of observation and amazing ability to or-
ganize detail led Bentz to invent "casing," elaborate reconnaissance of
banks. Although he sometimes put together his own gang to rob banks,
Bentz planned for dozens of bank-robbing gangs.

Traveling throughout the country, Bentz would visit a small but well-to-
do town. He would introduce himself as a cattle-buyer or investor and
take a room in a respectable boardinghouse.

Bentz would then visit the local library and, like a monk laboring in a
scriptorium, dig deep into several months' worth of the local newspaper.
He would study the advertisements of the bank which detailed assets and
liabilities.

Part of his elaborate note taking included the bank's cash on hand and
cash due from other banks, along with amounts owed the Federal
Reserve. Bentz would also carefully note the bank's bond inventory after
posing as a heavy depositor and obtaining involved bank statements.

Bentz then made allowances for deposits and withdrawals and was
mindful to note any changes brought about by commercial conditions. His
system of deductions became so accurate that he could determine within
$1,000 the amount of cash the bank would have on hand when a gang en-
tered the building to rob it.

Bentz then made detailed notes of side roads for escape routes, checking streetlights and the rounds of the local police. He estimated to the minute how much time each gang could safely spend inside a bank before detection.

Of the fifty banks Bentz personally robbed with professional bank robbers, his biggest score was the Lincoln National Bank and Trust Company of Lincoln, Nebraska, on September 17, 1930. He, Harvey Bailey and a few others took more than $1 million in cash, bonds and negotiable stocks. The theft caused a run on the bank and forced its eventual liquidation.

Bentz was so successful that he soon retired from active bank robbing. He acted strictly as a consultant for at least 200 bank robberies by high-powered gangs.

Dozens of gangs paid him with the negotiable stocks and bonds taken with the cash. The cash was all the bandits wanted—to them, the bonds were useless. Bentz, though, placed the bonds with lawyers and certain corrupt government officials, who paid him as much as seventy cents on the dollar. He was a multimillionaire by 1936.

Bentz only worked in good weather. He spent the winter at the South's best resorts or on the Riviera. On these trips, Bentz always took along five large trunks containing his rare coin sets and hundreds of first editions of the classics from Washington Irving to Anatole France. In fact, Bentz's love of books led to his downfall.

Federal agents, tipped that he had moved from a small town in upstate New York to Manhattan, trailed Bentz to a small rooming house by following a moving van hauling his library. Bentz surrendered without a fight.

"I'll wait it out," he said quietly. "When I get out of stir, I'll dig up the $5 million in bonds I have buried and retire."

Bentz never dug up those bonds, though. He was sentenced to twenty years for bank robbery and died dreaming of the illegal fortune he had made—and lost—as a result of a ravenous literary appetite.

THE PARK AVENUE BANDIT

Just after World War II, a unique criminal stepped forth to terrorize New York City's high society. Indeed, few stickup artists have rivaled the man known as "The Park Avenue Bandit."

The felon first struck on August 18, 1946, when he approached a limousine waiting at a Park Avenue curb. The young man, dressed in a tuxedo and sporting a head of red hair, smiled at the six wealthy passengers as he opened the vehicle's door and climbed in. Ordering the driver at gunpoint to proceed slowly into a dark street, the bandit worked fast, scooping up jewelry, furs and wallets.

The police were dumbfounded. No one on their rolls of suspects came close to matching the description of the robber. All they were able to gather from the victims was that he was well mannered, seemed highly educated and was a snappy dresser.

With the lack of substantial clues, the police could only assume the bandit was either a person new to crime or an experienced hand who had changed his modus operandi. Officers did agree, however, that the thief had "cased" his victims to find out their schedules, and that he had the right connections to fence the expensive items he had stolen.

Within months, the Park Avenue Bandit struck four more times, netting an estimated $200,000 in stolen goods. Despite exhaustive police searches, none of the loot was uncovered.

Investigators resorted to the only avenue of detection left open. They began to draw circles on a map indicating the spots where robbery had occurred, and guessed that the bandit parked his car nearby. Working in pairs, detectives interviewed hundreds of citizens, asking each if they had seen any strange cars parked on side streets and whether they recognized the suspect from a rough sketch.

This checking went on for months. The robberies continued, but the police net grew tighter, the circles on the map increasing and then overlapping, until they eventually intersected at East Forty-eighth Street, running from Fifth Avenue to the East River.

Police went from one apartment building to another in the pinpointed area. The suspect was finally identified as a resident of a small apartment in the heart of the Park Avenue Bandit's area of activity. Police waited for hours for the man to appear.

Finally, a red-haired, well-dressed young man came up the stairs. He was arrested and gave his name as Justin William McCarthy. He quickly admitted his guilt, but stated that because he was suffering from dysentery, "doctors have warned I have only three years to live." He also implicated a wealthy jewelry salesman as his fence.

The jewelry merchant went free for lack of solid evidence, but McCarthy, after a year and a half of legal and medical delaying tactics, was found guilty and given a ten-to-twenty-year sentence in prison.

Police had been correct in the assumption that McCarthy was new to crime; the twenty-five-year-old thief had no record. After his return from the war, McCarthy's first job had been that of a professional robber.

Apparently, McCarthy's doctors were wrong. He lived long enough to serve out a full sentence.

In the case of the Park Avenue Bandit, the police proved that wearisome routine work does pay off. "Cracking that one," a detective said, "wasn't glamorous at all. We just kept looking and looking. As long as he operated we could get closer and closer. That 'one more time' was his last."

Other notable events and personalities in robbery include:

London, 1671: The British Crown Jewels had been stolen by the usurper Oliver Cromwell in 1649 following the execution of Charles I, and, upon their recovery, great pains had been taken to protect these royal heirlooms. These priceless relics—crowns, orbs, state swords, scepters, spurs of chivalry, all gold and silver studded with countless jewels—had been placed in the Tower of London, which was surrounded by a detachment of dedicated guards.

It was the sole job of Talbot and Dolly Edwards, man and wife, to clean and protect the jewels. To that end, the couple actually lived with the gems, their apartment right above the jewel room in Martin Tower, which was part of the Tower of London. It was also Edwards' responsibility to greet any distinguished visitors permitted to view the jewels and explain their origin and history. One such visitor in April 1671 was a clergyman accompanied by his wife. This couple befriended the Edwardses and, after several social visits to the Tower, the minister stated that he knew of a well-bred, rich young gentleman who would be more than suitable as a husband for the Edwardses' pretty daughter. The parson agreed to bring the young suitor for Edwards' approval on his next visit.

The clergyman returned on May 9, 1671, accompanied by two friends. The minister's nephew, the so-called suitor, would be along within minutes, explained the parson to Edwards. "Until he gets here," mused the parson, "why don't we visit the jewel room? My friends are most anxious to see the ensigns of the king."

Edwards happily showed the trio downstairs. As soon as they entered the jewel room, the parson and his two friends leaped upon the elderly guardian of the Crown Jewels, knocking Edwards down, then binding his hands and feet and stuffing a gag into his mouth. When Edwards continued to struggle, the minister withdrew a wooden mallet from beneath his cloak and struck Edwards three blows that rendered him unconscious.

The parson used the mallet to smash the crown flat enough for him to stuff it into a leather pouch. The second man pocketed the gold ball of the royal orb while the third filed the scepter in halves, slipping them into specially made pockets in his cloak.

Just as the thieves turned to leave the treasure room they heard one of the Tower guards shout the alarm. The three robbers bolted down the stairs and raced to the main gate, where a fourth man waited with their horses. They rode away at a fast gallop but a squadron of fast-moving militia in hot pursuit overtook them, swarming over the thieves and knocking them to the ground. All four men were taken back to the Tower and locked up; it had been only an hour since the great robbery.

Once in custody, officials determined the fake parson and ringleader of the gang to be none other than Colonel Thomas Blood (born about 1618), an Irish rebel who had fought with Cromwell and had attempted many times to kidnap members of the royal family and topple the throne.

Blood refused to answer any questions by authorities, stating that he would not reply to interrogations "unless they are put to me by the king himself." Such outrageous airs, following the most spectacular theft in English history, intrigued King Charles II, who, on a whim, visited Blood in his cell and did, indeed, question that bold thief.

Blood's conversation so amused and startled Charles that the king not only dismissed the mandatory death sentence against him and his followers, but gave Blood a full pardon, restored his estates and conferred upon the imaginative burglar a yearly pension of 300 pounds. This magnanimous gesture did not alter Blood's attitude. He went on plotting against the crown until his death in August 1680.

England, 1855: The so-called "Great Train Robbery," the first train robbery on record, was masterminded by William Pierce, a professional thief. Pierce and a confederate, Edward Agar, bribed a train guard named Burgess to allow them into the coach carrying about 20,000 pounds in gold bullion on an express of the South Eastern Railway.

The gold was locked in tin boxes and the keys for these had been made

Gold thief Agar, who helped William Pierce commit the first great train robbery in 1857.

The train guard Burgess, who helped the thieves loot the gold from the train safes.

from impressions of the real keys borrowed momentarily for that use by a clerk named William George Tester, who worked in the railway's traffic department in London and who, like Burgess, had been handsomely bribed.

While the shipment was being trained from London, Pierce, Agar and Burgess unlocked the tin boxes in the gold car, took out the bullion and threw it to waiting henchmen at designated spots along the train's route. Lead was then substituted for the gold and the boxes locked. The theft was not discovered until the shipment arrived in Boulogne. By that time, the robbers were busy making plans to sail to America, but Agar was arrested on another charge, that of cashing forged checks. Pierce visited Agar in prison, promising to give Agar's share to his mistress. When Agar learned that Pierce had given his woman only a pittance of his share of the gold robbery, he became enraged and blurted out the entire fantastic story to police. Pierce and the others were promptly arrested. All drew long prison terms.

Malden, Massachusetts, 1863: The first bank robbery in America took place on December 15, 1863, when Edward W. Green, the postmaster of Malden, who had been drinking over his heavy debts, walked into the Malden bank to find only Frank Converse, the seventeen-year-old son of the president, in the building.

Green apparently got the idea to rob the bank on the spot, for he went home, got a gun, then returned to the bank, where he shot and killed Converse, taking a little more than $5,000 from the small safe. Green left Malden but was picked up a short time later when his wild spending drew suspicion. He confessed the robbery and murder and was executed on February 27, 1866.

St. Albans, Vermont, 1864: A band of Confederate soldiers, seeking to fund the depleted coffers of the South, which was clearly losing the Civil War by 1864, entered three banks in St. Albans, Vermont, on October 18, 1864, and looted the vaults of $114,522 in gold and currency. The robbers, twenty-two in number, then galloped out of town, raced across the Canadian border and buried the money.

Fourteen of the men were later arrested in Canada but the money was never recovered. It was later claimed that the thieves forgot where they buried the money and it still remains somewhere under the earth along the Canadian border.

Seymour, Indiana, 1866: The Reno brothers—Frank, John, Simon and William—along with a half dozen other men, committed the first train robbery in America on October 6, 1866, when they stopped the Ohio and Mississippi flyer outside of Seymour, Indiana, and took $10,000 in gold and currency from the Adams Express car.

Frank Reno of the Reno brothers, who robbed the first train in America. (Pinkerton, Inc.)

Liberty, Missouri, 1866: In their first raid, Jesse and Frank James, Cole Younger and others, on February 13, 1866, rode into the peaceful town of Liberty, Missouri, and robbed the Clay County Savings Bank of $60,000 in currency and non-negotiable bonds.

George Wymore, a resident of Liberty, stared at the two men as they rode out of town. Thinking he was going to give the alarm, one of the bandits shot him to death, then all the robbers, firing their weapons into the air, raced away. This was the first bank robbery in America by an organized band of thieves. (Some historians argue that Jesse James was not present during this robbery.)

Marshfield, Indiana, 1868: A passenger train of the Jefferson, Missouri and Indianapolis Railway came to a water stop outside of Marshfield, Indiana, on the night of May 22, 1868. When crew members got off to retrieve wood and water, the Reno brothers and others climbed onto the engine, knocking out the engineer and fireman and tossing them out of the cab. Uncoupling the passenger cars, the bandits took the engine and baggage car down the tracks for twenty miles, then looted the express car of $96,000 in gold, currency and government bonds. The Renos and their men were later tracked down and hanged by vigilantes on December 11, 1868.

New York City, 1869: Master bank burglar George Leonidas Leslie and accomplices, after weeks of studying their objective, broke into the Ocean National Bank on the night of June 27, 1869, and removed $786,879, an amount that staggered the burglars.

Leslie was a man of two lives, by day a cultured club-going gentleman, by night a master planner of bank thefts—he had, for handsome fees, planned dozens of bank burglaries along the eastern seaboard for a bevy of gangs. It was through his high social contacts in New York that Leslie learned not only the amounts on hand in banks but the intricate lock systems of their safes and vaults.

Corydon, Iowa, 1871: Jesse and Frank James, accompanied by the Younger brothers and three others, rode into the sleepy hamlet of Corydon, Iowa, on June 3, taking $45,000 in cash and gold from the Ocobock Brothers' Bank, a tremendous amount for that day. Only one clerk was on duty at the time and he was easily cowed into turning over the money. Before riding from town, Jesse James stopped at a local church to announce to the congregation that the bank had been robbed. He and the others, bursting with laughter, then rode pell-mell out of Corydon, a posse in pursuit. The outlaws outdistanced the posse and disappeared once back in Missouri.

Otterville, Missouri, 1875: The James gang stopped the Missouri Pacific express train on July 7, outside of Otterville, Missouri, looting the United Express car of $75,000, which members carried off in wheat

Sam Bass (shown here as a youth) committed his biggest robbery in 1877. (Western History Collection, University of Oklahoma)

sacks. "If you see any of the Pinkertons," Jesse told a terrified train guard, "tell 'em to come and get us!"

Big Springs, Nebraska, 1877: Outlaw Sam Bass and five others stopped a Union Pacific train near Big Springs, Nebraska, on September 18, 1877, taking from the express car a little more than $60,000 in gold which was being shipped from the Denver Mint. The outlaws also sauntered through the passenger cars, taking less than $1,000 in cash and jewelry from the passengers.

London, 1878: Adam Worth, a selective burglar with high artistic tastes, broke into the building owned by art dealers Agnew and Agnew on the night of May 25, 1878, a thick fog shrouding his actions, and removed the priceless Gainsborough painting *The Duchess of Devonshire*. Worth later wrote authorities that he would return this masterpiece if they would release his friend George Thompson, who had been jailed for forging checks.

When he learned that Thompson had been freed on a legal technicality, Worth decided to keep the painting, sending it to the United States. Worth dickered with Agnew and Agnew for decades, finally selling the Gainsborough back to the art firm in 1901 for a hefty but undisclosed sum. It did Worth little good since he was dying from tuberculosis at the time.

Gentleman art thief Adam Worth. (Pinkerton, Inc.)

New York City, 1878: The largest theft in U.S. history to date was that of the Manhattan Savings Institution, engineered by George Leonidas Leslie on October 27. Leslie and four others, using Leslie's architectural plans—he had labored for three years to obtain these plans and learn the location of the hidden vaults; his delicate burglary tools alone cost Leslie $3,000—dragged from the coffers of the bank $2,747,000, which the burglars stuffed into satchels. (The burglars overlooked another $2 million in sacks on the floor of the main vault.)

Gentleman burglar Leslie would be killed in 1884 by Ed Goodie in a fight over a girl, his body dumped at the base of Tramp's Rock in the Bronx.

Paris, 1911: Vincenzo Peruggia, a janitor in the Louvre Museum, waiting until the institution was closed for cleaning on August 21, 1911, cut the priceless *Mona Lisa* from its frame, then smuggled the painting out of the museum (Peruggia carried the *Mona Lisa* flat from the museum as Da Vinci had painted it on wood and it could not be rolled up like canvas). The thief took the painting to his apartment and placed it in the false bottom of a trunk, where it remained until 1913, when Peruggia tried to sell the *Mona Lisa* to Italy for a reported $95,000. He was suspected of the theft all along but the charges could not be proved; Peruggia walked into an art dealer's establishment, the story goes, in 1913, asking if the dealer could "clean a priceless painting." Yes, the dealer responded, but what painting? "The *Mona Lisa,*" said the somewhat dim-witted Peruggia, shrugging. Police arrested the man a short while later.

Peruggia insisted at his trial that he had stolen the painting for patriotic reasons, that he felt Da Vinci's work should be returned to Italy, the land where it was painted more than three hundred years earlier. This argument was accepted and he was given a light sentence.

Chantilly, France, 1912: Jules Bonnot, the first European thief credited with using an auto in a bank robbery, drove up to the largest bank in Chantilly, France, raced inside with the motor still running, took 80,000 francs at gunpoint, and shot to death three persons before fleeing. Bonnot and another man were killed later in a shoot-out involving more than two hundred French police. Bonnot took great pride in his inventive robbery techniques, stating in his will: "I am a celebrated man. Ought I to regret what I have done? Yes, perhaps, but I am not more guilty than the sweaters who exploit poor devils."

New York City, 1921: Professional thief Gerald Chapman and two others stopped a mail truck moving from Wall Street to the main New York post office on the night of October 27, taking thirty-three mail sacks which contained $1,424,129, the largest mail theft to that date, most of the loot being in the form of money orders, bonds and securities. Chapman had timed the routes of the mail trucks for weeks. After several adventures, Chapman was hanged on April 5, 1926, in Connecticut for killing a guard in a robbery.

Denver, Colorado, 1922: More than $500,000 in gold was taken out of the U. S. Mint in Denver in 1922; credited with that enormous robbery were Harvey Bailey and James Ripley.

Pampa, Texas, 1927: Oklahoma outlaws Matt and George Kimes and Ray Terrill robbed the bank in Pampa, Texas, in record time; the trio merely backed up a truck through the front window of the bank, ran inside and, tying the safe to a winch, drove off with the safe bouncing behind, a haul of $35,000 inside.

Lincoln, Nebraska, 1931: Harvey Bailey, Eddie Bentz and others robbed the Lincoln National Bank and Trust Company of more than $1 million in cash and negotiable securities, the largest armed bank robbery to that time.

Brooklyn, New York, 1934: An armored car of the U. S. Trucking Corp., stopping to deliver a payroll at the Rubel Ice Company on Bay and Nineteenth streets in Brooklyn on the morning of August 21, 1934, was surrounded by machine gunners just as its doors were opened. (One of the robbers had disguised himself as a pushcart vendor.) The cash, $427,950 in unmarked bills, was quickly transferred to cars which sped off within minutes of the robbery. The thieves were later identified and four sent to prison, but the money was never located.

Gerald Chapman stole more than $1 million in a New York mail theft in 1921; here he blithely puffs on a cigar after being told that he has been sentenced to death. (UPI)

Paris, 1941: Émile Buisson and two others stopped two bank messengers moving almost four million francs in a pushcart from the Crédit Industriel & Commercial to an office of the Bank of France on February 24. When one guard refused Buisson's order to put up his hands, he was killed by the robber, shot twice in the stomach. Buisson and the two others loaded the money into an unmarked Citroën and sped off. The money, which was never recovered, was being moved in such a primitive fashion to save the cost of gas.

Milan, Italy, 1958: A large truck cut off a delivery van of the Popular Bank of Milan on the morning of February 27, 1958, curbing the lightly armed truck on the Via Ospoppo. Six bandits, all wielding machine guns, looted the truck of 114,000,000 lire ($182,400) and about three quarters of a million dollars in securities, the largest theft in Italian history to that date. All six men were later apprehended.

Cheddington, England, 1963: England's "Great Train Robbery" of this century took place near Cheddington on August 8, 1963. Twelve masked men led by intellectual Bruce Reynolds, stopped the Glasgow-to-London mail train, removed 120 mailbags within forty-five minutes and fled in two Land Rovers, an army truck, two Jaguars and a motorcycle. The amount stolen shocked the world—$7,368,715, the largest train theft in history. All the thieves were eventually caught; after all their careful planning, they left their fingerprints in a nearby farmhouse. Less than $1 million of the stolen money has been recovered.

New York City, 1971: On December 31 the Hotel Pierre on Fifth Avenue was robbed of jewels unofficially estimated to be worth more than $5 million.

Cambridge, Massachusetts, 1973: Antique coins estimated to be worth $5 million were stolen from the Fogg Museum at Harvard University on December 2. Three men, Carl R. Dixon, Louis R. Mathis and Anthony B. Vaglica, were caught and given long prison terms.

Chicago, Illinois, 1974: Blowing a hole in the Purolator Building at 127 W. Huron in Chicago on the night of October 20, 1974, six men took from the vaults $4.3 million and fled to Ohio, where they flew to Florida. Some of the men tried to get to Costa Rica but all were rounded up and most of the money recovered.

Lebanon, 1976: At the height of the civil war in Lebanon in late January 1976, guerillas blew open the vaults of the British Bank of the Middle East in Bab Idriss, taking from the safety-deposit boxes between $20 and $50 million.

Montreal, Canada, 1976: On March 30, five men ambushed a Brink's delivery truck on a Montreal street, aiming an antiaircraft gun at the vehicle and taking more than $2.8 million from the truck, abandoning their escape cars some miles away on a golf course. This was the largest Brink's theft in history.

Palm Beach, Florida, 1976: About $6 million in jewels were taken from the safety-deposit boxes in the Palm Towers Hotel in Palm Beach on April 14, the largest hotel jewelry theft on record.

Nice, France, 1976: Tunneling into an underground vault of the branch bank of the Société Générale, ten burglars spent forty-eight hours rifling more than four hundred safety-deposit boxes and stealing between $8 and $10 million in cash, jewels, securities and bonds, one of the greatest thefts in history.

The burglars, led by professional thief, forty-five-year-old Albert Spaggiari, obtained the plans for the bank and entered the vault via a sewer system on the evening of July 16, 1976. So confident were the burglars that they brought along wine and lunches, which they consumed while they leisurely looted the bank. The burglars found some pornographic photos, allegedly kept by one of the depositors as a blackmail device, and foiled the blackmailer by plastering the safety-deposit box room with the photos.

Spaggiari was apprehended early the following year and brought to trial. Promising to hand the judge the detailed plan of the ingenious robbery, Spaggiari broke free of his guards in the courtroom, then leaped out a second-story window, to land on the roof of a car parked beneath the window, parked by design to break his fall. The thief, an ex-paratrooper, leaped into the car and sped off with his waiting accomplice; he is still being sought at this writing.

London, 1976: The largest bank robbery in English history involved the taking of $13.6 million from the Mayfair branch of the Bank of America. The eight holdup men responsible were captured within forty-eight hours of the crime and all received long prison terms. Most of the money was recovered.

Los Angeles, California, 1978: In a labyrinthine scheme, Stanley Mark Rifkin, a thirty-two-year-old computer consultant, robbed the Security Pacific National Bank of $10.2 million on October 25, 1978. The scheme involved transferring the money from the bank's transfer room through a secret code Rifkin had learned. He merely represented himself as being with the bank's international division and, using the code, had the money transferred to a New York bank, where he drew upon it.

Using the money, Rifkin purchased $8.1 million in polished diamonds in Switzerland, flying back to the United States, where he planned to sell the diamonds. Rifkin was arrested, the diamonds confiscated, and the balance of the money recovered in Belgium. All the bank's losses were recoverable. According to all sources, Rifkin's theft was the largest American bank robbery on record to date.

TERRORISM

A BRIEF HISTORY

Although terrorist groups around the United States have set off hundreds of bombs in the past few years, such political tactics are nothing new on the American scene. With the advent of huge waves of immigrants in the late nineteenth century, political terrorism increased alarmingly as radicals attempted to reform, reshape or totally abolish the structure of American government. Bombs were planted in front of the homes of leading political, financial and social leaders, but the "super rich" were the first victims.

Anarchist Alexander Berkman thought the way to change social inequities was by murdering American tycoons, and one day he barged into the lavish offices of Pittsburgh, Pennsylvania, steel magnate Henry Clay Frick and began shooting.

Despite being wounded in the attack, Frick jumped on Berkman and subdued him. Although he was well known for brutally crushing union-inspired strikes, Frick became a national hero.

The first large-scale terrorist act in American history took place May 4, 1886, in Haymarket Square in Chicago, Illinois, when a mass meeting of union members to protest the alleged shooting of working men by police turned ugly.

While squads of police gathered in the distance, Samuel Fielden, an English-born teamster, climbed on top of a wagon and harangued the Haymarket mob, saying, "You have nothing more to do with the law . . . Throttle it, kill it, stab it—do everything you can to wound it!"

Police soon moved forward, but the mob had been roused to bloodlust. Fielden jumped down from the wagon, and shouted, "We are peaceable!" to the advancing officers. However, many of the anarchists who had mingled with the legitimate workers had other ideas. One of them threw a

round, cast-iron, dynamite-filled bomb into the ranks of the police, instantly killing seven officers and wounding sixty-seven more.

Four avowed anarchists, August Spies, Adolph Fisher, George Engel and Albert Richard Parsons, were hanged for the crime, although the person who threw the bomb was never apprehended. The first three men were German-born labor agitators, but Parsons came from New England stock and his ancestors had fought in the American Revolution.

Parsons, like many other native Americans obsessed with violence as a means of changing the system of government, had published a newspaper called *Alarm,* in which he urged:

"Working men of America, learn the manufacture and use of dynamite. It will be your most powerful weapon."

Parsons might well have been talking to the radical political terrorists of almost a century later.

The second great wave of terrorism in the United States began during World War I. The most startling event of this bomb-throwing epoch occurred at 11:15 P.M., June 2, 1919, when two anarchists placed a bomb on the front doorstep of Attorney General A. Mitchell Palmer. The blast was premature, though, and while tearing half of Palmer's house away, it blew the fleeing terrorists to pieces. (Parts of their bodies were sent flying to the front doorstep of the man who lived across the street—Assistant Secretary of the Navy Franklin Delano Roosevelt.)

Palmer retorted by initiating the infamous "Red Raids" in January

1920, when hundreds of Communists and anarchists were rounded up and deported. In these violent raids, though, many innocent persons were beaten and wrongly arrested.

The terrorists retaliated by parking a wagonload of dynamite and scrap iron at the intersection of Broad and Wall streets in New York City, which went off in a terrific explosion at 11:59 A.M., September 16, 1920. Scores of offices, including those of J. P. Morgan, were ruined. Worse, thirty-eight persons working on Wall Street were killed and hundreds more wounded.

For years since then, non-political maniacs have also surfaced. In the early 1930s, a berserk New York bomber who called himself "3-X" appeared. About the same time, Sylvestre Matuschka blew up several trains in Austria and Hungary, killing scores of innocent passengers. When captured, Matuschka said he blew up trains to call attention to a new train safety device he had invented, a device the railroads had refused to purchase!

New York was plagued by a lone terrorist in the 1940s and 1950s. When George Peter Metesky, whom police dubbed "The Mad Bomber" was arrested, he said he planted the explosives because Consolidated Edison was responsible for his contracting tuberculosis. The bombs Metesky placed in Radio City Music Hall and Grand Central and Penn stations demonstrated his hatred for the power company, although it was never clear why he chose those sites.

Alexander Berkman attempting to kill steel tycoon Henry Frick.

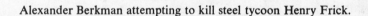

George Peter Metesky, New York's "Mad Bomber." (Wide World)

THE AMERICAN HISTORY OF HOSTAGE TAKING

The taking of hostages, such as the criminal seizure of the fifty Americans in Iran, for one perverse reason or another has been with us for centuries. The 134 hostages held by Hanafi Moslem leader Hamaas Abdul Khaalis and his fellow thugs in Washington, D.C., in 1977 ostensibly symbolized a wrong to correct a wrong. But the seizure was nothing less than brutal extortion of the government to release to the custody of the Hanafis those accused of killing four children in Khaalis' home in 1973.

In the past, hostage-taking had wholly different motives. In the twelfth century it became common to hold important warriors hostage, such as England's King Richard the Lion-Hearted, for the sake of ransom and ne-gotiations which led to favorable war terms and rich settlements of terri-tory. It took criminals little time to adopt the methods of their sovereigns.

Many an outlaw of America's young Wild West found it convenient to employ hostages while rickety bank safes were opened by hand-trembling cashiers. Jesse and Frank James, along with the Younger brothers, used hostages to escape Northfield, Minnesota, after an abortive and disastrous raid in 1876. The hardy pioneer residents of Northfield, however, were not impressed. Dozens of unarmed citizens ignored the hostages held by the outlaws with pistols to their heads and stoned the gang from the town streets.

The idea of using hostages as shields against police bullets became the craze of the 1930s, especially with bank robbers John Dillinger, Baby Face Nelson, Pretty Boy Floyd and Bonnie and Clyde.

Dillinger's first use of hostages occurred on November 20, 1933, when he and four of his gang held up the American Bank and Trust Company in Racine, Wisconsin. The bank robber "invited" the bank's president and its bookkeeper, Mrs. Henry Patzke, to ride with them until they were safely out of town. It was all very funny to Dillinger, who let the two terrified hostages out of the car some minutes later on a deserted road.

The humor went out of Dillinger's hostage taking on March 13, 1934, as he and five other gangsters scooped $52,000 from the vault of the First National Bank of Mason City, Iowa. In his escape, Dillinger and Baby Face Nelson ordered no less than twenty hostages to stand at gunpoint on the running boards of the gang's large touring car, as well as spread themselves over the hood, fenders and bumpers.

Sagging beneath this weight, the car barely managed to get out of town; Police Chief E. J. Patton realized the hostages would die if his anxious squads of police opened up on the car, and allowed the bank robbers to escape. (Among the hundreds of spectators witnessing the robbery and hostage taking was a musician named Meredith Willson, later to immortalize Mason City as "River City" in his smash musical *The Music Man*.)

Later, rival gangs throughout the country began to take hostages from the mobster ranks. The price of release was often ransom, but most sought was information about the activities of the opposition.

One such victim was a man named Muddy Kasoff, taken hostage by the Brownsville, New York, arm of Murder, Inc., on orders of Charles "Lucky" Luciano, who wanted to know about Kasoff's narcotics operations, which were cutting into his own.

Two psychotic killers, Harry Strauss, known as "Pittsburgh Phil," and Abe "Kid Twist" Reles, snatched Kasoff and held him hostage until he and his associates revealed the extent of their narcotics rings. Once the information was in hand, Reles blew off the top of Kasoff's head with a shotgun.

Recalling this grisly murder in his long confession before he himself was killed by parties unknown, Reles guffawed in court: "It handed Phil a laugh. We left the bum under a billboard that says 'Drive Safely.' Lucky was satisfied plenty."

Reles' inhuman attitude toward hostages has been largely shared by those taking hostages today, a perspective that regards life itself as cheap, hostages precious only as tools for bargaining or as a living weapon to achieve whatever end the hostage taker chooses.

UNDERWORLD LINGO

THE U.S.–SOME PECULIAR BEGINNINGS

Underworld terms that have crept into everyday usage stem from the most routine of criminal acts to meanings of dark and sinister proportions. A good example of the former is the word "hoodlum." It's used as commonly as is the word "turkey." (Incidentally, the word "turkey" is today used unabashedly by the misinformed to indicate stupidity, although it is a long-standing ethnic slur against the Irish.)

The use of "hoodlum" began in San Francisco, California, in the 1870s among the cutthroat gangs populating the Barbary Coast. When gang members spotted a wealthy tourist wandering into the district, they would surround the victim to shield their acts of robbery from view, shouting, "Huddle 'em, huddle 'em!" Hence the word hoodlum."

On the darker side is the word "thug," whose meaning stems from the ancient Indian killer cult Thuggee. The members of that organization worshiped the lethal goddess Kali and were obligated to strangle some innocent victim once a year to retain membership. Although the British colonial government ultimately suppressed the Thugs in the mid-nineteenth century, their American counterparts are alive and work for organized crime.

A word that is no longer in use but is often seen in historical accounts is "footpad," which was first employed by British writers a century before the American Revolution. A footpad was simply a purse snatcher who could not afford a horse to elevate himself to highwayman. Instead, the footpad had to stalk his victim on foot along a lonely street before striking. Today, he would be called a mugger.

The word "yegg," which originated about 1880 in San Francisco, is applied to criminal tramps, especially those experienced at breaking into safes. The term is a corruption of "yekk," a word from a Chinese dialect meaning "a beggar."

"Yegg" became a bone of great contention between criminal lexicographer Eric Partridge and detective writer Raymond Chandler. Partridge contended that such malefactors were "tough, itinerant bank robbers." Chandler, on the other hand, asserted, "A yegg is a safecracker, a box-man. He wouldn't go near a bank, because he couldn't open up a bank safe, even if it didn't have a time lock. He could only open a rather cheap and vulnerable safe . . . this yegg . . . might open the safe in a country grocery store."

Since the 1930s, the word "gunzel" (in all its various spellings) has come to mean an apprentice hoodlum who is much too fast with his trigger finger.

In Dashiell Hammett's *The Maltese Falcon,* the character Wilmer is depicted as just such a gunzel. Yet this same word, which was first used in a 1914 criminal opus entitled *The Gay Cat,* also means a passive male homosexual.

The derivation of gunzel is cloudy, but some dictionary specialists insist it comes from the Irish word "gossoon," which means man. Others, however, claim it comes from tramp idiom, where "gazooney" means a young hobo.

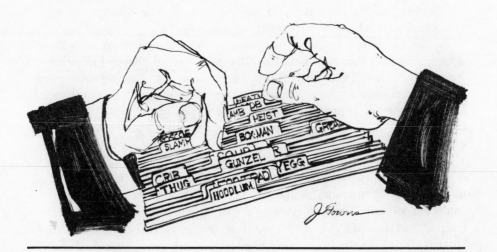

A perennial underworld word is "lam." Used as a verb, it simply means escape. The word first appeared and was explained as such in the April 1895 edition of *Popular Science Monthly*. However, some experts claim "lam" stems from the exploits of a bank robber named Herman K. Lamm.

Lamm was a baron and Prussian officer who was kicked out of the German Army before World War I for cheating at cards. Emigrating to Utah, Lamm put together the first modern-day bank-robbing gang. Using exact military precision, Lamm developed an almost foolproof bank-robbing system built on three steps.

First, Lamm would "case" the bank. Posing as a reporter or banking official, Lamm would investigate the bank's financial records, security and location in town.

Next, Lamm and his associates would draw up elaborate floor plans of the bank. They then often built a mock-up of the bank in a deserted building and practiced the robbery.

Third, the escape was planned to the second with getaway routes charted block by block by speedometer readings and practiced under all kinds of weather conditions.

For thirteen years Lamm and his associates successfully looted banks before December 16, 1930, when vigilantes in Clinton, Indiana, accidentally trapped the gang and killed the baron.

Lamm's escape system, many agree, created the real meaning of "taking it on the lam," and his methods were not forgotten. One of the baron's gang, Walter Dietrich, survived the Indiana shoot-out and was sent to Michigan City State Prison. While there, Dietrich told all he knew about Lamm's operation to another inmate, a man intensely interested in banks —John Herbert Dillinger.

BIBLIOGRAPHY

Myriad books, periodicals, pamphlets and reports, as well as extensive interviews and correspondence with police officials and criminals were employed in researching this work. What follows was the most helpful of published material.

Acton, William. *Prostitution*. London: Churchill, 1857.

Adam, H. L. *Trial of George Chapman*. London: William Hodge, 1930.

Adelman, Robert H. *The Bloody Benders*. New York: Stein and Day, 1970.

Alix, Ernest Kahlar. *Ransom Kidnapping in America*. Carbondale, Ill.: Southern Ill. Univ. Press, 1978.

Allsop, Kenneth. *The Bootleggers*. Garden City, N.Y.: Doubleday, 1961.

Almedingen, E. M. *The Romanovs*. New York: Holt, Rinehart and Winston, 1966.

Anderson, Sir Robert. *The Lighter Side of My Official Life*. London: Hodder and Stoughton, 1910.

Andrews, George, and Vinkenoog, Simon, eds. *The Book of Grass*. New York: Grove Press, 1967.

Andrews, Ralph W. *Historic Fires of the West*. New York: Bonanza Books, 1966.

Andrews, William. *Old-Time Punishments*. London: Tabard Press, 1960.

Anonymous. *Streetwalker*. London: Bodley Head, 1959.

Anslinger, Harry J. *The Protectors*. New York: Farrar, Straus, 1964.

Archer, Fred. *Ghost Detectives*. London: W. H. Allen, 1970.

Asbury, Herbert. *The Gangs of New York*. Knopf, 1927.

———. *Gem of the Prairie*. New York: Knopf, 1940.

———. *The French Quarter*. New York: Knopf, 1940.

Atholl, Justin. *The Reluctant Hangman*. London: John Long, 1956.

————. *Shadow of the Gallows*. London: John Long, 1954.

Atwell, Benjamin H. *The Great Harry Thaw Case*. Chicago: Laird & Lee, 1907.

Ayscough, Florence. *Chinese Women Yesterday and Today*. Boston: Houghton, 1937.

Baker, Peter. *Time Out of Life*. London: Heinemann, 1961.

Ball, Larry D. *The United States Marshals of New Mexico and Arizona Territories, 1846–1912*. Albuquerque: University of N.Me. Press, 1978.

Balsdon, J. P. V. D., ed. *The Romans*. New York: Basic Books, 1965.

Barker, Dudley. *Lord Darling's Famous Cases*. London: Hutchinson, 1936.

Barnard, Allan, ed. *The Harlot Killer*. New York: Dodd, Mead, 1953.

Barnes, David. *The Metropolitan Police*. New York: Baker & Godwin, 1863.

Barnes, Harry Elmer, and Teeters, Negley K. *New Horizons in Criminology*. Englewood Cliffs, N.J.: Prentice-Hall, 1959.

Barracato, John, with Michelmore, Walter. *Arson*. New York: Avon Books, 1976.

Barry, Iris. *D. W. Griffith, American Film Master*. New York: Museum of Modern Art, 1940.

Basedow, H. *The Australian Aboriginal*. Adelaide, Aus.: n.p., 1925.

Basserman, Lujo. *The Oldest Profession; the History of Prostitution*. New York: Stein and Day, 1968.

Battle, Breadan P., and Weston, Paul B. *Arson*. New York: Arco Pub., 1978.

Baugh, Jack W., and Morgan, Jefferson. *Why Have They Taken Our Children?* New York: Delacorte Press, 1978.

Baxter, John. *The Gangster Film*. New York: A. S. Barnes, 1970.

Bedford, Sybille. *The Faces of Justice*. New York: Simon & Schuster, 1961.

Bemis, George. *Report of the Case of John W. Webster*. Boston: Little, Brown, 1850.

Berg, Dr. Karl. *The Sadist*. London: Heinemann, 1932.

Bergamini, David. *Japan's Imperial Conspiracy*. New York: Morrow, 1971.

Besant, Walter. *East London*. London: Chatto & Windus, 1903.

————. *London in the Time of the Stuarts*. London: Adam & Black, 1903.

Besterman, Lujo. *Men Against Women: A Study of Sexual Relations*. London: Methuen, 1924.

Bishop, George. *Executions*. Los Angeles: Sherbourne, 1965.

Bleackley, Horace. *Ladies Fair & Frail: Sketches of the Demi-Monde During the Eighteenth Century*. London: Bodley Head, 1909.

Bohannan, P. *African Homicide and Suicide*. Princeton, N.J.: Princeton Univ. Press, 1960.

Bolitho, William. *Murder for Profit*. New York: Harper, 1926.

Borniche, Roger. *Flic Story*. Garden City: Doubleday, 1975.

Borowitz, Albert. *Innocence and Arsenic, Studies in Crime and Literature*. New York: Harper & Row, 1977.

Borrell, Clive, and Cashinella, Brian. *Crime in Britain Today*. London: Routledge & Paul, 1975.

Bowker, A. E. *A Lifetime with the Law*. London: W. H. Allen, 1961.

Brace, Charles Loving. *The Dangerous Classes of New York*. New York: Wynkoop & Hallenbeck, 1880.

Brearley, H. C. *Homicide in the United States*. Chapel Hill, N.C.: University of N.C. Press, 1932.

Breasted, James Henry. *A History of Egypt*. New York: Scribner, 1951.

Browne, Douglas G., and Brock, Alan. *Fingerprints*. London: Harrap, 1951.

————, and Tullet, E. V. *Bernard Spilsbury, His Life and Cases*. London: Harrap, 1951.

Bryan, Helen. *Inside*. New York: Houghton Mifflin, 1953.

Bullough, Vern L. *History of Prostitution*. New Hyde Park, N.Y.: Univ. Books, 1964.

Burns, Walter Noble. *The One-Way Ride*. Garden City: Doubleday, 1931.

Busch, Noel F. *TR*. New York: Apollo Eds., 1963.

Byrnes, Thomas. *Professional Criminals in America*. New York: Cassell, 1886.

Calvert, E. R. *Capital Punishment in the Twentieth Century*. London: Putnam, 1927.

Carter, W. N. *Harry Tracy. The Desperate Outlaw*. Chicago: Laird & Lee, 1902.

Castleman, Harvey N. *Sam Bass, The Train Robber*. Girard, Kan.: Haldeman-Julius, 1944.

Christoph, James B. *Capital Punishment and British Politics*. London: Allen & Unwin, 1962

Clark, Tim, and Penycate, John. *Psychopath*. London: Routledge & Paul, 1976.

Clarke, Donald Henderson. *In the Reign of Rothstein*. New York: Vanguard Press, 1929.

Clayton, Gerald Fancourt. *The Wall Is Strong*. London: John Long, 1958.

Cobb, Belton. *Critical Years at the Yard*. London: Faber & Faber, 1956.

Cohen, Louis H. *Murder, Madness and the Law*. New York: World Book, 1952.

Coles, Robert, M.D.; Brenner, Joseph H., M.D.; and Meagher, Dermot. *Drugs and Youth*. New York: Liveright, 1970.

Collins, Frederick Lewis. *The F.B.I. in Peace and War*. New York: Putnam, 1943.

Colquhoun, Patrick. *A Treatise on the Public Metropolis*. London: Joseph Mawman, 1800.

Cook, Fred J. *The F.B.I. Nobody Knows*. New York: Macmillan, 1964

Cooper, Courtney Riley. *Ten Thousand Public Enemies*. Boston: Little, Brown, 1935.

————. *Designs in Scarlet*. Boston: Little, Brown, 1939.

Crane, Milton, ed. *Sins of New York*. New York: Boni & Gaer, 1947.

Crapsey, Edward. *The Nether Side of New York*. New York: Sheldon, 1872.

Croy, Homer. *Jesse James Was My Neighbor*. New York: Duell, 1949.

Cullen, Tom. *Autumn of Terror*. London: Bodley Head, 1965.

Cummings, Homer. *Selected Papers*. New York: Scribner, 1939.

Cuthbert, C. R. M. *Science and the Detection of Crime*. New York: Philosophical Lib., 1958.

Davison, M. H. Armstrong. *The Casket Letters*. Washington, D.C.: University Press of Washington, and The Community College Press, 1965.

De Ford, Miriam Allen. *Murderers Sane and Mad*. New York: Abelard-Schuman, 1965.

De la Torre, Lillian. *The Truth About Belle Gunness*. New York: Gold Medal, 1955.

Demeter, Anna. *Legal Kidnapping*. Boston: Beacon Press, 1977.

Depewolff, Richard. *Famous Old New England Murders*. Brattleboro, Vt.: Daye, 1942.

Dew, Walter. *I Caught Crippen*. London: Blackie & Son, 1938.

Dickson, G. *Murder by Numbers*. London: R. Hale, 1958.

Dilnot, George. *Celebrated Crimes*. London: S. Paul, 1925.

Dineen, Michael P., ed. *Great Fires of America*. Waukesha, Wis.: Country Beautiful Corp., 1972.

Divall, Tom. *Scoundrels and Scallywags*. London: Benn, 1929.

Donavan, R. J. *The Assassins*. New York: Harper, 1955.

Douthwaite, L. C. *Mass Murder*. New York: Holt, 1929.

Drummond, Isabel. *The Sex Paradox*. New York: Putnam, 1953.

Duff, Charles. *A New Handbook on Hanging*. Chicago: Regnery, 1955.

Duffy, Clinton D. *San Quentin Story*. Garden City: Doubleday, 1950.

————, and Hirshberg, Al. *88 Men and 2 Women*. Garden City, N.Y.: Doubleday, 1962.

Duke, Thomas S. *Celebrated Cases of America*. San Francisco: James H. Barry, 1910.

Du Rose, John. *Murder Was My Business*. London: W. H. Allen, 1971.

Eames, Hugh. *Sleuths, Inc*. Philadelphia: Lippincott, 1978.

East, N. *Society and the Criminal*. Springfield, Ill.: C. C. Thomas, 1950.

Elliott, Robert G. *Agent of Death: The Memoirs of an Executioner*. New York: Dutton, 1940.

Eissler, K. R. *Searchlights on Delinquency*. New York: Int. Univs. Press, 1949.

English, O. S., and Pearson, G. H. J. *Common Neuroses of Children and Adults*. New York: Norton, 1937.

Epstein, Edward Jay. *Legend*. New York: Readers Digest Press, 1978.

Epton, Nina. *Love and the French*. London: Cassell, 1959.

Erickson, Gladys A. *Warden Ragen of Joliet*. New York: Dutton, 1957.

Everson, William K. *The Detective in Film*. Secaucus, N.J.: Citadel Press, 1972.

Farley, Philip. *Criminals of America*. New York: Farley, 1876.

Farson, Dan. *Jack the Ripper*. London: M. Joseph, 1972.

Feverwerker, Albert, ed. *Modern China*. Englewood Cliffs, N.J.: Prentice-Hall, 1964.

Finn, John T. *History of the Chicago Police*. Chicago: Police Book Fund, 1887.

Flexner, Abraham. *Prostitution in Europe*. New York: Century Co., 1914.

Floherty, John J. *Inside the F.B.I.* Philadelphia: Lippincott, 1943.

Foley, Doris. *The Divine Eccentric: Lola Montez and the Newspapers*. Los Angeles: Westernlore, 1969.

Ford, Clellan S., and Beach, Frank A. *Patterns of Sexual Behavior*. New York: Harper, 1951.

Fosdick, Raymond B. *American Police Systems*. New York: Century Co., 1920.

Fox, Lionel. *English Prison and Borstal Systems*. London: Routledge, 1952.

Frasca, Dom. *Ring of Crime*. New York: Crown, 1959.

French, Harvey M. *The Anatomy of Arson*. New York: Arco, 1979.

Friedlander, Ludwig. *Roman Life and Manners under the Early Empire*. Translated by Leonard Magnus. London: Routledge, 1940.

Furneaux, Rupert. *The Medical Murderer*. London: Elek, 1957.

———. *The World's Most Intriguing True Mysteries*. New York: Arco, 1966.

Gaddis, Thomas E. *Birdman of Alcatraz*. New York: Random House, 1955.

Gardiner, G. *Capital Punishment as a Deterrent and the Alternative*. London: Gollancz, 1956.

Ginzburg, Ralph. *100 Years of Lynchings*. New York: Lancer Books, 1962.

Glaister, J. *Medical Jurisprudence and Toxicology*. London: Livingstone Press, 1953.

Glueck, B. *Studies in Forensic Psychiatry*. London: Heinemann, 1916.

Goddard, Henry. *The Memoirs of a Bow Street Runner*. New York: Morrow, 1956.

Godwin, George. *Peter Kurten, A Study in Sadism*. London: Acorn Press, 1938.

————. *Killers Unknown*. London: Jenkins, 1960.

Goldberg, Isaac. *Queen of Hearts*. New York: Day, 1936.

Gosling, John, and Craig, Dennis. *The Great Train Robbery*. Indianapolis: Bobbs, 1964.

Gowers, Sir Ernest. *A Life for a Life*. London: Chatto & Windus, 1956.

Graves, Robert. *The Twelve Caesars*. Baltimore: Penguin Books, 1957.

Gribble, L. *Murders Most Strange*. London: John Long, 1959.

Griffiths, Major Arthur. *Mysteries of Police and Crime*. London: Cassell, 1898.

Grimal, Pierre. *Hellenism and the Rise of Rome*. New York: Delacorte Press, 1968.

Grinspoon, Lester, and Bakalar, James B. *Cocaine*. New York: Basic Books, 1976.

Gross, Hans. *Criminal Psychology*. Boston: Little, Brown, 1915.

Guttmacher, M. S. *The Mind of the Murderer*. New York: Farrar, Straus, 1960.

Hale, Leslie. *Hanged in Error*. London: Penguin Books, 1961.

Hall, Jerome. *General Principles of Criminal Law*. Indianapolis: Bobbs, 1947.

Halper, Albert, ed. *The Chicago Crime Book*. Cleveland: World Pub., 1967.

Hammerschlag, H. E. *Hypnotism and Crime*. London: Rider, 1956.

Harrison, Michael. *Clarence*. London: W. H. Allen, 1972.

Hart, Henry H. *Marco Polo*. Norman, Okla.: University of Okla. Press, 1967.

Hassler, Alfred. *Diary of a Self-Made Convict*. Chicago: Regnery, 1954.

Hayward, Arthur L. *Lives of the Most Remarkable Criminals Who Have Been Condemned and Executed*. London: Routledge, 1927.

Hayward, C. *The Courtesan*. London: Casanova Society, 1926.

Hect, Ben. *A Child of the Century*. New York: Simon & Schuster, 1954.

Henriques, Fernando. *Prostitution and Society*. 3 vols. London: MacGibbon, 1962–68.

Henriques, Dr. Fernando. *Modern Sexuality: Prostitution and Society*. Vol. 3. London: MacGibbon, 1968.

Hentig, Hans von. *The Criminal and His Victim: Studies in the Sociobiology of Crime*. New Haven: Yale Univ. Press, 1948.

Hinde, R. S. E. *The British Penal System, 1773–1950*. London: Duckworth, 1951.

Hirsch, Phil, ed. *Fires*. New York: Pyramid Books, 1971.

Hirschfeld, Magnus. *Sexual Anomalies and Perversions*. London: Encyclopedic Press, 1938.

Hodge, James H., ed. *Famous Trials*. No. 5. London: Penguin Books, 1955.

Höhne, Heinz. *The Order of the Death's Head*. New York: Coward-McCann, 1970.

Holdredge, Helen. *The Woman in Black*. New York: Putnam, 1955.

Hole, C. *A Mirror of Witchcraft*. London: Chatto & Windus, 1957.

Hollis, C. *Shadow of the Gallows*. London: Gollancz, 1951.

Holtzoff, H., ed. *Encyclopedia of Criminology*. New York: Philosophical Lib., 1949.

Holyroyd, James Edward. *The Gaslight Murders*. London: Allen & Unwin, 1960.

Holzman, Robert S. *The Romance of Firefighters*. New York: Bonanza Books, 1971.

Hoover, J. Edgar. *Persons in Hiding*. Boston: Little, Brown, 1938.

Howe, Cliff. *Scoundrels, Fiends and Human Monsters*. New York: Ace Books, 1958.

Howe, Sir Ronald. *The Pursuit of Crime*. London: Barker, 1962.

Huie, William Bradford. *He Slew the Dreamer*. New York: Delacorte Press, 1968.

Humphreys, Christmas. *Seven Murders*. London: Heinemann, 1931.

Hurwitz, Stephen. *Criminology*. London: Allen & Unwin, 1952.

Huson, Richard. *Sixty Famous Trials*. London: Daily Express, 1938.

Hyde, H. Montgomery. *Sir Patrick Hastings, His Life and Cases*. London: Heinemann, 1960.

Irving, H. B. *A Book of Remarkable Criminals*. New York: Doran, 1918.

James, John T. *The Benders in Kansas*. Wichita, Kan.: Kan-Okla Publishing Co., 1913.

James, T. E. *Prostitution and the Law*. London: Heinemann, 1951.

Jenkins, Elizabeth. *Six Criminal Women*. London: Low, 1949.

Jennings, Dean. *We Only Kill Each Other.* Englewood Cliffs, N.J.: Prentice-Hall, 1967.

Jesse, F. Tennyson. *Murder and Its Motives.* New York: Knopf, 1924.

Johnson, Malcolm. *Crime on the Labor Front.* New York: McGraw-Hill, 1950.

Johnston, James A. *Alcatraz Island Prison.* New York: Scribner, 1949.

Jonas, George, and Amiel, Barbara. *By Persons Unknown.* Toronto: Macmillan, 1977.

Jones, A. B., and Llewellyn, J. *Malingering.* London: Heinemann, 1917.

Jones, Howard. *Crime and Penal System.* London: University Tutorial Press, 1956.

Joyce, James Avery. *Capital Punishment, A World View.* New York: Nelson, 1962.

Karpman, B. *The Sexual Offender and His Offenses.* New York: Julian Press, 1954.

Kelly, Alexander. *Jack the Ripper: A Bibliography and Review of the Literature.* London: Assn. of Assistant Librarians, 1973.

Kenny, C. S. *Outlines of Criminal Law.* London: Cambridge Univ. Press, 1947.

Kershaw, Alister. *A History of the Guillotine.* London: J. Calder, 1958.

King, Veronica, and King, Paul. *Problems of Modern American Crime.* London: Heath Cranton, 1924.

Kingston, Charles. *Remarkable Rogues, Some Notable Criminals of Europe and America.* London: Lane, 1921.

————. *Dramatic Days at the Old Bailey.* New York: Stokes, 1924.

Kinsey, A. C., with Pomeroy, W. B., and Martin, C. E. *Sexual Behavior in the Human Male.* London: Saunders, 1948.

————. *Sexual Behavior in the Human Female.* London: Saunders, 1953.

Klare, Hugh J. *Anatomy of Prison.* London: Hutchinson, 1960.

Kneeland, George J. *Commercialized Prostitution in New York City.* New York: Century Co., 1913.

Koestler, Arthur. *Reflections on Hanging.* London: Gollancz, 1956.

Kraft-Ebing, Richard von. *Psychopathia Sexualis.* Chicago: W. T. Keener and Co., 1900.

Kramer, Samuel Noah. *History Begins at Sumer.* Garden City: Doubleday, 1959.

Lacky, William E. H. *History of European Morals.* 2 vols. New York: Harper, 1958.

Lane, Mark. *Rush to Judgment.* New York: Holt, 1966.

———— and Gregory, Dick. *Code Name "Zorro."* Englewood Cliffs, N.J.: Prentice-Hall, 1977.

Lawes, Warden Lewis E. *Twenty Thousand Years in Sing Sing.* New York: New Home Lib., 1942.

Lawrence, John. *A History of Capital Punishment.* New York: Citadel, 1950.

Lee, Raymond, and Van Hecke, B. C. *Gangsters and Hoodlums, The Underworld and the Cinema.* New York: Barnes & Noble, 1971.

Leek, Sybil and Sugar, Bert R. *The Assassination Chain.* New York: Corwin Books, 1976.

Leeson, Benjamin. *Lost London.* London: S. Paul, 1934.

Lefebure, Molly. *Evidence for the Crown.* London: Heinemann, 1955.

Lenotre, G. *The Guillotine and Its Servants.* London: Hutchinson, n.d.

Leopold, Nathan F. *Life Plus 99 Years.* Garden City: Doubleday, 1958.

Le Queux, William. *Things I Know about Kings, Celebrities and Crooks.* London: Everleigh, Nash & Grayson, Ltd., 1923.

Lesberg, Sandy. *Assassination in Our Times.* London: Peebles Press Int., 1976.

Lester, David, and Lester, Gene. *Crime of Passion.* Chicago: Nelson-Hall, 1975.

Lewinsohn, Richard. *A History of Sexual Customs.* New York: Harper, 1958.

Lewis, W. H. *The Splendid Century.* New York: Sloane, 1953.

Lombroso, C., and Ferrero, W. *The Female Offender.* New York: Appleton, 1899.

————. *Crime, Its Causes and Remedies.* Boston: Little, Brown, 1918.

Loomis, Stanley. *Paris in the Terror.* Philadelphia: Lippincott, 1964.

————. *A Crime of Passion.* Philadelphia: Lippincott, 1967.

————. *Du Barry.* Philadelphia: Lippincott, 1959.

Longford, Elizabeth. *Queen Victoria.* New York: Harper, 1965.

Lustgarten, Edgar. *Verdict in Dispute.* New York: Scribner, 1950.

Macardle, Dorothy. *The Irish Republic.* New York: Farrar, Straus & Giroux, 1965.

Macdonald, J. M. *Psychiatry and the Criminal.* Springfield, Ill.: C. C. Thomas, 1958.

Macnaghten, Sir Melville. *Days of My Years.* London: Edward Arnold, 1915.

Magnus, Philip. *King Edward the Seventh.* London: J. Murray, 1964.

Maine, C. E. *The World's Strangest Crimes.* New York: Hart, 1967.

Mannheim, Hermann. *Group Problems in Crime and Punishment.* New York: Humanities Press, 1955.

Marcus, Steven. *The Other Victorians.* London: Weidenfeld & Nicolson, 1966.

Martin, Raymond V. *Revolt in the Mafia.* New York: Duell, 1963.

Mass, Peter. *The Valachi Papers.* New York: Putnam, 1968.

Massie, Robert K. *Nicholas and Alexandra.* New York: Dell, 1967.

Matters, Leonard. *The Mystery of Jack the Ripper.* London: W. H. Allen, 1948.

Maurois, Simone Andre. *Miss Howard and the Emperor.* New York: Knopf, 1957.

Mayhew, Henry. *London's Underworld.* London: Kimber, 1950.

McClellan, John L. *Crime without Punishment.* New York: Duell, 1962.

McClintock, F. H. and Gibson, Evelyn. *Robbery in London.* New York: St. Martins Press, 1961.

McCord, W., and McCord, J. *Origins of Crime.* New York: Columbia Univ. Press, 1959.

McCormick, Donald. *The Identity of Jack the Ripper.* London: Jarrolds, 1959.

McGrady, Mike. *Crime Scientists.* Philadelphia: Lippincott, 1961.

McKelway, St. Clair. *True Tales from the Annals of Crime and Rascality.* New York: Random House, 1950.

McMillan, Priscilla Johnson. *Marina and Lee.* New York: Harper & Row, 1977.

McPhaul, Jack. *Johnny Torrio.* New Rochelle, N.Y.: Arlington House, 1970.

Mencken, August. *By the Neck.* New York: Hastings House, 1942.

Menninger, K. A. *Man Against Himself.* New York: Harcourt, 1938.

Mercier, C. *Criminal Responsibility.* London: Oxford, 1935.

Merrow, Smith; Harris, L. W.; and Harris, James. *Prison Screw.* London: Jenkins, 1962.

Meyer, Johann Jacob. *Sexual Life in Ancient India.* New York: Barnes & Noble, 1953.

Miller, Gene. *83 Hours till Dawn.* Garden City: Doubleday, 1971.

Miller, Tom. *The Assassination Please Almanac.* Chicago: Regnery, 1977.

Mitchell, Edwin Valentine, ed. *The Newgate Calendar.* Garden City: Garden City Pub., 1927.

Mooney, Martin. *Crime Incorporated.* New York: Whittlesey House, 1935.

Moorehead, Alan. *The Russian Revolution.* New York: Harper, 1958.

Morris, Norral. *The Habitual Criminal.* Cambridge, Mass.: Harvard Univ. Press, 1951.

Morris, R. B. *Fair Trial.* New York: Knopf, 1953.

Morris, Terence. *The Criminal Area.* New York: Humanities Press, 1958.

Mueller, Gerhard O. W., ed. *Essays in Criminal Science.* Hackensack, N.J.: Rothman, 1961.

Mullins, Claud. *Why Crime?* Philadelphia: Saunders, 1945.

Murray, George. *The Legacy of Al Capone.* New York: Putnam, 1975.

Murtagh, John M., and Harris, Sara. *Cast the First Stone*. New York: McGraw-Hill, 1957.

Nash, Jay Robert. *Dillinger: Dead or Alive?* Chicago: Regnery, 1970.
———. *Citizen Hoover, A Critical Study of the Life and Times of J. Edgar Hoover and His FBI*. Chicago: Nelson-Hall, 1972.
———. *Bloodletters and Badmen, A Narrative Encyclopedia of American Criminals from the Pilgrims to the Present*. New York: M. Evans & Co., 1973.
———. *Hustlers and Con Men, An Anecdotal History of the Confidence Man and His Games*. New York: M. Evans & Co., 1976.
———. *Darkest Hours*. Chicago: Nelson-Hall, 1976.
———. *Among the Missing, An Anecdotal History of Missing Persons from 1800 to the Present*. New York: Simon & Schuster, 1978.
———. *Murder America, Homicide in the United States from the Revolution to the Present*. New York: Simon & Schuster, 1980.
Neustatter, W. L. *The Mind of the Murderer*. London: C. Johnson, 1957.
Nordon, Pierre. *Conan Doyle*. New York: Holt, 1964.

O'Connor, John. *Broadway Racketeers*. New York: Liveright, 1928.
Odell, Robin. *Jack the Ripper in Fact and Fiction*. London: Harrap, 1965.
O'Donnell, B. *Should Women Hang?* London: W. H. Allen, 1956.
O'Hara, Albert R. *Position of Women in Early China*. Washington, D.C.: Catholic Univ. of America Press, 1945.
Olden, Marc. *Cocaine*. New York: Lancer Books, 1973.
Olmstead, A. T. *History of Assyria*. New York: Scribner, 1923.
Orchard, Harry. *The Confessions and Autobiography of Harry Orchard*. New York: Doubleday, Page, 1907.

Palmer, Stuart. *The Psychology of Murder*. New York: Crowell, 1960.
Parkenham, Frank. *Causes of Crime*. London: Weidenfeld, 1948.
Partridge, Ralph. *Broadmoor: A History of Criminal Lunacy and its Problems*. London: Chatto & Windus, 1953.
Pasley, Fred D. *Muscling In*. New York: Washburn, 1931.
Pearce, Charles E. *Unsolved Murder Mysteries*. London: Stanley Paul, 1924.
Pearl, Cyril. *The Girl with the Swansdown Seat*. Indianapolis: Bobbs, 1955.
Pearson, Edmund Lester. *Studies in Murder*. New York: Macmillan, 1924.
———. *Murder at Smutty Nose*. Garden City: Doubleday, 1927.
———. *Five Murders*. Garden City: Doubleday, 1928.
———. *More Studies in Murder*. New York: H. Smith, 1931.

Pearson, Michael. *Age of Consent*. London: David & Charles, 1972.

Pelham, Camden. *Chronicles of Crime, or the New Newgate Calendar*. 2 vols. London: Reeves and Turner, 1886.

Pilkington, Ian D. B. *The King's Pleasure*. London: Jarrolds, 1957.

Pinkerton, Alan. *Criminal Reminiscences and Detective Sketches*. New York: G. W. Dillingham, 1878.

Pinkerton, Matthew. *Murder in All Ages*. Chicago: Pinkerton & Co., 1898.

Platnick, Kenneth B. *Great Mysteries of History*. New York: Stackpole Books, 1971.

Playfair, Giles, and Sington, Derrick. *The Offenders*. New York: Simon & Schuster, 1957.

Pollack, Otto. *The Criminality of Women*. Philadelphia: University of Pa. Press, 1950.

Potter, John Deane. *The Art of Hanging*. Cranbury, N.J.: A. S. Barnes, 1969.

Pugh, Ralph B. *Imprisonment in Medieval England*. Cambridge, Eng.: Cambridge Univ. Press, 1968.

Purvis, James. *Great Unsolved Mysteries*. New York: Grosset & Dunlap, 1978.

Putnam, Samuel. *History of Prostitution*. 3 vols. Chicago: P. Covici, 1926.

Radzinowicz, L. *A History of English Criminal Law*. New York: Macmillan, 1948.

Raper, A. F. *The Tragedy of Lynching*. Chapel Hill: University of N.C. Press, 1933.

Ray, Chaplain, with Wagner, Walter. *God's Prison Gang*. Old Tappan, N.J.: Revell, 1976.

Reckless, Walter. *The Crime Problem*. New York: Appleton, 1950.

Rees, J. Taylor, and Usill, Harley V., eds. *They Stand Apart*. London: Heinemann, 1955.

Reichard, Gladys A. *Navaho Religion*. New York: Bollingen Foundation, 1950.

Reik, T. *The Compulsion to Confess*. New York: Farrar, Straus, 1959.

Reinhardt, James M. *Sex Perversions and Sex Crimes*. London: Thomas, 1957.

Reiter, P. J. *Antisocial or Criminal Acts and Hypnosis*. Springfield, Ill.: Thomas, 1958.

Reith, Charles. *A New Study of Police History*. London: Oliver, 1956.

Reiwald, P. *Society and Its Criminals*. New York: Int. Univs. Press, 1950.

Reynolds, Quentin. *Headquarters*. New York: Harper, 1955.

————. *I, Willie Sutton*. New York: Farrar, Straus, 1953.

Riasanovsky, Nicholas V. *A History of Russia*. New York: Oxford Univ. Press, 1969.

Richardson, Joanna. *The Courtesans*. Cleveland: World Pub., 1967.

Robinson, Cyril E. *History of Greece*. New York: Apollo Eds., 1965.

———. *History of Rome*. New York: Apollo Eds., 1965.

Rolph, C. H., ed. *The Police and the Public*. London: Heinemann, 1962.

———. *Women of the Streets*. London: Secker & Warburg, 1955.

Root, Jonathan. *The Life and Bad Times of Charlie Becker*. London: Secker & Warburg, 1962.

Rose, Gordon. *The Struggle for Penal Reform*. Chicago: Quadrangle Books, 1961.

Rosow, Eugene. *Born to Lose, The Gangster Film in America*. New York: Oxford Univ. Press, 1978.

Roughead, William. *The Murderer's Companion*. New York: Readers Club, 1941.

Rowan, David. *Famous American Crimes*. London: Muller, 1957.

Ruck, S. K., ed. *Paterson on Prisons*. London: Muller, 1951.

Rumbelow, Donald. *The Complete Jack the Ripper*. Boston: New York Graphic Soc., 1975.

Ryan, Michael. *Prostitution in London*. London: Bailliere, 1838.

Salusbury, G. T. *Street Life in Medieval England*. Oxford: Pen-in-Hand, 1948.

Sanger, William W. *History of Prostitution*. New York: Harper, 1858.

Sann, Paul. *Kill the Dutchman!* New Rochelle, N.Y.: Arlington House, 1971.

Sarkar, S. C. *Some Aspects of the Earliest Social History of India*. London: Oxford Univ. Press, 1928.

Sayers, Dorothy L. *Tales of Detection, Mystery and Horror*. London: Gollancz, 1928.

Scott, Sir Harold. *Scotland Yard*. New York: Random House, 1955.

Servadio, Gaia. *Mafioso*. New York: Dell, 1976.

Seward, Desmond. *The First Bourbon*. Boston: Gambit, 1971.

Sheldon, William H. *Varieties of Delinquent Youth*. New York: Harper, 1949.

Shew, E. Spencer. *A Companion to Murder*. New York: Knopf, 1961.

Shirer, William L. *The Rise and Fall of the Third Reich*. New York: Simon & Schuster, 1960.

Sichel, Walter. *Emma Lady Hamilton*. New York: Dodd, Mead, 1907.

Silver, Gary, ed. *The Dope Chronicles*. New York: Harper & Row, 1979.

Simpson, C. Keith. *Modern Trends in Forensic Medicine*. London: Butterworth, 1952.

Simpson, Keith. *Forty Years of Murder*. New York: Scribner, 1979.

Smith, Ann D. *Women in Prison*. Chicago: Quadrangle Books, 1962.

Smith-Hughes, Jack. *Unfair Comment Upon Some Victorian Murder Trials*. London: Cassell, 1951.

——. *Six Ventures in Villainy*. London: Cassell, 1956.

——. *Nine Verdicts on Violence*. London: Cassell, 1956.

Smith, Sir Henry. *From Constable to Commissioner*. London: Chatto & Windus, 1910.

Smith, Sydney. *Mostly Murder*. London: Harrap, 1959.

Soderman, Harry. *Policeman's Lot*. New York: Funk, 1956.

Sparrow, Judge Gerald. *The Great Assassins*. New York: Arco, 1969.

Spiering, Frank. *Prince Jack, The True Story of Jack the Ripper*. Garden City: Doubleday, 1978.

Stead, P. J. *The Police of Paris*. London: Staples, 1951.

——. *Vidocq*. New York: Roy Pubs., 1954.

Stekel, W. *Peculiarities of Behavior*. New York: Liveright, 1924.

Stern, Philip Van Doren. *The Man Who Killed Lincoln*. New York: Dell, 1955.

Stewart, William. *Jack the Ripper*. London: Quality, 1939.

Stow, John. *The Survey of London*. Edited by Henry Wheatley. London: J. M. Dent & Co., 1912.

Sullivan, Edward D. *Rattling the Cup on Chicago Crime*. New York: Vanguard Press, 1929.

Susskind, Richard. *The Crusades*. New York: Ballantine, 1962.

Sutherland, E. H., and Cressey, Donald R. *Principles of Criminology*. Philadelphia: Lippincott, 1959.

Sutton, Willie. *Where the Money Was*. New York: Viking Press, 1976.

Svensson, Arne, and Wendell, Otto. *Crime Detection*. London: Cleaver-Hume, 1955.

Taft, Donald R. *Criminology*. New York: Macmillan, 1956.

Tannenbaum, Frank. *Crime and the Community*. New York: Columbia Univ. Press, 1951.

Toch, Hans. *Violent Men*. Chicago: Aldine Pub., 1969.

Torgersen, Don Arthur. *Gandhi*. Chicago: Children's Press, 1968.

Touhy, Roger. *The Stolen Years*. Cleveland: Pennington Press, 1959.

Traini, Robert. *Murder for Sex*. London: Kimber, 1960.

Tredgold, R. F., and Soddy, K. *A Textbook of Mental Deficiency*. London: Balliere, Tindall and Cox, 1956.

Tuchman, Barbara W. *Stilwell and the American Experience in China, 1911–45*. New York: Macmillan, 1971.

Turner, Mertyn. *Safe Lodging*. London: Hutchinson, 1961.

Turner, R. F. *Forensic Science and Laboratory Techniques*. Springfield, Ill.: C. C. Thomas, 1949.

Tuska, Jon. *The Detective in Hollywood*. Garden City: Doubleday, 1978.

Tuttle, Elizabeth Orman. *The Crusade Against Capital Punishment in Great Britain*. Chicago: Quadrangle Books, 1961.

Tyler, Gus, ed. *Organized Crime in America*. Ann Arbor: University of Mich. Press, 1962.

Viglotti, Gabriel R. *The Girls of Nevada*. Secaucus, N.J.: Citadel Press, 1975.

Wagner, Margaret Seaton. *The Monster of Düsseldorf, The Life and Trial of Peter Kurten*. London: Faber, 1932.

Waller, George. *Kidnap*. New York: Dial Press, 1961.

Warren, Paul. *Next Time Is for Life*. New York: Dell, 1953.

Webb, Duncan. *Deadline for Crime*. London: Muller, 1955.

Weihofen, Henry. *The Urge to Punish*. New York: Farrar, Straus, 1956.

Wensley, Frederick Porter. *Forty Years of Scotland Yard*. New York: Garden City Pub., 1930.

Wertham, Fredric. *Dark Legend*. London: Gollancz, 1947.

———. *The Show of Violence*. Garden City: Doubleday, 1949.

———. *The Circle of Guilt*. New York: Rinehart, 1956.

West, R. *A Train of Powder*. New York: Viking Press, 1946.

Whitehead, Don. *Journey into Crime*. New York: Random House, 1960.

Wicker, Tom. *Investigating the FBI*. Garden City: Doubleday, 1973.

Wildeblood, Peter. *Against the Law*. London: Weidenfeld, 1955.

Williams, H. Noel. *Memoirs of Madame du Barry*. New York: Collier, 1910.

Williams, Roger L. *Gaslight and Shadow: The World of Napoleon III*. New York: Macmillan, 1957.

Williams, Watkins W. *The Life of General Sir Charles Warren*. Oxford: Blackwell, 1941.

Wilson, Colin. *A Casebook of Murder*. New York: Cowles, 1969.

Winick, Charles, and Kinsie, Paul M. *The Lively Commerce: Prostitution in the U.S.* Chicago: Quadrangle Books, 1971.

Winslow, L. Forbes. *Recollections of Forty Years*. London: John Ouseley, 1910.

Woolston, Howard B. *Prostitution in the United States*. New York: Appleton, 1921.

Wooton, Barbara. *Social Science and Social Pathology*. New York: Macmillan, 1959.

Zierold, Norman. *Little Charley Ross*. Boston: Little, Brown, 1967.

INDEX